New Perspectives on Faking in Personality Assessment

New Perspectives on Faking in Personality Assessment

EDITED BY

Matthias Ziegler
Carolyn MacCann
Richard D. Roberts

OXFORD
UNIVERSITY PRESS

OXFORD
UNIVERSITY PRESS

Oxford University Press, Inc., publishes works that further
Oxford University's objective of excellence in research,
scholarship, and education.

Oxford   New York
Auckland   Cape Town   Dar es Salaam   Hong Kong   Karachi
Kuala Lumpur   Madrid   Melbourne   Mexico City   Nairobi
New Delhi   Shanghai   Taipei   Toronto

With offices in
Argentina   Austria   Brazil   Chile   Czech Republic   France   Greece
Guatemala   Hungary   Italy   Japan   Poland   Portugal   Singapore
South Korea   Switzerland   Thailand   Turkey   Ukraine   Vietnam

Published by Oxford University Press, Inc.
198 Madison Avenue, New York, New York 10016
http://www.oup.com

Oxford is a registered trademark of Oxford University Press

Library of Congress Cataloging-in-Publication Data
Ziegler, Matthias, 1978-
   New perspectives on faking in personality assessment/Matthias Ziegler, Carolyn MacCann,
Richard D. Roberts.
      p. cm.
   Includes bibliographical references and index.
   ISBN-13: 978-0-19-538747-6 (hardcover) 1. Personality assessment. I. MacCann, Carolyn.
II. Roberts, Richard D. III. Title.
   BF698.4.Z54 2011
155.2'8—dc22   2010052039

Printing number: 9 8 7 6 5 4 3 2 1
Printed in the United States of America
on acid-free paper

■ CONTENTS

■ FOREWORD

Faking has long been the soft underbelly of personality research. Beneath the gaudy cavalcade of psychometric models and validity coefficients lurks the fear that respondents on personality questionnaires are simply "making it up." As may happen when people are confronted by an existential threat, stereotyped coping strategies develop. Some researchers deny the whole problem, or at best flaunt some reassuringly trivial correlations between the trait of interest and some social desirability measure. Others—especially in applied psychology—are apt to dismiss the whole field of personality assessment.

Neither denial of the problem nor disparagement of personality scales is conducive to a better understanding of faking. In this volume, Ziegler, MacCann, and Roberts have done an enormous service to personality researchers by systematically distilling what is known and unknown about faking, and deriving evidence-based practical recommendations.

Such an analysis is well past due. Faking is often seen as a petty nuisance that need only aggravate those foolhardy enough to use personality assessment in real-life settings. However, as the editors point out in their concluding chapter, around a quarter of people will fake in high-stakes settings, in contexts such as job seeking and making legal claims. Such faking leads to penalties for honest respondents, poor hiring decisions in industry, and outright fraud in the legal system.

The contributors to this book demonstrate conclusively the importance of a theoretical understanding of faking as a guide for practical countermeasures. The study of faking can indeed be set within the dominant interactionist paradigm for personality research. Faking behaviors are powerfully influenced by incentives and other situational factors. Not everyone will fake, however, even when the test environment seems to issue a siren call to encourage faking. Dispositional differences in willingness to fake interact with situational pressures to determine behavior. The book chapters also explore some of the critical motivational, cognitive, and emotional factors that may mediate the person–situation interaction.

This is a book that is both honest and brave in its analysis of faking. Editors and contributors are honest in lucidly setting out both solidly established research findings and areas of uncertainty. On a consensual note, the book firmly establishes the prevalence and real-life relevance of faking as well as the key role of motivational factors. Methodologies for investigating motivational factors through experimental manipulations of incentives and through sophisticated psychometric techniques have also been rigorously established. Personality factors including conscientiousness and neuroticism are shown to influence the willingness to fake.

More contentious are possible solutions to faking in high-stakes assessments. The reader of this book will be struck by the inventiveness and range of interventions available. Countermeasures based on detecting faking include the overclaiming technique (the respondent falsely recognizes bogus terms and concepts), detection of excessive social conformity, application of item response theory and other statistical techniques, and even analysis of the language used in documents such as cover letters and oral interview responses. All are intriguing, but none is yet ready for large-scale deployment in real-life settings. Similar uncertainties attach to methods for preventing faking through reducing the motivation to fake and independent verification of personality data, although this approach may be the more promising in the long run.

Research on faking is thus in a productive state of flux. Nevertheless, the editors are courageous enough to offer some definite practical recommendations in their concluding chapter. They challenge received wisdom in firmly rejecting the utility of social desirability scales. Indeed, they are skeptical concerning the value of trying to detect faking at all; prevention measures are to be preferred. Another novel recommendation is to use personality assessment more for weeding out those with entirely unsuitable traits than for identifying individuals with particularly high scores on wanted qualities.

This is a book that should be read by anyone using personality assessment in field settings—and not a few researchers may learn something from it, too. It does an admirable job of laying out the state-of-the-art approach in research and describing the most promising directions for future theoretical and applied work. Fakers should beware—at last, Ziegler et al. and their cohorts are making a systematic effort to maintain the fairness and integrity of personality assessment.

Gerald Matthews
University of Cincinnati
May 2010

◼ PREFACE

Faking on psychological assessments is a topic of enormous importance for many applications in psychology. Research on faking has been investigated for over six decades in many different contexts and countries, using many different methods and psychometric instruments. Given this lengthy and thorough research history we might assume that most of the questions on faking have been answered and that researchers are now united in their views, methods, and practices. Unfortunately for the field—but not for three vagabond scholars looking for a gritty topic on which to work together—this consensus has not quite been reached. Despite some points of agreement, there are still important research questions that have not been satisfactorily resolved. One of the complicating factors is that faking research is often fragmented, with researchers tackling diverse topics, often in isolation. Whereas some researchers are concerned with explaining or describing the phenomenon of faking, other researchers focus primarily on the impact of faking on the psychometric properties of assessment tools. Yet again, other researchers focus on identifying fakers and still others on the prevention of faking.

These multiple points of view allow for considerable heated debate on what is known, unknown, and unknowable in faking research. For a person first starting out in this discipline, it is very hard to wrap one's arms around the field and get a feeling for current points of agreement or the various, often steamy, controversies. With this background, this book serves two purposes. One goal is to compile a comprehensive summary of the present state-of-the-art approach on faking research and its practical implications. Second, by presenting and comparing a variety of conceptual models and findings, it serves as a tangible step toward resolving extant controversies. To achieve these two goals, the book includes a series of contrasting views on theoretical and practical issues in faking research. Theoretical issues include the fundamental nature of faking, different ideas as to why and how people fake, and whether this changes the nature of what it is that a test actually measures. Practical issues include the possibility of preventing faking before it happens, of detecting faking, of correcting "faked" scores, and the potential impact of faking on the consequential use of test scores. In addition, leading assessment experts in the fields of educational and clinical psychology describe how faking impacts their fields and where they see a need for further research.

Thus, the book presents an overview of faking research that is in line with what we perceived as four foundational topics:

1. Do people fake and does it matter?
2. Can we tell if people fake?
3. Can we stop people from faking?
4. Is faking a consequential issue outside a job selection context?

The structure of the book directly follows these questions. It also provides an overview of the issues in an introductory section and two attempts to integrate the answers to the posed questions in a concluding section.

In Part *One*, Ziegler, MacCann, and Roberts (Chapter 1) provide some important background literature concerning psychological assessment in general and the role that faking has played in research so far. Based on their review, they also provide a working definition of faking, as well as refining some of the key questions grappled with by respective authors throughout the book.

Part *Two* is entitled *Do People Fake and Does It Matter? The Existence of Faking and Its Impact on Personality Assessments*. The first, fundamental issue is whether people actually distort their statements in personality assessments. Although some researchers strongly advocate that faking exists only in laboratory situations and not in the real world, other researchers argue just as vehemently for the opposing position: That it happens regularly in all applied contexts. Chapter 2 (Ellingson) and Chapter 3 (Griffith and Converse) are primarily concerned with resolving this debate.

The second focus is the possible influence faking might have on selection decisions as well as on the psychometric properties of assessment instruments. Once again, there are opposing positions and contradictory points of view. In this instance, the issues are discussed first by Smith and McDaniel (Chapter 4), and then by Holden and Book (Chapter 5), again with the goal of arriving at some degree of consensus.

Part *Three* addresses a different set of concerns. Instead of questioning the existence of faking or its possible effects on personality scores, this part focuses on a research strand that aims to identify faked scores or correct for faking using a variety of analytic and methodological techniques. This is the most extensive section of the volume, addressing the issues that are of the most applied concern. Part three is titled *Can We Tell If People Fake? The Detection and Correction of Response Distortion*. Chapters in this part focus on several major issues: (1) which personality and individual differences variables might play a role in faking, (2) models and processes of faking, (3) methods for detecting faking, and finally (4) methods for correcting faking.

Chapter 6 (Heggestad) opens Part *Three* by considering the detection of faking from a process perspective. Detecting whether someone has faked their responses in a personality test requires an accurate model of faking. Heggestad suggests that model development has so far been a neglected topic of research. The remaining chapters discuss potential mechanisms to detect or correct for faking. Extensive reviews by Kuncel, Bornemann, and Kiger (Chapter 7) as well as Zickar and Sliter (Chapter 8) address different methods to detect faking based on investigating the items used in personality assessments. By contrast, Reeder and Ryan (Chapter 9) address methods of correcting for faking. The final two chapters of this part, Paulhus (Chapter 10) and Ventura (Chapter 11), present relatively new methods to measure faking, thus providing a glimpse of what the future of faking research might look like.

In applied settings, an alternative to correcting for faking is to prevent the behavior from occurring in the first place. Part *Four* (*Can We Stop People from Faking?*

Preventive Strategies) includes contributions by several experts who state their views on a variety of prevention mechanisms.

Basically, prevention strategies can be seen as either focusing on the test taker or the test items. Dilchert and Ones (Chapter 12) summarize the state of knowledge regarding different techniques that directly address the test taker. Subsequently, Bäckström, Björklund, and Larsson (Chapter 13) suggest a novel prevention strategy, based on the idea of reformulating item stems. In a similar vein, Stark, Chernyshenko, and Drasgow (Chapter 14) discuss their work on using forced-choice item formats, which appear to offer considerable promise. In the final chapter of this part, Lukoff (Chapter 15) introduces a new method, and some early data, in which people are warned not to fake if a certain answer pattern occurs within the first few items of a personality assessment.

Part *Five* (*Is Faking a Consequential Issue Outside a Job Selection Context? Current Applications and Future Directions in Clinical and Educational Settings*) examines applied perspectives on the issue of faking. This part addresses applications that lie outside of the implicit context of many of the early chapters: industrial-organizational psychology. Indeed, our aim here was to broaden the conversation, since it is clearly a topic that extends beyond personnel selection and personnel development. Faking also occurs in clinical and educational settings. Leading experts from educational and clinical psychology were invited to write about faking research from the perspective of their respective backgrounds, in particular focusing on the role of faking and the typical ways of dealing with faking in this domain.

Hall and Hall present an overview on faking and its impact as applied to the clinical field (Chapter 16). Burrus, Naemi, and Kyllonen (Chapter 17) discuss the role and impact of faking in a range of educational settings.

The concluding Part *Six* contains two chapters that represent separate attempts to synthesize the viewpoints expressed in the earlier chapters. Chapter 18 by MacCann, Ziegler, and Roberts and Chapter 19 by Sackett both aim at distilling the information from all chapters in this book and to paint an agenda for the next generation of faking studies.

All in all, this book provides a comprehensive summary and evaluation of conflicting findings and viewpoints in the existing literature, with a resolution of disputatious issues wherever possible. The book also serves as a resource for practitioners who might now make informed decisions on the best personality test to employ in their applied context (or to at least be savvy of various methods available to address "the little problem of faking"). Additionally, by summarizing what is known and what is unknown about faking, an agenda for future research is offered.

■ ACKNOWLEDGMENTS

The idea for this edited volume grew out of two miniconferences sponsored by the Educational Testing Service during April and October 2006, in Princeton, New Jersey. At these miniconferences, it became obvious to us, as well as to the many participants who attended these fact-filled events, that there was a need to systematically distill the vast repertoire of knowledge on faking and personality assessment in one, cogent volume. Our charge appeared not only to present a more contemporary account of faking than has hitherto been the case (many important advances have occurred during the past decade), but to offer a more diverse amalgam of theory, measures, and applications than has previously been offered. We followed up these miniconferences with further interactions with various contributors at a number of national and international conferences, including the International Congress of Applied Psychology, the American Psychological Association, and the Society for Industrial and Organizational Psychology. We are grateful to the Educational Testing Service initially, but subsequently wish to thank each of these organizations for their support of what became the catalyst for this edited volume.

During the writing of our respective chapters and the editing of this book, Humboldt Universität zu Berlin, The University of Sydney, and the Educational Testing Service (ETS) provided the facilities and resources necessary to undertake and complete this body of work. In addition, we would like to acknowledge the following senior staff and management from ETS who supported the project, including its broader vision, from its inception: Dr. Ida Lawrence (ETS Vice-President of Research and Development), Dr. Patrick C. Kyllonen (ETS New Constructs Center Director), and Dr. Cathy Wendler (ETS Foundational and Validity Research Principal Director). Although arriving later on the scene in terms of support, no less valuable were the efforts of senior management at The University of Sydney, including Professor Sally Andrews (The University of Sydney Head of the School of Psychology) and Professor Jill Trewhella (The University of Sydney Deputy Vice-Chancellor for Research).

Edited volumes can be difficult to produce as anyone who has set out on this onerous task would attest; the principle of "no pain, no gain" appears apposite. We are indebted to Mary Lucas and Dan Howard from ETS for their work pulling together the important preproduction pieces. Heartfelt appreciation is also extended to the production team at Oxford University Press for making the process tolerable, and to Lori Handelman, in particular, for both pushing and cajoling us, and answering many of our questions without a single hint of protest.

We are grateful to many people across the globe for other forms of support throughout the duration of this project. First and foremost it would be remiss not to acknowledge our respective partners—Romy Frömer, Robert Hynson, and Cristina Aicher—each of whom has variously lost us for days (and sometimes weeks) as we grappled with production issues; stole time away from home to write a word here, a page there; or reviewed one of the contributions by our distinguished panel of international experts. To each of you, we are grateful that you neither exhibited too much negative emotion nor faked your sentiments to an alarming degree. And to the following friends, family, students, and/or colleagues, many thanks for being conduits for our out-of-the-box thoughts, folks we can vent our frustrations on (and sometimes at), occasional motivators, or just plain being there: Caspian Sondre Aicher-Roberts, Jens Beckmann, Anthony Betancourt, Damian Birney, David Bowman, Markus Buehner, Erik Danay, T. J. Elliott, China Forbes, Eugene Gonzales, Moritz Heene, Daniel Howard, Teresa Jackson, Jihyun Lee, Anastasiya Lipnevich, Mary Lucas, Ann MacCann, Robert MacCann, Amirali Minbashian, Jennifer Minsky, Camille Morgan, Frank Rijmen, Matthew D. Roberts, John Sabatini, Franziska Schölmerich, Sabine Schulz, Ralf Schulze, and Namrata Tognatta.

Finally, an edited book would be nothing without its contributors. We are extremely grateful to each of the acclaimed scholars (given in the list of contributors) who we asked to give their time, expertise, and knowledge to address a series of pointed questions that we believed needed compelling answers. Indeed, we are indebted to each of you for the various chapters appearing in this volume. We appreciate your critical contributions, your willingness to cope with a challenging and often difficult task, and to respond to suggestions we raised so that the volume might cohere and be something that is both unique and compelling. Special thanks to Professor Paul Sackett, who agreed to pen a commentary chapter in rapid time and to Professor Gerald Matthews for agreeing to write the Foreword, in his usual inimitable style.

We hope this volume will provide readers with a deeper understanding and appreciation of the current state-of-the art research on faking and how it operates in personality assessment. We also hope it might guide future theory, research, and applications in this domain. Please do enjoy and do not hesitate to drop us a line should the book raise some burning questions: You will find us mighty accommodating, even if stretched across three continents.

Matthias Ziegler
Carolyn MacCann
Richard D. Roberts

■ CONTRIBUTORS

Martin Bäckström, Ph.D.
Professor
Department of Psychology
Lund University
Lund, Sweden

Fredrik Björklund, Ph.D.
Associate Professor
Department of Psychology
Lund University
Lund, Sweden

Angela S. Book, Ph.D.
Associate Professor
Brock University,
  St. Catharines
Ontario, Canada

Matthew Borneman
Graduate student
Psychology Department
University of Minnesota
Minneapolis, MN

Jeremy Burrus, Ph.D.
Associate Research Scientist
Center for Academic and Workplace
  Readiness and Success
Princeton, NJ

Oleksandr S. Chernyshenko, Ph.D.
Associate Professor
Nanyang Technological University
Singapore

Patrick D. Converse, Ph.D.
Associate Professor
College of Psychology and Liberal Arts
Florida Institute of Technology
Melbourne, FL

Stephan Dilchert, Ph.D.
Assistant Professor of Management
Department of Management
Zicklin School of Business,
  Baruch College, CUNY
New York, NY

Fritz Drasgow, Ph.D.
Professor
University of Illinois at Urbana-
  Champaign
Industrial-Organizational Division
Champaign, IL

Jill E. Ellingson, Ph.D.
Associate Professor
Department of Management
  and Human Resources
The Ohio State University
Columbus, OH

Richard L. Griffith, Ph.D.
Professor
College of Psychology and Liberal Arts
Florida Institute of Technology
Melbourne, FL

Richard C. W. Hall, M.D.
Professor Department of Medical
  Education, University of Central
  Florida College of Medicine
  Orlando, FL
Affiliate Professor
Department of Psychiatry and
  Behavioral Medicine
University of South Florida
Tampa, FL
Courtesy Clinical Professor of
  Psychiatry, University of Florida
  Gainesville, FL

Ryan C. W. Hall, M.D.
Affiliate Associate Professor
Department of Psychiatry and
  Behavioral Medicine
University of South Florida
Tampa, FL
Assistant Professor of Psychiatry
Department of Medical Education
University of Central Florida College
  of Medicine
Orlando, FL
Adjunct Faculty Member
Barry University Dwayne O. Andreas
  School of Law
Orlando, FL

Eric D. Heggestad, Ph.D.
Associate Professor of Psychology,
  Associate Professor of
  Organizational Science
University of North Carolina–
  Charlotte
Charlotte, NC

Ronald R. Holden, Ph.D.
Professor
Department of Psychology
Queen's University at Kingston
Kingston, Ontario, Canada

Thomas Kiger
Graduate student
Psychology Department
University of Minnesota
Minneapolis, MN

Nathan R. Kuncel, Ph.D.
Associate Professor
Psychology Department
University of Minnesota
Minneapolis, MN

Patrick C. Kyllonen, Ph.D.
Principal Research Scientist and
  Director
Center for New Constructs
Educational Testing Service
Princeton, NJ

Magnus R. Larsson, Ph.D.
Assistant Professor
Department of Psychology
Lund University
Lund, Sweden

Brian Lukoff, Ph.D.
Postdoctoral Fellow in Technology and
  Education
School of Engineering and Applied
  Sciences
Harvard University
Cambridge, MA

Carolyn MacCann, Ph.D.
Lecturer
School of Psychology
Faculty of Science
The University of Sydney
Sydney, Australia

Gerald E. Matthews, Ph.D.
Professor of Psychology
Department of Psychology
University of Cincinnati
Cincinnati, OH

Max McDaniel, Ph.D.
SWA Consulting
Raleigh, NC

Bobby D. Naemi, Ph.D.
Associate Research Scientist
Center for Academic and Workplace
  Readiness and Success
Educational Testing Service
Princeton, NJ

Deniz S. Ones, Ph.D.
Professor of Psychology
Psychology Department
University of Minnesota
Minneapolis, MN

Delroy L. Paulhus, Ph.D.
Professor of Psychology
Department of Psychology
University of British Columbia
Vancouver, Canada

Matthew C. Reeder
Graduate Student
Department of Psychology
Michigan State University
East Lansing, MI

Richard D. Roberts, Ph.D.
Principal Research Scientist
Center for Academic and Workplace
   Readiness and Success
Princeton, NJ

Ann Marie Ryan, Ph.D.
Professor
Department of Psychology
Michigan State University
East Lansing, MI

Paul R. Sackett, Ph.D.
Professor
Department of Psychology
University of Minnesota
Minneapolis, MN

Katherine A. Sliter
Graduate student
Department of Psychology
Bowling Green State University
Bowling Green, OH

D. Brent Smith, Ph.D.
Associate Dean of Executive Education
Associate Professor of Management
   and Psychology
Jones Graduate School of Business
Rice University
Houston, TX

Stephen Stark, Ph.D.
Associate Professor
Department of Psychology
University of South Florida
Tampa, FL

Matthew Ventura, Ph.D.
Associate Research Scientist
Center for New Constructs
Educational Testing Service
Princeton, NJ

Michael J. Zickar, Ph.D.
Associate Professor
Director of the Graduate Program in
   I-O Psychology
Department of Psychology
Bowling Green State University
Bowling Green, OH

Matthias Ziegler, Dr. phil. habil.
Associate Professor
Chair for Psychological Diagnostics
Institute for Psychology
Humboldt-Universität zu Berlin
Berlin, Germany

■ PART ONE
General Background

1 Faking

Knowns, Unknowns, and Points of Contention[1]

■ MATTHIAS ZIEGLER, CAROLYN MACCANN,
AND RICHARD D. ROBERTS

In contemporaneous society, it seems feasible to suggest that personality testing touches many different parts of an individual's life: work, school, family, and play. For example, if single, the dating process now commonly involves personality assessment with Internet services using personality testing to match people on a variety of salient dimensions. A range of personality assessments is also available on social networks like Facebook, both for personal insight and to maximize social networking. In many jobs, applicants routinely undergo psychological testing, including personality assessment, for selection, training, and career progression. With the availability of the standardized letter of recommendation for college admissions, personality testing may now also become routine in educational admissions (see Liu, Minsky, Ling, & Kyllonen, 2009). Personality tests are also used for diagnosis, in medicine (especially psychiatry) and clinical psychology, as well as in the schools (e.g., for the diagnosis of students with attention deficit hyperactivity disorder) and even for legal purposes (e.g., to establish diminished responsibility).

These personality assessments are undertaken by different groups of people for disparate reasons, in variegated contexts, with test scores interpreted according to different sets of expertise. There seem to be only two points of agreement that these instances of assessments share. First, that test scores are meant to be an accurate indication of the individual's level of some set of attributes. Second, this accurate information, distilled from the test scores, is expected to relate meaningfully to the individual's future behavior. In other words, test scores are valued because they are interpreted to mean something about what kind of partner a person will make, their likely success as a student or worker, their continued clinical symptoms, erratic behavior, or hyperactivity. This assumed link from test scores to future behavior is what allows employment testing to be a multibillion dollar international industry, for interpretations of personality profiles to affect sentencing in courts of law, and for professional interpretations of personality tests to be used as evidence that individuals should be confined to psychiatric institutions. In short, personality tests derive both their power and importance from the two pillars of accuracy and prediction. People value scores from personality assessments in so much as scores are seen as an accurate reflection of some attribute and can be used in some broad sense to predict the future.

1. The views expressed here are those of the authors and do not reflect on the Educational Testing Service, The University of Sydney, or Humboldt Universität zu Berlin.

The possibility that personality scores are fake, phony, inaccurate, or in some way counterfeit calls in question the first pillar of personality testing and leaves the second pillar equivocal. This then explains why faking is such a hotly disputatious topic. In the worst possible scenario (1) people *can* fake more desirable test scores, (2) people in fact *do* fake more desirable test scores, (3) faked scores are inaccurate, (4) faked scores no longer predict future behavior, (5) faking cannot be detected, and (6) faking cannot be stopped, and finally (7) faking has an impact on the use and interpretation of tests across a diverse array of applications. A range of viewpoints and empirical findings exists, such that depending on one's perspective there is support for either all or no components of this argument. A major feature of this book is that it allows debate on these issues from some of the primary researchers putting forth their various perspectives. In the spirit of this undertaking, the goal of this opening chapter is twofold. First, we wish to set a context for faking on personality testing by covering some of the early history, guiding theoretical frameworks for assessment, and expressing concerns that have plagued the field since its inception. Second, we wish to distil some of the more prominent research literature to highlight some of the knowns and unknowns surrounding the science of faking, which in turn sets the stage for more detailed treatment by the respective authors of each subsequent chapter.

■ HISTORICAL CONTEXT FOR PERSONALITY ASSESSMENT

Modern psychological testing gathered its major impetus from the Binet intelligence test, first published in France in 1905, and intended to identify children of below average cognitive ability (e.g., Binet, Simon, & Kite, 1916). Subsequently, intelligence tests were transported to the United States and administered to potential immigrants, as well as to the armed services during World War I (where the Army Alpha and Beta intelligence tests were developed). Despite the early dominance of intelligence testing (Roberts, Markham, Zeidner, & Matthews, 2005), researchers have always acknowledged that other personality traits besides intelligence might also be important for diagnosis, prediction, selection, and placement. The first objective personality assessment was ostensibly the Personal Data Sheet (Woodworth, 1919), developed by the U.S. military to diagnose people with symptoms of personality disorders so as to exclude them from military service. Several other personality scales followed shortly thereafter (see Boyle, Matthews, & Saklofske, 2008 for a brief overview or Gregory, 2006). Other personality assessments were developed in the field of clinical psychology. A notable example is the Minnesota Multiphasic Personality Inventory (MMPI), which was also created to differentiate between clinical client groups and undiagnosed individuals (Hathaway & McKinley, 1943). The MMPI included a protocol for detecting intentionally distorted answers, and thus demonstrates that the concern with faking dates back almost as far as the assessment of personality (see Baer, Wetter, Nichols, Greene & Berry, 1995).

After the initial development and use of psychological tests, the next phase in research involved establishing an agreed upon taxonomic structure of personality and of intelligence. These measurement frameworks guide much of the research and interpretation of psychological testing, and allow a common language across research groups, theorists, policy makers, and practitioners. Although there are competing theories, the current consensus on personality structure is that five broad dimensions best describe peoples' behavioral tendencies (Schulze & Roberts, 2006). These dimensions are defined slightly differently by various theories, but generally contain more points of similarity than differences. The Big Five framework first emerged in military research (Tupes & Christal, 1961) but did not become popularly acceptable until the late 1980s (see, e.g., Digmann, 1990; Goldberg, 1990; John, 1990; Kyllonen, Lipnevich, Burrus, & Roberts, 2011; Matthews, Deary, & Whiteman, 2009; Matthews, Zeidner, & Roberts, 2009). The five factors are outlined below, together with brief descriptions and example items from the International Personality Item Pool (IPIP, Goldberg et al., 2006).

(1) *Openness to Experience (O)*. High-O people are open to new thoughts, activities, and values, and tend to be interested in intellectual, imaginative, and artistic pursuits, whereas people low on O are less comfortable with new or unfamiliar ideas, activities, or values. Example item: "I enjoy hearing new ideas."

(2) *Conscientiousness (C)*. High-C people are generally orderly, self-disciplined, achievement striving, and focused on details, in contrast to low-C people, who tend to be unconcerned with achievement, and use few resources on striving to achieve. *Example item*: "I pay attention to details."

(3) *Extraversion (E)*. High-E people tend to be gregarious, social, active, and sensation seeking, whereas low-E people are quieter, more easily overstimulated, and have lower needs for social interaction. Example item: "I make friends easily."

(4) *Agreeableness (A)*. High-A people are trusting, kind, cooperative, and modest, whereas low-A people tend to be more skeptical, distrustful, ruthless, and scheming. Example item: "I trust what people say."

(5) *Neuroticism (N)*. High-N people tend to experience emotions easily and strongly and may quickly become anxious, depressed, irritable, or stressed out, whereas people low on N are calm and placid, experiencing few strong emotions. (To place all factors on the same pole, some researchers prefer to focus on the low end of N and refer to this construct as Emotional Stability.) *Example item*: "I worry about things."

This five-factor structure has been established through structural analysis in at least 14 different languages (Saucier & Goldberg, 2006). The five personality factors relate to important life outcomes, and are therefore frequently used in selection testing. In a widely cited meta-analysis, Barrick and Mount (1991) demonstrated that Conscientiousness consistently predicts workplace performance across all job types and that Extraversion predicts managerial and sales performance. In addition, Roberts, Kuncel, Shiner, Caspi, and Goldberg (2007) recently demonstrated that these five personality traits can be meta-analytically linked to mortality, divorce, and occupational attainment above and beyond socioeconomic status and cognitive ability. A further meta-analysis by Poropat (2009) showed a consistent link between Conscientiousness and academic achievement, and a recent empirical study also shows links between Conscientiousness and a variety of other valued educational outcomes, such as discipline and attendance (MacCann, Duckworth, & Roberts, 2009). Thus, Conscientiousness and perhaps Extraversion test scores can usefully predict future behavior in the workplace and in educational, social, and health-related domains. Lower order facets, representing the structure beneath the Big Five domains, have been shown to be even more promising predictors of educational outcomes as well (e.g., Lounsbury, Sundstrom, Loveland & Gibson, 2002; Ziegler, Danay, Schoelmerich & Buehner, 2010). In the current context, the important question is how strongly these relationships with valued future behaviors will hold if some proportion of test takers is willing and able to distort their responses on some proportion of test items.

■ SITUATIONAL DEMAND AND FAKING ON PERSONALITY ASSESSMENTS

Two of the most common uses of psychological tests are selection and diagnosis. In each of these scenarios, the test taker may have a vested interest in the outcome of the test. For example, an individual may want to gain a diagnosis of posttraumatic stress disorder (or some other psychological conditions) to claim compensation or early retirement or to gain a payout from a health insurance company. A test taker in this kind of situation who is asked how much they agree with the statement "I worry about things" may consider not only their actual level of worry, but also the level of worry that they suspect would be required for their desired diagnosis. This kind of response distortion is often called *malingering* and may also be referred to as *faking bad*. A considerable body of research has considered this type of faking (e.g., Aronoff et al., 2007; Chafetz, Abrahams, & Kohlmaier, 2007; Egeland & Langfjaeran, 2007; Schmidt-Atzert, Buehner, Rischen, & Warkentin, 2004).

A second obvious situation in which test takers may have a vested interest in obtaining a particular score in personality tests is for employment selection testing. In most cases, the test taker wants the job, and knows that selection is contingent on gaining a desirable score on the personality test. Under these conditions, test takers may concentrate on giving the most desirable response to personality items, rather than the most accurate responses. For example, consider a candidate applying for a proofreading job who is asked the extent of his or her agreement with the statement "I pay attention to details." It seems highly likely that the candidate's final rating will be based not only on whether they pay attention to details, but whether they think their potential employer would value attention to detail.

There are several factors that might influence the effect of this situational demand on the candidate's final rating. First, candidate's real or self-perceived level of the attribute may affect the extent of response distortion (i.e., if the candidate genuinely pays attention to details, the "desirable" answer may in fact be the same as the accurate, nonfaked answer). Second, the strength of the reward may influence the extent of faking (i.e., how much the candidate wants and needs the job).

The strength or possibility of reward is often described as the *stakes* of the testing situation. A low-stakes test has no or few important consequences whereas a high-stakes test may result in consequences that are highly valued by the test taker. Third, the candidate may first consider his or her own standing on the attribute and adjust for desirability, or may consider only the desirability of the attribute (tendencies that lead to slight faking or extreme faking; see Robie, Brown, & Beaty, 2007). Fourth, whether the candidate believes that he or she will get "caught out" by the test may affect his or her answers. Fifth, personal qualities such as cynicism or distrust may determine whether the candidate's primary goal is to obtain a desirable score or to present an accurate impression. This nonexhaustive list of the possible processes of faking illustrates the multiple situational and personal variables involved in the process.

■ TOWARD A WORKING DEFINITION OF FAKING

Commonalities among Different Models of Faking

Faking has been used synonymously with a number of different terms, including *response bias, response sets* and *response styles, response distortion, socially desirable responding,* and *malingering* (Hopwood, Morey, Rogers, & Ewell, 2007; Hough, Eaton, Dunnette, Kamp, & McCloy, 1990; Jackson & Messick, 1958; Paulhus, 2002; Ziegler & Buehner, 2009). Notably, this list is by no means exhaustive. Although each of these terms comes with its own precise definition and theoretical model, each shares one important characteristic: *There are one or more systematic sources of variation other than the attribute of interest that systematically affect test scores.* It is the nature of the systematic sources of variation affecting test scores that differentiates models.

Paulhus (2002) provides an excellent summary of different definitions and theoretical views before providing his own conceptualization of socially desirable responding, which he defines as "The tendency to give overly positive self-descriptions" (p. 50). One important implication of this definition is that a faked personality questionnaire no longer gives a realistic picture of the person who answered the questions. Thus, using information gained from faked personality questionnaires for predicting a person's behavior would not result in accurate predictions based solely on systematic trait differences. Ziegler and colleagues argue that faking could be considered as the interaction between a person and a situation (e.g., Ziegler & Buehner, 2009; Ziegler, Toomela, & Buehner, 2009; see also Heggestad, George, & Reeve, 2006). In other words, the situational demand differs across situations and interacts with the test takers' personality to create variance due to faking. The statistical term for such an interaction between situation and person characteristics is spurious measurement error (Schmidt, Le, & Ilies, 2003).

As an example of the interaction between personality and situation, consider two people with the same level of Conscientiousness applying for the same job. Mary is introverted, detail-oriented, and has low self-efficacy beliefs, whereas John is outgoing, ambitious, and has strong faith in his own abilities. Both John and Mary are administered a Conscientiousness test during the selection process and both want the job. Obviously, this can be regarded as a high-stakes situation. Both candidates may recognize the optimal answers dictated by the situation. However, individual differences in John and Mary's personality traits may influence the way they fake. John might be more willing to push his own image, believing that he can really live up to a highly (and distorted) conscientious self-portrayal, whereas Mary, with lower self-efficacy, may not believe that she could. Thus, John would score higher than Mary, although the situational demands and the "true" Conscientiousness level are the same, respectively. Thus, a model of faking on a personality test must distinguish among (1) "true" personality differences, (2) differences due to situational demand, (3) faking as the interaction between personality and situation, and (4) unsystematic error variance. Ziegler and Buehner (2009) have recently proposed a technique for measuring these various components, although it is outside the scope of the present chapter.

Formulating a Working Definition of Faking

Despite some differences, the definitions by Paulhus (2002) and Ziegler et al. (2009) have in common the notion that faking should not be viewed as a consistent behavior across time and questionnaires. Therefore, it must be considered as a response set and not a response style, which was defined as consistent across time and questionnaires (Jackson & Messick, 1958). One feature seemingly inherent in all the different views on faking is that the aim of the response distortion is a self-description that helps to achieve personal goals (e.g., getting a job, getting a disability pension, getting a compensation payout). Thus, a straightforward definition for faking could be as follows:

> *Faking represents a response set aimed at providing a portrayal of the self that helps a person to achieve personal goals. Faking occurs when this response set is activated by situational demands and person characteristics to produce systematic differences in test scores that are not due to the attribute of interest.*

There are several models of faking that flesh out the generalities of this definition in more detail, describing the characteristics of both the person and the situation that produce this response set (e.g., Mueller-Hanson, Heggestad, & Thornton, 2006; Snell, Sydell, & Lueke, 1999). These models typically involve the opportunity and intention to fake, as well as specific personality traits that increase the likelihood of faking. The model of Mueller-Hanson et al., based on Ajzen's (1991) theory of planned behavior, has been empirically tested. Faking in this model results from a multifactorial process in which person factors and situation factors interact to produce the intention to fake. It was found that the perception of the situation and especially subjective norms (Will faking help me reach my goal? Will I be able to fake successfully?) are major factors when building an intention to fake. Person factors influencing faking intentions included willingness to fake, Emotional Stability, and Conscientiousness.

■ KNOWNS AND UNKNOWNS IN FAKING RESEARCH

The effects of faking on questionnaire data have been studied extensively. The studies can be classified into three different categories with regard to the study aim, i.e., the effect of faking on

1. Means
2. Validity
3. Rank order.

Means

There is little doubt that people are capable and willing to fake if instructed to do so (Martin, Bowen, & Hunt, 2002; Viswesvaran & Ones, 1999; Ziegler, Schmidt-Atzert, Buehner, & Krumm, 2007). An early meta-analysis reported that instructions to fake increased mean scores on all five major personality traits (Viswesvaran & Ones, 1999). Scores increased by more than half a standard deviation ($d \approx 0.60$), and increases were roughly equal across all five personality traits. However, this meta-analysis was based solely on laboratory studies with fake good instructions and answered the question only of whether research volunteers *can* fake higher scores (Smith, Hanges, & Dickson, 2001).

A subsequent meta-analysis addressed the question of whether test takers do fake higher scores in real-world applications (Birkeland, Manson, Kisamore, Brannick, & Smith, 2006). Birkeland et al. found the greatest faking effects on the mean scores of Neuroticism ($d = 0.44$) and Conscientiousness ($d = 0.45$). Effect sizes for Extraversion ($d = 0.11$) and Openness ($d = 0.13$) were considerably lower than reported by Viswesvaran and Ones (1999). In addition, different personality traits showed different levels of mean increases for different types of jobs. That is, test takers distorted only responses on personality domains that they viewed as relevant for the job for which they were currently applying (see Ziegler et al., 2009). Thus, the practitioner cannot assume that these mean level increases for the different personality traits will generalize across all job types or all testing situations.

Summing up, research has demonstrated an effect of faking on mean scores of personality questionnaires. However, the magnitude of these changes varies according to the situations that the questionnaires have been administered. This situational specificity has important consequences for theory and measurement of faking in personality assessment.

Validity

When applicants fake, their obtained test scores may reflect both individual differences in the trait of interest, as well as individual differences in faking behavior. The larger the proportion of faking-related variance is, the smaller the proportion of variance due to the construct of interest. For example, if the majority of the differences between people on a Conscientiousness measure are due to differences in the extent people fake, then the obtained scores really measure faking rather than Conscientiousness. In this scenario, scores no longer measure the construct of interest, and faking has decreased the construct validity of the test interpretation. If faked Conscientiousness test scores were then used for selection, this would be equivalent to selecting people based on how much they were willing and able to fake. Unless the relationship of faking to performance is stronger than the relationship between Conscientiousness and performance, faking would also decrease the predictive validity of test score interpretations. Faking might thus affect both the construct validity of test scores as well as the test-criterion relationship.

Faking and Discriminant Validity Evidence

The question of a test score's construct validity is often investigated by looking at the test score's relationship to other variables. For example, scores on one particular test of Conscientiousness should have large correlations with scores on other Conscientiousness tests but should have low correlations with scores on other dimensions of personality (e.g., Neuroticism or Extraversion). If faking decreases construct validity, then faked Conscientiousness scores should show higher correlations with other dimensions of personality than nonfaked Conscientiousness test scores. Generalizing across all personality dimensions, if correlations between different dimensions of personality increase due to faking, this is evidence that faking reduces the discriminant validity of test scores by increasing the shared variance (faking variances).

There is some empirical evidence that faking indeed increases correlations between Big Five dimensions (Pauls & Crost, 2005; Schmit & Ryan, 1993; Ziegler & Buehner, 2009; Ziegler et al., 2009). Within the study by Schmit and Ryan (1993), the correlations gained so much in magnitude that the authors suggested that the best statistical model would be to aggregate all five personality scores to form one factor. Using an experimental design in combination with structural equation modeling, Ziegler and Buehner (2009) showed that correlational increases due to faking could be totally controlled for by modeling a latent variable capturing individual differences in faking. Both results confirm that faking can be considered as a source of systematic variance that is added to (or even replaces) the true score variance on a test. As a consequence, faked scores on different constructs will share more variance than unfaked scores on different constructs, demonstrating poor discriminant validity.

Validity of Scores in Motivated versus Unmotivated Samples

Not all research suggests that faking will necessarily impact validity. Smith and Ellingson (2002) examined factor loadings for motivated test takers (job applicants) versus nonmotivated test takers (student samples), and concluded that these were not different. Invariant factor loadings suggest that the (assumed) faking behavior of at least some of the applicants did not affect the validity of the items.

The issue of how strongly faking might affect the validity of scales remains a particularly fertile area for contemporary research.

Faking and Test-Criterion Relationship

For faking to influence the test-criterion relationship, a substantial part of the score's variance must be due to faking. In addition, this faking-related variance must relate to the criterion in question. Otherwise suppressor effects could occur. Studies examining the effect of instructed faking on test-criterion validities have found substantial decreases in validity (Holden, Wood, & Tomashewski, 2001; Holden, 2007; Topping & O'Gorman, 1997). In contrast, a meta-analysis by Ones, Viswesvaran, and Reiss (1996) showed that social desirability scales did not relate to job performance, and also did not moderate or mediate the relationships between personality and job performance. Moreover, controlling for social desirability scores did not affect the test-criterion relationship. However, given that social desirability scales relate to substantive personality variance, the meta-analysis might simply prove that one operationalization of personality (a social desirability scale) is not incrementally predictive over a different operationalization of personality (a trait questionnaire). Nevertheless, more recent studies using different approaches to model faking also support the conclusion that faking does not affect the test-criterion relationship (Ziegler & Buehner, 2009), at least on the domain level.

A further complication of this issue might be the difference between broad domains and narrow facets of personality. A recent study demonstrated that faking may have differential effects on different facets of personality: Faking decreased the test-criterion relationship for some facet scores, but increased the test-criterion relationship for others (Ziegler, Danay, Schölmerich, & Buehner, 2010). Overall, these changes are leveled out across one domain and so the domain score superficially seems unaffected.

Overall, the question of whether faking affects test-criterion relationships remains unresolved. Instructed faking studies, for example, suggest that faking decreases test-criterion relationships. Other methods, however, suggest little differences, with mixed results when personality facets are considered.

Changes in Rank Order

Actual selection processes do not take a group perspective as has been done in all the studies mentioned so far. Instead, individual test scores are looked at and decisions for single persons are made. Therefore, it is important that the prediction does not work only on the whole, but is accurate for the people selected. There are researchers calling for more caution regarding this issue (Holden, 2007, 2008). Simply looking at group statistics might not reveal the true impact faking might have. One of the most important arguments here is that faking has an adverse effect on decisions in a selection process. That is, depending on the selection rate, the people actually being selected based on faked scores differ from those who would have been selected if relying on honest scores. This issue depends on the changes to rank order that faking might cause.

A study by Mueller-Hanson, Heggestad, and Thornton (2003) sought to determine whether such changes in rank order and the connected changes in selection decisions also affect test-criterion correlations. In their study 444 participants were randomly assigned either to a control or an incentive group. Both groups were asked to fill out an achievement motivation questionnaire. Whereas the control group was given standard instructions asking them to provide honest answers, the incentive group was told that the following measure would be used to select participants for the second stage of the experiment. In that stage $20 could be earned, but they were told that only achievement-oriented participants would be selected. In the end, all participants were allowed to take part in the second stage, a performance test that served as a criterion measure. To investigate the effects of faking on selection decisions, both groups were combined. Not surprisingly, the fewer the number of people selected from this combined sample, the fewer the number of participants selected from the control group. Assuming that the two groups had on average equal levels of achievement motivation, but that the incentive group faked, it was concluded that faking affected selection decisions. Further analysis showed that on average the performance of those selected from the control group always exceeded the performance from selected incentive group members. In other words, participants from the incentive group did not live up to the distorted picture they had drawn of themselves. Participants from the control group who were selected really were as achievement-oriented as they portrayed themselves and therefore outperformed the fakers. Thus, the changes in rank order due to faking not only led to changes in selection but also decreased the predictive power of the selection instrument.

Summarizing, we can say that empirical research so far has yielded a number of disparate results. Some of the findings seem to be reassuring and suggest that personality measures might be used for selection and prediction purposes. Other studies cast a different light and call for a more cautious approach and certainly a more nuanced set of recommendations.

■ CONCLUDING COMMENTS

We trust that the issues raised throughout this introductory chapter serve as a context for the reader to appreciate the many knowns and unknowns of faking research with which our expert contributors were asked to grapple. Clearly, our perspective on some of these issues may contrast with some of these experts; resolving such discrepancies represents an important aspect of scientific discourse and advancement. In the chapters that follow, each contributor will attempt to tackle the issues posed from their particular perspective, armed with their specialized expertise in a given domain. The core areas covered include discussing whether faking occurs and an evaluation of its impact on personality assessment, attempts to detect and correct for response distortion, preventive strategies that can be used to combat faking, and the implications of faking on various applied fields, with various experts addressing these questions in five separate sections of this edited volume. Reflecting the complex interplay between each domain, doubtless we will find some contributors crossing over and addressing key questions in another topic area, but the demarcation is nonetheless important for tackling targeted issues that we believed required answers if ever a fully fledged science of faking was to emerge, resulting in improved personality assessment. Ensuing commentaries by the contributors will likely invite still further discussion of broad issues, which we will synthesize in a concluding chapter, along with another independent evaluation of each respective chapter, most graciously penned by Paul Sackett.

References

Ajzen, I. (1991). The theory of planned behavior. *Organizational Behavior and Human Decision Processes, 50,* 179–211.

Aronoff, G. M., Mandel, S., Genovese, E., Maitz, E. A., Dorto, A. J., Klimek, E. H., & Staats, T. E. (2007). Evaluating malingering in contested injury or illness. *Pain Practice, 7,* 178–204.

Baer, R. A., Wetter, M. W., Nichols, D. S., Greene, R., & Berry, D. T. R. (1995). Sensitivity of MMPI-2 validity scales to underreporting of symptoms. *Psychological Assessment, 7,* 419–423.

Barrick, M. R., & Mount, M. K. (1991). The Big Five personality dimensions and job performance: A meta-analysis. *Personnel Psychology, 44,* 1–26.

Binet, A., Simon, T., & Kite, E. (1916). *The development of intelligence in children: The Binet-Simon scale.* Baltimore, MD: Williams & Wilkins Company.

Birkeland, S. A., Manson, T. M., Kisamore, J. L., Brannick, M. T., & Smith, M. A. (2006). A meta-analytic investigation of job applicant faking on personality measures. *International Journal of Selection and Assessment, 14,* 317–335.

Boyle, G., Matthews, G., & Saklofske, D. (2008). *The SAGE handbook of personality theory and assessment* (Vol. 2). London: Sage Publications.

Chafetz, M. D., Abrahams, J. P., & Kohlmaier, J. (2007). Malingering on the social security disability consultative exam: A new rating scale. *Archives of Clinical Neuropsychology, 22,* 1–14.

Digman, J. M. (1990). Personality structure: Emergence of the five-factor model. *Annual Review of Psychology, 41,* 417–440.

Egeland, J., & Langfjaeran, T. (2007). Differentiating malingering from genuine cognitive dysfunction using the trail making test-ratio and Stroop interference scores. *Applied Neuropsychology, 14,* 113–119.

Goldberg, L. R. (1990). An alternative "description of personality": The Big-Five factor structure. *Journal of Personality and Social Psychology, 59,* 1216–1229.

Goldberg, L. R., Johnson, J. A., Eber, H. W., Hogan, R., Ashton, M. C., Cloninger, C. R., & Gough, H. C. (2006). The International Personality Item Pool and the future of public-domain personality measures. *Journal of Research in Personality, 40,* 84–96.

Gregory, R. J. (2006). *Psychological testing: History, principles, and applications* (5th ed.). Boston: Allyn & Bacon.

Hathaway, S., & McKinley, J. (1943). *Manual for administering and scoring the Minnesota Multiphasic Personality Inventory (MMPI).* Minneapolis: University of Minnesota Press.

Heggestad, E. D., George, E., & Reeve, C. L. (2006). Transient error in personality scores: Considering honest and faked responses. *Personality and Individual Differences, 40,* 1201–1211.

Holden, R. R. (2007). Socially desirable responding does moderate scale validity both in experimental and in nonexperimental contexts. *Canadian Journal of Behavioural Science, 39*, 184–201.

Holden, R. R. (2008). Underestimating the effects of faking on the validity of self-report personality scales. *Personality and Individual Differences, 44*, 311–321.

Holden, R. R., Wood, L. L., & Tomashewski, L. (2001). Do response time limitations counteract the effect of faking on personality inventory validity? *Journal of Personality and Social Psychology, 81*, 160–169.

Hopwood, C. J., Morey, L. C., Rogers, R., & Ewell, K. (2007). Malingering on the Personality Assessment Inventory: Identification of specific feigned disorders. *Journal of Personality Assessment, 88*, 43–48.

Hough, L. M., Eaton, N. K., Dunnette, M. D., Kamp, J. D., & McCloy, R. A. (1990). Criterion-related validities of personality constructs and the effect of response distortion on those validities. *Journal of Applied Psychology, 75*, 581–595.

Jackson, D. N., & Messick, S. (1958). Content and style in personality-assessment. *Psychological Bulletin, 55*, 243–252.

John, O. P. (1990). The "Big Five" factor taxonomy: Dimensions of personality in the natural language and in questionnaires. In L. A. Pervin (Ed.), *Handbook of Personality: Theory and Research* (pp. 66–100). San Francisco: Harper.

Kyllonen, P. C., Lipnevich, A. A., Burrus, J., & Roberts, R. D. (2011). *Personality, motivation, and college readiness: A prospectus for assessment and development.* Princeton, NJ: ETS.

Liu, O. L., Minsky, J., Ling, G., & Kyllonen, P. C. (2009). Using the Standardized Letters of Recommendation in selection: Results from a Multidimensional Rasch Model. *Educational and Psychological Measurement, 69*, 475–492.

Lounsbury, J. W., Sundstrom, E., Loveland, J. L., & Gibson, L. W. (2002). Broad versus narrow personality traits in predicting academic performance of adolescents. *Learning and Individual Differences, 14*, 65–75.

MacCann, C., Duckworth, A., & Roberts, R. D. (2009). Identifying the major facets of Conscientiousness in high school students and their relationships with valued educational outcomes. *Learning and Individual Differences, 19*, 451–458.

Martin, B. A., Bowen, C. C., & Hunt, S. T. (2002). How effective are people at faking on personality questionnaires? *Personality and Individual Differences, 32*, 247–256.

Matthews, G., Deary, I. J., & Whiteman, M. C. (2003). *Personality traits* (2 ed.). Cambridge: University Press.

Matthews, G., Zeidner, M., & Roberts, R. D. (2004). *Emotional intelligence: Science and myth*: The MIT Press.

McClelland, D. C. (1987). *Human motivation*: New York: Cambridge University Press.

McCrae, R. R. (1996). Social consequences of experiential openness. *Psychological Bulletin, 51*, 81–90.

Mueller-Hanson, R., Heggestad, E. D., & Thornton, G. C. (2003). Faking and selection: Considering the use of personality from select-in and select-out perspectives. *Journal of Applied Psychology, 88*, 348–355.

Mueller-Hanson, R., Heggestad, E. D., & Thornton, G. C. (2006). Individual differences in impression management: An exploration of the psychological processes underlying faking. *Psychology Science, 3*, 288–312.

Ones, D. S., Viswesvaran, C., & Reiss, A. D. (1996). Role of social desirability in personality testing for personnel selection: The red herring. *Journal of Applied Psychology, 81*, 660–679.

Paulhus, D. L. (2002). Socially desirable responding: The evolution of a construct. In H. I. Braun, D. N. Jackson, & D. E. Wiley (Eds.), *The role of constructs in psychological and educational measurement* (pp. 49–69). Mahwah, NJ: Lawrence Erlbaum Associates.

Pauls, C. A., & Crost, N. W. (2005). Effects of different instructional sets on the construct validity of the NEO-PI-R. *Personality and Individual Differences, 39,* 297–308.

Poropat, A. E. (2009). A meta-analysis of the Five-Factor Model of personality and academic performance. *Psychological Bulletin, 135,* 322–338.

Robie, C., Brown, D. J., & Beaty, J. C. (2007). Do people fake on personality inventories? A verbal protocol analysis. *Journal of Business and Psychology, 21,* 489–509.

Roberts, B. W., Kuncel, N. R., Shiner, R., Caspi, A., & Goldberg, L. R. (2007). The power of personality: The comparative validity of personality traits, socioeconomic status, and cognitive ability for predicting important life outcomes. *Perspectives on Psychological Science, 2,* 313–345.

Roberts, R. D., Markham, P. M., Zeidner, M., & Matthews, G. (2005). Assessing intelligence: Past, present, and future. In O. Wilhelm & R. W. Engle (Eds.), *Understanding and measuring intelligence* (pp. 333–360). Thousand Oaks, CA: Sage Publications.

Saucier, G., & Goldberg, L. R. (2006). Personality, character, and temperament: The cross-language structure of traits. *Psychologie Française, 51,* 265–284.

Schmidt, F. L., Le, H., & Ilies, R. (2003). Beyond alpha: An empirical examination of the effects of different sources of measurement error on reliability estimates for measures of individual-differences constructs. *Psychological Methods, 8,* 206–224.

Schmidt-Atzert, L., Buhner, M., Rischen, S., & Warkentin, V. (2004). Erkennen von Simulation und Dissimulation im Test d2 (Detection of malingering and dissimulation in d2 test). *Diagnostica, 50,* 124–133.

Schmit, M. J., & Ryan, A. M. (1993). The Big Five in personnel selection: Factor structure in applicant and nonapplicant populations. *Journal of Applied Psychology, 78,* 966–974.

Schulze, R., & Roberts, R. D. (2006). Assessing the Big-Five: Development and validation of the Openness Conscientiousness Extraversion Agreeableness Neuroticism Index Condensed (OCEANIC). *Zeitschrift für Psychologie, 214,* 133–149.

Smith, D. B., & Ellingson, J. E. (2002). Substance versus style: A new look at social desirability in motivating contexts. *Journal of Applied Psychology, 87,* 211–219.

Smith, D. B., Hanges, P. J., & Dickson, M. W. (2001). Personnel selection and the five-factor model: Reexamining the effects of applicant's frame of reference. *Journal of Applied Psychology, 86,* 304–315.

Snell, A. F., Sydell, E. J., & Lueke, S. B. (1999). Towards a theory of applicant faking: Integrating studies of deception. *Human Resource Management Review, 9,* 219–242.

Topping, G. D., & O'Gorman, J. G. (1997). Effects of faking set on validity of the NEO-FFI. *Personality and Individual Differences, 23,* 117–124.

Tupes, E., & Christal, R. (1961). Recurrent personality factors based on trait ratings (ASD-TR-61-97). *Lackland Air Force Base, TX: Aeronautical Systems Division, Personnel Laboratory.*

Viswesvaran, C., & Ones, D. S. (1999). Meta-analyses of fakability estimates: Implications for personality measurement. *Educational and Psychological Measurement, 59,* 197–210.

Woodworth, R. (1919). Examination of emotional fitness for warfare. *Psychological Bulletin, 16,* 59–60.

Zeidner, M., Matthews, G., & Roberts, R. D. (2009). *What we know about emotional intelligence: How it affects learning, work, relationships, and our mental health.* Cambridge, MA: MIT Press.

Ziegler, M., & Buehner, M. (2009). Modeling socially desirable responding and its effects. *Educational and Psychological Measurement, 69,* 548–565.

Ziegler, M., Danay, E., Schoelmerich, F., & Buehner, M. (2010). Predicting academic success with the Big 5 rated from different points of view: Self rated, other rated and faked. *European Journal of Personality, 24,* 341–355.

Ziegler, M., Schmidt-Atzert, L., Buehner, M., & Krumm, S. (2007). Fakability of different measurement methods for achievement motivation: Questionnaire, semi-projective, and objective. *Psychology Science, 49,* 291–307.

Ziegler, M., Toomela, A., & Buehner, M. (2009). A reanalysis of Toomela (2003): Spurious measurement error as cause for common variance between personality factors. *Psychology Science Quarterly, 51,* 65–75.

PART TWO

Do People Fake and Does It Matter?

The Existence of Faking and Its Impact on Personality Assessments

2 People Fake Only When They *Need* to Fake[1]

■ JILL E. ELLINGSON

In the extant faking literature, researchers have sought with great persistence to answer the question of whether people fake on personality assessments when they should be motivated to do so. Whereas it is clear that individuals are capable of faking their responses when asked (Viswesvaran & Ones, 1999), it is not at all clear that individuals will engage in faking of their own accord when responding to personality questions as part of a hiring process or other high-stakes assessment context. Previous research on the question of whether people will fake in operational, high-stakes settings has resulted in two distinct bodies of evidence within the faking literature. These are research supporting the conclusion that faking does not occur at meaningful levels (e.g., Ellingson, Sackett, & Connelly, 2007; Ellingson, Smith, & Sackett, 2001; Hogan, Barrett, & Hogan, 2007; Hough, Eaton, Dunnette, Kamp, & McCloy, 1990; Ones & Viswesvaran, 1998; Smith, Hanges, & Dickson, 2001) and research that suggests the opposite conclusion (e.g., Birkeland, Manson, Kisamore, Brannick, & Smith, 2006; Donovan, Dwight, & Hurtz, 2003; Griffith, Chmielowski, & Yoshita, 2007; Hough, 1998a; Mueller-Hanson, Heggestad, & Thornton, 2003; Rosse, Stecher, Miller, & Levin, 1998). The charge of this chapter was to discuss the first body of research supporting the statement that people do not fake with the intention of pairing it with another chapter charged with arguing that people do fake based on the second body of research. The faking literature is full of such "take sides" discussions; I would propose that our ability to build a solid foundation of knowledge on the issue of faking has suffered for it. The diametrically opposed results signal that our universalistic approach has merely served to position the resulting evidence at unnecessary odds. As with most debates on social science phenomena, the answer sought within this discussion probably lies somewhere between the two perspectives. In short, the question of do people fake when responding to personality assessments in high-stakes contexts belies a definitive "yes" or "no" answer.

This chapter seeks a resolution to this discussion by reframing the question from "Do people fake?" to "*When* do people fake?" The position that individuals will not under any circumstances distort their responses to a personality assessment is unreasonable and unverifiable. Granting this statement precludes the conclusion

1. Portions of this chapter were presented as part of a symposium conducted at the annual meeting of the Society for Industrial and Organizational Psychology, April 2009, New Orleans, LA. Correspondence concerning this chapter should be addressed to Jill E. Ellingson, Department of Management and Human Resources, The Ohio State University, 734 Fisher Hall, 2100 Neil Avenue, Columbus, OH, 43210. E-mail: ellingson@fisher.osu.edu.

that people do not fake, but importantly, *it does not also connote that people will fake.* Instead, the position put forth in this chapter is that faking is a behavior in which individuals will engage under certain circumstances. This position is consistent with recent research suggesting that faking is transient in nature—it varies across assessment occasions within individuals due to temporal fluctuations and context-specific factors (Heggestad, George, & Reeve, 2006; Ziegler & Buehner, 2009). The context-specific factors of interest here are those that are self-defined by the individual. Previous work characterizes an assessment situation in terms of salient structural aspects (e.g., item type, warnings, administration medium) that differ from one assessment context to the next (e.g., Christiansen, Burns, & Montgomery, 2005; Dwight & Donovan, 2003; Heggestad, Morrison, Reeve, & McCloy, 2006; Richman, Kiesler, Weisband, & Drasgow, 1999). These are important elements to consider. Nonetheless, I argue that an individual's personal perspective or situation can actively mitigate the high-stakes nature of an assessment situation and shape behavior within that situation.

The idea that faking behavior will be partially determined by one's personal situation has been acknowledged in previous theoretical work (e.g., Snell, Sydell, & Lueke, 1999). Yet, there has been little focus on explicating the manner by which personal circumstances impact faking. When personality assessments are used to allocate opportunity, faking should emerge when (1) an individual perceives such behavior as necessary for gaining access to that opportunity, (2) that individual believes she is capable of faking, and (3) that opportunity has personal value to that individual. The value of an opportunity will vary among individuals presumably on the basis of personal circumstances. Dramatic between-individual differences in value perceptions could represent an important explanatory factor.

This chapter will explore the nature of individual differences in value perceptions as a predictor of when faking behavior will occur. The chapter is divided into five sections. The first section defines faking and positions it as a motivated behavior. Drawing from classic motivation theory, expectancy theory is introduced as a mechanism for reviewing current models of faking behavior. The second section outlines how current conceptualizations of faking incorporate expectancy and instrumentality judgments as determining factors in the choice to fake. The third section questions the lack of attention to valence judgments in theoretical models of faking. Heterogeneity in individuals' perceptions of the value of a given opportunity is put forth to dispute the assumption that high-stakes assessment contexts are universally perceived as such. The fourth section discusses methods for introducing the concept of valence into current models of faking behavior. Three constructs that manifest valence beliefs are reviewed: marketability, job search self-efficacy, and job desirability. Finally, the fifth section offers some closing thoughts on how we might proceed in investigating the role of valence in faking research.

■ FAKING AS A CHOICE BEHAVIOR

The term *faking* has been used synonymously with other terms such as social desirability, impression management, response bias, lying, and dissimulation.

Although potentially related, these other concepts are interpreted differently within their respective literatures and invoke different configuration elements (Bolino, Kacmar, Turnley, & Gilstrap, 2008; Bond & DePaulo, 2006; Furnham, 1986; Leary & Kowalski, 1990; Zerbe & Paulhus, 1987). For the purposes of this discussion, faking is viewed as distinct from these concepts. Specifically, faking is defined here as a volitional behavior. Individuals knowingly choose to answer personality questions in a manner that provides an inaccurate characterization or facade. Although certain individuals may be predisposed to fake due to certain traits, faking as conceptualized here is a manifest behavior and not a trait. From the perspective of operational users, faking is maladaptive since it prohibits decisions based on full and accurate information consistent with an individual's typical behavior. Yet faking, again as defined here, generally lacks malicious intent. It is viewed as a behavior engaged in to support or to benefit one's own interests. Although the behavior may harm others, such consequences are a byproduct of the behavior and not the motive of the behavior.

This characterization of faking implies that it is an effortful behavior. Individuals choose to direct energy toward the creation and provision of inaccurate responses. Viewed in this manner, faking behavior requires a motivating force (Leary & Kowalski, 1990). Indeed, faking researchers work hard to create viable methodologies wherein research participants should be "motivated to fake." And yet, once that methodology is selected, we simply assume that such motivation will emerge. For example, it is common practice within the faking literature to call for research designs that draw on job applicants as a sample (e.g., Ellingson et al., 2001; Griffith et al., 2007; Smith & Robie, 2004). We assume that applicants will be universally "motivated to fake" because they are competing for a job opportunity that we believe they value. Perhaps we have erred in that assumption. Motivation results from the interaction of both individual and environmental factors (Pinder, 1998). Faking will surface only when both individual *and* situational factors motivate that behavior. We have spent very little time exploring the question of whether our "motivated" samples are really motivated to fake.

By viewing faking behavior through a motivational lens, we can draw on classic expectancy theory as a framework for conceptualizing the psychological elements necessary for motivating faking behavior (Kanfer, 1991; Vroom, 1964). Relative to other motivation theories such as reinforcement theory or need theory, expectancy theory has long been identified as well-suited for predicting choice behaviors when such behaviors are linked to valued extrinsic outcomes (e.g., Landy & Becker, 1987; Wanous, Keon, & Latack, 1983). Also, expectancy theory is formulated from an episodic perspective for the purpose of considering specific behaviors in specific situations (Kanfer, 1991). High-stakes assessment contexts involve the allocation of valued, competitive opportunities such as being hired, receiving a promotion, or gaining entrance into a university or degree program based on the assessment results. Each assessment context is unique and independent. When individuals are asked to complete a personality assessment as part of the process for accessing a valued opportunity they are faced with the choice of whether to fake. When making this choice, individuals with positive estimates of expectancy, instrumentality, and valence should be motivated to engage in faking behavior as a method for securing that opportunity.

Expectancy judgments concern one's perceived ability to fake successfully in a given high-stakes assessment situation. Do individuals believe they have the capability to fake? Do they believe that they have the skills and knowledge necessary? Does the situation appear to facilitate this behavior? Individuals who feel more confident in their ability to fake on a given assessment tool should be more likely to do so. Valence judgments capture the perceived value of the allocated opportunity to the individual. Such judgments reflect the degree to which the opportunity of interest is preferred among other options and the belief that this opportunity will bring personal satisfaction. Instrumentality judgments reflect the perception that faking is necessary in this assessment context. Faking is a critical vehicle for competing effectively against others for this valued opportunity. Each factor has the potential to play a key role in an individual's choice to fake.

■ EXPECTANCY AND INSTRUMENTALITY JUDGMENTS

Current theoretical models of faking behavior focus predominantly on factors that drive expectancy and instrumentality judgments. As displayed in Figure 2.1, the variables put forth in these models can be sorted based on the type of belief that a particular variable is likely to impact. Differences in personality, intelligence, knowledge, and experience are thought to position an individual as more or less capable of faking (Griffith, Malm, English, Yoshita, & Gujar, 2006; McFarland & Ryan, 2000; Raymark & Tafero, 2009; Riggio, Salinas, & Tucker, 1988; Snell et al., 1999). Persons who are highly methodical, perceptive, self-monitoring, and knowledgeable of the assessment context in terms of the nature of the opportunity and the constructs being assessed should be more capable of faking. Situational factors such as the degree of

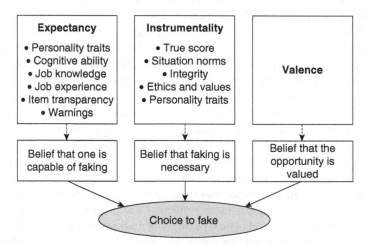

Figure 2.1 Elements of expectancy theory as represented by the situational and individual difference variables found in current models of faking behavior.

item transparency and the usage of warnings about verification or the presence of a lie scale are also identified as influential in determining faking behavior (McFarland & Ryan, 2000; Snell et al., 1999). Assessments that incorporate subtle questions or the receipt of specific instructions about the potential for detection should impact individuals' judgments about their capability of faking. Capability judgments based on both person and situation factors should, in turn, determine expectancy judgments. Specifically, individuals who feel efficacious in their ability to fake because they possess the characteristics necessary and encounter an assessment situation that facilitates this behavior should exhibit positive expectancy beliefs.

Instrumentality judgments may be impacted by multiple theoretical factors included in faking models. McFarland and Ryan (2000) identified an individual's true score as an important determinant of faking behavior. They highlighted the evident fact that individuals whose true scores on the personality traits of interest match operational needs will lack the opportunity to fake. Respondents can fake only when their true characterization differs from expected requirements. Necessarily, this should reflect the presence of negative instrumentality beliefs. If someone already possesses the required traits, then there is little reason to view faking as a critical behavior. Other variables likely to impact instrumentality judgments are those that capture individuals' perceptions of situation norms. Snell et al. (1999) and Boyce (2005) noted the importance of considering individuals' perceptions of others' behavior and attitudes as potential determinants of faking. When faking is thought to be a common and accepted behavior among the individuals assessed, such individuals should be more likely to view faking as necessary for competing successfully.

Current models also discuss the role of personal codes of behavior. McFarland and Ryan (2000) identified morals, values, and religious beliefs as potential indicators of whether faking is considered to be acceptable behavior. Boyce (2005) highlighted the role of personal ethics as an important determinant. Similarly, Snell et al. (1999) discussed the significance of considering personal attitudes toward faking. Individuals whose values or moral stance preclude actions of deception may reaffirm those personal standards through a belief that faking is not necessary. The desire to avoid dissonance may lead these individuals to reduce instrumentality beliefs concluding that the outcome of interest is obtainable without such questionable behavior (Festinger, 1957). Researchers have also theorized that certain personality traits should differentiate individuals on the basis of their perspective on faking behavior (Griffith et al., 2006; McFarland & Ryan, 2000; Snell et al., 1999). Personality traits characterize individuals' behavior, interpretations, and attitudes (Hogan, 1991). Individuals high in integrity may view faking as inappropriate and thus may choose to abstain from faking behavior (Griffith et al., 2006; Hogan et al., 2007; Snell et al., 1999). In contrast, other traits may lead individuals to be partial toward faking and to frame situations as requiring such behavior. Individuals high on manipulativeness, for example, should be more likely to view faking behavior as acceptable and necessary for accomplishing their goals, thereby increasing instrumentality beliefs. In short, both trait differences and one's personal code of behavior should impact how a given respondent approaches and perceives the assessment situation in terms of the criticality of engaging in faking.

■ WHERE IS VALENCE?

When framed within the tenets of expectancy theory, current models of faking behavior have much to say about factors that support expectancy and instrumentality beliefs and very little to say about factors that contribute to the perceived value of the allocated opportunity. This is a conspicuous absence. Shiflett and Cohen (1982, p. 75) found evidence that valence judgments may be the more potent determinant of behavior compared to expectancy or instrumentality judgments and noted that "what you don't have, but want, determines behavior." The primary feature that defines an assessment situation is the opportunity being allocated. McClelland (1985) emphasized that situational demands are effective in inducing action only when they connect to personal incentives. Furthermore, how one's motives translate into behavior is partially dependent on what one values and deems important. Leary and Kowalski (1990) stressed that individuals will be motivated to alter the impression made on others when doing so has implications for an individual's ability to fulfill personal, valued goals. Schlenker (1980) discussed the proposition that behavior designed to manage the impressions of others is rooted in hedonic principle; these actions are designed to maximize expected rewards. Similarly, deception research demonstrates that individuals lie out of self-interest (e.g., DePaulo & Bell, 1996). Individuals should be motivated to fake when they value the allocated opportunity because they believe attainment of that opportunity is integral to personal expectations of satisfaction.

The trend in past faking research has been to prescriptively identify opportunities as valued. We assume that since a job or degree program is a scarce resource (not everyone who desires it can be satisfied) then it must have positive valence. Yet, all such opportunities are not equally valued in the eyes of individuals. Heterogeneity due to differences in valence beliefs may begin to explain why the literature is fraught with discrepant findings. Consistent with this idea, research using upper-level, professional, or managerial samples tends to find lower levels of faking behavior (e.g., Bartram, 1995; Ellingson et al., 2007; Robie, Zickar, & Schmit, 2001; Smith & Robie, 2004; Tsaousis & Nikolaou, 2001), whereas research using nonexempt, lower-level type applicants tends to find higher levels of faking behavior (e.g., Boyce, 2005; Griffith et al., 2007; Hunt, 2006; Schmit & Ryan, 1993; Smith & Canger, 2006). Admittedly, this is a crude dichotomization, but it hints that we may have missed the notion of need as a driving force of faking.

The idea of considering individual differences in the degree to which an opportunity is valued has surfaced in previous work. Snell et al. (1999) noted that the motivation to fake should be dependent on the personal needs of an applicant. Individuals who are desperate for a job should be more likely to fake, presumably because feelings of desperation increase the valence of the opportunity. McFarland and Ryan (2000) included "desire for job" in their model of faking behavior. They positioned the variable as a moderator and suggested that the desirability of the outcome may outweigh an individual's personal stance on faking. In other words, valence beliefs may override instrumentality beliefs in determining faking behavior. However, they stopped short of offering a detailed account of the variable. Ten years later, this remains an avenue that faking researchers have yet to explore. The remainder of this chapter delineates how we might conceptualize the concept of valence as it pertains to choices about faking behavior for the purpose of stimulating research in this direction.

■ CONSTRUCTS THAT MANIFEST VALENCE

Understanding if an opportunity is valued requires a comparative evaluation of options (Vroom, 1964). Given a set of outcomes, positively valent beliefs arise when we identify a preference for one outcome over another. It is a subjective valuation based on the nature of potential alternatives. The depiction of one's set of possible outcomes, then, drives perceptions of value. For example, when an applicant's possible outcomes with respect to a given job opening are limited to being employed or being unemployed, the valence of the job opportunity at hand likely increases dramatically. In contrast, when an applicant enjoys access to multiple job opportunities or is currently employed, valence judgments should shift by comparison. This suggests that measuring valence judgments in the context of operational, high-stakes assessment requires identifying one or more constructs that capture individual differences in perceptions about one's set of potential outcomes. As a starting point, there are three such constructs that could serve to reflect the perceived value of a given opportunity relative to other outcomes: job desirability, marketability, and job search self-efficacy. The following discussion provides a theoretical justification for interpreting these constructs as representative of valence judgments. To support this dialogue, Figure 2.2 presents a comparative summary of the three constructs based on the content discussed.

	Job desirability	Marketability	Job search self-efficacy
Definition	The degree to which a given job is wanted or needed.	An individual's personal perception regarding one's value to employers.	An individual's self-evaluation of one's capacity to perform job search behaviors and obtain employment.
Manifestation of valence	Proximal	Distal	Distal
Potential antecedents	Judgment of fit or match Need for employment Perceived lack of opportunities	Extensive skill sets More experience Advanced education Developed networks	Advanced education Extensive academic portfolios Job search experience Job search training
Sample items[1]	This is the perfect job for me. I need this job. While I have other opportunities available to me, this is the job that I want most. Obtaining this job is of primary importance to me. I'll do whatever is necessary to get this job. I want this job regardless of what it takes to be competitive.	There are a lot of employment possibilities for people with my education and background. I could easily obtain a comparable job with another employer. There are many jobs available for me given my skills and experience. Given my skills and experience, organizations will veiw me as a value-added resource.	I feel certain about my ability to get the job that I want. I have what it takes to get a good job. I am certain that my job search will be successful.

[1]Marketability and job search self-efficacy items taken from Eby, Butts, & Lockwood (2003), Chapman & Webster (2006), and Moynihan, Roehling, LePine, & Boswell (2003).

Figure 2.2 Summary of three constructs that manifest valence.

Job Desirability

Asking applicants to evaluate the desirability of a given job opportunity represents a proximal measure of the degree to which the allocated opportunity is valued. Indeed, valence is typically measured by obtaining individuals' ratings on the desirability of various outcomes (e.g., Ilgen, Nebeker, & Pritchard, 1981; Klein, 1991; Lawler & Suttle, 1973; Leon, 1981; Shiflett & Cohen, 1982). In most high-stakes assessment contexts, we cannot know an individual's set of potential outcomes a priori, which precludes gathering comparative valence ratings across outcomes. Yet, this comparative process is surely taking place within the minds of individuals. In addition, Vroom (1964, p. 16) stated that "means acquire valence as a consequence of their relationship to ends." In other words, if the actions that are required to compete for a job opportunity run counter to an individual's preferences, the presence of those required actions will serve to decrease the valence of the outcome. A job desirability measure would capture the emergent internal valuation process through items that facilitate that comparison by targeting its result.

Figure 2.2 provides some sample items that reflect how we could begin to quantify this process. Note that the level of measurement present in these statements is generalized as opposed to being specific to characteristics of the job such as pay, location, corporate values, or responsibilities that determine an individual's attraction to a job or fit with a job. Although these elements can certainly contribute to an individual's conclusion about the desirability of an opportunity, it is important to capture desirability judgments independent of specific job characteristics because job desirability can also function independent of job attraction or job match. For example, individuals desperate for employment may actively pursue unattractive positions because being employed in a position that is less attractive may be judged as a better outcome relative to remaining unemployed. Hence, the job opportunity is viewed as desirable even though it contains characteristics that are unattractive. Presumably, individuals who evaluate the allocated opportunity as more desirable will hold positively valent beliefs about the job. These individuals should then be more motivated to fake as a means of increasing the potential of securing that valued opportunity.

Marketability

Research in vocational and career development established the construct of marketability to refer to an individual's personal perception regarding their value to employers (Eby, Butts, & Lockwood, 2003; Veiga, 1983). The construct captures a sense of confidence in one's abilities and an understanding of one's worth in the marketplace. Individuals with extensive skill sets, more experience, higher levels of education, and strong internal and external networks tend to perceive themselves as more marketable (Cable & Judge 1996; Eby et al., 2003; Eddleston, Baldrige, & Veiga, 2004; Sullivan, Carden, & Martin, 1998). Reflective of this characterization, marketability is typically measured by asking applicants to rate their perceived favorability using items such as those presented in Figure 2.2.

The competencies of highly marketable individuals are transferable, and are applicable in many different organizational settings. As any graduate from a top-ranked degree program can attest (and empirical research bears out), individuals who are highly marketable are sought after, often enjoying multiple competing offers (Chapman & Webster, 2006). They receive offers of higher compensation from organizations attempting to retain them and organizations attempting to attract them (Fossum & Fitch, 1985; Gowan & Lepak, 2007). Thus, individuals high in marketability believe they possess a valued human capital profile that should afford greater labor market mobility and increased job opportunity (Blau, 1992; Chapman & Webster, 2006).

Marketability provides for greater degrees of freedom in applicant behavior. Cable and Judge (1996) found that individuals who perceived themselves as having more opportunities in the job market were more likely to reject a job offer. Bauer, Maertz, Dolen, and Campion (1998) argued that applicants with more options should be more likely to reject organizations when the selection practices used are viewed as procedurally unjust. Liden and Parsons (1986) demonstrated that applicants with multiple job possibilities were less likely to indicate intentions to accept job offers even when they found the recruiting experience to be positive relative to applicants who had few alternatives. For marketable individuals, any given opportunity is less necessary and has less personal value in the presence of other equally competitive opportunities. In other words, they are less dependent on the allocated job at hand. This implies that persons who are high in marketability will judge any given job opportunity as having less valence since they readily perceive that other options are available.

With valence reduced, the likelihood of faking should be reduced as well. Marketable individuals have the option to choose not to engage in faking even if it means the loss of a job opportunity. Furthermore, when faced with evaluating multiple opportunities, highly marketable individuals should be motivated to present an accurate portrayal of themselves in order to maximize fit and realize the value of a given opportunity. For talented applicants, answering honestly supports their interests because it allows them to sort opportunities efficiently. In short, marketability provides the leverage necessary to enjoy the luxury of honesty.

Job Search Self-Efficacy

Job search self-efficacy refers to an individual's self-evaluation of their capacity to perform the job search behaviors necessary to obtain employment (Kanfer & Hulin, 1985; Saks & Ashforth, 1999). It reflects an individual's confidence in their ability to land a job (Moynihan, Roehling, LePine, & Boswell, 2003; Saks, 2006; Vinokur, Price, & Schul, 1995). Individuals who are high in job search self-efficacy are self-assured in their ability to conduct a successful job search; they expect to do well. These individuals often possess greater levels of education and stronger academic portfolios (Moynihan et al., 2003; Saks & Ashforth, 1999; Wanberg, Watt, & Rumsey, 1996). Measures of job search self-efficacy constructed at an intermediate level of specificity best represent this general feeling of job search confidence and personal assurance that one's efforts will produce positive results (Lent & Hackett, 1987). Intermediate job search self-efficacy scales ask applicants to rate their generalized job search confidence using items such as those presented in Figure 2.2.

High job search self-efficacy gives individuals the self-assurance to act more freely in accordance with personal expectations, preferences, or standards. LaHuis (2005) found that individuals high in job search self-efficacy were more likely to associate fairness perceptions with job pursuit intentions. In other words, those who are more confident in their ability to obtain other job offers are more likely to select-out of a hiring process that they deem unfair (Gilliland & Steiner, 2001). Saks (2006) provided evidence that job search self-efficacy moderates the relationship between the number of offers received and employment status. Individuals who were high in job search self-efficacy were more likely to reject in-hand job offers and remain unemployed in favor of pursuing the best employment opportunity.

Confidence in one's job search capability also gives an individual greater latitude in valuing any given job opportunity. Necessarily, any opportunity can have less value since other opportunities are reasoned to be available and accessible. Essentially, high job search self-efficacy increases one's perception of the set of possible outcomes. With other options available, valence beliefs regarding the particular opportunity allocated are free to be less positive. When valence is reduced, the likelihood that individuals will choose to fake should be less as well. They may be capable of faking and they may view faking as important for obtaining the job at hand. Yet, because the opportunity allocated has less value they choose not to engage in faking.

In contrast, the perception that one has few options in the labor marketplace or a lack of confidence in one's job search capability will predetermine a given opportunity as positively valent. Individuals who question their competitiveness or their ability to search effectively face an uncertain future. This limits their ability to forgo the option at hand—they need to land this job. Their actions are restricted by these self-perceptions, and it follows that this restriction should substantially increase the value of the allocated opportunity. These individuals should be strongly motivated to fake as a means of increasing the potential of securing that opportunity.

It is not anticipated that models of faking behavior would need to incorporate all three constructs. The constructs are theoretically distinct, but are likely to be related. For example, the two distal measures of marketability and job search self-efficacy may not increment above and beyond the proximal measure of job desirability. A strong emotional desire for a job could be the most effective measure of valence. There is also a need to consider the extent to which marketability and job search self-efficacy are distinct constructs. It seems likely that an individual who is highly marketable should also possess high job search self-efficacy, suggesting a notable degree of overlap. However, the reverse may not hold true. For example, individuals who reenter the labor market after a long absence from employment may improve their job search self-efficacy through training in the search process, but still question the degree to which their skills are valued in the marketplace. Indeed, research conducted by Eden and Aviram (1993) demonstrates that unemployed individuals' self-efficacy can be increased through the training technique of behavior modeling independent of whether such individuals view themselves as marketable. Ultimately, these issues represent empirical questions that, although ripe for conceptual speculation, should be explored through data collection and construct validation methods.

■ **FINAL THOUGHTS**

Theoretical models of faking may benefit from recognizing that individuals are diverse not only in terms of their ability and disposition, but also in terms of their personal circumstances. Perceptions that individuals hold about their personal situation and needs may explain significant variance in faking behavior. Introducing the third component of valence into our conceptualizations of faking would help account for respondent heterogeneity, better clarifying when and under what conditions faking occurs. When individuals judge that they are capable of faking and that faking is required in order to compete successfully for an opportunity that they value, they are more likely to choose to fake. However, when individuals question their ability to fake, question the necessity of faking, or fail to value the outcome of interest, they should be less likely to fake.

Given this perspective, taking a closer look at research samples and methodology should increase the precision of our investigations into faking behavior. Clearly, the assumption that respondents are a single motivated entity is problematic. This raises concerns about meta-analytic work that has typically treated applicants as homogeneous (e.g., Birkeland et al., 2006; Hough, 1998b; Ones & Viswesvaran, 1998), and thus may mask key patterns in faking behavior. Snell et al. (1999) noted that characteristics of the samples may help explain discrepancies in research addressing whether faking impacts the criterion-related validity of personality assessments. We might expect that the discrepant results observed in research on the impact of faking on personality assessment factor structure (see Ellingson et al., 2001 and Schmit & Ryan, 1993 for an example of diverging construct validity evidence) partially result from this issue as well. If valence judgments differ among individuals, then we must take care to gather information on this variable for the purpose of either controlling or exploring those differences. Experimental treatments should include a manipulation check to confirm that participants are in fact equally motivated by the artificial context. Field research should include measures of valence in addition to more typical predictors of faking behavior. Essentially, failing to measure this difference among individuals may decrease our ability to understand the effects of faking on the psychometric properties of personality assessments and on selection decisions made using these tools.

As it is hoped that faking researchers will begin to explore for differences in judgments about the degree to which individuals value a given outcome, some comments on additional options for exploration would seem to be in order. First, although this chapter introduces three constructs (job desirability, marketability, and job search self-efficacy) that are based in the employment literature, we could conceptualize the development of similar constructs based in the education literature. When education institutions rely on personality assessment tools as a means of differentiating student applicants, these individuals may make similar judgments—judgments about their marketability to schools, their ability to get accepted into degree programs, and the desirability of a given degree program. Although the item frame of reference may be different, these valence beliefs may be equally able to motivate faking behavior. The majority of the faking literature is based in the context of internal or external hiring; it may be time to broaden our perspective to include other high-stakes contexts.

Second, defining the situation in terms of the value of the allocated opportunity introduces the potential for an individual's desires to interact with structural aspects of the situation in ways that render either element moot. For example, high levels of job desirability may reduce the controlling effect of warnings about answering dishonestly. Individuals who want the job badly enough may be willing to risk detection and choose to fake regardless. In contrast, individuals less desirous of the opportunity may be particularly sensitive to warnings. Future research might explore the potential for this interaction in order to shed light on salient elements of the assessment situation. Lastly, it would be interesting to track the relationship between self-perceptions of marketability or job search self-efficacy and faking behavior longitudinally. Individuals who remain unemployed longer than they anticipated may respond with decreased judgments of marketability and job search self-efficacy that should be associated with an increase in faking behavior. Future research might seek to identify and better understand those critical points when an applicant shifts from choosing *not* to fake to choosing *to* fake.

References

Bartram, D. (1995). The predictive validity of the EPI and 16PF for military flying training. *Journal of Occupational and Organizational Psychology, 68*, 219–236.

Bauer, T. N., Maertz, C. P., Dolen, M. R., & Campion, M. A. (1998). Longitudinal assessment of applicant reactions to employment testing and test outcome feedback. *Journal of Applied Psychology, 83*, 892–903.

Birkeland, S. A., Manson, T. M., Kisamore, J. L., Brannick, M. T., & Smith, M. A. (2006). A meta-analytic investigation of job applicant faking on personality measures. *International Journal of Selection and Assessment, 14*, 317–335.

Blau, D. M. (1992). An empirical analysis of employed and unemployed search behavior. *Industrial and Labor Relations Review, 45*, 738–752.

Bolino, M. C., Kacmar, K. M., Turnley, W. H., & Gilstrap, J. B. (2008). A multi-level review of impression management motives and behavior. *Journal of Management, 34*, 1080–1109.

Bond, C. F., & DePaulo, B. M. (2006). Accuracy of deception judgments. *Personality and Social Psychology Review, 10*, 214–234.

Boyce, A. S. (2005, April). An investigation of faking: Its antecedents and impacts in applicant settings. In D. Ones (Chair), *Usefulness of Social Desirability Scales, Faking Scores, and Potential Alternatives.* Symposium conducted at the annual meeting of the Society for Industrial and Organizational Psychology, Los Angeles, CA.

Cable, D. M., & Judge, T. A. (1996). Person-organization fit, job choice decision, and organizational entry. *Organizational Behavior and Human Decision Processes, 67*, 294–311.

Chapman, D., & Webster, J. (2006). Toward an integrated model of applicant reactions and job choice. *International Journal of Human Resource Management, 17*, 1032–1057.

Christiansen, N. D., Burns, G. N., & Montgomery, G. E. (2005). Reconsidering forced-choice item formats for applicant personality assessment. *Human Performance, 18*, 267–307.

DePaulo, B. M., & Bell, K. L. (1996). Truth and investment: Lies are told to those who care. *Journal of Personality and Social Psychology, 71*, 703–716.

Donovan, J. J., Dwight, S. A., & Hurtz, G. M. (2003). An assessment of the prevalence, severity, and verifiability of entry-level applicant faking using the randomized response technique. *Human Performance, 16*, 81–106.

Dwight, S. A., & Donovan, J. J. (2003). Do warnings not to fake reduce faking? *Human Performance, 16,* 1–23.

Eby, L. T., Butts, M., & Lockwood, A. (2003). Predictors of success in the era of the boundaryless career. *Journal of Organizational Behavior, 24,* 689–708.

Eddleston, K. A., Baldridge, D. C., & Veiga, J. F. (2004). Toward modeling the predictors of managerial career success: Does gender matter? *Journal of Managerial Psychology, 19,* 360–385.

Eden, D., & Aviram, A. (1993). Self-efficacy training to speed reemployment: Helping people to help themselves. *Journal of Applied Psychology, 78,* 352–360.

Ellingson, J. E., Sackett, P. R., & Connelly, B. S. (2007). Personality assessment across selection and development contexts: Insights into response distortion. *Journal of Applied Psychology, 92,* 386–395.

Ellingson, J. E., Smith, D. B., & Sackett, P. R. (2001). Investigating the influence of social desirability on personality factor structure. *Journal of Applied Psychology, 86,* 122–133.

Festinger, L. (1957). *A theory of cognitive dissonance.* Stanford, CA: Stanford University Press.

Fossum, J. A., & Fitch, M. K. (1985). The effects of individual and contextual attributes on the sizes of recommended salary increases. *Personnel Psychology, 38,* 587–602.

Furnham, A. (1986). Response bias, social desirability and dissimulation. *Personality and Individual Differences, 7,* 385–400.

Gilliland, S. W., & Steiner, D. D. (2001). Causes and consequences of applicant perceptions of unfairness. In R. Cropanzano (Ed.), *Justice in the workplace, Vol. 2* (pp. 175–196). Mahwah, NJ: Lawrence Erlbaum.

Gowan, M. A., & Lepak, D. (2007). Current and future value of human capital: Predictors of reemployment compensation following a job loss. *Journal of Employment Counseling, 44,* 135–144.

Griffith, R. L., Chmielowski, T., & Yoshita, Y. (2007). Do applicants fake? An examination of the frequency of applicant faking behavior. *Personnel Review, 36,* 341–355.

Griffith, R., Malm, T., English, A., Yoshita, Y., & Gujar, A. (2006). Applicant faking behavior: Teasing apart the influence of situational variance, cognitive biases, and individual differences. In R. L. Griffith & M. H. Peterson (Eds.), *A closer examination of applicant faking behavior* (pp. 151–178). Greenwich, CT: Information Age.

Heggestad, E. D., George, E., & Reeve, C. L. (2006). Transient error in personality scores: Considering honest and faked responses. *Personality and Individual Differences, 40,* 1201–1211.

Heggestad, E. D., Morrison, M., Reeve, C. L., & McCloy, R. A. (2006). Forced-choice assessments of personality for selection: Evaluating issues of normative assessment and faking resistance. *Journal of Applied Psychology, 91,* 9–24.

Hogan, R. (1991). Personality and personality measurement. In M. D. Dunnette & L. M. Hough (Eds.), *Handbook of industrial and organizational psychology, Vol. 2* (pp. 873–919). Palo Alto, CA: Consulting Psychologists Press.

Hogan, J., Barrett, P., & Hogan, R. (2007). Personality measurement, faking, and employment selection. *Journal of Applied Psychology, 92,* 1270–1285.

Hough, L. M. (1998a). Effects of intentional distortion in personality measurement and evaluation of suggested palliatives. *Human Performance, 11,* 209–244.

Hough, L. M. (1998b). Personality at work: Issues and evidence. In M. Hakel (Ed.), *Beyond multiple choice: Evaluating alternatives to traditional testing for selection* (pp. 131–166). Hillsdale, NJ: Lawrence Erlbaum.

Hough, L. M., Eaton, N. K., Dunnette, M. D., Kamp, J. D., & McCloy, R. A. (1990). Criterion-related validities of personality constructs and the effect of response distortion of those validities. *Journal of Applied Psychology, 75,* 581–595.

Hunt, S. T. (2006, May). Risks associated with using measures of conscientiousness to predict job performance. In R. R. Sinclair & S. T. Hunt (Chairs), *Staffing the Entry Level Workforce: Selection, Fit, and Climate Considerations*. Symposium conducted at the annual meeting of the Society for Industrial and Organizational Psychology, Dallas, TX.

Ilgen, D. R., Nebeker, D. M., & Pritchard, R. D. (1981). Expectancy theory measures: An empirical comparison in an experimental simulation. *Organizational Behavior and Human Performance, 28,* 189–223.

Kanfer, R. (1991). Motivation theory and industrial and organizational psychology. In M. D. Dunnette & L. M. Hough (Eds.), *Handbook of industrial and organizational psychology, Vol. 1* (pp. 75–170). Palo Alto, CA: Consulting Psychologists Press.

Kanfer, R., & Hulin, C. L. (1985). Individual differences in successful job searches following lay-off. *Personnel Psychology, 38,* 835– 847.

Klein, H. J. (1991). Further evidence on the relationship between goal setting and expectancy theories. *Organizational Behavior and Human Decision Processes, 49,* 230–257.

LaHuis, D. M. (2005). Individual differences in applicant reactions: A job-search perspective. *International Journal of Selection and Assessment, 13,* 150–159.

Landy, F. J., & Becker, W. S. (1987). Motivation theory reconsidered. In L. L. Cummings & B. M. Staw (Eds.), *Research in organizational behavior* (pp. 1–38). Greenwich, CT: JAI.

Lawler, E. E., III., & Suttle, J. L. (1973). Expectancy theory and job behavior. *Organizational Behavior and Human Performance, 9,* 482–503.

Leary, M. R., & Kowalski, R. M. (1990). Impression management: A literature review and two-component model. *Psychological Bulletin, 107,* 34–47.

Lent, R. W., & Hackett, G. (1987). Career self-efficacy: Empirical status and future directions. *Journal of Vocational Behavior, 30,* 347–382.

Leon, F. R. (1981). The role of positive and negative outcomes in the causation of motivational forces. *Journal of Applied Psychology, 66,* 45–53.

Liden, R. C., & Parsons, C. K. (1986). A field study of job applicant interview perceptions, alternative opportunities, and demographic characteristics. *Personnel Psychology, 39,* 109–122.

McClelland, D. C. (1985). *Human motivation.* Glenview, IL: Scott Foresman.

McFarland, L. A., & Ryan, A. M. (2000). Variance in faking across noncognitive measures. *Journal of Applied Psychology, 85,* 812–821.

Moynihan, L. M., Roehling, M. V., LePine, M. A., & Boswell, W. R. (2003). A longitudinal study of the relationships among job search self-efficacy, job interviews, and employment outcomes. *Journal of Business and Psychology, 18,* 207– 233.

Mueller-Hanson, R., Heggestad, E. D., & Thornton, G. C., III. (2003). Faking and selection: Considering the use of personality from select-in and select-out perspectives. *Journal of Applied Psychology, 88,* 348–355.

Ones, D. S., & Viswesvaran, C. (1998). The effects of social desirability and faking on personality and integrity assessment for personnel selection. *Human Performance, 11,* 245–269.

Pinder, C. C. (1998). *Work motivation in organizational behavior.* Upper Saddle River, NJ: Prentice Hall.

Raymark, P. H., & Tafero, T. L. (2009). Individual differences in the ability to fake on personality measures. *Human Performance, 22,* 86–103.

Richman, W. L., Kiesler, S., Weisband, S., & Drasgow, F. (1999). A meta-analytic study of social desirability distortion in computer-administered questionnaires, traditional questionnaires, and interviews. *Journal of Applied Psychology, 84,* 754–775.

Riggio, R. E., Salinas, C., & Tucker, J. (1988). Personality and deception ability. *Personality and Individual Differences, 9,* 189–191.

Robie, C., Zickar, M. J., & Schmit, M. J. (2001). Measurement equivalence between applicant and incumbent groups: An IRT analysis of personality scales. *Human Performance, 14,* 187–207.

Rosse, J. G., Stecher, M. D., Miller, J. L., & Levin, R. (1998). The impact of response distortion on preemployment personality testing and hiring decisions. *Journal of Applied Psychology, 83,* 634–644.

Saks, A. M. (2006). Multiple predictors and criteria of job search success. *Journal of Vocational Behavior, 68,* 400–415.

Saks, A. M., & Ashforth, B. E. (1999). Effects of individual differences and job search behaviors on the employment status of recent university graduates. *Journal of Vocational Behavior, 54,* 335–349.

Schlenker, B. R. (1980). *Impression management.* Monterey, CA: Wadsworth.

Schmit, M. J., & Ryan, A. M. (1993). The big five in personnel selection: Factor structure in applicant and nonapplicant populations. *Journal of Applied Psychology, 78,* 966–974.

Shiflett, S., & Cohen, S. L. (1982). The shifting salience of valence and instrumentality in the prediction of perceived effort, satisfaction, and turnover. *Motivation and Emotion, 6,* 65–77.

Smith, D. B., Hanges, P. J., & Dickson, M. W. (2001). Personnel selection and the five-factor model: Reexamining the effects of applicant's frame of reference. *Journal of Applied Psychology, 86,* 304–315.

Smith, D. B., & Robie, C. (2004). The implications of impression management for personality research in organizations. In B. Schneider & D. B. Smith (Eds.) *Personality and organizations* (pp. 111–138). Mahwah, NJ: Lawrence Erlbaum.

Smith, M. A., & Canger, J. M. (2006, May). *Within-person Inconsistency of Personality Scores Between Applicant and Volunteer Situations.* Poster session presented at the 21st annual conference of the Society for Industrial and Organizational Psychology, Dallas, TX.

Snell, A. F., Sydell, E. J., & Lueke, S. B. (1999). Towards a theory of applicant faking: Integrating studies of deception. *Human Resource Management Review, 9,* 219–242.

Sullivan, S. E., Carden, W. A., & Martin, D. F. (1998). Careers in the next millennium: Directions for future research. *Human Resource Management Review, 8,* 165–185.

Tsaousis, I., & Nikolaou, I. (2001). The stability of the five-factor model of personality in personnel selection and assessment in Greece. *International Journal of Selection and Assessment, 9,* 290–301.

Veiga, J. F. (1983). Mobility influences during managerial career stages. *Academy of Management Journal, 26,* 64–85.

Vinokur, A. D., Price, R. H., & Schul, Y. (1995). Impact of the JOBS intervention on unemployed workers varying in risk for depression. *American Journal of Community Psychology, 23,* 39–74.

Visweswaran, C., & Ones, D. S. (1999). Meta-analyses of fakability estimates: Implications for personality measurement. *Educational and Psychological Measurement, 59,* 197–210.

Vroom, V. H. (1964). *Work and motivation.* New York: John Wiley.

Wanberg, C. R., Watt, J. D., & Rumsey, D. J. (1996). Individuals without jobs: An empirical study of job-seeking behavior and reemployment. *Journal of Applied Psychology, 81,* 76–87.

Wanous, J. P., Keon, T. L., & Latack, J. C. (1983). Expectancy theory and occupational and organizational choices. *Organizational Behavior and Human Performance, 32,* 66–85.

Zerbe, W. J., & Paulhus, D. L. (1987). Socially desirable responding in organizational behavior: A reconception. *Academy of Management Review, 12,* 250–264.

Ziegler, M, & Buehner, M. (2009). Modeling socially desirable responding and its effects. *Educational and Psychological Measurement, 69,* 548–565.

3

The Rules of Evidence and the Prevalence of Applicant Faking

■ RICHARD L. GRIFFITH AND
PATRICK D. CONVERSE

When the editors of this book approached us to contribute a chapter, we were asked to comment on the question "Do applicants tend to fake?" This is a common question often used to frame the issue of faking, and a seemingly logical starting point to any examination of the phenomenon. A variation of this apparently simple question ("do applicants fake?") has accompanied the majority of faking articles written in the past decade. However, upon closer inspection, the nature of this research question may have contributed to the stunted growth of our knowledge regarding applicant faking behavior.[1] Therefore, before we address the substance of the question, we will first comment on some of the properties of this inquiry that we find problematic.

Our first concern regarding the opening question is the form of logical argument it entails. Posing the question "do applicants fake?" introduces a false dilemma into our research psyche. A false dilemma is a form of logical fallacy in which two opposing alternatives are held to be mutually exclusive, and viewed as the only possible answers to the question (Waller, 2004). Research questions of this nature fail to consider one or more genuine alternatives. Our collective adoption of the false dilemma has led to the search for a conclusive "yes" or "no" answer, and slowed the search for a range of other possibilities. Unfortunately, this has led researchers to stake out extreme positions on the topic, and rigorously defend them. This type of black and white thinking has bred more argument than scientific discovery. Finding answers in this area of research is more difficult if we are asking the wrong questions.

Very few categories of human behavior fall into a "do" or "do not" dichotomy, and we would expect that faking behavior is no different. Contemporary psychological research generally avoids a typological approach to research questions. We have found that the notion of a continuum of behaviors better reflects the nature of the participants we study. Thus, we rarely ask the question "*does* a particular group engage in a behavior." Rather, we ask, "*to what extent* might a member of that group engage in a behavior"? Our science is also fond of answering those

---

1. Lest the pot call the kettle black, we too were guilty of falling into this semantic trap.

types of questions with the qualifier "it depends," which is a simple way of discussing possible moderators to the magnitude of the behavior. We would expect that applicant faking behavior, like all behaviors, would vary considerably across samples and situations.

The second concern we have regarding the question of "do applicants fake?" is congruence of the question with our methods of inquiry in the behavioral sciences. Inquiries regarding the existence of a behavior are actually a very unusual line of questioning in psychological research. In the course of contemporary research, we frequently encounter questions regarding the existence of a construct.[2] When these questions arise, we have well-established principles to develop a nomological network to provide some evidence of the construct validity of the proposed latent trait. We are also often concerned with *why a behavior occurred*, and thus gather evidence of the internal validity of our proposed explanation by isolating the effects of the independent variable on the dependent variable. But rarely do we have to establish proof that a behavior occurs. We simply observe the behavior and that is proof enough. However, applicant faking is difficult to directly observe because it is a cognitive or internal behavior.

Researchers examining the faking phenomenon increasingly find their work held to this uncommon standard (i.e., proving that a behavior occurs). For example, Smith and Robie (2004) capitulate that although faking may be observed in applicant samples, the body of research does not "provide definitive proof that impression management does occur" (p. 125). Thus, by asking whether applicants fake, we have given ourselves the unenviable task of proving the unprovable. The combination of the false dilemma argument and the epistemological puzzle of proving the existence of faking has painted us into a scientific corner.

Our goal for this chapter is to untangle this scientific knot and provide some clarity on what should be a simple question. We will begin this discussion with a reframing of the focal question and ask instead, "What is the prevalence of applicant faking behavior?"[3] Thus, our goal will be to shed light on the degree to which faking behavior is present in applicant settings. It is our intention to present evidence that may illustrate whether faking is substantially present in applicant samples (to the point at which faking may compromise the testing process), or a trivial artifact of personality measurement. Rather than attempting to provide a definitive static percentage of applicant fakers, we will present an estimate of the range of applicant faking based on accumulated evidence. We expect the degree to which faking will be present in a sample will depend on many moderators (e.g., sample characteristics, construct measured, measurement format) and, thus, it should vary accordingly.

---

2. Although some authors (e.g., Tett, Anderson, Ho, Yang, Huan, & Hanvongse, 2006) view faking as a construct, we do not hold this opinion. We view applicant faking as a behavior that may have multiple independent and interacting motivations.

3. This reframed question subsumes the original question "Do applicants fake?" in that we may observe a prevalence of 0% or 100%, but also allows us to find an answer in the middle. It is likely that we will see a percentage between those extreme poles.

■ APPLYING THE RULES OF EVIDENCE

Given the unusual nature of the original question posed to us, we will approach this intellectual exercise with an equally unusual approach for psychological research. Although in our field it is rare to prove a behavior exists, this approach is common in most Western societies and forms the basis of western judicial systems. Our societal norms hold the standard that the accused is innocent until proven otherwise. If an individual is accused of a crime, evidence must be collected and presented to establish that the offense did in fact occur. In a court of law, our burden would be to produce evidence sufficient to establish a fact and to persuade a jury that there is no reasonable doubt about the fact's existence, based on the evidence introduced (Keane, 2008). Therefore, to address our focal research question we will also take this approach and use the rules of evidence as a metaphor and an organizing framework. To address the question of whether applicants fake, and the prevalence of this behavior, we will do a little detective work and collect evidence to build our case.

■ OPENING ARGUMENTS

In the matter of the prevalence of faking behavior we contend that a substantial portion of applicants can, and do attempt to present a more favorable appearance than is warranted when responding to personality measures. We will present both direct and indirect evidence of the occurrence of this behavior in the applicant setting, and we will demonstrate that when taken as a whole, the alternative explanations offered are implausible. The evidence we will present suggests that in any given personnel selection effort roughly 30% of applicants (plus or minus 10%) engage in applicant faking, and this variability can be attributed to a number of moderators (see Chapter 2 for a discussion of how applicant marketability may impact the prevalence of faking). At the conclusion of our presentation of the evidence, we will ask the reader to decide if the weight of the evidence supports this contention. We begin our presentation with the indirect evidence.

■ INDIRECT EVIDENCE

Until recently, the evidence surrounding applicant faking behavior has been largely circumstantial. Circumstantial evidence indirectly proves a fact by providing support for inferences that lead to a presumption that the fact exists (Hails, 2005). This evidence takes the form of a chain of established facts, which together may lead to a reasonable conclusion. Although we often think of circumstantial evidence as having less weight than direct evidence, it is no less important and intrinsically no different than direct evidence in establishing a fact (Keane, 2008). Circumstantial evidence is most effective when it provides different relevant facts that all point to the same conclusion. With this type of evidence there may be a combination of circumstances, no one of which would raise a reasonable suspicion, but taken together lead naturally to a sound inference (Keane, 2008). Thus, when presenting circumstantial evidence, it is necessary that the facts are not only consistent with guilt, but also inconsistent with any other reasonable conclusion. The key piece of circumstantial evidence in the examination of faking is differences found in personality scores between applicant and incumbent respondents.

The majority of research examining possible differences across administration contexts suggests that applicants score significantly higher on personality measures than incumbents (Hough, 1998; O'Connell, Bott, Ramakrishnan, & Doverspike, 2007; Rosse, Stecher, Miller, & Levin, 1998; Robie, Zickar, & Schmit, 2001; Stark, Chernyshenko, Chan, Lee, & Drasgow, 2001; Smith & Robie, 2004; Stokes, Hogan, & Snell, 1993). Birkeland, Manson, Kisamore, Brannick, and Smith (2006) conducted a meta-analysis and found substantial score differences between applicants and incumbents. They report uncorrected d effect sizes ranging from 0.11 (extraversion) to 0.45 (conscientiousness) with corrected effect sizes[4] exceeding one-half standard deviation. In a more recent study, O'Connell et al. (2007) found d effect sizes larger than one full standard deviation. With few exceptions (e.g., Hough, Eaton, Dunnette, Kamp, & McCloy, 1990), research has consistently demonstrated that applicant scores are significantly higher than incumbent scores. One possible explanation for this difference is that applicants are motivated to get the job and thus may elevate their scores to improve their chances, whereas incumbents have less motivation to raise their scores (Bott, O'Connell, Ramakrishnan, & Doverspike, 2007). Thus, applicant/incumbent differences may be the consequence of applicant faking, and may constitute the "fingerprints of the crime."

Skeptics of faking research, however, suggest that there may be alternative explanations for this phenomenon that have not been ruled out. Because subjects are not randomly assigned to conditions in applicant/incumbent comparisons it is impossible to eliminate potential confounds by classic experimental methods. Thus, one possible explanation for this divergence is that other characteristics of the samples may account for the observed mean level differences. The first possible issue is sampling error, in which sample differences simply reflect chance. However, if this explanation accounted for differences in the magnitude of personality scores we should see mixed results rather than a consistent pattern of higher applicant scores. Another possible confound is that there are true differences in personality across the samples. The pattern of scores does not support this alternative explanation. The Attraction, Selection, and Attrition (ASA) model (Schneider, 1987), in combination with personality change over time (Robins, Fraley, Roberts, & Trzesniewski, 2001), would tend to favor the incumbent in these comparisons. Incumbents are likely to be older, and may have been prescreened on personality measures, or at least on selection procedures (such as an interview) that are correlated with desired personality traits. Thus, incumbent personality scores should evidence range restriction (Ones & Viswesvaran, 2003; Satterwhite, Fleenor, Braddy, Feldman, & Hoopes, 2009) and be closer to the desired score than a comparison applicant sample.

A third possible explanation is that applicants and incumbents adopt a different frame of reference (Bing, Whanger, Davidson, & Van Hook, 2004; Schmit, Ryan,

---

4. Corrected for sampling error and reliability.

Stierwalt, & Powell, 1995) when completing personality measures. If applicants respond to a personality measure by reporting their behavior as it would occur in a work context, these responses may differ from incumbents' responses in a research setting. Without explicit instructions regarding the frame of reference, an incumbent may choose a more general frame of reference. In general, the data suggest that frame of reference does not account for the full difference across samples. In an experimental study examining this issue, the *d* effect size between applicant and nonmotivated conditions was reduced when frame of reference was held constant but significant differences remained (Griffith, Malm, English, Yoshita, & Gujar, 2006). Taking frame of reference into account, between 17% (Openness) and 25% (Conscientiousness) of applicants were still categorized as fakers. In addition, if applicants adopt a work frame of reference we should see higher criterion-related validities in comparison to incumbent samples (Hunthausen, Truxillo, Bauer, & Hammer, 2003). But, we do not. This brings us to our second source of indirect evidence.

An examination of criterion-related validities of personality measures reveals that, in general, applicant samples produce lower validity coefficients than incumbent samples (Dunnette, McCartney, Carlson, & Kirchner, 1962; Hough, 1998; Ones, Viswesvaran, & Schmidt, 1993). Hough (1998) reported an average difference of 0.07 between these validity coefficients across the two sample types, with applicant validities being lower. Two plausible causes for the attenuation of validity in applicant samples are changes in rank order (Christiansen, Goffin, Johnston, & Rothstein, 1994; Griffith, Chmielowski, & Yoshita, 2007; Rosse et al., 1998) and nonlinearity (Haaland & Christiansen, 1998), both of which would occur if applicants who fake rise in the applicant distribution. Smith and Robie (2004) offered an alternative explanation and suggested that it is also possible that range restriction could account for these differences in validity coefficients.[5]

Douglas, McDaniel, and Snell (1996) provided a method to estimate the prevalence of faking that would be associated with the differences in validity found in the Hough (1998) meta-analysis. They conducted a Monte Carlo study that examined the criterion-related validities of Conscientiousness and Agreeableness measures when faking was present in the sample. They first calculated the validity of each measure using personality scores collected in nonmotivated conditions. They then varied the percentage of fakers introduced into the sample, and recalculated the validities. As you would expect, as more fakers were introduced into the sample, validities were attenuated. We used this approach to reanalyze the Hough (1998) coefficients to estimate the number of fakers necessary to achieve a given attenuation in validity across the two samples.

5. The authors suggest that range restriction may also occur in applicant samples, and without specific information regarding the corrections applied in Hough (1998), differences in validity should be interpreted with caution. Thus, their statement suggests the possibility that unless corrections were applied uniformly across predictive and concurrent designs, the validity differences observed in Hough (1998) may have been artifactual in nature. However, range restriction corrections were not applied in the Hough study. Thus, the validity gap is likely to be wider than reported (>0.07).

Hough (1998) reported a 0.07 difference in validity across samples, but this difference was averaged across eight constructs. To more accurately estimate the prevalence of faking, we restricted our reanalysis to include the same constructs as Douglas et al. (1996). When examining the results of the Hough meta-analysis, validities for Conscientiousness (dependability) were an average of 0.12 lower for predictive samples, which resulted in a 55% drop in validity. According to the estimates of Douglas et al., more than 39% of the sample would need to have faked to attain this degree of attenuation. A similar pattern of results emerged for the construct of Agreeableness, which evidenced a 67% attenuation of validity in the predictive sample (which suggested that 49% of the applicants in the sample engaged in faking behavior). Thus, the data would suggest that between 39% and 49% of applicants engaged in faking behavior in the predictive study results reported by Hough (1998).

The circumstantial evidence regarding faking does lend some support to the notion that a substantial number of applicants are engaging in the behavior. Nevertheless, there are other plausible explanations for these findings. Thus, with this circumstantial evidence alone, definitively establishing the existence of faking may at first appear to be a difficult prospect. However, a strong case can be built on circumstantial evidence if the prosecutor can convince the jury of the MMO (means, motive, and opportunity) of the perpetrator. We will now present the facts regarding the opportunity presented to applicants, their ability to fake personality measures, and their motivation to do so.

■ OPPORTUNITY

Opportunity refers to the potential for applicants to fake on personality measures. Opportunity to fake has been included in models of faking, sometimes as a factor separate from the ability to fake (McFarland & Ryan, 2000) and sometimes as a factor influencing the ability to fake (McFarland & Ryan, 2006). One basic factor influencing the opportunity to fake is the extent to which applicant responses are not constrained in terms of image management. Although self-report personality measures may constrain responses more than some other types of assessments (e.g., unstructured interviews), applicants are nonetheless free to agree or disagree with each item on most personality inventories given the common use of the Likert-scale format. Thus, within the context of the items in the measure, applicants have the opportunity to present themselves as they wish.

Another factor influencing opportunity to fake is the extent to which applicant responses are verifiable (i.e., additional information could be obtained to confirm item responses). If applicant responses were verifiable, opportunity to fake would be reduced or eliminated in the sense that (1) applicants would likely perceive less chance that they could fake without detection (which also speaks to applicant motivation) and (2) inaccurate (faked) responses could be identified and eliminated from further consideration. However, in applicant settings responses to many personality items are almost impossible to verify. Take, for example, an item drawn from the International Personality Item Pool (Goldberg, Johnson, Eber, Hogan, Ashton, Cloninger, & Gough, 2006) measuring the construct of Prudence,

"I don't know why I do some of the things I do." Only the respondent and his or her creator may know the veracity of the response to this item. Evidence suggests that applicants are sensitive to this issue of verifiability (Cascio, 1975; Doll, 1971). For instance, Becker and Colquitt (1992) examined faking on a 25-item biodata form and found that the items that appeared to be faked in practice were less verifiable than the other items.

A related factor associated with the opportunity to fake is the ability of the applicant to elude detection through approaches other than verification. Once the foxes have entered the henhouse, we have not been effective at catching them. The predominant method of faking detection has been the use of lie scales and embedded social desirability (SD) measures. Although these scales have been used almost as long as personality measures have existed (Burns & Christiansen, 2006; Zickar & Gibby, 2006), empirical evidence supporting their use in applicant settings is almost nonexistent. Griffith and Peterson (2008) suggest that SD scales are poor proxy measures for faking and bear no statistical relationship to the behavior they are intended to reflect. In addition to being poor predictors of faking behavior, they yield high false-positive and false-negative rates (Griffith & Peterson, 2008; Peterson, Griffith, O'Connell, & Isaacson, 2008), essentially rendering them useless in operational settings.

Finally, one other factor influencing opportunity is the applicant's true score for the construct at hand. If the applicant has a high true score, there would be little opportunity to fake because the individual has limited room for score inflation. This issue has been discussed previously (e.g., McFarland & Ryan, 2000) and is certainly a factor that reduces some applicants' opportunity to fake. However, this is a severe limitation only for those individuals whose true scores are extremely high for the given construct. Assuming a relatively normal distribution of true scores for personality constructs, most individuals would have the opportunity to produce an observed score significantly higher than their true score.

■ MEANS

Given that applicants appear to have the opportunity to fake, the next logical issue to address would be the extent to which they are capable of doing so. Numerous studies have indicated that, in general, individuals are able to substantially alter their responses to personality measures. The most direct evidence for faking ability comes from studies comparing responses obtained under honest instructions with those obtained under faking instructions. Viswesvaran and Ones (1999) meta-analytically summarized this area of research and reported strong support for the notion that individuals can fake. For example, mean effect sizes for studies involving "fake-good" instructions and between-subjects designs ranged from 0.48 (agreeableness) to 0.65 (openness to experience), meaning individuals instructed to fake scored noticeably higher across the Big Five dimensions.

Ability to fake has also been included as an important factor in models of faking (e.g., McFarland & Ryan, 2000; Snell, Sydell, & Lueke, 1999). These models have identified several variables that are likely to influence the ability to fake (e.g., self-monitoring, knowledge of the construct being measured), suggesting that ability varies across individuals. Empirical evidence is consistent with this idea of variability in faking ability across people (e.g., Alliger, Lilienfeld, & Mitchell, 1996; Pauls & Crost, 2005). Nonetheless, it is also clear from the studies reviewed by Viswesvaran and Ones (1999) that, on average, individuals are able to substantially fake their responses to personality measures.

■ MOTIVE

Motive is the logic or reasoning that constitutes the root cause of a behavior. To establish motive, we must provide plausible answers to the question, "why would applicants fake?" Often, the rationale behind the motives of the applicant is implied rather than investigated in detail. By applying for a job, it is assumed that the applicant does in fact desire the job, and this motivation may lead some to attempt to manage their impression in such a way that they are seen as a desirable employee. Dilchert, Ones, Viswesvaran, and Deller (2006) suggest that "When assessments are made for the purpose of making decisions that affect the employment of test takers (e.g., getting a job or not, getting promoted or not, et cetera), those assessed have an incentive to produce a score that will increase the likelihood of the desired outcome" (pp. 210–211). However, few researchers have examined the motivation of the faker in depth.

Snell et al. (1999) concluded that three factors contribute to the motivation to fake: (1) demographic variables (e.g., young adults may be more prone to unethical behavior such as cheating), (2) dispositional variables (e.g., individuals high in Machiavellianism often engage in deception to obtain a desired goal), and (3) applicant perceptions regarding the behavior of other applicants (e.g., if applicants believe that others are engaging in faking behavior they in turn are more likely to fake). McFarland and Ryan (2000) also proposed that an applicant's attitudes regarding faking are linked to motivation. They suggest that an individual's values and morals will influence his or her beliefs regarding the appropriateness of faking behavior, which will in turn influence their intention to fake. McFarland and Ryan (2006) extended this model by incorporating the theory of planned behavior (Ajzen, 1991). The theory of planned behavior has proven to be a powerful meta-theory that explains a wide range of human behaviors. McFarland and Ryan (2006) apply this theory to applicant responding and suggest that attitudes toward faking serve as a predictor of faking intentions. They found that attitudes toward faking, subjective norms, and perceived behavioral control were all strongly related to the intention to fake, and thus directly impact motivation. The study also revealed a strong relationship between faking intentions and actual faking behavior. Mueller-Hanson, Heggestad, and Thornton (2006) tested a model that combined elements of the work by Snell et al. and McFarland and Ryan and found support for both dispositional and attitudinal predictors of faking behavior.

Griffith and McDaniel (2006) offer some additional insight into the applicant's motivation to fake. Beginning with a broad view of deceptive behavior, they suggest that deception is an adaptive characteristic that has a basis in evolution (Smith, 2004). In nature, deception is used to gain a competitive advantage, and the employment setting can be viewed as a socially constructed extension of that environment. They argue that deception is common in our social interactions, with evidence indicating that most individuals lie every day (Depaulo, Kashy, Kirkendol, Dwyer, & Epstein, 1996). Furthermore, Griffith and McDaniel suggest that the conditions that may inhibit deception are usually absent in the application process. Two factors that may reduce the motivation to deceive are the fear of getting caught and guilt (Ekman & Frank, 1993). These emotions are not likely to be present in the applicant setting in that the perceived likelihood of getting caught is minimal and the applicant is not likely to have a relationship with the target (in this case the organization). Applicants may, in fact, believe that *not faking* leaves them at a competitive disadvantage if they consider the behavior to be widespread. English, Griffith, Graseck, and Steelman (2005) reported that 74% of applicants believed that other applicants were engaging in faking behavior.

Finally, there is ample evidence to suggest that deception is in fact the *modus operandi* of the applicant. Modus operandi (MO) is a Latin phrase meaning method of operation, and refers to similarities of behavior by the accused in the act of committing a crime. The linkage between the MO of a perpetrator and the offense in question is often entered as evidence of motivation or intent.

Personality tests are not the only portion of a selection battery that can be falsified. Dilchert et al. (2006) see falsification as an inevitable outcome of a high-stakes assessment in which the applicant has an opportunity to deceive. They state, "In general, response distortion seems to be a concern in any assessment conducted for the purposes of distributing valued outcomes (e.g., jobs, promotions, development opportunities), regardless of the testing tool or medium (e.g., personality test, interview, assessment center). In fact, all high-stakes assessments are likely to elicit deception" (p. 210). Whereas cheating on cognitive ability tests requires some effort, and may be perceived as risky, deception on some forms of assessment is considerably less difficult.[6]

Two selection tools that are particularly vulnerable to distortion are the interview and the resume. Evidence suggests that applicants engage in a substantial amount of falsification on both. Levashina and Campion (2007) examined the base rate of faking on the employment interview utilizing a self-report methodology. The data suggested that over 90% of respondents had engaged in some form of impression management during the interview and between 28% and 70% engaged in severe forms of falsification. Callahan (2004) cited reports in which 41% of applicants report falsifying their resumes. In addition, routine background checks reveal that 20% of applicant resumes have falsified educational claims. Aamodt (2003) examined the frequency of resume fraud across 15 independent studies and reported a median percentage of 25%.

---

6. Arthur et al. (2010) found a considerably lower prevalence of cheating on cognitive ability tests when compared to the prevalence of faking on personality tests.

■ DIRECT EVIDENCE

The combination of circumstantial evidence and a demonstration that applicants have the opportunity, means, and motivation to fake personality measures might alone be enough to make our case. However, recent developments in faking research allow us to present a more compelling and conclusive argument. In addition to the circumstantial evidence that a substantial number of applicants fake, we have the direct evidence of both eyewitness testimony and a confession.

The essence of eyewitness testimony is that an individual observed the behavior in question first hand. Although the act of faking is an internal behavior, the results of faking can be observed and measured. Thus, researchers have attempted to directly observe the results of faking in several ways and their reports can be viewed as a sort of eyewitness testimony. Note that the eyewitness accounts involved in court proceedings can often be unreliable (Loftus, 2003), but in the current context this should be less of a concern because we are dealing with systematic observation stemming from empirical studies with researchers as the witnesses.[7]

One method that has been used to observe faking is the inclusion of bogus statements in personality or biodata assessments. Bogus statements ask applicants to report their experience on nonexistent equipment or processes that superficially resemble actual job-related tasks. Therefore, if an applicant responds in the affirmative across several of these statements, the inference often drawn is that the applicants have intentionally misrepresented themselves. However, an alternative explanation, that the applicants may have carelessly responded or misunderstood the content of the items, is plausible. Anderson, Warner, and Spencer (1984) asked applicants to report their experience on a list of tasks that included a subset of bogus tasks. The authors stated that 45% of job applicants reported that they engaged in one or more bogus tasks. Pannone (1984) asked a group of applicants for an electrician position to report their experience on job-related tasks, and found that 35% of respondents self-reported using a nonexistent piece of equipment. In a study conducted by Donovan, Dwight, and Schneider (2008), 21% of applicants strongly endorsed items indicating that they had experience with at least three (there were five total items) bogus tasks. Although carelessness or misunderstanding may account for endorsing a single item, it is unlikely to account for the responses to three or more items. Thus, the Donovan et al. study calls into question the alternative explanation for the endorsement of these items.

Previous designs often attempted to capture faking at a group level by comparing two samples of people who differ on motivation to fake (e.g., applicants and incumbents), or manipulating instructional sets. However, recent research has focused on within-subjects designs in applicant settings. In this design, the personality test data are collected from the same person in an unmotivated context,

---

7. Unlike the subjects in eyewitness testimony studies, who are often innocent bystanders surprised by being in the wrong place at the wrong time, researchers are focused on the phenomenon. Thus, this eyewitness testimony is more similar to detectives on a stakeout. However, we don't get free donuts.

and then again when they apply for a job.[8] By comparing the two responses, we can perform analyses to determine how much *an individual* faked his or her score, and *how many individuals faked*, rather than inferring how much faking occurred by examining differences in group means. Utilizing this design we have the opportunity to observe which applicants faked, and by how much. Thus, if analyzed properly, it is well suited to our research question of directly examining the prevalence of faking behavior.

Griffith et al. (2007) conducted a within-subjects design in an applicant setting. They collected data on a 30-item measure of conscientiousness from a sample of temporary workers at the application stage. One month later, the same respondents were asked to complete a research survey that contained the same items as the selection measure embedded in a longer research instrument. The survey was mailed from an independent institution and included an honest instructional set and an assurance that their employer would not have access to the data. When the data were compared across the two administration conditions, a significant amount of faking occurred at the group level ($d = 0.61$). In addition to the group level analysis, Griffith et al. examined the percentage of individuals in the sample who faked their score. To conduct this analysis, they created a set of confidence intervals around each respondent's honest score, and if an individual's applicant score exceeded the upper bound of the interval, they were categorized as a faker. To account for the measurement error inherent in the personality instrument, two intervals were calculated. The first interval was calculated by multiplying the standard error of the measurement (SEM) by 1.96; thus the applicant score should fall within this interval with a 95% probability. When this interval was used as the threshold to detect faking, 31% of applicants were categorized as fakers. Given that the honest score also contained measurement error, a more conservative confidence interval based on the standard error of the difference (SED) was calculated. Twenty-two percent of applicants were categorized as fakers when this operational definition of faking was used.

Peterson, Griffith, O'Connell, and Isaacson (2008) replicated this study with a sample of applicants for manufacturing positions and found similar results. The mean level differences were once again significant; however, the effect size was smaller than in the Griffith et al. (2007) study ($d = 0.26$). Using the two-SEM cutoff methodology established in Griffith et al. (2007), 26% of the sample met the criterion for being identified as having faked the personality assessment.

Donovan et al. (2008) also conducted a study utilizing a within-subjects design collecting personality data in motivated and nonmotivated contexts. They collected personality data on two job-related constructs (Potency and Achievement Striving) from 198 applicants for a pharmaceutical sales position. Data on the same measures were then collected 1 month later during an employee training program, and employees were informed that the measure was being used for developmental purposes and that their responses would not affect their job assignment.

---

8. We excluded discussion of Hogan, Barrett, and Hogan (2007) for this reason. Hogan et al. collected data twice in an applicant setting, so no unmotivated assessment served as a baseline measure.

Donovan et al. reported that scores under the applicant condition were significantly higher than in the developmental condition. In addition, 27% of the applicants were classified as fakers on the Achievement Striving dimension, and 19% of the applicants were classified as fakers on the Potency dimension (based on a two-SEM cutoff). Donovan et al. also employed a bogus statement methodology, and using this identifier of faking behavior, 21% of applicants would have been classified as fakers.

Arthur, Glaze, Villado, and Taylor (2010) found a similar pattern of results for an unproctored Internet personality assessment. Two-hundred and ninety-six participants completed the Guilford–Zimmerman Temperament Survey and the Differential Personality Inventory in an applicant setting. The same participants completed the measures again 1 year later as part of a research study. Arthur et al. then mapped the measures onto a five-factor structure using the scheme established by Birkeland et al. (2006). They established a confidence interval around the nonmotivated research scores using the standard error of measurement of the difference score (SEM_d), and participants who exceeded this interval in the applicant setting were categorized as fakers. Once again, scores were significantly higher in the applicant condition (with the exception of the construct of Openness). Arthur et al. reported that a substantial number of participants exceeded the confidence interval and thus were classified as fakers (35.81% on Agreeableness, 34.12% on Conscientiousness, 33.11% on Emotional Stability, 35.81% on Extraversion, and 14.53% on Openness). They replicated the design using a different Big Five measure in a second study and found a remarkably similar pattern of results.

Results from one additional study, however, do not appear to be consistent with these findings. Ellingson, Sackett, and Connelly (2007) located individuals who had taken the California Psychological Inventory (CPI), a 434-item survey measuring 20 personality dimensions, twice within a 7-year period. In some instances, participants responded in a developmental context, in which the employees would likely be less motivated to fake. In other instances, the assessment tools were used for the purposes of promotion, where the respondent is likely more motivated to fake by economic and status changes in their organization. After the parameters were adjusted to account for the confounding variables of time lag and developmental feedback, the average effect size across the development/selection and the selection/development conditions was 0.075. It was concluded that "results from these data suggest that individuals will engage in a limited degree of response distortion when asked to complete a personality measure for the purposes of selection relative to the responses that they would provide if asked to complete that measure for development purposes" (p. 393).

We believe this concluding statement is not supported by the analysis conducted by Ellingson et al. (2007). The conceptual disagreement we have with the authors revolves around the levels of analysis issue, in that relatively precise estimates of the number of individuals who fake (and by how much) requires individual-level analyses rather than group-level analyses. Specifically, although the overall effect size may be 0.075, this increase in scores may occur many ways. All candidates for promotion may raise their scores a small amount, or most can vary normally around their true score while some engage in extreme faking. Ellingson et al. seem to adopt the first interpretation. They state, "intentional distortion accounts for applicants receiving a score on the Flexibility scale, for example, that is 0.3 points higher than they would receive if assessed under nonmotivating conditions. The difference between receiving a score of 14.3 and 14.6 is unlikely to produce a notable change in selection decisions" (p. 393). Given this statement, they seem to conclude that all motivated respondents fake to the same degree. Previous studies have demonstrated considerable variation in applicant faking (Griffith et al. 2006; Griffith & Peterson, 2008). We simulated the results of the Ellingson et al. study to examine how much faking could have occurred with an average effect size of 0.075. In a worst-case scenario, as many as 20% of applicants could have raised their scores over one half standard deviation without exceeding the reported effect size for the total sample.

The eyewitness testimony provided by examining within-person score change yields compelling evidence that a substantial number of applicants attempt to elevate their scores on personality measures. These studies produced comparable results, finding that between 20% and 40% of applicants exceed established confidence intervals. These studies also call some of the alternative explanations for score shifts into question. First, the nonmotivated scores were collected in several contexts (research and job-relevant settings) ruling out alternative frame of reference explanations for this score change. Second, nonmotivated scores were collected shortly after the applicant condition (ranging from 1 month to 1 year), ruling out potential changes in actual trait levels of the respondents. Finally, experimental manipulations using the same methodology (Peterson, Griffith, & Converse, 2009) find similar results, and control for the order effects that might be considered a threat to internal validity of the field studies.

■ THE CONFESSION

The last piece of evidence we will introduce comes directly from the applicants: namely, confessing to attempts at faking. In a fairly obscure study, McDaniel, Douglas, and Snell (1997) took a novel approach to determine the prevalence of fakers in an applicant sample. Instead of relying on statistical analysis for this estimation, they simply asked participants to self-report the behavior. McDaniel et al. surveyed respondents from an Internet job site, and 42% reported that they had given false impressions about themselves when completing personality measures. Donovan, Dwight, and Hurtz (2003) improved on the design by incorporating the randomized response technique, which is designed to improve the respondent's reactions regarding the perception of anonymity of the survey (see Fox & Tracy, 1986). They suggested that this was necessary to establish an accurate baseline for the behavior because respondents in the McDaniel et al. (1997) study may have been reluctant to report dishonesty, which would lead to conservative estimates of faking behavior. Donovan et al. asked recent job applicants to rate 29 true/false items that assessed faking behaviors that may occur during the application process. The average percentage of endorsement across all behavioral items was 29%, whereas items specifically tapping behaviors related to the completion of a personality assessment had an average endorsement rate of 39%. Donovan et al.

concluded that the prevalence of faking is nontrivial, but noted that the majority of faking did occur on the least severe and most transparent items.

Robie, Brown, and Beaty (2007) conducted a qualitative study examining the prevalence and form of faking behavior. They recruited a sample of 12 participants through a local newspaper advertisement. The advertisement asked for participants to complete a research survey and informed the applicants that the three top respondents would receive $100. Participants completed the Criterion International Service Inventory—Short Form (CISI-S) as if applying for a retail position while also having their verbal protocol recorded. Verbal Protocol Analysis is a method in which participants are encouraged to think out loud and verbalize cognitive steps in which they may be engaging while completing a task (Brannick, Levine, & Morgeson, 2007). Robie et al. then coded the protocols and categorized the participants as honest (only accessing self-relevant information), slight fakers (beginning with self-relevant information, but then shading toward the idealized response), or extreme fakers (only referencing idealized responses for the position). Out of 12 respondents, one was categorized as an extreme faker, two were categorized as slight fakers, and the rest fell into the honest category. Thus, 25% of the sample was composed of fakers. Robie et al. (2007) not only give us convergent evidence regarding the prevalence of faking, but some insight into the process of faking as well.

■ CLOSING ARGUMENTS

Ladies and gentlemen of the jury, we will now ask you to carefully weigh the evidence in the case of the prevalence of applicant faking. It is our contention that a substantial number of applicants misrepresent themselves when completing personality measures for selection purposes. The circumstantial evidence tells us that applicant scores are elevated in comparison to incumbent scores, and that criterion-related validity decays in predictive designs. These patterns are pervasive, despite the fact that mean score differences should be reversed given findings related to the ASA model and validity differences should be reversed given frame of reference effects. The applicant has the means, motive, and opportunity to fake these measures and has established a modus operandi of deception in the applicant setting. The applicant has repeatedly been caught in the act of faking through within-subjects designs and the controversial use of bogus statements. Finally, the applicant has confessed to the offense.

This evidence, gathered through multiple means of data collection, indicates that roughly 30% of applicants are engaging in faking behavior (±10%). The evidence is particularly compelling given the convergence of these estimates of the prevalence of faking from different methodologies and different contexts (see Table 3.1). In addition, as summarized in Table 3.2, alternative explanations for the evidence presented work in isolation, but it appears that of the potential explanations discussed, only applicant faking fits the full set of findings. In addition, the alternative explanations for the effects of faking fall short and are often contradictory in that an explanation may hold for one piece of evidence, but if true, would lead to results that are at odds with other evidence.

TABLE 3.1 *Estimates of the Prevalence of Faking*

Research Study	Construct	Percentage[1]
Hough (1998) reanalysis	Conscientiousness	39%
Hough (1998) reanalysis	Agreeableness	49%
Aamodt (2003) estimate of resume fraud	~	25%
Levashina and Campion (2007) average interview falsification	~	49%
Bogus Item Methodology		
Anderson et al. (1984)	~	45%
Pannone (1984)	~	35%
Donovan et al. (2008)	~	21%
Within-Subjects Design		
Griffith and Peterson (2007)	Conscientiousness	$31\%_1$
	Conscientiousness	$22\%_2$
Griffith et al. (2008)	Conscientiousness	$26\%_1$
	Conscientiousness	$15\%_2$
Donovan et al. (2008)	Achievement Striving	$27\%_1$
	Potency	$19\%_1$
Arthur et al. (2010)	Agreeableness	$36\%_3$
	Conscientiousness	$34\%_3$
	Emotional Stability	$33\%_3$
	Extraversion	$36\%_3$
	Openness	$15\%_3$
Peterson et al. (2009)	Conscientiousness	$19\%_2$
Self-Report		
McDaniel et al (1997)	~	42%
Donovan et al. (2003)	~	29%
Robie et al. (2007)	Conscientiousness Agreeableness	25%
Mean %		30.5%

[1]1 = Standard Error of Measurement (SEM), 2 = Standard Error of the Difference (SED),
3 = Standard Error of Measurement of the Difference (SEM_d).

TABLE 3.2 *Potential Explanations for Evidence Related to Applicant Faking*

	Sampling Error	True Personality Differences	Frame of Reference	Range Restriction	Applicant Carelessness	Applicant Faking
Elevated applicant means	✓	✓	✓			✓
Attenuated criterion-related validity	✓			✓		✓
Bogus item endorsement					✓	✓
Within-subjects score change			✓			✓
Rank order change	✓					✓
Self-reported faking						✓

We contend that this convincing evidence proves beyond a reasonable doubt that a substantial portion of applicants fakes personality measures. Like all human behaviors, we expect applicant faking to vary across a population (Zickar, Gibby, & Robie, 2004). Not all applicants fake, and those that do fake, do so to different degrees and for different reasons (Griffith et al., 2006). Because of these varying response patterns and motivations, the effects of faking are disputed, and largely unknown. We will leave those issues for subsequent chapters of this text to explore.

We rest our case.

References

Aamodt, M. G. (2003). How common is resume fraud? *Assessment Council News*, February, 6–7.

Ajzen, I. (1991). Theory of planned behavior. *Organizational Behavior and Human Decision Processes*, *50*, 179–211.

Alliger, G. M., Lilienfeld, S. O., & Mitchell, K. E. (1996). The susceptibility of overt and covert integrity tests to coaching and faking. *Psychological Science*, *7*, 32–39.

Anderson, C. D., Warner, J. L., & Spencer, C. C. (1984). Inflation bias in self-assessment examinations: Implications for valid employee selection. *Journal of Applied Psychology*, *69*, 574–580.

Arthur, W., Jr., Glaze, R. M., Villado, A. J., & Taylor, J. E. (2010). The magnitude and extent of cheating and response distortion effects on unproctored Internet based tests of cognitive ability and personality. *International Journal of Selection and Assessment*, *18*, 1–16.

Becker, T. E., & Colquitt, A. L. (1992). Potential versus actual faking of a biodata form: An analysis along several dimensions of item type. *Personnel Psychology*, *45*, 389–406.

Bing, M. N., Whanger, J. C., Davidson, H. K., & Van Hook, J. B. (2004). Incremental validity of the frame-of-reference effect in personality scale scores: A replication and extension. *Journal of Applied Psychology*, *89*, 150–157.

Birkeland, S. A., Manson, T. M., Kisamore, J., Brannick, M., & Smith, M. A. (2006). A meta-analytic investigation of job applicant faking on personality measures. *International Journal of Selection and Assessment*, *14*, 317–335.

Bott, J. P., O'Connell, M. S., Ramakrishnan, M., & Doverspike, D. D. (2007). Practical limitations in making decisions regarding the distribution of applicant personality test scores based on incumbent data. *Journal of Business & Psychology*, *22*, 123–134.

Brannick, M. T., Levine, E. L., & Morgeson, F. (2007). *Job analysis: Methods, research and applications for human resource management*. Thousand Oaks, CA: Sage.

Burns, G. N., & Christiansen, N. D. (2006). Sensitive or senseless: On the use of social desirability measures in selection and assessment. In R. L. Griffith & M. H. Peterson (Eds.), *A closer examination of applicant faking behavior* (pp. 115–150). Greenwich, CT: Information Age.

Callahan, D. (2004). *The cheating culture*. Orlando, FL: Harcourt, Inc.

Cascio, W. F. (1975). Accuracy of verifiable biographical information blank responses. *Journal of Applied Psychology*, *60*, 767–769.

Christiansen, N. D., Goffin, R. D., Johnston, N. G., & Rothstein, M. G. (1994). Correcting the 16PF for faking: Effects on criterion-related validity and individual hiring decisions. *Personnel Psychology*, *47*, 847–860.

Depaulo, B. M., Kashy, D. A., Kirkendol, S. E., Dwyer, M. M., & Epstein, J. A. (1996). Lying in everyday life. *Journal of Personality and Social Psychology*, *70*, 979–995.

Dilchert, S., Ones, D. S., Viswesvaran, C., & Deller, J. (2006). Response distortion in personality measurement: Born to deceive, yet capable of providing valid self-assessments? *Psychology Science, 48*, 209–225.

Doll, R. E. (1971). Item susceptibility to attempted faking as related to item characteristic and adopted fake set. *Journal of Psychology, 77*, 9–16.

Donovan, J. J., Dwight, S. A., & Hurtz, G. M. (2003). An assessment of the prevalence, severity and verifiability of entry-level applicant faking using the randomized response technique. *Human Performance, 16*, 81–106.

Donovan, J. J., Dwight, S. A., & Schneider, D. (2008, April). Faking in the real world: Evidence from a field study. In R. L. Griffith & M. H. Peterson (Chairs), *Examining faking using within-subjects designs and applicant data*. Symposium conducted at the 23rd Annual Conference for the Society for Industrial and Organizational Psychology, San Francisco, CA.

Douglas, E. F., McDaniel, M. A., & Snell, A. F. (1996). The validity of non-cognitive measures decays when applicants fake. Proceedings of the Academy of Management, Cincinnati, OH.

Dunnette, M. D., McCartney, J., Carlson, H. C., & Kirchner, W. K. (1962). A study of faking behavior on a forced-choice self-description checklist. *Personnel Psychology, 15*, 13–24.

Ekman, P., & Frank, M. G. (1993). Lies that fail. In M. Lewis & C. Saarni (Eds.), *Lying and deception in everyday life*. London: The Guilford Press.

Ellingson, J. E., Sackett, P. R., & Connelly, B. S. (2007). Personality assessment across selection and development contexts: Insights into response distortion. *Journal of Applied Psychology, 92*, 386–395.

English, A., Griffith, R. L., Graseck, M., & Steelman, L. A. (2005). Frame of reference, applicant faking and the predictive validity of non-cognitive measures: a matter of context. Unpublished manuscript.

Fox, J. A., & Tracy, P. E. (1986). *Randomized response: A method for sensitive surveys*. Beverly Hills, CA: Sage.

Goldberg, L. R., Johnson, J. A., Eber, H. W., Hogan, R., Ashton, M. C., Cloninger, R. C., & Gough, H. G. (2006). The international personality item pool and the future of public-domain personality measures. *Journal of Research in Personality, 40*, 84–96.

Griffith, R. L., Chmielowski, T., & Yoshita, Y. (2007). Do applicants fake? An examination of the frequency of applicant faking behavior. *Personnel Review, 36*, 341–355.

Griffith, R. L., Malm, T., English, A., Yoshita, Y., & Gujar, A. (2006). Applicant faking behavior: Teasing apart the influence of situational variance, cognitive biases, and individual differences. In R. L. Griffith & M. H. Peterson (Eds.), *A closer examination of applicant faking behavior* (pp. 151–178). Greenwich, CT: Information Age.

Griffith, R. L., & McDaniel, M. A. (2006). The nature of deception and applicant faking behavior. In R. L. Griffith & M. H. Peterson (Eds.), *A closer examination of applicant faking behavior* (pp. 1–19). Greenwich, CT: Information Age.

Griffith, R. L., & Peterson, M. H. (2008). The failure of social desirability measures to capture applicant faking behavior. *Industrial and Organizational Psychology: Perspectives on Science and Practice, 1*, 308–311.

Haaland, D., & Christiansen, N. D. (1998). Departures from linearity in the relationship between applicant personality test scores and performance as evidence of response distortion. Paper presented at the 22nd Annual International Personnel Management Association Assessment Council Conference, Chicago, IL.

Hails, J. (2005) *Criminal evidence* (5th ed.). Belmont, CA: Thompson Wadsworth.

Hogan, J., Barrett, P., & Hogan, R. (2007). Personality measurement, faking, and employment selection. *Journal of Applied Psychology, 92,* 1270–1285.

Hough, L. M. (1998). Personality at work: Issues and evidence. In M. D. Hakel (Ed.), *Beyond multiple choice: Evaluating alternatives to traditional testing for selection* (pp. 131–166). Mahwah. NJ: Lawrence Erlbaum Associates.

Hough, L. M., Eaton, N. K., Dunnette, M. D., Kamp, J. D., & McCloy, R. A. (1990). Criterion-related validities of personality constructs and the effects of response distortion on those validities. *Journal of Applied Psychology Monograph, 75,* 581–595.

Hunthausen, J. M., Truxillo, D. M., Bauer, T. N., & Hammer, L. B. (2003). A field study of frame-of-reference effects on personality test validity. *Journal of Applied Psychology, 88,* 545–551.

Keane, A. (2008). *The modern law of evidence.* New York: Oxford University Press.

Levashina, J., & Campion, M. (2007). Measuring faking in the employment interview: Development and validation of an interview faking behavior scale. *Journal of Applied Psychology, 92,* 1638–1656.

Loftus, E. (2003). Our changeable memories: Legal and practical implications. *Nature Reviews Neuroscience, 4,* 231–234.

McDaniel, M. A., Douglas, E. F., & Snell, A. F. (1997, April). A survey of deception among job seekers. In G. J. Lautenschlager (Chair), *Faking on non-cognitive measures: The extent, impact, and identification of assimilation.* Symposium conducted at the 12th annual conference of the Society for Industrial and Organizational Psychology, St. Louis, MO.

McFarland, L. A., & Ryan, A. M. (2000). Variance in faking across noncognitive measures. *Journal of Applied Psychology, 85,* 812–821.

McFarland, L. A., & Ryan, A. M. (2006). Toward an integrated model of applicant faking behavior. *Journal of Applied Social Psychology, 36,* 979–1016.

Mueller-Hanson, R. A., Heggestad, E. D., & Thornton, G. C. III (2006). Individual differences impression management: An exploration of the processes underlying faking. *Psychology Science, 48,* 288–312.

O'Connell, M. S., Bott, J. P., Ramakrishnan, M., & Doverspike, D. (2007). Practical limitations in making decisions regarding the distribution of applicant personality test scores based on incumbent data. *Journal of Business and Psychology, 22,* 123–134.

Ones, D. S., & Viswesvaran, C. (2003). Job-specific applicant pools and national norms for personality scales: Implications for range-restriction corrections in validation research. *Journal of Applied Psychology, 88,* 570–577.

Ones, D. S., Viswesvaran, C., & Schmidt, F. L. (1993). Comprehensive meta-analysis of integrity test validities: Findings and implications for personnel selection and theories of job performance. *Journal of Applied Psychology, 78,* 679–703.

Pannone, R. D. (1984). Predicting test performance: A content valid approach to screening applicants. *Personnel Psychology, 37,* 507–514.

Pauls, C. A., & Crost, N. W. (2005). Effects of different instructional sets on the construct validity of the NEO-PI-R. *Personality and Individual Differences, 39,* 297–308.

Peterson, M. H., Griffith, R. L., & Converse, P. D. (2009). Examining the role of applicant faking in hiring decisions: Percentage of fakers hired and hiring discrepancies in single and multiple predictor selection. *Journal of Business and Psychology, 24,* 373–386, DOI: 10.1007/s10869-009-9121-5.

Peterson, M. P., Griffith, R. L., O'Connell, M. S., & Isaacson J. A. (2008, April). Examining faking in real job applicants: A within-subjects investigation of score changes across applicant and research settings. Paper presented at the 23rd annual meeting for the Society for Industrial and Organizational Psychology, San Francisco, California.

Robie, C., Brown, D. J., & Beaty, J. C. (2007). Do people fake on personality inventories? A verbal protocol analysis. *Journal of Business and Psychology, 21*, 489–509.

Robie, C., Zickar, M. J., & Schmit, M. J. (2001). Measurement equivalence between applicant and incumbent groups: An IRT analysis of personality scales. *Human Performance, 14*, 187–207.

Robins, R. W., Fraley, R. C., Roberts, B. W., & Trzesniewski, K. H. (2001). A longitudinal study of personality change in young adulthood. *Journal of Personality, 69*, 617–640.

Rosse, J. G., Stecher, M. D., Miller, J. L., & Levin, R. A. (1998). The impact of response distortion on preemployment personality testing and hiring decisions. *Journal of Applied Psychology, 83*, 634–644.

Satterwhite, R. C., Fleenor, J. W., Braddy, P. W., Feldman, J., & Hoopes, L. (2009). A case for homogeneity of personality at the occupational level. *International Journal of Selection and Assessment, 17*, 154–164.

Schmit, M. J., Ryan, A. M., Stierwalt, S. L., & Powell, A. B. (1995). Frame-of-reference effects on personality sale scores and criterion related validity. *Journal of Applied Psychology, 80*, 607–620.

Schneider, B. W. (1987). The people make the place. *Personnel Psychology, 40*, 437–453.

Smith, B., & Robie, C. (2004). Implications of impression management for personality research in organizations. In B. Schneider & D. B. Smith (Eds.), *Personality and organizations* (pp. 111–138). Mahwah, NJ: Laurence Erlbaum Associates.

Smith, D. L. (2004). *Why we lie. The Evolutionary roots of deception and the unconscious mind.* New York: St. Martin's Press.

Snell, A. F., Sydell, E. J., & Lueke, S. B. (1999). Towards a theory of applicant faking: Integrating studies of deception. *Human Resource Management Review, 9*, 219–242.

Stark, S., Chernyshenko, O. S., Chan, K., Lee, W., & Drasgow, F. (2001). Effects of the testing situation on item responding: Cause for concern. *Journal of Applied Psychology, 86*, 943–953.

Stokes, G. S., Hogan, J. B., & Snell, A. F. (1993). Comparability of incumbent and applicant samples for the development of biodata keys: The influence of social desirability. *Personnel Psychology, 46*, 739–762.

Tett, R. P., Anderson, M. G., Ho, C., Yang, T. S., Huang, L., & Hanvongse, A. (2006). Seven nested questions about faking on personality tests: An overview and interactionist model of item-level response distortion. In R. L. Griffith & M. H. Peterson (Eds.), *A closer examination of applicant faking behavior* (pp. 43–83). Greenwich, CT: Information Age Publishing.

Viswesvaran, C., & Ones, D. S. (1999). Meta-analyses of fakability estimates: Implications for personality measurement. *Educational and Psychological Measurement, 59*, 197–210.

Waller, B. N. (2004). *Critical thinking: Consider the verdict* (5th ed.). Englewood Cliffs, NJ: Prentice Hall.

Zickar, M. J., & Gibby, R. E. (2006). A history of faking and socially desirable responding on personality tests. In R. L. Griffith & M. H. Peterson (Eds.), *A closer examination of applicant faking behavior* (pp. 21–42). Greenwich, CT: Information Age Publishing.

Zickar, M. J., Gibby, R. E., & Robie, C. (2004). Uncovering faking samples in applicant, incumbent, and experimental data sets: An application of mixed-model item response theory. *Organizational Research Methods, 7*, 168–190.

4   Questioning Old Assumptions

Faking and the Personality–Performance Relationship

■   D. BRENT SMITH AND MAX McDANIEL

> [F]urther explorations of impression management [faking] need to
> be grounded in a broader theoretical approach to understanding the
> construct. We are at the stage of ignoring theory and attempting
> either to prove or disprove the deleterious effects of an ambiguous
> construct. Attempts to understand impression management need to
> be grounded in the broader psychological, social-psychological, and
> sociological literature relevant for the topic. Furthermore,
> understanding impression management can only be achieved with
> reference to a particular theoretical model explaining what responses
> to a personality questionnaire mean … we need to step back and
> reground ourselves in the theoretical history of the debate unless we
> are interested in repeating that history.
>
> (SMITH & SCHNEIDER, 2004, p. 399)

We were asked to write a chapter reviewing the literature on the effects of response distortion and faking on the personality–performance relationship with the intent of suggesting that the effects are minimal. We must admit from the outset that we have a slightly different agenda. Although we do intend to briefly summarize the tenor of the current debate and discuss some of the evidence supporting the conclusion that faking is neither as prevalent as some might intuitively believe nor as damaging to criterion-related validity or selection utility as some have suggested, our primary goal, consistent with the above passage, is to suggest that it is time to break from the past and explore a new research agenda grounded in the broader psychological and social-psychological traditions. We intend to question some of the basic assumptions that have guided faking research and provide an alternative view—a view grounded in a social-cognitive perspective on personality that deviates from the largely applied focus of current conceptualizations of faking. This is, of course, not to suggest that past research has been misguided or failed to advance our understanding of faking[1] (response distortion, impression management, socially-desirable responding, etc.). This is surely not the case. Rather, our review of the literature suggests we are at an impasse. Rather than calling for a moratorium on faking research (as has been done), we hope our thoughts imply new

---

1. We recognize that terminology has been the source of frequent discussion. For purposes of this chapter, we will use the term faking to describe motivated impression management and, where applicable, differentiate faking from other forms of response distortion (e.g., self-deception).

research questions that will redirect and, hopefully, reinvigorate research on faking.

In this chapter, we will examine (albeit briefly) the central questions that serve as the focus or framing of the preponderance of faking research, discuss theoretical perspectives on personality and item responding [Personality and Role Identity Structural Model (PRISM), Roberts & Donahue (1994), and the Behavioral Process Model of Personality (BPMP), Back, Schumkle, & Egloff, (2009)] and discuss implications of a social-cognitive view for faking research, and, in conclusion, provide a summary of new research directions.

▪ CURRENT FRAMING OF FAKING RESEARCH

Two questions dominate research on faking as it relates to personality assessment: Do people fake when placed in a motivated context (e.g., applying for a job, being evaluated for a promotion) and, if they do, does faking adversely affect the predictive validity of personality measures. The number of books (this one included), chapters, and articles that organize their review of the faking literature around these two questions and the dissimilarity of their conclusions are what suggest to us that we have reached an impasse. Given definitional and methodological differences in the research literature, it is not surprising that conclusions are inconsistent and have failed to yield an answer to this longstanding debate.

Of the two questions, the first, "do people fake," is paramount. If they do, we can then evaluate the impact of faking on predictive validity and/or selection utility. If, however, faking is not as prevalent as some might believe or occurs infrequently or uniformly for those in a motivated context, then it makes little sense to belabor the consequences of faking. In other words, we must demonstrate that it occurs before we investigate "if it matters." Unfortunately, the limitations inherent in existing research designs make it difficult (arguably impossible) to establish a base rate for faking or to track the situational influences on faking motivation. Nonetheless, the conclusions drawn from this research are often interpreted as definitive evidence for or against the occurrence and pervasiveness of faking. Although it is clear that many academics and practitioners believe that faking occurs [Rees & Metcalf (2003) report that managers believe that more than 50% of all test takers fake], conventional wisdom is no substitute for externally valid empirical findings. Before we question conventional wisdom, we would like to offer a few comments on the limitations of existing research designs.

Three methodologies are typically employed to investigate the frequency of faking—directed faking instruction sets (either within or between-subjects designs), applicant-incumbent comparisons (again, either within or between-subjects designs), and direct measurement of faking using response distortion scales (social desirability, impression management, etc.).[2] As many have noted, each design has limitations that restrict the generalizability of our conclusions

---

2. Compare Mesmer-Magnus and Viswesvaran (2006) for a review of limitations of current research designs.

and constrain our ability to determine the base rate of faking behavior. Although a few other designs have been used to make inferences regarding the prevalence of faking (e.g., endorsement of obviously false statements, response latencies), they are few in number and similarly fraught with interpretive difficulties.

Directed Faking Studies

Historically, the use of instruction sets represents the most common methodology for investigating faking behavior. Using a within or between subjects design, study participants are asked to respond to a personality questionnaire under a "respond honestly" or a "motivated" condition (as if they were applying for a job, for instance). However, directed faking studies, by definition and design, cannot provide an indication of the extent to which people are motivated to fake in a real world setting. They do provide valuable insights into the extent to which people can fake when instructed to do so and, perhaps, represent the upper bound of faking behavior (Smith & Ellingson, 2002). Regardless, it is precisely the issue of "motivation" that is removed in directed faking studies limiting our understanding of the actual extent of faking behavior. As Smith and Robie (2004) noted, "we believe that laboratory research on impression management (including directed faking studies, whether conducted in the lab or not), provide little insight into impression management beyond the fact that when instructed to do so people can alter their scores on a personality assessment . . . we believe the research evidence suggests that laboratory research (as it is typically conducted using a directed faking approach) is probably an inappropriate vehicle for studying impression management issues" (p. 114). Although this sentiment has been frequently expressed, examination of faking prevalence using directed faking studies continues.

Applicant-Incumbent Comparison

Several researchers (cf. Ellingson, Smith & Sackett, 2001; Hough, 1998; Hough, Eaton, Dunnette, Kamp, & McCloy, 1990; Michaelis & Eysenck, 1971; Rosse, Stecher, Miller, & Levin, 1998; Schwab & Packard, 1973; Smith & Ellingson, 2002) have made comparisons of mean personality scale scores between groups where faking motivation is assumed to vary naturally. While this design does overcome some of the limitations of directed faking studies, conclusions are limited by the inherent differences that exist between the groups being compared. Mount and Barrick (1995) concluded that applicant-incumbent comparisons violate the basic assumption of between-group designs—that our groups are sufficiently equivalent to rule out alternative explanations for observed mean differences—and, therefore, conclusions drawn from this research are limited. The assumption of equivalent groups can rarely be supported with most published research using the applicant-incumbent design. In fact, we would expect applicant and incumbent samples to be notably different due to the selection processes, potential demographic differences between groups, and range restriction. Demonstrating that applicants differ from incumbents can provide us with clues regarding the extent of response distortion; however, it cannot provide definite proof that faking is commonplace.

Interestingly, the results are mixed with roughly as many studies suggesting meaningful mean differences between applicant-incumbent groups as those that do not (Morgeson, Campion, Dipboye, Hollenbeck, Murphy, & Schmitt, 2007).

Recently, two studies have been published that attempt to redress this criticism of nonequivalence in applicant-incumbent comparisons. Ellingson, Sackett, and Connelly (2007) examined within-person differences in responses to the California Psychological Inventory (CPI) across selection (motivated) and development (unmotivated) contexts. There are several notable aspects of the study of Ellingson et al. that warrant mention. First, the study had a large sample size relatively rare in within-subjects comparisons. One of the primary criticisms of previous applicant-incumbent research demonstrating insignificant mean differences between groups was small sample size (compared to the larger sample sizes that tend to show differences). Second, because the sample consisted of respondents who had taken the CPI in different contexts and in different orders (selection then development, development then selection), they could account for time, practice, and feedback effects. Simplifying greatly, their results suggest that intentional distortion explains an increase of approximately 0.075 standard deviation units in a selection context with relatively little changes in rank order (correlations approximated the 5-year test-retest of the CPI). They conclude that such a small increase is unlikely to cause significant effects on selection decisions.

Similarly, Griffith, Chmielowski, and Yoshita (2007) conducted a within-subjects investigation of faking behavior. In their study, applicants completed a task-related measure of conscientiousness and, once hired, were asked to complete the assessment under an "honest responding" condition. They interpreted their results to suggest that applicants can and do fake (effect size of 0.61 between the applicant and honest responding condition) and this does affect the rank ordering of candidates during selection. Interestingly, the results of the study of Griffith et al. suggest that faking in real world situations is smaller in magnitude than the results typically found in directed faking studies. However, the design of their study has limitations that, we believe, urge caution in accepting their conclusions. Most notably, the use of an "honest responding" instruction set during the incumbent retest could yield a demand characteristic that deflates respondents' scores. If respondents, now hired, are asked to retake a personality assessment and are asked to respond honestly, the instruction (not present during the applicant phase) could cause them to be both more cautious and more conservative in their responses. Additionally, the study has a comparatively small sample (61 participants), cannot control for practice or feedback effects, fails to take into account test–retest unreliability of the instrument, and focused on a single aspect of personality, conscientiousness. Although we do give greater credence to the results of Ellingson & Sackett, we would suggest that the evidence supporting faking from applicant-incumbent comparisons remains mixed.

Impression Management Scales

Response distortion scales have been used extensively in both directed faking studies and applicant-incumbent comparison. However, given the subset of research that examines the prevalence of faking based on scores on such scales (independent of context or instruction), we believed it appropriate to make a few brief comments on the value of measures of impression management scales for faking research. Although often taken for granted, we largely agree with Burns and Christiansen (2006) that the evidence supporting the ability of impression management scales to detect faking (particularly in applicant contexts) is questionable. More importantly, there is considerable evidence that many impression management scales measure substantive trait variance that overlaps significantly with the five-factor model (Smith & Ellingson, 2002) and may be conceptually distinct from faking. Given these limitations it seems prudent to accept the conclusions of research using impression management scales as indicators of the prevalence of faking with some caution. If it is the case that impression management scales overlap with substantive traits (primarily neuroticism, agreeableness, and conscientiousness), then the assumed frequency of faking will be driven by these substantive characteristics rather than true faking behavior.

Obviously, this brief review of research methodologies was not intended to be exhaustive. Our point is that we have yet to identify a research design without significant limitations that allows for an unambiguous test of the extent to which people distort their responses to personality and other noncognitive measures. Although Ellingson, Sackett, and Connelly's (2007) results are promising, they deserve replication and extension with other measures of personality with greater control over lag between test and retest, context, and personality feedback processes.

■ QUESTIONING CONVENTIONAL WISDOM

As we noted in the introduction to this chapter, faking research originated from concerns driven by the predominantly applied focus of personality research to selection decisions and faking is typically considered to be both prevalent and problematic (particularly by practitioners and test takers). If, however, we were to begin with the premise that faking occurs infrequently, what theory and evidence could be advanced to support this conclusion? We offer this question not to indicate that faking is rare, but to shift attention to organizational and psychological theory that may suggest that faking could be more infrequent than is often assumed.

First, it is important to realize that the job and vocational choice process is not random. As Walsh (2004) noted, "The notion that personality relates in meaningful ways to the kinds of careers people select and their performance and satisfaction in those careers has a long and significant history in vocational psychology. There is a substantial database indicating that people tend to move toward, enter, and remain in occupational environments congruent with their personality traits" (p. 141). In addition, numerous studies indicate that when personality matches job demands, people are more satisfied, less likely to turn over, and experience less stress (see Kristoff, 1996 and Walsh, 2004 for reviews). This suggests that the extent of faking would be naturally constrained by restriction in the range of applicants for a particular job. Take, for instance, the job of sales person. We would suspect that applicants for sale positions involving significant customer interaction and direct selling are unlikely to be predominantly introverted. If we accept (hypothetically) that extraversion is related to sales effectiveness and primarily extraverts apply for sales positions, the amount of faking that would be necessary is constrained by the sorting process (for job choice) that occurs prior to applying for the job. Someone could fake the extent of their extraversion, but it would seem unlikely that an introvert would put himself or herself in a situation that requires extraversion. We grant this is a simplification and we do not intend to suggest that introverts are incapable of being effective at sales or that introversion/extraversion is a dichotomy. However, it seems reasonable to suspect that faking behavior will be constrained by the nonrandom process by which people with particular personality characteristics apply for particular types of jobs. Additionally, the same motivation that leads to specific vocational preferences (i.e., avoiding a career/job that is disconsonant with your personality preferences or underlying motives) should operate to inhibit faking in the extreme.

Second, there is a long-standing tradition of research in social psychology on self-consistency (Aronson, 1968; Festinger, 1957; Lecky, 1945; Swann, 1983). The basic premise of self-consistency research is that people form stable identities and seek to maintain a stable identity in their social interactions, choices of environments, and opportunities. Although a full elaboration of psychological self-consistency theories is beyond the scope of this chapter, Swann's research on self-verification theory is illustrative and provides an interesting counterpoint to the perspective of much research on faking. Self-verification theory posits that people develop chronic and stable self-views and then seek to "verify" these self-views in their social worlds. In contrast to a self-enhancement perspective suggesting people need to view themselves and be viewed by others positively (to maintain and enhance self-esteem), Swann's research has clearly indicated that people attempt to verify both positive and negative self-views through feedback seeking, and choice of (among other things) social situations, roommates, and relationships. The research on self-verification has uncovered surprising findings. For instance, people with negative self-views often seek feedback supportive of their negative self-view, and if given feedback to the contrary, ignore it or consider it invalid (Bosson & Swann, 1999; Swann, Wenzlaff, Krull, & Pelham, 1992). In other words, whether good or bad, people attempt to "validate" their self-views rather than attempt to invalidate them. So, what implications does this have for faking research? If self-consistency and self-verification are dominant motives, it would suggest that faking (placing oneself in a situation in which the self may not be verified because the demands of the job are misaligned with personal traits) would be psychologically harmful (producing anxiety and distress) because it places a person in a situation in which his or her identity is at risk. Furthermore, self-enhancement theory would argue that people would not want to place themselves in a situation involving potential failure (and be viewed negatively by others) by faking traits they do not possess.

Placing the question of faking motivation in the broader context of vocational and social psychological theories (particularly theories of self-consistency and identity formation and maintenance) would suggest that there are constraints that belie the conventional wisdom that faking (or the motivation to fake) is common-place. However, this does require us to shift our perspective away from the empirical and psychometric focus of current research and draws us into the general theoretical debate regarding what responses to personality questionnaires actually mean. The meaning of faking behavior and its implications are quite disparate given one's theoretical explanation for personality item responding and before addressing the question of the impact of faking on criterion-related validity; to frame our perspective on this question, we will provide two opposing views and review two recently developed models from a social-cognitive perspective on personality.

■ THEORETICAL PERSPECTIVES ON PERSONALITY

Historically, there have been a variety of theoretical explanations for personality item responding (cf. Hogan & Hogan, 1998 for a comprehensive review). However, our reading of the literature in applied psychology suggests that most research begins with the premise that responses to a personality questionnaire are veridical reports of a person's underlying psychological traits—a perspective that has been termed the trait-realist position (Allport, 1937). For trait-realists, a person's standing on personality traits is constant across situations, is available to conscious introspection, and represents mental structures that "explain" consistencies in behavior across time and context. From this perspective, faking represents a threat to the validity of personality assessments because true scores for personality traits will be contaminated if it occurs. This can be contrasted to a social-constructionist perspective [drawing on the work of Mead (1913) and Goffman, (1956)] that suggests that consistency in behavior is a function of stable self-presentation strategies (for a review of this perspective see Johnson & Hogan, 2006). Hogan's (1983) socio-analytic theory of personality is an example of a social-constructionist view of personality. If, for the moment, we reject the trait-realist view and consider personality responding to be a form of self-presentation whereby respondents are engaged in the process of negotiating their identity with others, it places personality assessment in the larger context of social interaction governed by the general rules of identity negotiation and maintenance. This tradition, uncommon in the applied psychology literature, has a substantial history in the social psychology of identity and presumes that people may have multiple "selves" (James 1890; Markus & Nurius, 1986; Stryker, 2007)—a concept considered incompatible with the trait-realist position. Nonetheless, considering faking from a self-presentational view would suggest that (assuming consistency of self-presentation strategy by context or role) faking is normal and valid variance not error.

Although this position is relatively rare in the faking literature (with the exception of work grounded in Hogan's socioanalytic theory), the view that explicit reports on personality questionnaires represent identity negotiation strategies related to context or role-specific "selves" is commonplace in the larger personality and social-psychological literature (cf. Roberts & Donahue, 1994). More importantly, building on recent research in social cognition, there is an emerging trend to view identity (implicit personality) and self-presentation (explicit personality) as two interrelated aspects of a broader personality self-concept. We believe this integration of social-cognitive perspectives with traditional trait psychology offers important insights for faking research. We review select social-cognitive models next with a focus on Roberts and Donahue's (1994) PRISM model and the BPMP (Back et al., 2009).

■ MULTIPLE SELVES AND THE PERSONALITY SELF-CONCEPT

Both PRISM and the BPMP make distinct yet related contributions to our understanding of personality processes. PRISM attempts to explain how an individual can possess multiple role specific identities (selves) related to a general identity and was developed in response to the central debate between dispositionalists and social-constructionists. BPMP, developed from the emerging work on dual process models in social psychology, recognizes the possibility of both dual identities or self-concepts (implicit and explicit) and provides a model of the relationship between these self-concepts and behavior. Although space does not allow a full elaboration of each theory, we will next provide a short overview of the primary elements of each.

■ PERSONALITY AND ROLE IDENTITY STRUCTURAL MODEL (PRISM)

The PRISM (Woods & Roberts, 2006) was developed to address a persistent criticism of dispositional models—that they fail to account for the effect of context (roles) on individuals' stable self-presentation strategies (personality). Hogan and Roberts (2000) suggested that the "situation" often absent in dispositional models of personality could be conceptualized as the psychological meaning people ascribe to the various roles they play in social life. There are four elements of the PRISM model relevant to the current discussion [cf. Woods & Roberts (2006) for a full elaboration and supporting research].

First, people have multiple identities that are hierarchically organized. At the highest level of the hierarchy, people have a general identity that serves to organize their self-concept. General identity refers to how we see ourself across time, roles, and situations and represents the decontextualized aspects of individual identity (personality). At a more detailed level people have role-specific identities that represent perceptions of narrower, context-specific dispositions (e.g., work role identity, family identity, friendship identity). By their very nature, most measures of normal personality are intended to assess general identity, however, PRISM implies that if people are cued to a specific role during the assessment process, a general personality measure will target role-specific identity rather than or in addition to general identity.

Second, general identity constrains the amount of variation that exists (or can exist without inducing stress) in role-specific identities. Furthermore, consistency in role identities should be explained by general identity.

Third, role-specific behaviors (e.g., being conscientious at work) should be fully mediated by role-specific identities. In other words, the relationship between general identity and role-related behaviors should be mediated by role-specific identities.

Lastly, the extent to which a role identity will be invoked or the salience and importance an individual has for a particular role identity will be based on the individual's social or emotional commitment to and satisfaction with his or her performance in that role (Hoelter, 1983; Stryker, 1987).

Roberts and Donahue (1994) and Woods and Roberts (2006) provide evidence supporting the theoretical propositions of PRISM. Their results suggest that people do, in fact, possess multiple role-related identities. These role identities represent stable and consistent self-presentation strategies that, although constrained by general identity, can explain role-specific behavior. PRISM provides a perspective on the research on frame of reference effects in personality measurement (Schmit, Ryan, Stierwalt, & Powell, 1995) whereby contextualized personality measures (with the inclusion of "at work" tags to specific items) have been shown to be more predictive of work behavior than decontextualized measures. Providing a frame of reference cues a specific role identity leading to responses that should be more related to role-specific behavior. The implications of PRISM will be discussed following an overview of the BPMP model.

■ BEHAVIORAL PROCESS MODEL OF PERSONALITY (BPMP)

The BPMP was developed as an extension of work on implicit social cognition and dual-process models of social behavior (Back et al., 2009). It focuses on the distinction between implicit and explicit aspects of the personality self-concept and the relationship between these aspects of the personality self-concept and automatic versus controlled behavior. Prior to elaborating on the BPMP model, we would first like to discuss the two components of personality that the BPMP model attempts to integrate: the personality self-concept and information-processing models.

First, it is possible that with regard to our personality, many of our associations in memory are hidden from conscious awareness. Prior work in implicit social cognition has differentiated between two similar, but distinct components of the personality self-concept: *implicit* and *explicit* components (Schnabel, Asendorpf, & Greenwald, 2007). Specifically, Schnabel and colleagues proposed a hierarchical structure of personality in which *implicit* and *explicit personality self-concept* are distinct latent constructs under the umbrella of a second-order latent construct, the *personality self-concept*. Refer to Figure 4.1 for an illustration of this distinction.

The *explicit personality self-concept* is based on propositional representations of the personality self-concept. For instance, the concepts of "self" and "outgoing" can be linked to form the statement "I am outgoing" or "I am not outgoing." The process of deciding whether either of these propositional statements is true is a conscious reasoning process based on introspection. The *implicit personality*

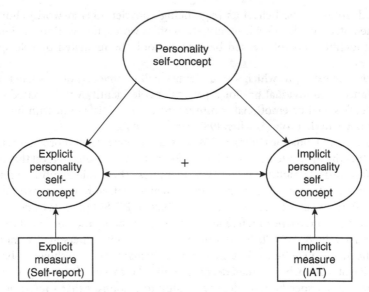

Figure 4.1 Model of personality self-concept and distinction between explicit and implicit components of personality.

self-concept consists of associative networks between concepts of the self (e.g., "I", "me") and attributes describing personality traits that typically operate outside of conscious awareness and are not always available via conscious introspective processes.

The distinction between *implicit* and *explicit personality self-concept* is important because these constructs are related to different modes of information processing that determine and guide behavior (Back et al., 2009). To understand how personality is related to actual behavior, it is vital to consider the processes that determine and guide behavior. Previous research has made a distinction between two different modes of processing that determine behavior: *controlled* and *automatic* (Fazio, 1990).

Theories of controlled and automatic processing have facilitated the development of dual-process theories in social and personality psychology research. One such theory is Fazio's (1990) Motivation and Opportunities as Determinants of Processing model (MODE). The model is an integration of spontaneous processing and deliberative processing models. The spontaneous model states that attitudes are associations in memory between an object and an individuals' evaluation of that object, and to the extent that the association is strong, the attitude should be automatically activated when the object is present. The deliberative model suggests that conscious processes are involved in attitude-behavior consistency, and to the extent that a person is able to recognize and monitor attitudes the resulting behavior will be intentional.

MODE posits that both processes can occur depending on the extent to which a behavioral decision involves effortful, deliberate reasoning or a dependence on preexisting associations. Unique to MODE is the importance placed on motivation and opportunity. Specifically, deliberative processing will occur only when an individual is sufficiently motivated and has the opportunity (i.e., time) to engage in effortful processing. When unable to consciously monitor behavior and thoughts, individuals will rely on spontaneous processing.

Similarly, Strack and Deutsch's (2004) Reflective and Impulsive Determinants of Social Behavior (RIDSB) model posits that perception, thought, and social behavior are functions of two different information-processing systems. The RIDSB model builds upon MODE by accounting for both direct influences of dual information-processing systems on behavior and interactions between the dual systems in triggering behavior. The two information-processing systems in this model are the *reflective* and *impulsive* systems. The *reflective* system is defined by dependence on cognitive resources and reliance on behavioral intentions and is analogous to the controlled or deliberative system reviewed earlier. In this system, aspects of a situation are perceived on a conscious level, allowing individuals to engage in effortful thinking and deliberation. During this process, behavioral response options are reviewed and weighted before a conscious decision to engage in a behavioral act occurs. Conversely, the *impulsive* system is represented by associations and schemata in memory and is analogous to the automatic or spontaneous system (Strack & Deutsch, 2004). In the *impulsive* system, information that is perceived triggers behavioral schema in the associative network and this activation leads to automatic initiation of the behavioral sequences that are encoded in the schema.

Although these models focus on attitude-behavior relationships and not personality, they are relevant because they suggest that (1) social information is processed on both conscious and unconscious levels, and (2) behavioral actions can be either spontaneous or controlled in nature. Prior research has supported the distinction between spontaneous and controlled behavior within the personality domain (Asendorpf, Banse, & Mücke, 2002; Steffens & Kőnig, 2006). Based on the MODE model, Asendorpf et al. (2002) proposed that implicit personality measures would better predict behavior thought to operate on an unconscious level, whereas explicit personality measures would better predict deliberate behavior. The results showed that an implicit association test (IAT) measure of shyness predicted spontaneous facial movements and speech illustrators (behaviors categorized as spontaneous and thought to derive from automatic information processing) better than an explicit measure of shyness. In addition, Asendorpf et al. (2002) also found that the explicit measure of shyness was better able to predict behaviors such as speech and duration of body movements (behaviors thought to derive from controlled information processing) than implicit measures.

In a subsequent study, Steffens and König (2006) examined whether IATs designed to measure all of the Big Five factors predicted behavior. Results showed that implicit measures of extraversion and conscientiousness predicted behavior that the explicit measure of personality did not predict. Specifically, the IAT measure of conscientiousness predicted spontaneous behavior related to a concentration task. Steffens and König hypothesized that individuals higher on implicitly measured conscientiousness would complete the self-paced task more slowly and make fewer errors and the results confirmed their hypothesis. Moreover, the IAT

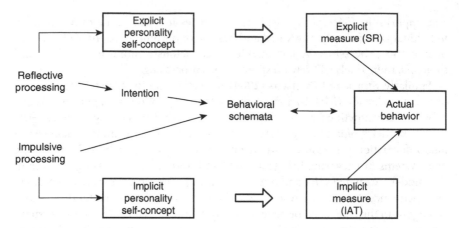

Figure 4.2 Adaptation of the Behavioral Process Model of Personality (BPMP; Back et al., 2009).

measure of extraversion predicted spontaneous behaviors related to the amount of time subjects spent in a social interaction.

The BPMP is the first social-cognitive model to fully integrate dual-process models and theories of multiple aspects of the personality self-concept. The model is essentially a personality oriented adaptation of the RIDSB model (see Figure 4.2 for an adaptation of the BPMP model; Back et al., 2009) and proposes that two information-processing paths can determine personality-relevant behavior. Trait expression results from both impulsive and reflective processes, with reflective processes representing how people normally perceive situations, which behavioral actions they prefer in a given situation, and how they deliberately initiate the behavior via propositional representations (e.g., I am a person who is organized). The information-processing system that is engaged determines which aspect of the personality self-concept is activated and subsequently whether implicit or explicit personality measures will predict the behavior.

The BPMP model suggests that reflective processes are represented in the *explicit personality self-concept*. Impulsive processes represent the automatic processing of information in well-established associative links in the associative network representing the *implicit personality self-concept*. As such, explicit personality measures should tap in to the *explicit personality self-concept* because both are based on the same conscious reasoning processes (i.e., introspection; Schnabel et al., 2007). The key idea here is that the explicit personality self-concept is determined, to a large extent, by the way a person perceives himself or herself and/or how he or she wants others to perceive him or her (self-presentation). In contrast, implicit measures of association strength in memory tap in to the associative representations that are part of the *implicit personality self-concept*. This suggests that the implicit personality self-concept is more likely to reflect aspects of an individual's personality independent of self-presentation (identity).

■ INTEGRATION OF PRISM AND BPMP

Although these two models have different histories, we believe they make unique contributions to our understanding of personality processes generally, and faking behavior in applied personality measurement specifically. First, both models assume the existence of different levels of personality measurement (general versus specific identities for PRISM and implicit versus explicit personality self-concept for BPMP). Rather than focusing on a unitary self, these theoretical models suggest the measurement of personality needs to be more nuanced and needs to reflect the complexities of underlying personality processes. Although this proposition may seem somewhat controversial to the dispositionalist perspective that guides applied research on personality assessment, it does reflect a long-standing tradition in personality and social psychology (Funder & Colvin, 1991).

Second, both models presume that responding to a self-report measure of personality is a reflective process guided by the motivation to negotiate our identity and/or describe the explicit (and contextualized) self-concept. This is in contrast to the trait-realist position that assumes that respondents are reporting, veridically, the traits that underlie their general identity. Interestingly, McCrae and Costa (1996), often considered proponents of the trait-realist perspective, propose a model of personality grounded in the five-factor model suggesting a distinction between "basic tendencies" and "characteristic adaptations." Basic tendencies represent underlying psychological traits that guide behavior, whereas characteristic adaptations are learned behavioral patterns developed in response to the environment. These could be considered analogous to general identity and role-specific identity or implicit and explicit personality self-concept.

Third, both models assume specific identities are constrained by general or implicit self-concept. Rather than assuming, as James (1890) suggested, that "man has as many social selves as there are individuals who recognize him" (p. 294), both models recognize that general identity places a limit on the plasticity of human behavior. Although unique role-related identities (or explicit self-concepts) may emerge based on experience in a given context, they will not deviate substantially from a person's general identity or implicit self-concept. This proposition allows for the continuity or coherence observed in behavior across time and satisfies the primary agenda of dispositional research.

Lastly, both models suggest that the prediction of behavior will improve if we put greater thought into the aspects of self-concept that guide behavior. Woods and Roberts (2006), drawing on the bandwidth-fidelity debate, suggest that the measurement of role-specific identities is more likely to predict role-relevant behavior. Back et al. (2009) suggest that measures of the explicit personality self-concept are more likely to predict controlled (reflective) behavior whereas measures of implicit self-concept are more likely to predict automatic (impulsive) behavior.

These propositions and the research supporting them suggest an alternative view of faking in applied personality measurement as well as problems with our current conceptualization of the personality–performance relationship. In the next section, we will discuss the implications of these alternative personality process models for theory and research on faking.

■ IMPLICATIONS FOR FAKING RESEARCH AND NEW RESEARCH DIRECTIONS

The introductory quotation for this chapter suggested that examining the broader psychological, social-psychology, and sociological literature germane to motivated impression management would advance our understanding of faking on personality measures. We have presented two recent models of personality processes that depart from the traditional trait-realist position that dominates current thinking in applied personality psychology. Although the debate concerning the meaning of personality item responses continues, the emerging evidence supporting the propositions of these models is encouraging and suggests an alternative view of faking and its potential impact on criterion-related validity. In conclusion, we would like to return to the two central questions in the faking literature, and examine the implications of an alternative view of personality for the ongoing debate.

■ DO PEOPLE "FAKE" AND THE MEANING OF "FAKING"

As we have noted, faking can be seen as a source of error in personality true scores or as an element of identity negotiation representing a consistent (and role-specific) self-presentation strategy. Contrasting the trait-realist and social-constructionist views provides insights regarding the meaning of "faking." If differences in a person's responses to a personality assessment across contexts (general responding versus motivated responding) represent differences in underlying role identities primed by the response condition, then "faking" not only represents valid variance, it is essential variance—artificially suppressing this variance with instruction sets and corrections are likely to diminish the predictive ability of personality assessments. Furthermore, this suggests that incorporating measures of role identity and role salience in examinations of faking prevalence and the personality-performance relationship could provide clues regarding the extent to which faking or responding consistent with an internalized role identity explains differences in personality scores across different contexts. In other words, role identity could serve as a useful moderator of within-subjects differences in personality scores across response conditions (particularly general versus applicant).

More importantly, however, the broader psychological literature suggests new avenues of research on faking motivation. Our review of the faking literature suggests that faking motivation is often assumed rather than seriously investigated. Although most of the theoretical models of faking include individual differences in faking motivation (cf. McFarland & Ryan, 2006; Mueller-Hanson, Heggestad, & Thornton, 2006; Snell, Sydell, & Lueke, 1999), there is remarkably little research on the underlying psychological mechanisms or contextual factors that contribute to faking motivation and even less research that builds on the broader vocational and social-psychological literature on job choice, impression management, reputation maintenance, and self-consistency. This literature begs several questions that are substantially more complex than our current view of faking motivation. For instance, recognizing that person–job misfit is a source of stress and leads to job dissatisfaction, when would a person choose to set aside his or her own preferences and present a false portrait of his or her character for the sake of getting a job? It is interesting that research suggests that knowledge of job requirements is necessary for successful faking (Griffith & McDaniel, 2006; Vasilopoulos, Reilly, & Leaman, 2000). However, this would also imply that "fakers" would have knowledge that job requirements do not match their personality characteristics. This might suggest that understanding faking motivation requires a broader understanding of the psychological process underlying decision-making when personal goals are in conflict, the relative weighting of different motives (status, economic gain, competitiveness, etc.) in applying for a job, how thoughtful applicants are regarding the extent to which person-job misfit can be a source of distress. Although we cannot answer these questions in this chapter, they do suggest fruitful avenues of future research that illuminate the complexities of faking motivation.

■ FAKING AND CRITERION-RELATED VALIDITY

We have often been struck by the assumption that the motivation to fake to attain a job would not carry over into a similar motivation to perform effectively on the job. The faking literature seems to presume that job attainment is more motivating than job retention, at least with regard to managing impressions. Again, if we assume that successful faking requires knowledge of job demands and job requirements (Griffith & McDaniel, 2006; Vasilopoulos, Reilly, & Leaman, 2000), it seems reasonable to suspect that successful fakers would perform their jobs consistent with performance expectations. In other words, they would fake on the job just as they would fake during the selection process. This suggests to us that we need to expand our conceptualization of faking motivation to the broader context of motivation to meet job-relevant performance criteria. As we have noted, this would be consistent with psychological self-consistency theories as well as implicit theories in the social-cognition literature.

More importantly, however, the BPMP model suggests that we need to expand our conceptualization of job performance to include automatic versus controlled behaviors. A basic proposition of the BPMP model is that implicit personality is more likely to be predictive of automatic behaviors that occur outside of conscious reasoning, whereas explicit personality is more predictive of controlled behaviors representing reflective processes. It could be the case that our often coarse measures of the criterion domain of job performance do not adequately separate automatic from controlled aspects of performance. It may be the case that for the types of jobs for which personality is a valid predictor of performance, controlled behaviors drive job performance. Recall, for the moment, our discussion of sales performance. We would consider a sales episode to be dominated primarily by a reflective process and, perhaps, more related to explicit personality than implicit personality. In the end, this suggests the need to be thoughtful regarding the criterion we are using in our studies of the faking phenomenon and, at the very least, differentiate between aspects of job performance that are more likely to be driven by automatic as opposed to controlled behaviors.

Our intent with this chapter was to provide a different perspective on faking and the personality-performance relationship by questioning the central assumption of the trait-realist position. We believe the basic propositions of the PRISM and BPMP provide fruitful avenues for future research and suggest many testable propositions that could advance our understanding of personality processes. More importantly, both models place faking in a dramatically different light than our current theoretical models grounded in specific assumptions regarding the meaning of personality item responses. We do hope that future work on faking broadens in perspective and incorporates more of the emerging literature in personality and social psychology.

References

Allport, G. (1937). *Personality: A psychological interpretation.* New York: Holt, Rinehart, & Winston.

Aronson, E. (1968). Dissonance theory: Progress and problems. In R. P. Abelson, E. Aronson, W. J. McGuire, T. M. Newcomb, M. J. Rosenberg, & P. H. Tannenbaum (Eds.), *Cognitive consistency theories: A source book* (pp. 5–27). Skokie, IL: Rand McNally.

Asendorpf, J. B., Banse, R., & Mücke, D. (2002). Double dissociation between implicit and explicit personality self-concept: The case of shy behavior. *Journal of Personality and Social Psychology, 83*, 380–393.

Back, M. D., Schumkle, S. C., & Egloff, B. (2009). Predicting actual behavior from the explicit and implicit self-concept of personality. *Journal of Personality and Social Psychology, 97*, 533–548.

Bosson, J., & Swann, W. B., Jr. (1999). Self-liking, self-competence, and the quest for self-verification. *Personality and Social Psychology Bulletin, 25*, 1230–1241.

Burns, G., & Christiansen, N. D. (2006). Use of social desirability in correcting for motivated distortion. In R. Griffith (Ed.), *A closer examination of applicant faking behavior* (pp. 115–150). Greenwich, CT: Information Age Publishing.

Ellingson, J. E., Sackett, P. R., & Connelly, B. S. (2007). Personality assessment across selection and development contexts: Insights into response distortion. *Journal of Applied Psychology, 92*, 386–395.

Ellingson, J. E., Smith, D. B., & Sackett, P. R. (2001). Investigating the influence of social desirability on personality factor structure. *Journal of Applied Psychology, 86*, 122–133.

Fazio, R. H. (1990). Multiple processes by which attitudes guide behavior: The MODE model as an integrative framework. In M. P. Zanna (Ed.), *Advances in the study of social psychology* (pp. 75–105). San Diego, CA: Academic Press.

Festinger, L. (1957). *A theory of cognitive dissonance.* Stanford, CA: Stanford University Press.

Funder, D. C., & Colvin C. R. (1991). Explorations in behavioral consistency: Properties of persons, situations, and behaviors. *Journal of Personality and Social Psychology, 60*, 773–794.

Goffman, E. (1956). *The presentation of self in everyday life.* Edinburgh: University of Edinburgh.

Griffith, R. L., Chmielowski, T. S., & Yoshita, Y. (2007). Do applicants fake? An examination of the frequency of applicant faking behavior. *Personnel Review, 34*, 341–355.

Griffith, R. L., & McDaniel, M. (2006). *A Closer Examination of Applicant Faking Behavior.* Charlotte, NC: Information Age Publishers.

Hoelter, J. W. (1983). The effects of role evaluation and commitment on identity salience. *Social Psychology Quarterly, 46*, 140–147.

Hogan, R. (1983). A socioanalytic theory of personality. In M. M. Page (Ed.), *Nebraska symposium on motivation 1982: Personality-current theory and research* (pp. 55–89). Lincoln: University of Nebraska Press.

Hogan, R., & Hogan, J. (1998). Theoretical frameworks for assessment. In R. Jeanneret & R. Silzer (Eds.), *Individual psychological assessment: Predicting behavior in organizational settings* (pp. 27–53). San Francisco, CA: Jossey-Bass.

Hogan, R. T., & Roberts, B. W. (2000). A Socioanalytic perspective on person/environment interaction. In W. B. Walsh, K. H. Craik, & R. H. Price (Eds.), *New directions in person-environment psychology* (pp. 1–24). Mahwah, NJ: Erlbaum.

Hough, L. M. (1998). Effects of intentional distortion personality measurement and evaluation of suggested palliatives. *Human Performance, 11*, 209–244.

Hough, L. M., Eaton, N. K., Dunnette, M. D., Kamp, J. D., & McCloy, R. A. (1990). Criterion-related validities of personality constructs and the effect of response distortion on those validities. *Journal of Applied Psychology, 75*, 581–595.

James, W. (1890). *The principles of psychology* (2 vols.). New York: Holt.

Johnson, J. A., & Hogan, R. (2006). A socioanalytic view of faking. In R. Griffith (Ed.), *A closer examination of applicant faking behavior* (pp. 209–231). Greenwich, CT: Information Age Publishing.

Kristof, A. L. (1996). Person-organisation fit: An integrative review of its conceptualizations, measurement, and implications. *Personnel Psychology, 49*, 1–49.

Lecky, P. (1945). *Self-consistency: A theory of personality*. New York: Island Press.

Markus, H., & Nurius, P. (1986). Possible selves. *American Psychologist, 41*, 954–969.

McCrae, R. R., & Costa, P. T., Jr. (1996). Toward a new generation of personality theories: Theoretical contexts for the five-factor model. In J. S. Wiggins (Ed.), *The five-factor model of personality: Theoretical perspectives* (pp. 51–87). New York: Guilford.

McFarland, L. A. & Ryan, A. M. (2006). Toward an integrated Model of Applicant Faking Behavior. *Journal of Applied Social Psychology, 36*, 979–1016.

Mead, G. H. (1913). The social self. *Journal of Philosophy, 10*, 374–380.

Mesmer-Magnus, J. R., & Viswesvaran, C. (2006). Assessing response distortion in personality tests: A review of research designs and analytic strategies. In R. Griffith & M. Peterson (Eds.), *A closer examination of applicant faking behavior* (pp. 85–113). Greenwich, CT: Information Age Publishing.

Michaelis, W., & Eysenck, H. J. (1971). The determination of personality inventory factor patterns and intercorrelations by changes in real-life motivation. *The Journal of Genetic Psychology, 118*, 223–234.

Morgeson, F., Campion, M., Dipboye, R., Hollenbeck, J., Murphy, K., & Schmitt, N. (2007). Reconsidering the use of personality tests in personnel selection contexts. *Personnel Psychology, 60*, 683–729.

Mount, M. K., & Barrick, M. R. (1995). The Big Five personality dimensions: Implications for research and practice in human resources management. In G. R Ferris (Ed.), *Research in personnel and human resources management, Vol. 13*. Greenwich, CT: JAI Press.

Mueller-Hanson, R. A., Heggestad, E. D., & Thornton, G. C. III. (2006). Individual differences in impression management: An exploration of the psychological processes underlying faking. *Psychological Science, 48*, 288–312.

Rees, C. J., & Metcalfe, B. (2003). The faking of personality questionnaires: Who's kidding whom? *Journal of Managerial Psychology, 18*, 156–165.

Roberts, B. W., & Donahue, E. M. (1994). One personality, multiple selves: Integrating personality and social roles. *Journal of Personality, 62*, 201–218.

Rosse, J. G., Stecher, M. D., Miller, J. L., & Levin, R. A. (1998). The impact of response distortion on preemployment personality testing and hiring decisions. *Journal of Applied Psychology*, *83*, 634–644.

Schmit, M. J., Ryan, A. M., Stierwalt, S. L., & Powell, S. L. (1995). Frame-of-reference effects on personality scores and criterion-related validity. *Journal of Applied Psychology*, *80*, 607–620.

Schnabel, K., Asendorpf, J. B., & Greenwald, A. G. (2007). Using implicit association tests for the assessment of implicit personality self-concept. In G. J. Boyle, G. Matthews, & H. Saklofske (Eds.), *Handbook of personality theory and testing*. (pp. 508–528). London: Sage.

Schwab, D. P., & Packard, G. L. (1973). Response distortion on the Gordon Personality Inventory and the Gordon Personal Profile in a selection context: Some implications for predicting employee tenure. *Journal of Applied Psychology*, *58*, 372–374.

Snell, A. F., Sydell, E. J., & Lueke, S. B. (1999). Towards a theory of applicant faking: Integrating studies of deception. *Human Resource Management Review*, *9*, 219–242.

Smith, D. B., & Ellingson, J. E. (2002). Substance versus style: A new look at social desirability in motivating contexts. *Journal of Applied Psychology*, *87*, 211–219.

Smith, D. B., & Robie, C. (2004). The implications for impression management for personality research in organizations. In B. Schneider & D. B. Smith (Eds.), *Personality and organizations*. Mahwah, NJ: Lawrence Erlbaum Associates.

Smith, D. B. & Schneider, B. (2004). Where we've been and where we're going: Some conclusions regarding personality and organizations. In B. Schneider, & D. B. Smith (Eds.), *Personality and organizations* (pp. 387–404). Hillsdale, NJ: Lawrence Erlbaum Associates.

Steffens, M. C., & König, S. S. (2006). Predicting spontaneous big five behavior with implicit association tests. *European Journal of Psychological Assessment*, *22*, 13–20.

Strack, F., & Deutsch, R. (2004). Reflective and impulsive determinants of social behavior. *Personality and Social Psychology Review*, *8*, 220–247.

Stryker, S. (1987). Identity theory: Developments and extensions. In Honess, T. & Yardley, K., (Eds.), *Self and Identity: Psychosocial Perspectives* (pp. 89–103). London: John Wiley.

Stryker, S. (2007). Identity theory and personality theory: Mutual relevance. *Journal of Personality*, *75*, 1083–1102.

Swann, W. B., Jr. (1983). Self-verification: Bringing social reality into harmony with the self. In J. Suls & A. G. Greenwald (Eds.), *Social psychological perspectives on the self, Vol. 2* (pp. 33–66). Hillsdale, NJ: Erlbaum.

Swann, W. B., Jr., Wenzlaff, R. M., Krull, D. S., & Pelham, B. W. (1992). The allure of negative feedback: Self-verification strivings among depressed persons. *Journal of Abnormal Psychology*, *101*, 293–306.

Vasilopoulos, N. L., Reilly, R. R., & Leaman, J. A. (2000). The influence of job familiarity and impression management on self-report measure scale scores and response latencies. Journal of Applied Psychology, *85*, 50–64.

Walsh, W. B. (2004). Vocational psychology and personality. In B. Schneider & D. B. Smith (Eds.), *Personality and organizations* (pp. 141–162). Mahwah, NJ: Lawrence Erlbaum Associates.

Wood, D., & Roberts, B. W. (2006). Cross-sectional and longitudinal tests of the Personality and Role Identity Structural Model (PRISM). *Journal of Personality*, *74*, 779–810.

5 Faking Does Distort Self-Report Personality Assessment

■ RONALD R. HOLDEN AND ANGELA S. BOOK[1]

The impact of faking on personality assessment can be substantial. In our evaluation of the influence of faking, we present what we consider to be three relevant issues:

1. The nature and dimensionality of faking: How is faking defined, theorized, operationally established, and measured?
2. Differences between experimentally induced and naturally occurring faking: Do results from directed faking studies differ from corresponding findings for real-world faking circumstances and, if so, for which psychometric properties are differences present?
3. Validity for a scale versus validity for individual test respondents: If scale validity is not affected by faking, does it follow that faking does not affect the meaningful interpretation of individual respondents' scale scores?

■ THE NATURE AND DIMENSIONALITY OF FAKING

We define faking as intentional misrepresentation in self-report. This definition intends to imply three key features:

1. Faking is intentional (i.e., conscious, deliberate, or occurs with active awareness).
2. Faking has some degree of deception associated with it.
3. Faking is oriented toward others (as opposed to deceiving the self).

Synonyms for faking include impression management (although some suggest impression management can be automatic and not conscious or without involving active awareness), response distortion (assumed to be intentional), and dissimulation. Faking is not necessarily lying or giving a nontruthful response. Consider that, in some instances, providing a truthful response may be congruent with the goal of impression management or faking. That is, a truthful answer may be given because it supports the respondent's intention of deceiving others rather than because the response is truthful.

1. This research was supported by the Social Sciences and Humanities Research Council of Canada.

Terms related to, but not synonymous with, faking include socially desirable responding, malingering, and acting. Faking may be only one of various facets of socially desirable responding. Another type of socially desirable responding would be self-deceptive enhancement. Malingering is only one type of faking. There, the focus is on faking in terms of negativity or in regard to a particular type of psychological problem or diagnosis. In acting (i.e., explicit role playing), the actor and audience collaborate to accept the persona of the actor. There is no intent to deceive, although the actor strives to have observers accept the role being portrayed.

Theories of faking on personality scales are not particularly well developed. Few empirical data exist as to what respondents actually do when they dissimulate on a personality test (but see Robie, Brown, & Beaty, 2007). Kroger and Turnbull (1970, 1975; Kroger, 1967) suggest that when faking, individuals may assume roles that are influenced by respondent characteristics, the method of assessment, and the social cues of the testing situation. Paulhus (1993) refers to an Automatic and Controlled Self-Presentation model in which faking is a process that is intentional, flexible, and requires attention. In his model, attention is necessary and involves consideration both of detailed self-presentational goals and of the specific audience for the self-presentation. Leary (1996) suggests that completing a personality scale may be a form of self-presentation that is not unlike the self-presentation in everyday social interactions. Self-presentation serves to influence others, to enhance identity and protect self-esteem, and to foster positive emotions. Johnson and Hogan (2006) posit that test dissimulation is a form of social interaction in which respondents have agendas and item responding is used as a communication device to advance these agendas. Because of different agendas, dissimulation will have different emphases for different people and may vary across different contexts for the same individual.

What is the dimensionality of faking? A consensus on this does not currently exist (see Table 5.1). Empirical research does not support faking as a unidimensional phenomenon. Experimental research with offenders (Holden & Kroner, 1992) and university students (Holden, Book, Edwards, Wasylkiw, & Starzyk, 2003) suggests that faking good and faking bad can be distinct dimensions and that, therefore, experimental faking can be at least two dimensional. Others have suggested or provided evidence that faking may be even more multidimensional than involving two distinct axes. For evaluations by mental health clinicians, Rogers and Cruise (2000) report three separate deception components: Implausible Presentation, Denial, and Conning and Manipulation. Analyses of the Minnesota Multiphasic Personality Inventory (MMPI)-2 indicate that some of its validity scales (i.e., L, F, K) load on orthogonal dimensions (Butcher, Dahlstrom, Graham, Tellegen, & Kaemmer, 1989). In experimentally inducing faking, Holden and Evoy (2005) were able to create four independent dimensions of faking: Personal Effectiveness, Sociability, Bold Innovation, and Open Disclosure. Jones and Pittman (1982) indicate that self-presentation strategies include ingratiation, intimidation, self-promotion, exemplification, and supplication. Lanyon (1996) identifies six types of deception (but not necessarily faking as defined here) present when responding to personality inventories: Extreme Virtue, Extreme Adjustment,

TABLE 5.1 *Possible Dimensions or Strategies of Faking*

Number	Source	Dimensions or Strategies
1	Lay Conception	Negativity ← Honesty → Positivity
2	Holden et al. (2003)	Faking Good
	Holden and Kroner (1992)	Faking Bad
3	MMPI-2 (Butcher et al., 1989)	L scale (Faking Well-Adjusted)
		F scale (Malingering)
		K scale (Faking Good)
3	Rogers and Cruise (2000)	Implausible Presentation
		Denial
		Conning and Manipulation
4	Holden and Evoy (2005)	Personal Effectiveness
		Sociability
		Bold Innovation
		Open Disclosure
5	Jones and Pittman (1982)	Ingratiation
		Intimidation
		Self-Promotion
		Exemplification
		Supplication
6	Lanyon (1996)	Extreme Virtue
		Extreme Adjustment
		Unaware Self-Enhancement
		Patient Stereotype
		Symptom Overendorsement
		Random
Multiple	Kroger and Turnbull (1970, 1975)	Role-Playing
Multiple	Paulhus et al. (1991)	Goal-Oriented
Multiple	Johnson and Hogan (2006)	Agenda-Based

Unaware Self-enhancement, Patient Stereotype, Symptom Overendorsement, and Random. Kroger and Turnbull (1970, 1975) conceive of faking as role playing and, consequently, imply an unlimited dimensionality to faking. Paulhus, Bruce, and McKay (1991), in indicating that faking has various implicit instrumental applications rather than an absolute meaning, suggest that faking needs to be defined as quite goal specific, varying from context to context.

Overall, therefore, there is no firm agreement on the structure of faking. Intuitively, theoretically, and empirically, we may appreciate that there are many different types of faking, but the specifics of what these are and of their rates of occurrence remain to be articulated.

Faking is typically assessed through the use of self-report validity scales. Most common are measures that rather than having the label of faking or lying incorporated in their names, have the term social desirability or a variant of it as part of their label [i.e., Edwards Social Desirability Scale (Edwards, 1957); Marlowe–Crowne Social Desirability Scale (Crowne & Marlowe, 1960); Personality Research Form Desirability Scale (Jackson, 1984); Balanced Inventory of Desirable Responding (Paulhus, 1998)]. This labeling difference highlights an important potential differentiation—faking and socially desirable responding are not isomorphic concepts but faking is only one aspect of socially desirable responding. Indeed, Holden (2007) indicates that although fakers will score at the extreme on scales of socially desirable responding, extreme scorers on scales of socially desirable responding are not necessarily fakers. Consequently, in addition to the standard limitations of any self-report scale in terms of psychometric properties such as reliability, commonly used operationalizations of faking may tend to be overinclusive in their coverage and assess more than just faking (e.g., other response styles or substance as well as style). As an example, respondents' scores on the Marlowe–Crowne Social Desirability Scale (a measure used to detect faking) are associated significantly with ratings by significant others on constructs of extraversion, agreeableness, and conscientiousness (Kurtz, Tarquini, & Iobst, 2008). Furthermore, faking detection scales that are not balanced for direction of keying may yield measures that are inadvertently confounded with acquiescent responding (Paulhus, 1998).

■ DIFFERENCES BETWEEN EXPERIMENTALLY INDUCED AND NATURALLY OCCURRING FAKING

Between induced and naturally occurring faking studies, different research designs and operationalizations of faking are typically used. For induced faking studies using a between-subjects design, respondents are randomly assigned to control or faking groups or, for a within-subjects approach, respondents are assigned (randomly or not) to a particular sequence (often balanced) of instructional conditions. Analytically, faking may be operationalized as instructional group membership or as a score on a faking scale. Statistical analyses can involve computing scale psychometric properties per instructional condition and then comparing across instructional conditions or can involve analyzing whether instructional condition (or faking scale score) moderates the psychometric property of the scale. Although most directed faking studies involve faking positivity (e.g., getting hired for a job), there are a substantial number that focus on negativity (e.g., malingering). For directed faking studies, there is an assumption that the instructions given are followed by each individual respondent and that the instructions to fake or respond honestly have construct validity for representing real-world faking or standard responding. Furthermore, when faking is operationalized through a faking scale (e.g., a scale of socially desirable responding) there is an assumption that the scale has construct validity for the measurement of faking in the context given. These assumptions, of course, may have limited tenability.

For naturally occurring faking, there are no randomly assigned experimental groups. One approach is to use a faking scale to create subgroups of respondents who have completed a personality scale. Another approach is to employ a differential prevalence design in which differential faking is assumed (e.g., job applicants versus job incumbents). For the former approach, it is possible to create a subgroup in which low scores on a scale of socially desirable responding (a proxy for faking) may occur and could, consequently, represent a naturally occurring group of respondents who could be interpreted as faking negativity. For the differential prevalence design, research on groups with naturally occurring faked negativity is more problematic. Consider that, whereas job application contexts represent commonly occurring situations where faking positivity is present, contexts

TABLE 5.2 *Findings for Substantial Effects of Faking*

Scale Property	Experimentally Induced Faking	Naturally Occurring Faking
Mean score	Generally Yes (e.g., Viswesvaran & Ones, 1999)	Generally Yes (e.g., Rosse et al., 1998)
Correlational structure	Generally Yes (e.g., Topping & O'Gorman, 1997)	Generally No (e.g., Ellingson et al., 2001)
Validity	Generally Yes (e.g., Douglas et al., 1996)	Mixed Results (e.g., Hough et al., 1990 versus White et al., 2001)

for faking negativity are relatively uncommon in our society and, consequently, have rarely been studied psychometrically at the group level (but see Chapters 16 and 17).

In evaluating the effects of faking on self-report personality assessment, arguably important distinctions have been drawn between experimentally induced (or directed) dissimulation and the faking that may occur in real-world contexts (e.g., job application contexts, forensic evaluations, worker injury assessments, child custody cases). Empirical findings for faking may also vary depending on whether the focus is on scale scores, correlational structures, or validities. Additionally, some of the distinctions between experimental and naturally occurring faking may interact with specific psychometric properties of the personality scale. For this reason, we present differences between experimentally induced and naturally occurring faking as a function of particular psychometric properties (see Table 5.2). Furthermore, although in many instances there are a plethora of research studies (cf. Morgeson, Campion, Dipboye, Hollenbeck, Murphy, & Schmitt, 2007), we highlight what we believe are the more prominent investigations and perspectives as well as what we consider some noteworthy contrary findings.

Faking Effects on Scale Means

Viswesvaran and Ones (1999) have undertaken a meta-analysis of the effects for instructed faking. Results indicated that across Big Five dimensions (i.e., agreeableness, conscientiousness, emotional stability, extraversion, and openness to experience), effects on mean scale scores are about half a standard deviation for instructions to fake good. For scales of socially desirable responding, effect sizes are approximately one standard deviation. For instructions to fake bad, corresponding effect sizes appear to be even greater than for those associated with instructed faking good. Interestingly, across Big Five factors, effects are reported generally as not varying by personality dimension. However, Topping and O'Gorman (1997) and Holden, Wood, and Tomashewski (2001) indicate that openness appears to be less susceptible to faking effects than are other Big Five dimensions. Whether this discrepancy reflects dimensional, scale, instructional, or other differences is unclear.

For naturally occurring faking, Dunnette, McCartney, Carlson, and Kirchner (1962), in studying industrial salespeople, suggest that 14% of job applicants may fake.

Their data indicate that differences between established salespeople and applicants constituted approximately a quarter to a third of a standard deviation for scores on personality scales. In a study involving airline pilot positions, Butcher, Morfitt, Rouse, and Holden (1997) reported that 27% of applicants activated personality inventory validity indices (i.e., were identified as "fakers" by validity scales) and that, for this group, mean differences from applicants who did not activate validity indices were less than a medium effect size. Rosse, Stecher, Miller, and Levin (1998) found differences between ski resort job applicants and incumbents of approximately two-thirds of a standard deviation for personality scales and more than a standard deviation for a response distortion scale. Stark, Chernyshenko, Chan, Lee, and Drasgow (2001) indicate small to large effect size differences for job applicant versus job incumbent groups on the 16PF. Hough, Eaton, Dunnette, Kamp, and McCloy (1990) compared military applicants and incumbents on measures including the Assessment of Background and Life Experiences (ABLE). Interestingly, although small to medium differences emerged on personality scale scores, the groups did not differ on scores for the socially desirable responding scale. In comparing groups of soldiers who were assessed either for research or for operational selection purposes, Putka and McCloy (2004) reported a large effect size difference between groups for a scale of Adaptability on the Assessment of Individual Motivation (AIM).

In general, data indicate that experimentally directed faking good produces an average of a medium effect size on personality scale mean scores. These effect sizes are, typically, larger than those for naturally occurring faking. Some differences may exist among personality dimensions and some naturally occurring contexts can yield large effect sizes for faking good. The specific instances in which dimensional differences (e.g., for openness) exist are unclear as are the details on when large faking effects naturally occur. For faking bad, experimentally directed faking yields, on average, a large effect size on personality scale mean scores. Effect sizes associated with naturally occurring faking bad are largely unknown.

Faking Effects on Correlational Structure

For instructed faking, research on MMPI dissimulation measures (Wiggins, 1959), Basic Personality Inventory response style scales (Helmes & Holden, 1986), NEO-FFI scales (Topping & O'Gorman, 1997), and Holden Psychological Screening Inventory scales (Holden, 1995) all indicate that scales become more highly correlated under instructions to fake (either fake good or fake bad). In a somewhat dissenting interpretation, Paulhus, Bruce, and Trapnell (1995) suggest that such convergence is attributable to spurious heterogeneity of responding associated with respondents directed to fake who do not follow instructions.

For naturally occurring faking, Ellingson, Smith, and Sackett (2001) compared factor structures for high and low socially desirable responding individuals for each of the ABLE ($N > 10,000$), California Psychological Inventory ($N > 6,000$), 16PF ($N > 13,000$), and revised Hogan Personality Inventory ($N > 2,000$). Differences as a function of level of socially desirable responding did not emerge. Smith and Ellingson (2002) found no factor structure differences on the revised Hogan

Personality Inventory (and supplementary social desirability scales) between job applicant and student groups. Marshall, De Fruyt, Rolland, and Bagby (2005), for the NEO-PI-R, found no factor structure differences either among job applicants subgrouped by relative amount of socially desirable responding ($N > 12,000$), or among applicant, counseling, and normative groups. In contrast to these null effects, Schmit and Ryan (1993) found NEO-FFI factor structure differences between job applicants and students ($N \sim 600$). Furthermore, Brown and Barrett (1999) have reported some factor structure differences on the 16PF between job applicant and nonapplicant samples. The source of discrepancies among these studies of factor structure for putatively naturally occurring faking is unclear. Among possible factors, consider that if faking is multidimensional and job specific, the combining of job applicants for different positions into one population of applicants could serve to attenuate faking effects that might be more strongly present for a more homogeneous group of applicants.

Overall, results suggest that experimentally directed faking good produces substantial convergence among personality scales. For naturally occurring circumstances using subgroups defined by socially desirable responding scale scores or using prevalence group designs, the effects of faking appear to be either nonexistent or small.

Faking Effects on Validity

In experimentally induced faking, Douglas, McDaniel, and Snell (1996) report that for undergraduates instructed to fake in a job application simulation, personality scale validity decreased. Similar decreases have been found for scales of the Basic Personality Inventory (Holden & Jackson, 1981, 1985) and the NEO-FFI (Holden et al., 2001; Holden, 2007; Topping & O'Gorman, 1997). In general, instructed faking (either fake positively or fake negatively) reduces criterion validity substantially with the effects for faking bad being even greater than those for faking good.

For naturally occurring faking, the effects on validity are mixed. In a study of naturally occurring response distortion among 319 long-haul driver applicants, Barrick and Mount (1996) reported that partialling out either of two operationalizations of socially desirable responding did not affect the validity of Big Five scales in predicting supervisor performance ratings or job turnover 6 months later. Perhaps importantly, analyses evaluated mediation but not moderating effects on validity for response distortion. Hough et al. (1990), in a study of over 8,000 military personnel, report that validities for ABLE scales for criteria of effort and leadership, personal discipline, and physical fitness were not a function of socially desirable responding. Of note, however, 10 of 33 validity comparisons were significant and 22 of 31 (with two ties) validities were greater for their accurate group than their overly desirable group. Piedmont, McCrae, Riemann, and Angleitner (2000) with studies of 178 students and more than 1,700 twins found little evidence that validities (based on correlations with peer report) for NEO-PI-R or Multidimensional Personality Questionnaire scales were affected by validity scale scores (including scales of socially desirable responding). Kurtz et al. (2008), in a study of 222 college students, found no evidence that Marlowe–Crowne Social Desirability scale scores moderated the validity of self-report on the NEO-FFI when either roommate or parent ratings were used as criteria.

In contrast, for a follow-up study to Hough et al. (1990) involving thousands of military recruits in a longitudinal study, White, Young, and Rumsey (2001) indicate that the effect of naturally occurring socially desirable responding on ABLE scale validity "severely curtailed the criterion-related validity of temperament measures" (p. 550). Additionally, Putka and McCloy (2004), in an investigation of thousands of military recruits, indicate an operational sample of soldiers manifested much more faking on the AIM, a successor to the ABLE, than did a research sample of soldiers. Furthermore, a validity scale was not particularly effective in detecting this faking. Ultimately, the validity of the AIM for predicting attrition was only about one-third of that associated with their research sample. Holden (2007), in a study of 420 undergraduates, reported that across Big Five personality scales, naturally occurring variations in socially desirable responding accounted for an average of 10–15% of the variability of the prediction in peer criterion ratings. That is, validity of self-report personality measures was substantially lower for those respondents scoring higher rather than lower on a scale of socially desirable responding that is regarded as a faking index.

In general, whereas the effect of instructed faking has substantial impact on the validity of self-report personality scales, the influence of naturally occurring faking seems quite mixed with some research indicating negligible effects and other indicating substantial results. Discrepancies in findings for naturally occurring variations in faking could, among other possibilities, reflect differences in assessment contexts (e.g., military, university, job applicant settings) and associated base rates for faking, criteria used (e.g., performance evaluations, peer ratings, attrition), samples (e.g., military personnel, university students, job candidates), operationalizations of faking (prevalence group design, established versus ad hoc scales of socially desirable responding), or analytic methods (covariance, moderator, or independent groups analyses). Furthermore, some have suggested that a more crucial distinction may be between high-stakes versus low-stakes testing situations (White, Young, Hunter, & Rumsey, 2008) rather than the currently focused differentiation between experimental and nonexperimental research.

■ VALIDITY FOR A SCALE VERSUS VALIDITY FOR INDIVIDUAL TEST RESPONDENTS

The difference between scale validity and the validity of individual protocols (see Table 5.3) represents an important distinction that is related to decision making. Christiansen, Goffin, Johnston, and Rothstein (1994), in a study of 495 assessment center candidates, indicated that whereas corrections for faking resulted in no significant changes in validity for 16PF scales, the choice of candidates to be selected was affected by correcting for faking. Without a statistically significant difference in validity, Christiansen et al. indicated that a change of rank ordering (and, potentially, individual hiring) could occur for more than 85% of job applicants. The magnitude of the number of different hires that would occur was an

TABLE 5.3 *An Anecdote Regarding Validity for a Scale versus Validity for an Individual Protocol*

Two psychometricians (Robert and Andrew) pull a prank on a colleague (Susan) who, as an industrial/organizational psychologist, consults for a company that is hiring workers for one of its production plants. As part of the prank, the two psychometricians apply for jobs as workers with this company and in doing so, complete a self-report personality scale.

A few days later, Robert, Andrew, and Susan meet. Robert and Andrew recount their job application experiences to Susan. Robert indicates that on the self-report personality measure, he faked so as to maximize the chances of being hired for the job. Susan, however, has read the literature (i.e., Barrick & Mount, 1996; Hough et al., 1990; Piedmont et al., 2000) and states that faking does not affect the validity of a self-report scale and is, consequently, a red herring (Ones et al., 1996) for personnel testing. In particular, Susan cites the research of Piedmont et al. indicating that various response styles (including faking as measured by scales of unlikely virtues or positive presentation management) do not affect scale validity. Robert seems a little perplexed but accepts Susan's interpretation of the literature and thinks that even though he faked, his test results must still have validity.

Andrew then recounts his approach to the self-report personality scale and reports that he responded randomly. Susan rebuts this issue, again citing the Piedmont article whereby a wide variety of response styles (including random responding measured by a number of response inconsistency scales) did not affect scale validity. Like Robert, Andrew now seems perplexed by this but he does not accept Susan's rebuttal. Andrew indicates that he did not generate the random responses himself but used his pocket calculator's random number generator to yield answers. How can a random number generator produce tests results that, for Andrew, have validity?

Comment:

In thinking about Robert's experiences and Susan's responses, we might believe that if scale validity is not affected by faking, it follows that Robert's test results should have validity. The belief could be that even if someone faked, their faked scores still reflect something that has accuracy for measuring that individual's standing on the assessed personality construct. Although this reasoning might appear true, the fault in logic becomes apparent when, as for Andrew, responses are generated by a source independent of the test respondent. Consideration of this faulty reasoning highlights the important distinction to be drawn between validity for a scale and validity for a respondent's scale score. These may be quite separate issues. Although the validity of a scale may be a necessary condition, it is not sufficient for ensuring the validity of an individual's score on a scale. Consequently, even if faking is (arguably) a red herring for scale validity, faking or any other type of nonaccurate responding is always an issue for the validity of an individual testing protocol and any subsequent meaningful interpretation.

inverse function of the selection ratio. Rosse et al. (1998) concur with the perspective that response distortion has a significant effect on which specific job applicants are hired and Mueller-Hanson, Heggestad, and Thornton (2003) indicate that the percentage of fakers hired for a job rises rapidly as the selection ratio decreases. Thus, faking can attenuate the usefulness of personality scales in hiring procedures by changing the rank ordering of applicants' personality scale scores (Stark et al., 2001).

In general, therefore, without affecting scale validity significantly, differences in hiring decisions can occur as a function of faking. These differences can be

TABLE 5.4 *Proposed Impact of Faking as a Function of Faking Rates and Scale versus Individual Focus (Holden, 2006)*

If 90% of respondents fake, will this influence:	
scale validities?	Probably
scale mean scores?	Probably
the valid interpretation of an individual protocol for someone who faked?	Definitely
If 20% of respondents fake, will this influence:	
scale validities?	Unclear
scale mean scores?	Probably
the valid interpretation of an individual protocol for someone who faked?	Definitely
If 2% of respondents fake, will this influence:	
scale validities?	Probably not
scale mean scores?	Probably not
the valid interpretation of an individual protocol for someone who faked?	Definitely

substantial in size, more so as selection ratios get smaller and when top-down selection is implemented.

In summarizing the effects of faking, Holden (2006) highlighted issues of base rates for faking and of scale versus individual protocol validity (Table 5.4). Subsequently, discrepancies between the impacts of faking on the validity of an individual test protocol versus the validity of a scale were explored further (Holden, 2007). In that research using an extraversion scale, directed faking of a very large effect size was induced in an experimental group. For a control group in which the extraversion scale had notable validity, randomly selected members of the experimental group manifesting substantial faking effects were sequentially added to the control group and the moderating effects of faking on scale validity were calculated. In general, even with substantial faking effects present at the individual respondent level, the moderating effects of faking on scale validity were nonsignificant. If less than 12% of the analyzed sample consisted of substantial fakers, the null hypothesis of no moderating effects for faking could not be rejected. Consider, therefore, that one would conclude that the effect of faking on scale validity is trivial even though 10% of a sample demonstrates substantial faking effects on their individual scale scores. Holden (2007, 2008) indicates that discrepancies between effects on the validity of individual scale scores and on the validity of scales depend on base rates for faking, the construct validity of operationalizations of faking, and the statistical power of different analytic techniques used to detect the moderating effects of faking. Consider further, however, that base rates associated with faking may vary widely across job application, clinical, legal, etc. contexts. In circumstances in which selection ratios are relevant (e.g., employment contexts), how base rates for faking combine with varying selection ratios remains to be fully specified.

■ SUMMARY

1. Defined as the conscious distortion of self-report, faking is a multidimensional process that is goal dependent and context dependent. The appropriateness of generalizing from one type of faking (e.g., communal-related,

directed, low-stakes faking) to another (e.g., agency-related, naturally occurring, high-stakes faking) may be questionable.

2. The effects of faking on personality scale psychometric properties can be substantial, particularly when the rates of faking are nontrivial.

3. Faking at the individual respondent level exists as an issue, regardless of whether faking affects personality scale mean scores, correlational structures, or validities.

The interpretation of research on faking must consider issues of the type of faking being investigated, base rates for faking, selection ratios for decision making, the construct validity of the operationalization of faking, and whether the focus is on a personality scale or on the individual scale scores of respondents. Prudent users of self-report personality measures should be alert to issues of faking and to any other sources of potentially invalid responding before making or recommending general or individual decisions based on personality scale scores.

References

Barrick, M. R., & Mount, M. K. (1996). Effects of impression management and self-deception on the predictive validity of personality constructs. *Journal of Applied Psychology, 81,* 261–272.

Brown, R., & Barrett, P. (1999, June). *Differences between applicant and non-applicant personality questionnaire data.* British Psychological Society Test User Conference, Scarborough. In published Conference Proceedings, pp. 76–86. Leicester: British Psychological Society.

Butcher, J. N., Dahlstrom, W. G., Graham, J. R., Tellegen, A., & Kaemmer, B. (1989). *Manual for administration and scoring of the MMPI-2.* Minneapolis: University of Minnesota Press.

Butcher, J. N., Morfitt, R. C., Rouse, S. V., & Holden, R. R. (1997). Reducing MMPI-2 defensiveness: The effect of specialized instructions on retest validity in a job applicant sample. *Journal of Personality Assessment, 68,* 385–401.

Christiansen, N. D., Goffin, R. D., Johnston, N. G., & Rothstein, M. G. (1994). Correcting the 16PF for faking: Effects on criterion-related validity and individual hiring decisions. *Personnel Psychology, 47,* 847–860.

Crowne, D. P., & Marlowe, D. (1960). A new scale of social desirability independent of psychopathology. *Journal of Consulting Psychology, 24,* 349–354.

Douglas, E. F., McDaniel, M. A., & Snell, A. F. (1996). The validity of non-cognitive measures decays when applicants fake. In J. B. Keyes & L. N. Dosier (Eds.), *Proceedings of the Academy of Management* (pp. 127–131). Madison, WI: Omnipress.

Dunnette, M. D., McCartney, J., Carlson, H. C., & Kirchner, W. K. (1962). A study of faking behavior on a forced-choice self-description checklist. *Personnel Psychology, 15,* 13–24.

Edwards, A. E. (1957). *The social desirability variable in personality assessment and research.* New York: Dryden.

Ellingson, J. E., Smith, D. B., & Sackett, P. R. (2001). Investigating the influence of social desirability on personality factor structure. *Journal of Applied Psychology, 86,* 122–133.

Helmes, E., & Holden, R. R. (1986). Response styles and faking on the Basic Personality Inventory. *Journal of Consulting and Clinical Psychology, 54,* 853–859.

Holden, R. R. (1995). Faking and its detection on the Holden Psychological Screening Inventory. *Psychological Reports, 76,* 1235–1240.

Holden, R. R. (2006, April). *Faking on noncognitive self-report: Seven primary questions.* Paper presented to the Educational Testing Services (ETS) Technical Advisory Group (TAG) Conference on Faking in Non-cognitive Assessment, Princeton, NJ.

Holden, R. R. (2007). Socially desirable responding does moderate scale validity both in experimental and in nonexperimental contexts. *Canadian Journal of Behavioural Science, 39*, 184–201.

Holden, R. R. (2008). Underestimating the effects of faking on the validity of self-report personality scales. *Personality and Individual Differences, 44*, 311–321.

Holden, R. R., Book, A. S., Edwards, M. J., Wasylkiw, L., & Starzyk, K. B. (2003). Experimental faking in self-reported psychopathology: Unidimensional or multidimensional? *Personality and Individual Differences, 35*, 1107–1117.

Holden, R. R., & Evoy, R. A. (2005). Personality inventory faking: A four-dimensional simulation of dissimulation. *Personality and Individual Differences, 39*, 1307–1318.

Holden, R. R., & Jackson, D. N. (1981). Subtlety, information and faking effects in personality assessment. *Journal of Clinical Psychology, 37*, 379–386.

Holden, R. R., & Jackson, D. N. (1985). Disguise and the structured self-report assessment of psychopathology: I. An analogue investigation. *Journal of Consulting and Clinical Psychology, 53*, 211–222.

Holden, R. R., & Kroner, D. G. (1992). Relative efficacy of differential response latencies for detecting faking on a self-report measure of psychopathology. *Psychological Assessment, 4*, 170–173.

Holden, R. R., Wood, L. L., & Tomashewski, L. (2001). Do response time limitations counteract the effect of faking on personality inventory validity? *Journal of Personality and Social Psychology, 81*, 160–169.

Hough, L. M., Eaton, N. K., Dunnette, M. D., Kamp, J. D., & McCloy, R. A. (1990). Criterion-related validities of personality constructs and the effect of response distortion on those validities. *Journal of Applied Psychology, 75*, 581–595.

Jackson, D. N. (1984). *Personality Research Form manual* (3rd ed.). Port Huron, MI: Sigma Assessment Systems.

Johnson, J. A., & Hogan, R. (2006). A socioanalytic view of faking. In R. L. Griffith & M. H. Peterson (Eds.), *A closer examination of applicant faking behavior* (pp. 209–231). Greenwich, CT: Information Age Publishing.

Jones, E. E., & Pittman, T. S. (1982). Toward a general theory of strategic self-presentation. In J. Suls (Ed.), *Psychological perspectives on the self* (Vol. 1, pp. 231–262). Hillsdale, NJ: Erlbaum.

Kroger, R. O. (1967). Effects of role demands and test-cue properties upon personality test performance. *Journal of Consulting Psychology, 31*, 304–312.

Kroger, R. O., & Turnbull, W. (1970). Effects of role demands and test-cue properties on personality test performance: Replication and extension. *Journal of Consulting and Clinical Psychology, 35*, 381–387.

Kroger, R. O., & Turnbull, W. (1975). Invalidity of validity scales: The case of the MMPI. *Journal of Consulting and Clinical Psychology, 43*, 48–55.

Kurtz, J. E., Tarquini, S. J., & Iobst, E. A. (2008). Socially desirable responding in personality assessment: Still more substance than style. *Personality and Individual Differences, 45*, 22–27.

Lanyon, R. I. (1996). Assessment of specific deception strategies used by personality inventory respondents. *American Journal of Forensic Psychology, 14*, 37–53.

Leary, M. R. (1996). *Self-presentation: Impression management and interpersonal behavior.* Boulder, CO: Westview Press.

Marshall, M. B., De Fruyt, F., Rolland, J. P., & Bagby, R. M. (2005). Socially desirable responding and the factorial stability of the NEO PI-R. *Psychological Assessment, 17*, 379–384.

Morgeson, F. P., Campion, M. A., Dipboye, R. L., Hollenbeck, J. R., Murphy, K., & Schmitt, N. (2007). Reconsidering the use of personality tests in personnel selection contexts. *Personnel Psychology, 60*, 683–729.

Mueller-Hanson, R., Heggestad, E. D., & Thornton, G. C., III (2003). Faking and selection: Considering the use of personality from select-in and select-out perspectives. *Journal of Applied Psychology, 88*, 348–355.

Ones, D. S., Viswesvaran, C., & Reiss, A. D. (1996). Role of social desirability in personality testing for personnel selection: The red herring. *Journal of Applied Psychology, 81*, 660–679.

Paulhus D. L. (1993). Bypassing the will: The automization of affirmations. In D. M. Wegner & J. W. Pennebaker (Eds.), *Handbook of mental control* (pp. 573–587). Englewood Cliffs, NJ: Prentice Hall.

Paulhus, D. L. (1998). *Paulhus Deception Scales (PDS): The Balanced Inventory of Desirable Responding–7.* North Tonawanda, NY: Multi-Health Systems.

Paulhus, D. L., Bruce, M. N., & McKay, E. (1991, August). *Effects of self-presentation on self-report of personality during job applications.* Paper presented at the American Psychological Association Annual Convention, San Francisco.

Paulhus, D. L., Bruce, M. N., & Trapnell, P. D. (1995). Effects of self-presentation strategies on personality profiles and their structure. *Personality and Social Psychology Bulletin, 21*, 100–108.

Piedmont, R. L., McCrae, R. R., Riemann, R., & Angleitner, A. (2000). On the invalidity of validity scales: Evidence from self-reports and observer ratings in volunteer samples. *Journal of Personality and Social Psychology, 78*, 582–593.

Putka, D. J., & McCloy, R. A. (2004). Preliminary AIM validation based on GED Plus program data. In D. J. Knapp, E. D. Heggestad, & M. C. Young (Eds.), *Understanding and improving the Assessment of Individual Motivation (AIM) in the Army's GED Plus program* (pp. 3-19–3-30). (Study Note 2004-03.) Alexandria, VA: U.S. Army Research Institute for the Behavioral and Social Sciences.

Robie, C., Brown, D. J., & Beaty, J. C. (2007). Do people fake on personality inventories? A verbal protocol analysis. *Journal of Business and Psychology, 21*, 489–509.

Rogers, R., & Cruise, K. R. (2000). Malingering and deception among psychopaths. In C. B. Gacono (Ed.), *The clinical and forensic assessment of psychopathy: A practitioner's guide* (pp. 269–284). Mahwah, NJ: Lawrence Erlbaum.

Rosse, J. G., Stecher, M. D., Miller, J. L., & Levin, R. A. (1998). The impact of response distortion on preemployment personality testing and hiring decisions. *Journal of Personality and Social Psychology, 83*, 634–644.

Schmit, M. J., & Ryan, A. M. (1993). The Big Five in personnel selection: Factor structure in applicants and nonapplicant populations. *Journal of Applied Psychology, 78*, 966–974.

Smith, D. B., & Ellingson, J. E. (2002). Substance versus style: A new look at social desirability in motivating contexts. *Journal of Applied Psychology, 87*, 211–219.

Stark, S., Chernyshenko, O. S., Chan, K. Y., Lee, W. C., & Drasgow, F. (2001). Effect of testing situation on item responding: Cause for concern. *Journal of Applied Psychology, 86*, 943–953.

Topping, G. D., & O'Gorman, J. G. (1997). Effects of faking set on validity of the NEO-FFI. *Personality and Individual Differences, 23*, 117–124.

Viswesvaran, C., & Ones, D. S. (1999). Meta-analyses of fakability estimates: Implications for personality measurement. *Educational and Psychological Measurement, 59,* 197–210.

White, L. A., Young, M. C., Hunter, A. E., & Rumsey, M. G. (2008). Lessons learned in transitioning personality measures from research to operational settings. *Industrial and Organizational Psychology, 1,* 291–295.

White, L. A., Young, M. C., & Rumsey, M. G. (2001). ABLE implementation issues and related research. In J. P. Campbell & D. J. Knapp (Eds.), *Exploring the limits of personnel selection and classification* (pp. 525–558). Mahwah, NJ: Erlbaum.

Wiggins, J. S. (1959). Interrelationships among MMPI measures of dissimulation under standard and social desirability instructions. *Journal of Consulting Psychology, 23,* 419–427.

6 A Conceptual Representation of Faking

Putting the Horse Back in Front of the Cart

■ ERIC D. HEGGESTAD

Research has well documented that scores on personality measures obtained in nonmotivated testing settings, such as when completing the assessment for research purposes or for self-exploration, tend to be lower than scores on the same measure obtained in motivated settings, such as in the context of applying for a job (Dunnette, McCartney, Carlson, & Kirchner, 1962; Hough, 1998; Hough, Eaton, Dunnette, Kamp, & McCloy, 1990; Rossé, Stecher, Miller, & Levin, 1998). The term *faking* has been used to refer to this increase in scores typically associated with motivated settings. The implication here is that test takers respond differently to items in motivated settings than they do in nonmotivated settings in an effort to create a favorable impression of their personality and to improve their score on the assessment. Organizational scholars have committed considerable effort to researching various issues associated with faking on personality assessments. Specifically, research has examined whether people fake personality assessments in applicant contexts, ways of detecting whether an applicant is faking, the effects on the criterion-related validity and utility of the scores, methods of discouraging people from faking or making it harder for them to do so, and statistical procedures for correcting scores for the influence of faking. As suggested by this list of research issues, the scientific literature on faking is fairly large.

Yet, relatively little work has been directed toward developing a conceptual framework for understanding faking. As noted by Mueller-Hanson, Heggestad, and Thornton (2006), "the lack of clear definition, measurement, and understanding of the psychological processes that underlie faking has further complicated the debate regarding the impact of faking on test scores and selection decisions" (p. 289). Likewise, Griffith, Malm, English, Yoshita, and Gujar (2006) commented that "little is known about the characteristics of the faker and how these characteristics, as well as situational influences, combine to form the phenomenon of faking" (p. 152). As such, it seems that we may have put the cart before the horse when it comes to faking personality assessments in applicant settings. That is, researchers have been documenting the effects of the problem and researching possible solutions to remedy it without first identifying and defining the nature of that problem. Although the solutions that have been proposed may ultimately prove useful, a more complete conceptual representation of faking should lead to a better understanding of why they work and to new, potentially more powerful means for detecting faking and deterring applicants from engaging in such behavior.

I have already defined faking in the context of personality assessment as a change in responses to the items on a personality test between motivated settings and nonmotivated settings (of course, the dichotomy between motivated and non-motivated settings is largely false, as all settings have some degree of motivation to cast ourself in a favorable manner). This definition is consistent with the thinking of Hogan, Barrett, and Hogan (2007), who suggested that "faking can only be understood as a motivated and significant change from a natural baseline condition of responding" (p. 1271). Based on these statements regarding the nature of faking, I see two key ideas that should serve as a foundation for a conceptual model of faking: (1) that faking is a behavior rather than a psychological construct and (2) that faking is, at its core, a measurement issue. Just as waving hello to a friend or greeting a stranger in an elevator involves context-specific behaviors rather than psychological constructs, faking is a behavior that occurs within a particular social context at a particular point in time. As a behavior, it can be expected that faking is determined by some combination of individual, attitudinal, and situational factors relevant to a particular assessment occasion. Thus, a good conceptual model of faking will identify the factors leading an individual to engage in faking behavior at a particular point in time. To date, a rather small number of papers have sought to explicitly identify such factors (e.g., Griffith et al., 2006; Levashina & Campion, 2006; McFarland & Ryan, 2000; Mueller-Hanson et al., 2006; Pauls & Crost, 2005; Snell, Sydell, & Lueke, 1999), with only a subset of these (i.e., Griffith et al., 2006; McFarland & Ryan, 2000; Mueller-Hanson et al., 2006; Pauls & Crost, 2005) providing empirical examinations of the relationships between these predictors and faking behavior.

Given the notion that faking is a measurement issue, a good conceptual model of faking must also be situated in the context of psychometric theory. Although several scholars have discussed faking from a measurement perspective (e.g., Komar, Brown, Robie, & Komar, 2008; Schmitt & Oswald, 2006), none has explicitly incorporated the factors believed to underlie faking into the psychometric model. Thus, a complete conceptual model of faking will situate the individual, attitudinal, and situational predictors of faking behavior within a broader framework of psychometric theory to understand how these predictors result in different responses to items between motivated and nonmotivated responding conditions.

My goal in this chapter is to expand our conceptual understanding of faking by considering how the predictors of faking behavior can be incorporated into psychometric theory. I begin by examining the dispositional, attitudinal, situational, and demographic factors that have been discussed as predictors or determinants of faking behavior. I then present a discussion of how these factors can be represented within Classical Test Theory, resulting in a more comprehensive understanding of how faking influences personality test scores. Finally, I offer future research directions and discuss the implications of this conceptual framework for detecting and preventing faking behavior.

■ PREDICTORS OF FAKING

To date, at least six key papers (Griffith et al., 2006; Levashina & Campion, 2006; McFarland & Ryan, 2000; Mueller-Hanson et al., 2006; Pauls & Crost, 2005; Snell et al., 1999) have been published in which the authors identify predictors of faking behavior. One of these papers, Levashina and Campion (2006), examined faking in the context of the employment interview, although I include it here as several of the factors they identify are likely relevant to personality assessment as well. As these papers have not evolved independently, there is considerable similarity in the predictors identified. Thus, rather than orienting my discussion around the perspectives and integrative models presented in these papers, I orient the discussion around the predictors identified within the set of papers. To this end, Table 6.1 contains a listing of the predictors identified.

TABLE 6.1 *Factors Proposed in the Literature as Determinants of Faking Behavior*

Construct	Expected Relationship to Faking	Empirical Support
Dispositional Factors		
Cognitive ability[1,2,4,5]	+	Mixed[1,5]
Conscientiousness[3,4]	−	Yes[3,4]
Emotional intelligence[6]	+	
Emotional stability[3,4]	−	Yes[3,4]
Impression mangement[1,5,6]	−	No[1,5]
Integrity[1,2,3,6]	−	Yes[1,3]
Locus of control (internal)[1,6]	−	Yes[1]
Machiavellianism[4,6]	+	Yes[4]
Manipulativeness[6]	+	
Need for approval[2]	+	
Stage of moral development[6]	−	
Rule consciousness[4]	−	Yes[4]
Self-monitoring[1,2,3,4]	+	No[1,3,4]
Attitudinal Factors		
Others' frequency[6]	+	
Perceived fairness of the test[6]	−	
Perceived behavioral control[4,5]	+	Yes[4,5]
Personal attitude toward faking[6]	+	
Subjective norms[4,6]	+	Yes[4]
Situational Factors		
Importance of the outcome[6]	+	
Knowlege of job requirements[2,6]	+	
Knowledge of how the test will be used[2,6]	+	
Demographic Factors		
Age[6]		
Sex[6]		

[1]Griffith et al. (2006).
[2]Levashina and Campion (2006).
[3]McFarland and Ryan (2000).
[4]Mueller-Hanson et al. (2006).
[5]Pauls and Crost (2005).
[6]Snell et al. (1999).

I have organized the potential predictors of faking behavior into broad categories: dispositional, attitudinal, situational, and demographic.[1] I provide, where appropriate, an indication as to the expected direction of the relationship between the predictor and faking behavior. For example, the "+" for cognitive ability indicates that individuals higher in cognitive ability have been hypothesized to engage in faking behavior more often and to a greater extent than individuals lower in cognitive ability. Finally, I provide an indication as to whether the predictor has been empirically investigated and whether support has been provided for the proposed relationship.

Dispositional Factors

As shown in Table 6.1, the largest set of factors identified across the papers falls into the dispositional category. The listing includes cognitive ability and personality characteristics. With respect to cognitive ability, it has been suggested that more intelligent people should be more successful at engaging in faking behavior as they will be better able to identify responses that correspond to the impression they wish to create. Based on a review of the recent literature, Griffith et al. (2006) concluded that the limited research has provided mixed results. Highlighting these mixed findings, Pauls and Crost (2005) found notable correlations between a measure of cognitive ability and measures of faking whereas Griffith et al. (2006) found no evidence of such a relationship. For most traditional personality assessments, identifying the socially desirable response is an easy endeavor. As such, I suspect cognitive abilities, especially the aspects of the construct space related to fluid intelligence, are not likely to be key predictors of faking behavior on typical self-report personality assessments. In more cognitively complex assessments, however, such as an interview, these abilities are more likely to be related to faking behavior (Levashina & Campion, 2006).

Among the personality characteristics identified, there is a clear clustering of characteristics related to a willingness to engage in deceitful or manipulative behavior, including integrity, Machiavellianism, manipulativeness, rule consciousness (i.e., a tendency to follow rules), and stage of moral development. The prevailing logic here is that people who are willing to manipulate others or are less constrained by rules will be more likely to engage in faking behavior. As shown in Table 6.1, there has been some empirical support for these characteristics as predictors of faking behavior. Mueller-Hanson et al. (2006), for instance, found that Machiavellianism and rule consciousness were correlated with faking behavior across a number of personality dimensions (r's ranged from 0.11 to 0.23 for Machiavellianism and from −0.08 to −0.20 for rule consciousness). With respect to integrity, McFarland and Ryan found that integrity scores were negatively correlated with faking on a set of

---

1. Of course, other organizing structures could have been used. For example, Snell and Fluckinger (2006) identified and defined a set of justification mechanisms—reasoning processes that applicants go through when deciding how to respond to personality measures—that they argued represent the determinants of faking behavior. As I see it, many of the more specifically defined predictors identified in Table 6.1 could be organized around the justification mechanisms discussed by these authors.

Big Five scores (*r*'s ranged from −0.09 to −0.27). Griffith et al. (2006), however, reported mixed results, finding that scores on an integrity measure were generally unrelated to faking on the NEO-FFI scales but negatively correlated with faking on a modified version of the NEO-FFI in which the items were contextualized within a work frame of reference (*r*'s ranged from −0.18 to −0.31).

Of course, it is not surprising that impression management and self-monitoring are on this list. These characteristics are associated with a concern regarding how one is perceived by others and a willingness and capability to adjust one's behavior to create a positive impression. As such, individuals high on impression management and self-monitoring are expected to adjust their responses to personality items to create a favorable impression. In many ways, engaging in faking behavior in a specific context can be thought of as state impression management; it is the extent to which the person is engaging in impression management in a particular situation. This state-trait notion does not, however, preclude the possibility of other factors also predicting faking behavior. As an analogy, whether you greet a stranger who enters an elevator with you tomorrow afternoon will likely be predicted by your trait sociability, but your behavior is also likely to be predicted by factors such as the number of people in the elevator and your mood at the time. Thus, although trait impression management may be a good predictor of faking behavior at a particular point in time, it certainly will not be the only predictor of that behavior.

Somewhat surprisingly, only Griffith et al. (2006) and Pauls and Crost (2005) have investigated impression management as a predictor of faking behavior. Quite unexpectedly, impression management scores were unrelated to faking in both of these studies. Consistent with these findings, no support has been provided for the relationship between self-monitoring and faking behavior. Both McFarland and Ryan (2000) and Mueller-Hanson et al. (2006) reported small correlations (all below 0.15) between self-monitoring and faking behavior. A compelling explanation for these unexpected findings was offered by McFarland and Ryan (2000), who speculated that the applicant context may represent a strong situation in which most applicants will engage in a relatively high level of self-monitoring (and impression management) thereby washing out the impact of individual differences in these traits on faking behavior.

Attitudinal Factors

Five attitudinal factors have been proposed to influence an individual's faking behavior. Of these, two ("Others' Frequency" and "Subjective Norms") have to do with the test taker's beliefs about other people. Specifically, the others' frequency attitude represents the test taker's ideas about the frequency with which others engage in faking whereas the subjective norms attitude captures the test taker's beliefs about whether other people condone faking behavior. It is expected that people will be more likely to engage in faking behavior when they believe that others are also engaging in such behavior and/or do not perceive faking as a problem. Related to subjective norms, the attitude labeled Personal Attitude toward Faking refers to the individual's own beliefs about the acceptability of faking behavior. With respect to the attitudes about the fairness of the test, it has been argued that test takers who see the test as a fair way of evaluating applicants will be less likely to engage in faking behavior. Finally, the attitude of perceived behavioral control represents a person's confidence in his or her ability to achieve higher scores by engaging in faking behavior. It could be argued that this concept is akin to a faking self-efficacy.

To date, only two of these attitude constructs have been empirically investigated. Mueller-Hanson et al. (2006) found fairly strong correlations between measures of perceived behavioral control and subjective norms and faking behavior on a personality measure. For example, they found that perceived behavioral control and subjective norms correlated $r = 0.43$ and 0.25, respectively, with faking on an achievement striving scale. Pauls and Crost (2005) found that scores on their Efficacy of Self-Presentation measure, which was defined similarly to perceived behavioral control, was related to faking behavior on the traits of neuroticism, extraversion, and conscientiousness. These results suggest that people are more likely to engage in faking behavior to the extent that they believe that they can effectively raise their scores and that other people are likely to attempt to do so as well. Although the available data are limited at this time, the results presented in the Mueller-Hanson et al. (2006) study suggest that attitudinal constructs are more strongly correlated with faking behavior than are dispositional factors (e.g., Machiavellianism, self-monitoring, rule consciousness). Although pure speculation, these results might suggest that the effects of dispositions on faking behavior are mediated by attitudinal factors.

Situational Factors

Three situational factors have been proposed as predictors of faking behavior. These factors include the importance that the applicant places on the outcome of the test, knowledge of the characteristics that are important to the employer for the job, and knowledge of how the test scores will be used. With regard to the latter factor, Snell et al. (1999) suggested that if applicants had knowledge that the number of applicants was far greater than the number of positions (i.e., a small selection ratio), then they might be more willing to engage in faking behavior. They also argued, along with Levashina and Campion (2006), that applicants will be more likely to engage in faking behavior when they hold strong beliefs regarding the characteristics important for the job and/or those desired by the employer. Of course, test takers who value the outcome (i.e., getting the job) to a greater degree than others are also expected to be more likely to engage in faking behavior.

In addition to the factors listed in Table 6.1, I believe it is likely that there are other situational determinants of faking behavior that have yet to be fully discussed or investigated. Further thinking is necessary to more precisely define the situational factors that may lead a person to engage in faking behavior. For instance, the "importance of the outcome" predictor may be too broad. It may be better to consider more specific factors such as the person's financial situation, the number of jobs available to him or her (based on qualifications, economic factors, etc.), and the individual's reason for applying for the job (e.g., extra money, looking for a better fit, to meet financial needs). I suspect that these situational factors may be relatively strong determinants of a person's propensity to engage in faking behavior.

Interestingly, these factors could be expected to act at both the individual and group levels. At the group level, for instance, changes in broad economic factors may lead to higher or lower propensities to fake across an applicant population. In an economic downturn during which available jobs are scarce, applicants may be more likely, on average, to engage in faking behavior than during good economic periods when jobs are more plentiful. In such good times, the applicant may feel that faking is not necessary as he or she can simply apply and compete for alternative jobs should he or she not be accepted for the present position. Of course, despite the fact that broad economic factors are likely to influence most of the applicants in a similar way, personal economic factors will also play a part in determining a particular applicant's propensity to engage in faking. In fact, it seems likely that personal economic factors may moderate the influences of the macroeconomic factors on faking behavior.

Demographic Factors

The demographic factors of age and sex were identified by Snell et al. (1999), who suggested that these factors may moderate the relationships between traits and perceptual factors and faking behavior; however, no specific hypotheses were offered. Findings by Ziegler (2006) suggest more of a direct effect. Specifically, he found that being young and being male were associated with a greater probability of being classified as an extreme faker.

Summary

Theory and research on the predictors of faking behavior suggest that it is a complex behavior. The decision by an individual to engage in faking behavior and the extent to which he or she does so is likely to be determined by a combination of personal dispositional factors, the attitudes he or she holds toward faking and its usefulness for attaining the desired outcome, personal and societal economic conditions, and knowledge of how and why the test is being used. What's more, I expect this list will grow as the literature evolves.

■ CONCEPTUALIZING FAKING WITHIN PSYCHOMETRIC THEORY

The identification of specific predictors of faking behavior is important. But, as I argued previously, faking is fundamentally a measurement issue; it is a behavior that affects a person's responses to particular personality items within a particular testing setting. Thus, to better understand faking we need to consider the predictors of faking behavior within the framework of psychometric theory. Although a generalizability theory approach could be taken (and, in fact, would likely be preferred by some scholars), in this section I discuss how these predictors of faking behavior can be incorporated into the Classical Test Theory perspective. Specifically, I will show how these predictors can be incorporated into expressions for a particular test taker's observed score on a personality assessment and for the variation in a set of observed scores collected in a motivated testing situation.

As is well understood, the central premise of Classical Test Theory is that an individual's observed score on a test can be expressed as a function of his or her true score and error, such that

$$X = T + E,$$

where X is the observed score (i.e., the score the individual obtains on the assessment), T is the true score, and E is random error. Moving from the consideration of a single observed score for an individual test taker to a set of observed scores for a sample of test takers, the variance in the observed scores can be expressed as a function of the variance in the true scores and the variance of the errors, such that

$$\sigma_X^2 = \sigma_T^2 + \sigma_E^2.$$

It should be noted that this expression is based on the assumption that error is random, and, as such, is completely unrelated to true scores.

Before we can incorporate faking into these expressions, we need to understand true and error scores. As noted by Schmidt, Le, and Ilies (2003), random error "is caused by momentary variations in attention, mental efficiency, distractions, and so forth within a given occasion" (p. 208). They further suggest that random error can be thought of rather simply as noise in the central nervous system (see also Schmidt & Hunter, 1999). True score, in contrast, is defined as the expected mean score for an individual if he or she were to complete the assessment across a large number of identical testing situations. In the context of personality assessment, it is often assumed that true score is synonymous with standing on the trait. This conceptualization, however, is not technically an accurate way to think about true score. Crocker and Algina (1986) noted that, "any systematic errors or biasing aspects of a particular test for an individual contribute to that person's psychological true score" (p. 110). Thus, true score is really a composite made up of the standing on the trait being assessed and any number of other unknown systematic or biasing factors.

As an example, consider a test taker known to have a rather low standing on the trait of neuroticism. Imagine that before taking the assessment, our test taker had a big fight with a loved one and is in a negative mood. Imagine also that on the way to the assessment our test taker drank several cups of strong coffee and now feels a bit jittery. These things may lead our test taker to obtain an observed score that is not an accurate reflection of his or her standing on the trait of neuroticism; our test taker's mood and jitteriness may lead to an observed score that is higher than would otherwise be expected. If we were to give this person the test over and over again under exactly identical conditions, our test taker's poor mood and jitteriness would be expected to impact his or her score in the same way each time. Thus, these factors clearly do not meet the definition of random error, and therefore have to be accounted for within the true score. As such, our test taker's observed score could be more accurately expressed as follows:

$$X_{Neuroticism\ Score} = (T_{Neuroticism} + T_{Mood} + T_{Jitteriness}) + E,$$

where $T_{Neuroticism}$ represents the true score due to the standing on the trait, T_{Mood} represents the true score due to the systemic influence of mood, and $T_{Jitteriness}$ represents the true score due to the systematic factor of jitteriness resulting from caffeine. Now, considering a sample in which all test takers have some level of mood and jitteriness and that these factors are associated with neuroticism scores, we can express the variance in the neuroticism observed scores as

$$\sigma^2_{NeuroticismScores} = (\sigma^2_{T_{Neuroticism}} + \sigma^2_{T_{Mood}} + \sigma^2_{T_{Jitteriness}} + 2\sigma_{T_{Neuroticism}T_{Mood}}$$
$$+ 2\sigma_{T_{Neuroticism}T_{Jitteriness}} + 2\sigma_{T_{Mood}T_{Jitteriness}}) + \sigma^2_E.$$

Note that when we incorporate these additional systematic factors into the true score composite we also have to consider the covariances between them. Thus, in our example, the variance of the observed neuroticism scores would be larger than the variance of the true neuroticism scores to the extent that mood and jitteriness vary within the sample of test takers and the extent to which these sources of variance covary positively with one another and with true neuroticism scores. Of course, it is our hope that most of the variance in observed neuroticism scores is due to variation in true neuroticism. Indeed, it is reasonable to think that this is the case, at least in nonmotivated settings, given that scores on many personality assessment instruments have shown evidence of construct validity.

Incorporating Faking

Given how we have defined true and error scores, the incorporation of faking into the Classical Test Theory perspective is rather simple. Clearly, the increase in observed scores associated with faking cannot be due to random error. Faking must therefore be conceptualized as a component of psychological true score. In other words, we can define faking as a systematic source of variance that impacts observed scores in motivated testing contexts but not in nonmotivated testing contexts, or at least not to the same degree (see also Ziegler & Buehner, 2009).

Conceptualizing faking as a single, unitary source of systematic variance has been the norm in psychometric approaches to faking. For instance, in recent simulation studies by Komar et al. (2008) and Schmitt and Oswald (2006) faking was modeled as a single score. However, given the previous discussion of the predictors of faking, it becomes clear that conceptualizing faking as a single source of systematic variance is an oversimplification. Faking is a complex behavior, such that the choice to engage in faking behavior and the degree to which one fakes is a function of dispositional, attitudinal, and situational factors. Thus, from a psychometric perspective, the term faking is really a generic term for a set of systematic factors that influences a person's observed score to a greater degree in a particular motivated testing situation than in a nonmotivated testing situations (see also Ziegler & Buehner, 2009). It would be more accurate and informative to directly include the set of individual, attitudinal, and situational factors related to faking behavior into the expression of an observed score when that score is obtained in a motivated setting. More specifically, in a motivated setting we can express observed scores as follows:

$$X_{Motivated} = (T_T + (T_{F1} + T_{F2} + T_{F3} + \ldots + T_{Fn})) + E$$

where T_{F1} to $+ T_{Fn}$ are the systematic individual, attitudinal, and situational factors that influence observed scores in motivated contexts to a notably greater extent than in nonmotivated contexts. Considering a sample of scores, we can express the variance in observed scores obtained in a motivated setting as follows:

$$\sigma^2_{X_{Motivated}} = (\sigma^2_{T_T} + (\sigma^2_{F1} + \sigma^2_{F2} + \ldots + \sigma^2_{Fn}) + (2\sigma_{T_T,F1} + \ldots + 2\sigma_{Fn-1,Fn})) + \sigma^2_E \ ,$$

where $\sigma^2_{T_T}$ is the variance due to the true score on the trait being assessed, σ^2_{F1} to σ^2_{Fn} are the variances due to the factors that influence observed scores in motivated contexts, and $2\sigma_{T_T,F1}$ to $2\sigma_{Fn-1,Fn}$ are the covariance terms between all the possible combinations of these factors.

Considerations

A few things are worthy of note given that this is a rather different way of conceptualizing faking. First, it should be noted that some of the predictors of faking are likely to impact observed scores in nonmotivated settings as well. For example, when completing an assessment of conscientiousness as part of a research project, test takers high on the trait of impression management may inflate their responses to some degree whereas test takers lower on this trait dimension might be less likely to inflate their responses. Thus, although variation in impression management may explain some of the variance in observed scores in nonmotivated settings, the amount of variance explained by this factor would be expected to be much higher in motivated testing settings.

Second, although any one of the predictors might explain very little of the overall observed score variation in a motivated setting, in combination they could explain a notable degree of the overall variation in observed scores. Third, in the context of a multitrait assessment, it must be recognized that the factors that determine faking on one trait scale may not impact faking on another trait scale. For example, within a motivated testing setting, individual differences in rule consciousness may explain the variation in observed scores on a conscientiousness scale but not on an openness scale (assuming that rule consciousness is not actually a component of conscientiousness).

■ FUTURE DIRECTIONS, IMPLICATIONS, AND OTHER MATTERS

Future Theory and Research

Although several predictors of faking behavior have been discussed in the literature, I expect that further critical thinking on the issue will result in improved specifications of these predictors and the identification of additional predictors. At present, the empirical literature base is limited and additional research is needed to demonstrate the relationships between the proposed predictors and faking behavior. Beyond simply identifying a predictor as being related to faking behavior in motivated testing settings, efforts are needed to identify the amount of variation in observed scores that can be accounted for by relevant sets of predictors. Identifying the predictors that account for the largest amounts of variance will allow researchers to develop interventions targeted to reduce faking behavior. Although I have used classical test theory as the psychometric framework for the present study, researchers should give strong consideration to adopting a generalizability theory approach for empirically investigating the variance in observed scores accounted for by the predictors.

There are at least two key difficulties with research in this area. The first is the use of difference scores to represent faking behavior, the key dependent variable. McFarland and Ryan (2000), Griffith et al. (2006), and Mueller-Hanson et al. (2006) all used difference scores between scales administered in motivated and nonmotivated settings to operationalize faking behavior. Indeed, given the definition of faking, this practice appears to be the most direct way to assess faking.[2] The problem with difference scores is that they are often unreliable. Consistent with this notion, Mueller-Hanson et al. (2006) reported difference score reliabilities that were quite low, ranging from 0.28 for faking on an Extroversion scale to 0.64 for faking on an Achievement Striving scale. Some potentially good news for this line of research is that difference score reliability is inversely related to the correlation between the scores on the two measures. Thus, the most fakable scales should produce the highest reliability estimates for the faking measures.[3]

The second difficulty is that the results of any study may be quite situation specific. As I have noted, faking is a situation-specific behavior. As such, the factors that predict

2. There have been some recent attempts to represent faking in latent variable models. For instance, Mueller-Hanson et al. (2006) developed a latent variable model in which difference scores (between motivated and nonmotivated responding conditions) were used as indicators. Alternatively, Ziegler and Buehner (2009) modeled faking as a "methods" factor. Specifically, they fitted a four factor model with six indicator variables for each factor. They then modeled a method factor which was related to all of the indictors. They were able to show that the indicators were more strongly related to the method factor and that the latent mean of the method factor was larger when the indicator scales were completed in a motivated setting than when they were completed in a nonmotivated setting. They interpreted this latent method variable as a faking factor. Although these methods of representing faking show promise and should continue to be explored, they represent faking differently than do difference scores. That is, although the difference scores represent differences in responding at the level of individual scales, the latent variable models represent faking behavior as something that is common to faking on each of the individual scales.

3. The basic idea here is that scales that are more fakable will result in greater changes in the rank ordering of individuals between the nonmotivated and motivated testing situations than will less fakable scales. Consequently, scores obtained in the motivated setting should be less correlated with scores obtained in nonmotivated settings for these more fakable scales. As the reliability of the difference score is inversely related to the correlation between the two scores, scales that are subject to a greater degree of faking should result in faking behavior scores (i.e., the difference score) that are more reliable than faking behavior scores for scales that are less susceptible to faking.

faking in one setting may well differ from the factors that predict faking in another setting. For example, personal economic factors may be a particularly important predictor of faking behavior during an economic downturn, whereas dispositional factors may be more strongly related to faking behavior during healthy economic times. Thus, estimates of how much variance in observed scores is accounted for by a particular predictor could be expected to change from setting to setting.

Implications for Detecting Faking

The detection of faking behavior is a difficult endeavor. The root of the problem here is that we have one equation with two unknowns. That is, we know that our observed score is a function of true score and faking behavior (and of course error). Considering an applicant who obtained a high score on a conscientiousness scale given as part of the application process for a desirable job, for example, we cannot know if the high score indicates that the applicant has a high standing on the trait of conscientiousness, has a moderate standing on the trait of conscientiousness but has engaged in some faking behavior to raise his or her score, or has a low standing on conscientiousness and has engaged in considerable faking behavior. Trait standing and faking behavior are completely confounded; we cannot disentangle the influences of trait standing and faking behavior on any single observed score.

Of course, if we had information about one of the unknowns in the equation, then we would be able to solve for the other. More specifically, if we had information about a person's faking behavior and his or her observed personality trait score, then we could know his or her trait standing (which would still be confounded with error). This, of course, is the basic logic behind using measures, such as impression management scales, social desirability scales, or lie scales to detect faking behavior and statistically adjust the observed score to account for it. However, the extent to which an individual engages in faking behavior on a particular scale at a particular time is a function of many different factors. As such, no one factor is likely to be a good indicator of faking for all test takers across all scales assessed and across all unique testing occasions. Thus, attempting to accurately assess or capture faking behavior on a multitrait inventory with a simple social desirability or impression management scale is an endeavor destined to fail.

Rather than using a single indicator of faking behavior, the ideas presented in this chapter suggest that it might be possible to develop a faking propensity measure that assesses test takers on several of the factors that have been linked to faking behavior, such as Machiavellianism, rule consciousness, subjective norms, and the individual's personal situation. However, this approach would work only to the extent that these factors are general predictors of faking behavior; they are related to faking behavior across all scales assessed and across different testing situations and occasions. I suspect that this would be a losing battle. That is, as I have already suggested, I expect that the factors that lead to faking behavior will differ by trait scale and by testing situation. Setting aside this concern, and adopting the notion that there may be a set of factors that predicts faking behavior across traits and settings, the approach would be successful only to the extent that we accurately model faking behavior. Without an excellent (or at least really good) model of faking behavior, the use of this measure to identify individuals as having engaged in faking behavior would, no doubt, be a highly error-prone process. And, in the end, such an approach is rather impractical as it would require an accurate assessment of each of the predictor variables.

Implications for Preventing Faking

As suggested above, the real impact of the approach that I have described here will come when research starts to identify which of the predictors explain the largest amount of variance in observed scores within motivated testing settings. With this information interventions can be designed to target these specific predictor constructs. For example, if a particular attitudinal factor can be shown to relate to a propensity to engage in faking behavior, then an intervention could be created to influence the attitudes of test takers prior to the administration of the test (McFarland & Ryan, 2000). Of course, the identification of predictors that explain variance in observed scores across different personality scales and distinct motivated response settings would be ideal as this could lead to interventions that are generalizable to a range of trait dimensions and testing situations.

The approach offered may also be used to develop theory around the interventions already used to reduce faking. For instance, warning statements have been shown to be at least somewhat effective at reducing faking behavior (e.g., Dwight & Donovan, 2003). It seems likely that warning statements are effective because they are related to at least one of the predictors of faking behavior. It could be hypothesized, for example, that warnings are particularly effective among rule-conscious individuals. That is, when no warning is present, both high and low rule-conscious individuals may engage in similar amounts of faking behavior. In contrast, in the presence of a warning statement, the heightened awareness that faking is a violation of the rules may lead all test takers to engage in less faking behavior than they would without the warning, with more significant reductions in faking behavior coming for individuals high in the trait of rule consciousness. If this were found to be the case, then other interventions could be designed for other predictors of faking behavior. Ultimately, a combination of methods designed to work on different determinants of faking behavior is likely to be the best prescription.

The Cart and the Horse

I think that we, as faking researchers, have put the proverbial cart before the horse when it comes to the phenomenon of faking. That is, we have studied the expected effects of faking and explored potential solutions to the problem it presents without first developing a thorough understanding of its nature. In this chapter, I have reviewed the literature on the determinants of faking behavior and have offered a psychometric framework that I hope will help us develop a better understanding of what faking behavior is and how it operates to influence our assessments. A key message here is that faking is a complex phenomenon. The expressions for an observed score and for the variance of observed scores when those scores are obtained in a motivated setting strongly suggest that there will be no single, simple solution to the detection or prevention of faking. But, using this conceptual perspective, we can begin to develop and evaluate theory-based approaches to the detection and prevention of faking in applicant settings. By developing this conceptual understanding of faking behavior, my hope is that we have begun to lead the horse to a position in front of the cart.

References

Crocker, L., & Algina, J. (1986). *Introduction to classical and modern test theory*. Belmont, CA: Wadsworth Group/Thompson Learning.

Dunnette, M. D., McCartney, J., Carlson, H. C., & Kirchner, W. K. (1962). A study of faking behavior on a forced-choice self-description checklist. *Personnel Psychology, 15*, 13–24.

Dwight, S. A., & Donovan, J. J. (2003). Warning: Proceed with caution when warning applicants not to dissimulate. *Human Performance, 16*, 1–23.

Griffith, R., Malm, T., English, A., Yoshita, Y., & Gujar, A. (2006). Applicant faking behavior: Teasing apart the influence of situational variance, cognitive biases, and individual differences. In R. L. Griffith & M. H. Peterson (Eds.), *A closer examination of applicant faking behavior* (pp. 151–178). Greenwich, CT: Information Age Publishing.

Hogan, J., Barrett, P., & Hogan, R. (2007). Personality measurement, faking, and employment selection. *Journal of Applied Psychology, 92*, 1270–1285.

Hough, L. M. (1998). Effects of intentional distortion in personality measurement and evaluation of suggested palliatives. *Human Performance, 11*, 209–244.

Hough, L. M., Eaton, N. K., Dunnette, M. D., Kamp, J. D., & McCloy, R. A. (1990). Criterion-related validities of personality constructs and the effect of response distortion on those validities. *Journal of Applied Psychology, 75*, 581–595.

Komar, S., Brown, D. J., Robie, C., & Komar, J. A. (2008). Faking and the validity of conscientiousness: A Monte Carlo investigation. *Journal of Applied Psychology, 93*, 140–154.

Levashina, J., & Campion, M. A. (2006). A model of faking likelihood in the employment interview. *International Journal of Selection and Assessment, 14*, 299–316.

McFarland, L. A., & Ryan, A. M. (2000). Variance in faking across noncognitive measures. *Journal of Applied Psychology, 85*, 812–821.

Mueller-Hanson, R., Heggestad, E. D., & Thornton, G. C. III. (2006). Impression management strategy and faking behavior. *Psychology Science, 48*, 288–312.

Pauls, C. A., & Crost, N. W. (2005). Cognitive ability and self-reported efficacy of self-presentation predict faking on personality measures. *Journal of Individual Differences, 26*, 194–206.

Rossé, J. G., Stecher, M. D., Miller, J. L., & Levin, R. (1998). The impact of response distortion on preemployment personality testing and hiring decisions. *Journal of Applied Psychology, 83*, 634–644.

Schmidt, F. L., & Hunter, J. E. (1999). Theory testing and measurement error. *Intelligence, 27*, 183–198.

Schmidt, F. L., Le, H., & Ilies, R. (2003). Beyond alpha: An empirical examination of the effects of different sources of measurement error on reliability estimates for measures of individual differences constructs. *Psychological Methods, 8*, 206–224.

Schmitt, N., & Oswald, F. L. (2006). The impact of corrections for faking on the validity of noncognitive measures in selection settings. *Journal of Applied Psychology, 91*, 613–621.

Snell, A. F., & Fluckinger, C. D. (2006). Understanding responses to personality selection measures: A conditional model of the applicant reasoning process. In R. L. Griffith &

M. H. Peterson (Eds.), *A closer examination of applicant faking behavior* (pp. 179–208). Greenwich, CT: Information Age Publishing.

Snell, A. F., Sydell, E. J., & Lueke, S. B. (1999). Towards a theory of applicant faking: Integrating studies of deception. *Human Resource Management Review, 9*, 219–242.

Ziegler, M. (2006). Situational demand and its impact on construct and criterion validity of a personality questionnaire: State and trait, a couple you just can't study separately! Unpublished doctoral dissertation.

Ziegler, M., & Buehner, M. (2009). Modeling socially desirable responding and its effects. *Educational and Psychological Measurement, 69*, 548–565.

7 Innovative Item Response Process and Bayesian Faking Detection Methods

More Questions Than Answers

■ NATHAN R. KUNCEL, MATTHEW BORNEMAN, AND THOMAS KIGER

Interest in detecting or preventing "bad" responses has been an ongoing and keen interest for psychology. Early research on the detection and prevention of what were termed "response sets" reached a peak in the 1960s capturing the attention of major names including Cronbach, Block, and Jackson. Although this debate subsided, psychology has continued to grapple with two unambiguous realities: People are not always honest and test takers can easily alter their responses to test items when instructed to do so, which makes the applied use of test scores a concern. The latter concern, coupled with an increasing use of personality measures for decision making, has ignited renewed interest in the detection and prevention of faking behavior.

Our focus in this chapter is to concentrate on new directions and innovations, after a brief review of what has come before. Rather than simply list methods, we also offer a conceptual framework for considering faking that we use to organize our thinking. We conclude that real progress has been made in the field's understanding and detection of faking behavior when faking behavior is defined as a deliberate effort to distort responses to obtain a desirable outcome.

Many of these methods are relatively new. This is positive in that it is an exciting time to be involved in faking research with so many new ideas to consider. However, the consequence is that our review focused equally on future questions and current knowledge. We attempt to identify the research questions that we think are the most urgent. We are optimistic that a decade of thoughtful research may result in at least partial remedies for this applied issue.

■ FAKING FROM A SOCIAL INTERACTION PERSPECTIVE

We advocate considering faking from an item response process perspective and view responses from the perspective of people engaging in a social interaction with others such as an employer, a clinician, or an admissions officer. We pose the question: How do people think about responding to one or more personality items given their interpersonal goals? We think it will be most productive to first focus research at the level of the item response. This provides an approach that has several advantages.

To start, the item-level response provides a pragmatically manageable focus for laboratory and field research. Scale-level or test-level effects may obscure important processes. It also helps avoid assumptions that the frame of reference of the researcher is the same as that of the test takers. Frame of reference is important because it is clear that participants taking personality tests do not have the same frame of reference or assumptions that are made by us, the experts. Many test takers clearly do not think about the summing of items to total scores. In other words, the implicit theory of test takers for how tests function is not classical test theory (see Kuncel & Tellegen, 2009). Understanding how they fake on an item will require understanding how they think about items and tests.

An item response focus avoids confusion that can occur from aggregate-level analyses of data. Faking is an individual-level phenomenon and although aggregate-level analyses can provide insights, they can also mislead about the nature of the response process. For example, average response latency is longest across all subjects for items with average difficulty. Using height as an example, items that ask about heights in the average range (Are you 5 feet 9 inches tall?) will tend to get the longest latencies. At an individual level, latency is greatest when items are closest to the *individual's* ability level (Kuncel & Kuncel, 1995). For example, Kuncel is about 6 feet 5 inches tall and a 5 feet 9 inches question requires no contemplation. But the question "Are you 6 feet 5 inches tall?" requires reflection. With or without shoes? If I stand up straight or not? As a consequence, latency increases. Thus, aggregate-level analyses can lead to confusion about the true item response process (i.e., items close to the individual's theta can require slower active processing).

Finally, our research on faking detection (Kuncel & Borneman, 2007) as well as item response theory (IRT)/paired comparison methods (see Chapters 8 and 14) and Bayesian methods has demonstrated some promising results. All are anchored in manipulating or measuring the individual response process to individual items. We see this as one useful area for theory development that should compliment broader theories of faking.

Our framework assumes that responding to personality items is fundamentally a social interaction not unlike an interview or conversation. Subjects engage in these interactions with one or more interpersonal goals in mind including getting a job, keeping the job, and getting along with future co-workers. We believe that a subject's reaction to a personality test item includes both conscious and unconscious elements, and, depending on the item, subjects engage in both automatic and controlled processing of test item information. Specifying the test takers' goals may be complex, but previous research on interpersonal goals (Fitzsimons & Bargh, 2003) has suggested 13 goal categories: *success in life, self-presentational concerns*, care for partner, show care for partner, help and support, *get along*, duties of relationship maintenance, *understanding/communication*, have fun, ideal self, relationship maintenance, *establish relationship*, and *self-benefit* (Fitzsimons & Bargh, 2003, p. 164). The goals we believe are most salient for the application setting have been italicized.

This research provides a starting point, but needs modification for three reasons. First, this interpersonal goal research does not include the supervisor (or a more amorphous employer) who may elicit different goals. Second, this previous research was not focused on the narrower goals likely to be relevant in the generally one-way applicant or admission testing interaction (the test responses given to the prospective supervisor, human resources professional, or admissions officer). Third, the purpose of the interaction is narrower than relationships in general and intimate ones in particular. However, we suggest that the purposes can be far broader than is often considered including developing friendships and avoiding conflict. We suggest that this interaction has three basic goals.

Responding to a single item comes down to wanting to be impressive, credible, and true to the self. Being impressive involves giving the response to a given item that is believed to be viewed as maximally desirable by the target audience without violating short- or long-term credibility or providing responses that are too inconsistent with the participant's "self."

The desirability of different response options will naturally be a function of the strength of the stimulus and the participant's understanding of the nature of the target audience and job. As a result, the best response does not necessarily involve the strongest response option. For many traits "weaker" responses are often seen as fundamentally more desirable by the majority of subjects (Kuncel & Borneman, 2007; Kuncel & Tellegen, 2009). For example, being talkative is desirable only up to a point.

Short-term credibility involves a guess of whether a response will be seen as credible by others in light of the specific response as well as previous responses. We believe this consideration matters even when the most desirable response is actually true of the test taker. Modesty effects appear to influence some subjects to avoid responses that they feel accurately characterize their behavior. Long-term credibility is a concern about saying something about the self that one will regret in the future. Creating unattainable expectations or a perception of the self that will eventually be falsified can create interpersonal conflict and tensions.

Finally, a subject's sense of self anchors item responses. Even when instructed and provided with incentives to maximally inflate scores (even involving dishonesty), subjects will frequently avoid extreme responses with the explanation that the response would be too inconsistent with their self (Kuncel & Tellegen, 2009).

■ FAKING AND SOCIAL DESIRABILITY

Our survey of the literature suggests that social desirability scales are the most commonly used and studied operationalizations of faking behavior. Additionally, they are frequently employed as either a proxy or direct measure of faking behavior. This research highlights the major challenge that psychologists face when attempting to detect inaccurate responding to personality measures: One person's deceptive response looks the same as another's honest self-report. As noted by Paulhus, Harms, Bruce, and Lysy (2003), "it is difficult to verify that these self-report instruments truly capture inflation of self-descriptions" (p. 890).

Social desirability scales were one of the earliest efforts to address this issue. Social desirability scales appear to capture a response style that is the tendency to respond not to the content of the item, but instead to the socially desirable content of the item. It was argued that both conscious and unconscious motives drove this response style and instruments were developed to measure this distinction (Paulhus, 1984). Although logically appealing, its utility for the detection of faking behavior in applied settings has been disappointing. In directed faking studies, social desirability scales do a reasonably accurate job of differentiating between subjects who are instructed to deliberately fake items and those who are not because social desirability scales show some of the largest average score changes in these studies (e.g., Viswesvaran & Ones, 1999). However, their effectiveness at improving the average performance of the passing group has been a failure. The scales themselves are uncorrelated with subsequent job performance and their use as a control has not resulted in meaningful improvements in predictive power (Ones, Viswesvaran, & Reiss, 1996).

The underlying problem is that social desirability variance appears to be valid trait variance. Indeed, Jackson (1970), who originally formulated a scale construction method that included steps for eliminating socially desirable items, later recognized that assessment of some characteristics requires measuring the presence of socially undesirable behaviors (Jackson, 1989). In their review of the history of social desirability in the assessment of personality in general and psychopathology in particular, Tellegen et al. (2006) note that "The most important and sophisticated program of inventory development to have been predicated on the idea of a general and separately measurable social desirability dimension ended up abandoning that construct" (p. 150).

Since this time several alternative methods have been developed. Two things have become clear. First, research on faking detection is in a period of rapid change and innovation. Second, conceptualizations of faking behavior have become increasingly complex and sophisticated.

For a detection method to be effective it needs to meet the following criteria. First, its detection rate needs to be high while avoiding false positives. The costs of false-positive and false-negative rates will need to be balanced against the benefits of detecting distorted tests. For example, if applicants are numerous and the cost of a distorted test is high then a high false-positive rate may be desirable. Second, the method should not capture valid organizationally relevant trait variance or eliminate top candidates. For example, extreme scores may reflect misrepresentation or ideal applicants. Those who say they are always diligent actually may be very diligent. Third, the method should ideally be resistant to coaching and instruction; this would help avoid situations in which there is incentive to coach applicants to pass the test (e.g., recruiters).

■ UNLIKELY VIRTUES

Unlikely virtue items have been discussed as an alternative to more traditional social desirability scales (although the distinction is often blurred). Unlikely virtue scales are composed of extreme items that present questions about always being kind, never swearing, and life-long truthfulness. Hough, Eaton, Dunnette, Kamp, and McCloy (1990) have demonstrated that unlikely virtue scale scores increase sharply, more so than other scales, when subjects are directed to fake (see also Ellingson, Sackett, & Hough, 1999). As such, they do a reasonable job of detecting this form of intentional distortion when contrasting instructed fakers with sub-jects responding under honest conditions. Unfortunately, correction with unlikely virtue scales does little to improve scores (Ellingson et al., 1999) much like social desirability scales (Christiansen, Goffin, Johnston, & Rothstein, 1994; Ones et al., 1996).

We speculate that unlikely virtue items represent a responding problem for test takers. Test developers make the assumption that test takers will approach them logically. Honest respondents are assumed to think, "Everyone lies, including me, so I cannot endorse the item, *I never lie*." Yet, when confronted with the question *True or False—I never lie*, a nonzero number of subjects will endorse the item. Endorsement is then assumed to reflect either conscious or unconscious dishon-esty because endorsement is rationally impossible. However, an equally reasonable interpretation of endorsement is that the subject is being confronted with an irra-tional and unreasonable statement. Of course everyone has lied, so the real issue is frequency of lying, situation, cost to the self, and cost to others. A very honest person, who very rarely lies and does so even when the personal cost is dear, could reasonably endorse "True" because that is the only reasonable response. Otherwise, the item might as well ask about whether one rides a green flying pig to work because the question is not a sensible query.

■ OVERCLAIMING/BOGUS ITEMS

The appeal of social desirability and unlikely virtue scales is anchored in the logic of essentially trapping dishonest respondents in a deception. Paulhus and col-leagues have built on this basic notion and developed a measure of self-enhance-ment that reduces concerns about the legitimacy of subject responses. They accomplish this by asking test takers to identify things that they recognize. The catch is that the scale contains a percent of illegitimate (i.e., nonexistent) people, places, or things (Paulhus et al., 2003). A measure of accuracy (indicating knowl-edge of legitimate items) acts as a self-report measure of knowledge and is moder-ately to strongly correlated with measures of cognitive ability. Their measure of bias demonstrates moderate correlations with other measures of self-enhancement and small but positive correlations with cognitive ability. Of characteristics exam-ined, the consistently largest relationship with bias is a measure of Narcissism. Even when subjects are warned about the basic nature of the measure, it continues to operate as intended and has demonstrated initial utility in detecting when people are intentionally distorting their responses (i.e., when directed to do so in a laboratory).

Overall, we see this method as having potential for use in applied settings. The approach is objective and initial results suggest that it is coaching resistant. However, its correlations with cognitive ability, although not unexpected, are potentially problematic for applied use. If higher scores are correlated with cognitive ability and are screened out, then the hired group will tend to be, on average, lower in cognitive ability. This effect could inadvertently produce adverse impact or result in lower quality hires.

The construct validity of the overclaiming or bogus items measure will, like most of the methods presented in this chapter, require additional research. In particular, we note that memory is associative and people with more knowledge are more likely to have many associations. One likely consequence is that knowledgeable people are more likely to have legitimate but inaccurate recognition for foil items. That is, they will truly believe, without any intent at deception, that they recognize foil items. Paulhus et al. (2003) note this issue and cite the example of an item "cholarine" that is quite close to the real "chlorine" (and, we note, "chloramine"). Both chemicals are commonly used in municipal water treatment and the foil item certainly activates the others. Is an endorsement overclaiming or spelling skill? Is accidentally endorsing the item overclaiming? In this sense, endorsement has the same confound that is seen with social desirability scales when detecting deliberate faking. We do not know, but must infer, intention.

For the purpose of detecting faking behavior in personality assessments an additional question needs to be addressed about the construct validity of the overclaiming technique. Overclaiming knowledge is not necessarily the same behavior or psychological process as faking personality items. More data are needed to better establish the construct validity of this approach. The number of known items that were not claimed by the subject is important information that cannot be quantified, that is, the number of items the subject really did know but, due to uncertainty or other reasons, they elected to not claim. Regardless, the method developed and tested by Paulhus et al. (2003) appears to be a novel and effective measure of tendency to overclaim knowledge, but its utility for detecting deliberately faked personality measures in applied settings remains to be seen.

■ BAYESIAN TRUTH SERUM

This novel approach effectively pits respondents against each other and is designed to reward honest responding by increasing the value assigned to different responses (Prelec, 2004) such that honest responses will receive higher expected scores. In order to work, Bayesian Truth Serum (BTS) methodology requires two pieces of information to be collected from each person: the person's response to the item and the person's estimation of how many people in the population will respond in the same manner. If the observed frequency of a response exceeds the collective predicted frequency, the response is "surprisingly common" and is given a higher value. This approach capitalizes on the empirically supported assumption that people will use their own behavior, values, and preferences as information for making judgments about the frequency of popularity of an item in the general population. The consequence is that they will tend to overestimate the frequency of the behavior or preference.

Note that this scoring approach requires a reasonable amount of group-level information that is scored and combined at the time of assessment. The method assumes that individual estimates of frequencies do not affect the geometric mean of the predicted frequencies across subjects. That is, there must be a sample size sufficient so that one subject cannot "push around" or bias the average. One way around this assumption in small sample settings (selection decisions for small applicant groups) might be to use previously collected data to score new data.

We present the math here for the interested reader. The sample frequencies are indexed as the following:

$$\overline{x_k} = \frac{1}{n}\sum_{i=1}^{n} x_k^r \tag{1}$$

where n is the number of persons and x_k^r is the score on response option r for person i on item k. An additional constraint is placed such that the $\sum x_k^r = 1$, where a person's response can only be {0,1}, such that 1 is the chosen response option and 0 is assigned to all other response options. The predicted frequencies, estimates of how many people in the population will respond in the same manner, is indexed as the following:

$$\log \overline{y_k} = \frac{1}{n}\sum_{i=1}^{n} \log y_k^r \tag{2}$$

where n is the number of persons and y_k^r is individual i's rating of the probability of occurrence for response option r on item k. This leads to an "information" score that is the log-ratio of actual endorsements to the predicted endorsements frequencies. This is indexed by

$$\log \frac{\overline{x_k}}{\overline{y_k}} \tag{3}$$

where terms are defined from Equations (1) and (2). The total score for a specific respondent is a combination of the information scores and prediction scores

$$\sum_k x_k^r \log \frac{\overline{x_k}}{\overline{y_k}} + \sum_k \overline{x_k} \log \frac{y_k^r}{\overline{x_k}} \tag{4}$$

where all terms are as defined previously.

Like most of the approaches previously discussed, there is comparatively little evidence relating to the effectiveness of this technique. Weaver (2008) presents a series of studies that examine resistance of the method to several simulated deception strategies (e.g., attempts to imitate someone else). Overall, deception strategies were not effective with a few exceptions that bear replication. Specifically, one was when a category of items (in this case humor) was consistently surprisingly funny (finding them funny was surprisingly common. People rated them as funny more frequently than was estimated for the overall population) and several strategies rewarded deceptively endorsing items as funny. This pattern may be relevant for homogeneous personality scales.

In a separate experiment, subjects were told they would be given a reward for a high BTS score (top third) and this was combined with incentives (10 cents) for claiming knowledge of items from the Paulhus et al. (2003) overclaiming measure. The BTS scoring reduced the amount of overclaiming apparently because subjects also desired the reward for honest responding ($25). The use of BTS and the use of an incentive appear to motivate subjects to respond honestly, thereby reducing bias and increasing accuracy.

Although this technique has the benefit of being able to detect faking within (and beyond) a single data-collection experience, the drawback is that it requires the collection of additional data beyond what is typically collected for selection. Given that many organizations feel time pressures for evaluating data, this could be a serious negative. Although there seems to be promise for this technique, further research is needed to determine its effectiveness in applied use for personnel selection.

We see future research needs surrounding a few topics. First, there are questions concerning the utility of BTS in practice with rolling hiring systems. Second, there is the degree to which the scoring method can be coached by experts to beat it. Third, there are concerns about the effects of frame of reference. Do subject's beliefs about the nature of the population against which they are being compared affect responding behavior? Finally, does the approach work due to the process proposed by Prelec (2004) or do bogus pipeline effects account for some of the efficacy of the method? That is, did the experiment by Weaver work because of a belief that dishonesty can be detected? The subject instructions used in Weaver (2008) establishes the conditions for a state similar to the bogus pipeline, "BTS Scoring is a method recently invented by an MIT professor, and published in the academic journal *Science*. . . . Even though there is no way for anyone to know if your answers are truthful . . . your score will be higher on average if you tell the truth" (Weaver, 2008, pp. 97–98). How does the subject's perception of the certainty of the method affect responding and if this belief is removed or damaged, does responding change meaningfully?

■ IDIOSYNCRATIC ITEM RESPONSES

Kuncel and Borneman (2007) began with three facts to develop a deliberate faking detection method (based on study results ultimately published in Kuncel & Tellegen, 2009). First, test takers consistently judge the relationship between trait level and desirability to be nonlinear for most traits. For example, it is generally desirable to be tidy but less desirable to be extremely tidy (which can become pathological). Second, desirability of different trait levels is not universally agreed upon by subjects, particularly for some items and traits (e.g., conservative). Finally, the relationship between trait level and desirability varies, sometimes sharply, depending on the context. For example, being above average in *strong and forceful* is viewed as more desirable at work than for life in general.

From these data, we hypothesized that test takers would produce unusual response patterns during deliberate distortion if the most desirable level of the trait was unclear, ambiguous, or debatable. In this case, subjects would tend to avoid intermediate responses and focus on extreme endorsements. We reasoned that test takers would be forced to select extremes of endorsement or play it safe with a completely neutral endorsement. In a study in which over half of the subjects responded honestly and the remainder were directed to intentionally distort responses, a set of items demonstrated a trimodal or bimodal response pattern under the directed faking conditions and roughly normal distributions under honest conditions. We argued that items such as "Complex" or "Daring" create a challenge for intentional distortion because it is unclear if being a complex or daring person is desirable or not in a work setting. Test takers then need to select a response that will convey the best impression of them as a potential hire. On a scale with 9 points, the three most common choices are 9 "very high," 1 "very low," or 5 "average." A scale of 11 keyed items detected 20% and 37% of faked personality measures with only a 1% false-positive rate in cross-validation samples (with 56% of all test takers responding honestly). The scale was also largely uncorrelated with other personality scales (under honest conditions) and cognitive ability. Finally, it would be challenging to provide effective coaching for such items.

Although we are optimistic that this approach can prove to be even more effective with further development and refinement, we note there are multiple future research questions that need to be answered. Most importantly would be the effect of scale use on criterion-related validity. Like other methods discussed here, if they have no effect on the quality of hired personnel or admitted students, their utility will remain low.

Study subjects were the ubiquitous introductory psychology college student and this may affect which items work. Real applicants may find less ambiguity for some items if they know the job and its requirements. Similarly, different items and keys may be necessary for some jobs due to the real or perceived fit between certain characteristics and performance. For example, there may be a consensus among sales applicants that high levels of "Daring" are desirable.

Furthermore, it is possible that subjects could detect the two types of items that yield idiosyncratic patterns (ambiguity about the optimal trait level such as "Daring" and confusion about the item's meaning such as "Unenvious," which is a nonstandard English word). If test takers can do so, they could be coached to defeat the scale. The confusing items seem more likely to be readily detectable.

■ KEYING METHODS

Keying methods consist of attempts to predict an outcome through the differential weighting of items. They include both rational/theoretical methods to weight items as well as empirical methods. Empirical keying involves selecting and weighting items based on the item's ability to discriminate between individuals on a criterion. Empirically keyed biodata inventories generally have been found to result in higher criterion-related validity relative to other, more rationally based, methods of keying (Mitchell & Klimoski, 1982; Stokes & Searcy, 1999).

The idiosyncratic item response method is one possible application of a keying method. In this case unusual items are being keyed. Despite a robust tradition in other areas of research such as personality and biodata measures, keying methods have not received much attention in the study of faking behavior until recently.

Traditional keying methods (vertical and horizontal percent) have a long history. Long and Sandiford (1935), for example, conducted a review of 23 different methods. Neither of these methods considers the possibility that item responses share information. If the majority of items are redundant, then a smaller number of effective items could be washed out. The use of either regression or decision tree methods with large samples provides keys that consider information redundancy among item responses and results by Lukoff, Heggestad, Kyllonen, and Roberts (2007) suggest that this may be a productive approach.

We believe that maximally effective use of keying methods will require large data sets and good performance and faking criteria. Keying efforts may also be facilitated by heterogeneous collections of items. Squeaky clean item banks may not be optimal for finding good faking detection items. If these conditions are met, a comparison of an item-level response key built on real applicant data for a good performance criterion with an item response level key built on personality responses between honest and faked conditions could prove interesting.

■ CONCLUSIONS

Although social desirability scales have yielded useful scientific knowledge, it has become clear that test takers do not approach deliberate faking in a simplistic manner and social desirably scales are ineffective for the detection and correction of scores. Recent efforts have put forward a variety of distinct and thoughtful methods that generally conceptualize faking as more than a straightforward score inflation process. Instead, the test taker's frame of reference and decision process are being considered as levers for detecting and controlling faking behavior. We see this as a promising start and encourage additional work on how test takers consider responding to test items. We believe that the greatest progress will be made with a clear understanding of how subjects consider and respond to personality items. Without this knowledge we are just faking it.

References

Christiansen, N. D., Goffin, R. D., Johnston, N. G., & Rothstein, M. G. (1994). Correcting the 16PF for faking-effects on criterion-related validity and individual hiring decisions. *Personnel Psychology, 47*, 847–860.

Ellingson, J. E., Sackett, P. R., & Hough, L. M. (1999). Social desirability corrections in personality measurement: Issues of applicant comparison and construct validity. *Journal of Applied Psychology, 84*, 155–166.

Fitzsimons, G. M., & Bargh, J. A. (2003). Thinking of you: Nonconscious pursuit of interpersonal goals associated with relationship partners. *Journal of Personality and Social Psychology, 84*, 148–164.

Hough, L. M., Eaton, N. K., Dunnette, M. D., Kamp, J. D., & McCloy, R. A. (1990). Criterion-related validities of personality constructs and the effect of response distortion on those validities. *Journal of Applied Psychology, 75*, 581–595.

Jackson, D. N. (1970). A sequential system for personality scale development. In C. D. Spielberger (Ed.), *Current topics in clinical and community psychology, Vol. 2* (pp. 61–96). New York: NY: Academic Press.

Jackson, D. N. (1989). Basic personality inventory manual. Port Huron, MI: Sigma Assessment Systems.

Kuncel, N. R., & Borneman, M. J. (2007). Toward a new method of detecting deliberately faked personality tests: The use of idiosyncratic item responses. *International Journal of Selection and Assessment, 15*, 220–231.

Kuncel, R. B., & Kuncel, N. R. (1995). *Response-process models: Toward an integration of cognitive-processing models, psychometric models, latent-trait theory, and self-schemas.* Shrout, Patrick E [Ed]; Fiske, Susan T [Ed]. (1995). Personality research, methods, and theory: A festschrift honoring Donald W. Fiske.

Kuncel, N. R., & Tellegen, A. (2009). A conceptual and empirical reexamination of the measurement of the social desirability of items: Implications for detecting desirable response style and scale development. *Personnel Psychology, 62*, 201–228.

Long, J. A., & Sandiford, P. (1935). *The validation of test items.* Toronto, Canada: University of Toronto Department of Education.

Lukoff, B., Heggestad, E., Kyllonen, P. C., & Roberts, R. D. (2007). Using decision trees to detect faking in noncognitive assessments. Paper presented at the 2007 American Psychological Association Conference, San Francisco, CA.

Mitchell, T. W., & Klimoski, R. J. (1982). Is it rational to be empirical? A test of methods for scoring biographical data. *Journal of Applied Psychology, 67*, 411–418.

Ones, D. S., Viswesvaran, C., & Reiss, A. D. (1996). Role of social desirability in personality testing for personnel selection: The red herring. *Journal of Applied Psychology, 81*, 660–679.

Paulhus, D. L. (1984). Two-component models of socially desirable responding. *Journal of Personality and Social Psychology, 46*, 598–609.

Paulhus, D. L., Harms, P. D., Bruce, M. N., & Lysy, D. C. (2003). The over-claiming technique measuring self-enhancement independent of ability. *Journal of Personality and Social Psychology, 84*, 890–904.

Prelec, D. (2004). A Bayesian truth serum for subjective data. *Science, 306*, 462–466.

Stokes, G. S., & Searcy, C. A. (1999). Specification of scales in biodata form development: Rational vs. empirical and global vs. specific. *International Journal of Selection and Assessment, 7*, 72–85.

Tellegen, A., Ben-Porath, Y. S., Sellbom, M., Arbisi, P. A., McNulty, J. L., & Graham, J. R. (2006). Further evidence on the validity of the MMPI-2 restructured clinical (RC) scales: Addressing questions raised by Rogers, Sewell, Harrison, and Jordan and Nichols. *Journal of Personality Assessment, 87*, 148–171.

Viswesvaran, C., & Ones. D. S. (1999). Meta-analysis of fakability estimates: Implications for personality measurement. *Educational and Psychological Measurement, 59*, 197–210.

Weaver, R. (2008). Three essays on decision making. Unpublished doctoral dissertation: Massachusetts Institute of Technology.

8 Searching for Unicorns

Item Response Theory-Based Solutions
to the Faking Problem

■ MICHAEL J. ZICKAR AND
KATHERINE A. SLITER

Throughout the history of research on the use of personality inventories, numerous attempts have been made to solve the so-called "faking problem." In fact, as Zickar and Gibby (2006) demonstrated, concerns about faking began to emerge soon after the creation of the first formal personality inventories during the 1920s. Since then, many solutions have been proposed to address the faking problem, such as social desirability scales, measurement of reaction times, polygraphs, and handwriting verification. Many of these proposed solutions are evaluated in this book; the purpose of our chapter, however, is to evaluate another, more recent set of approaches to solving the faking problem: item response theory (IRT) approaches to detecting faking.

As alluded to in the title, we believe that the faking problem has not been solved despite the many attempts to find a solution; much like the mythical unicorn, a solution to the faking problem in personality testing has been an exciting but elusive quarry. Despite continued research into the topic, we still do not have a method for accurately and consistently detecting faking behavior. We believe that the research on IRT-based techniques shows that they currently do not warrant operational usage in large-scale personality testing programs for the purposes of detecting faking. However, we do believe that there is much to be learned from using IRT techniques that might help in furthering our understanding of the faking problem.

In this chapter, we first review the basics behind IRT-based techniques, especially appropriateness measurement (i.e., measures of "person fit" to the model of test responding), detail the previous research that has been conducted on IRT, and examine possible applications of IRT to personality measurement and faking. Next, we provide our conclusions, which we have foreshadowed as being somewhat cynical. Despite this cynicism, we end with a roadmap for future researchers and practitioners who are still considering the use of appropriateness measurement to address the faking problem. We also provide suggestions for improving appropriateness measurement in future research; in a sense, we provide advice for those who wish to continue the search for the unicorn. We cannot know for sure if there are any unicorns out there to be found, but it sure would be great if there were. Rumors abound, so we hope to provide fellow unicorn seekers with the knowledge and tools necessary to be successful in their quest.

■ BACKGROUND: ITEM RESPONSE THEORY AND APPROPRIATENESS MEASUREMENT

Item Response Theory

IRT is a theory that links characteristics of items and characteristics of respondents in order to predict how individuals will respond to particular test items. Many researchers have viewed it as an advance over classical test theory, the theory that underlies many of the popular psychometric techniques such as coefficient alpha, item-total correlations, and standard error of measurement (see Zickar & Broadfoot, 2009). One advantage over classical test theory is that its parameters are invariant across populations. Second, the theory is empirically falsifiable. Third, IRT has more specific parameters than classical test theory, which may be extremely impor-tant for faking applications. IRT has several specific *item characteristic parameters* (e.g., discrimination, difficulty, and pseudoguessing), as well as a *person parameter*. Fourth, IRT can describe the measurement precision of a test at different levels of ability (e.g., a test may more finely differentiate among test takers at the high end of a scale versus at the low end). These characteristics are advantages that help advance the understanding of faking beyond that possible with classical test theory.

The Person Parameter

The person parameter, commonly denoted by the Greek letter theta (i.e., θ), is related to the underlying trait measured by the inventory. This parameter is typi-cally distributed like a z-score, with a mean of zero and standard deviation of one, and provides an indication of an individual's standing on the latent trait of interest relative to others. Thus, a high theta value is indicative of a higher-than-average standing on the trait whereas a low theta value indicates the opposite. To review IRT, it makes sense to discuss the various parameters included in typical models.

Item Parameters

One of the cornerstones of IRT is the item response function (IRF), which relates theta to the expected probability of affirming an item. The shape of the IRF is determined by item parameters, which vary in number and type based upon the model chosen by the researcher. For example, a one-parameter model includes only an item difficulty (b) parameter, a two-parameter model also includes an item discrimination (a) parameter, and a three-parameter model includes a third parameter, the pseudoguessing (c) parameter. Figure 8.1 provides a graphic depiction of the parameters that would be estimated by the latter of these, the three-parameter logistic model. We will now describe these parameters in more detail.

 Discrimination (a) provides an indication of how well an item discriminates among those with varying levels of theta. An item with a high discrimination parameter will more finely discriminate between low-and high-performing test takers, for instance, than will an item with a very low discrimination parameter.

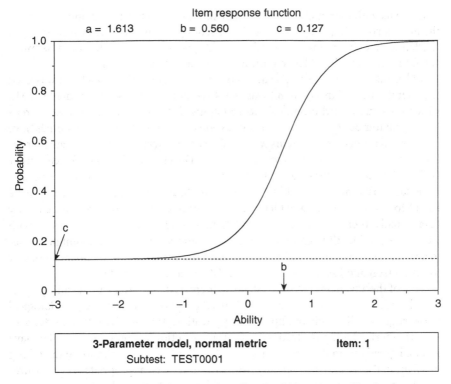

Figure 8.1 Graphic depiction of the parameters that would be estimated by the three-parameter logistic model.

Item difficulty (*b*) indicates the level of the latent trait at which the item is most discriminating. When comparing the discrimination and the item difficulty parameters, the former indicates how *well* the item distinguishes among theta levels whereas the difficulty parameter indicates *where* on the trait continuum it does this the best. Items with low difficulty will be endorsed by nearly all respondents, even those with low theta levels. By contrast, items with high difficulty will be endorsed only by respondents with large positive theta levels. The item in Figure 8.1 has a difficulty parameter (*b*) of 0.56 and because theta is a standard normal variable, this indicates that the item is a moderately difficult item (an item with a difficulty value of zero would be of average difficulty). The relationship between theta and difficulty is possible because the two are on the same scale.

Pseudoguessing (*c*) is useful in cases in which guessing could result in a "correct" answer (one indicating a higher standing on the latent trait). For instance, even though extremely low theta respondents may not know the correct answer to a multiple choice test item, these respondents will be able to correctly guess the item with a probability of 1 divided by the number of options. The pseudoguessing (*c*) parameter provides an estimate of the probability that an individual with an extremely low theta will answer an item correctly. The item in Figure 8.1, for example, has a pseudoguessing parameter (*c*) of 0.13. This value indicates that even individuals with extremely low theta will still have about a 13% chance of getting the item correct simply by guessing. The pseudoguessing parameter is most often needed with ability items and in other situations in which people would be motivated to guess, making it less common in personality assessment.

IRT models can vary along a variety of characteristics. The model that was used to generate the IRT in Figure 8.1 was the three-parameter logistic model (3PLM), which is useful for dichotomously scored items. Other models can be used to represent polytomous (i.e., more than two response options) items; these models have been useful for personality items which often have Likert response formats that are ordered with some anchors such as Strongly Disagree to Strongly Agree. Other IRT models have multiple latent traits that are used to determine item responses; these latter IRT models could be used for multidimensional data and might be useful for personality data, which are often more complex than cognitive ability data. Finally, there are other IRT models that combine latent class analysis with IRT models to identify different classes of respondents who use different processes to answer items. For more information about the basics of IRT, we refer the reader to Embretson and Reise (2000), DeAyala (1993), and Zickar (1998).

One of the advantages of IRT is that the increased precision and flexibility allow for advanced psychometric tools that, if used properly, can advance psychological knowledge as well as help in improving applications that involve testing. Advances in computerized adaptive testing as well as detection of item and test bias have profited greatly from the development of IRT. Two advances relevant to the faking problem that have benefited greatly from IRT have been appropriateness measurement and computational modeling. We will review both of these applications as well as review the research relevant to the faking problem.

Appropriateness Measurement

In confirmatory factor analysis, there is a lot of concern for testing overall model fit with various indexes used to determine whether the proposed model fits the observed data. In IRT, there are similar indexes that can be used to determine whether a particular model fits the data well or whether there are other models that might fit better. This approach of model–data fit is understood by most researchers when it applies to the fit of individual items or to models that represent that data. Appropriateness measurement looks at fit in another way, though. It automatically assumes that a particular model fits the data well overall. So, for example, the 3PLM might have been determined to be an acceptable way to characterize items for a particular personality inventory. Even though the model might have fit the overall sample fairly well, there is still the possibility that individual respondents might not fit the model acceptably. Appropriateness measurement takes into account how the data of individuals fit with the model.

These indexes are called person-fit statistics and can be construed similarly to outlier detection techniques such as those used in multiple regression and related techniques. Appropriateness indexes were first proposed to identify aberrant respondents who were cheating on an ability examination or were responding in a haphazard manner. For example, someone who responds as a below-average test taker for 80% of a mathematics examination but who cheats off his or her high-ability neighbor for 20% of the examination while the proctor leaves the room would have an inconsistent response pattern. For most of the test, he appears to be a low theta respondent but for a small number of items, he appears to be extremely high in ability. Similarly, a worker who does not understand English might complete a job attitudes inventory because of fear of being identified as not understanding the language. The worker's responses might appear extremely inconsistent to the best fitting model because he or she was not responding to the content of individual items; for some items he or she might appear to be strongly in favor of company policies whereas for others strongly against.

Appropriateness indexes work in a variety of ways. In general, though, they work by figuring out the maximum likelihood value of theta and then examining some version of the likelihood function that can be used to determine whether a level of theta is likely or unlikely. As a result, extreme values on the appropriateness index indicate that a particular respondent's pattern of responding does not fit the model. Based on these extreme values, test administrators may use these indexes to investigate reasons for the aberrance or may use that aberrance as evidence to dismiss particular test scores. There have been studies using appropriateness measurement to detect cheating on ability examinations (Drasgow, Levine, & McLaughlin, 1987), to identify individuals who are untraited (i.e., whose responses cannot be reliably mapped on a particular personality dimension) on personality inventories (Reise & Waller, 1990), to uncover inconsistent response patterns on cognitive measures (Tasuoka & Tasuoka, 1982), and even to assess the effects of test anxiety on responding (Birenbaum, 1986).

In terms of the faking problem, several researchers have proposed to use appropriateness measurement to identify fakers. The idea is that people who are faking will have high appropriateness indexes compared to those responding honestly. This is because people who engage in faking are purposely altering their natural response pattern to increase their scores. Appropriateness indexes should, then, be able to pick up on these altered patterns and alert examiners to their presence of intentional response distortion.

■ DETECTING FAKING USING APPROPRIATENESS MEASUREMENT: PREVIOUS RESEARCH

In this section, we would like to present a number of studies that have examined the use of IRT appropriateness indexes in relation to personality test faking. Specifically, we wish to highlight the successes and limitations found when appropriateness measurement techniques are used to detect faking. We will begin by outlining the first article in which appropriateness measurement was applied to faking detection and will then cover several articles examining this process with different appropriateness measurement subtypes.

Appropriateness Measurement and Faking: The Beginning

In the first study to investigate faking and appropriateness measurement, Zickar and Drasgow (1996) analyzed personality scales that were part of the Assessment of Background and Life Events (ABLE), a test designed to identify people likely to drop out of the military (White, Nord, Mael, & Young, 1993). The military had conducted an experiment in which they instructed respondents to either respond honestly or to "fake good" (answer in a way that would make them look the best to the Army); the fake good respondents were further randomly assigned to one of two groups: one which received no specific advice on how to fake and a group that received pretest coaching on how to effectively fake (Young, White, & Oppler, 1991). Zickar and Drasgow (1996) used dichotomous and polytomous IRT models to fit the data for the honest respondents and then conducted appropriateness measurement analyses to determine whether those indexes could be used to differentiate the coached and the ad-lib fakers (i.e., no instructions on how to fake) from the honest respondents. One limitation of their method was that it assumed that people in the instructed-honest condition responded in a manner similar to those people who respond honestly when applying for a job. As will be seen in a follow-up study, this assumption is probably not accurate.

One particularly important thing to consider when evaluating a device for identifying fakers is that it is necessary to examine the hit rate (i.e., the percentage of fakers correctly identified as fakers) in conjunction with the false-positive rate (i.e., the percentage of honest respondents incorrectly identified as fakers). There is a consistent relationship between these two rates: As hit rate increases, the false alarm rate will generally also rise. The question becomes what is the maximal false-positive rate that an organization (such as a testing company) is willing to tolerate and what is the corresponding hit rate at that false alarm rate. Most testing organizations are reluctant to label someone as a cheater or a faker unless there is strong, conclusive evidence to support that allegation.

Zickar and Drasgow found that appropriateness indexes, even under the best conditions, performed at about the same rate as a social desirability scale in terms of identifying fakers and neither technique performed particularly well. At 5% false alarm rates, the best scenario resulted in the detection of about 40% of those coached to fake good and about 20% of the ad lib fakers. They concluded that using appropriateness measurement, at least in their situation, was not a panacea for detecting faking but did warrant further research.

Standardized Log-Likelihood Index

Ferrando and Chico (2001) also examined the effectiveness of IRT models by comparing IRT methods with traditional social desirability techniques in detecting faking behavior on personality measures. Participants in Ferrando and Chico's study completed Spanish translations of the Extraversion, Neuroticism, and Psychoticism subscales of the Eysenck Personality Questionnaire–Revised (Aguilar, Tous, & Andrés, 1990) as well as Crowne and Marlowe's (1960) Social Desirability Scale. The Crowne and Marlow scale was intended to catch those respondents answering in a socially desirable but realistically unlikely manner (e.g., stating that you have never hurt another person's feelings). The undergraduate students completing the measures were randomly assigned to receive either standard completion instructions or instructions openly asking them to "fake good," or to answer in the way they thought would be seen as most desirable by employers.

When comparing the effectiveness of IRT to that of social desirability (SD) measures in detecting faking, Ferrando and Chico specifically examined an IRT fit statistic known as the standardized log-likelihood index, or *lz* index (Drasgow, Levine, & Williams, 1985). The *lz* index is similar to the general log-likelihood (*lo*) index in that it is based upon the idea that the likelihood function of a given response pattern will be larger when that response pattern fits with the overall IRT model and smaller when it is inconsistent. With either index, a pattern of responding that is consistent with the model will produce an index score that is larger and more positive whereas an inconsistent response pattern will produce a lower, negative score. Scores that are strongly negative are seen as possible indications of faking. The main reason for utilizing the *lz*, rather then the *lo*, index is that it is standardized, meaning that it is robust to the effects of test length and model choice and can be interpreted similarity to a z-score.

Ferrando and Chico used discriminant analyses to compare the relative effectiveness of *lz* indices and the SD measure method at detecting faked responses. Although the scores on the Extraversion, Neuroticism, and Psychoticism scores differed significantly across the two instruction conditions (indicating that significant faking had occurred), they concluded that the person-fit indices were unable to detect the faking to a practically useful extent. Furthermore, when compared, they indicated that the SD measures actually outperformed the person-fit indices in detecting faking. Although the detection accuracy of the *lz* indices were only about 10.2% above that expected by chance, the accuracy afforded by the SD method was approximately 78.6% higher than chance alone.

Hybrid Rasch-Latent Class Modeling

More recently, Holden and Brooks (2009) analyzed the ability of an IRT technique known as hybrid Rasch-latent class modeling to detect faking behavior. Undergraduate participants in Holden and Book's study were asked to imagine that they were being screened for entry into the military while completing the NEO-Five Factor Inventory personality measures (NEO-FFI; Costa & McCrae, 1992) and a set of social desirability measures from the Balanced Inventory of Desirable Responding (BIDR; Paulhus, 1998). They completed these measures under one of three instruction sets: standard responding, fake good (answer in such a way as to increase chances of being accepted into the military), and fake bad (answer in such a way as to decrease chances of being accepted into the military).

It was hypothesized that the use of the hybrid Rasch-latent class modeling technique would not only produce better detection of latent classes (i.e., would better distinguish among the three response patterns) but would provide incremental validity beyond use of social desirability measures as the sole method for detecting faking. This IRT technique combines the benefits of both traditional Rasch modeling and latent class modeling, thus allowing for a posteriori identification of subgroups and generation of item response patterns for individuals that are specific to their subgroup.

Holden and Brooks' results proved to be more promising than those of previous studies utilizing IRT for faking detection. Whether two or three classes were used, the hybrid Rasch-latent class model effectively distinguished those who were faking good from those who were responding in standard fashion or in an attempt to fake bad. Furthermore, the effectiveness of the IRT method added incremental validity above and beyond the use of the social desirability measures alone. Although generalizability to real-life, high-stakes situations, such as those encountered in a preemployment testing situation, could not be established, it was rightfully pointed out that the results of the study are encouraging for proponents of IRT.

Z_3 and F_2 Indexes

Brown and Harvey (2003) examined the effectiveness of two specific forms of appropriateness measurement, Z_3 and F_2, in detecting intentional faking. The former, Z_3 appropriateness measurement, involves generating an index based upon the height of the likelihood function after controlling for the fact that the maximum value of the likelihood function may vary across latent trait levels. A lower Z_3 index value indicates a lower maximum value of the likelihood function, which, in turn, indicates that the response pattern is not consistent with the item characteristics. The latter form of appropriateness measurement, F_2, involves the computation of an index based upon a comparison of a test taker's given responses to those predicted based upon the item characteristics and his or her estimated theta level. The higher the level of inconsistency between predicted and observed scores for a given test taker (the F_2 value), the greater the indication that the response pattern is not reflective of the test taker's true latent trait level. The internal inconsistencies indicated by decreased Z_3 values and increased F_2 values can be viewed as signs that response distortion is present.

Brown and Harvey (2003) used both forms of appropriateness measurement to try to detect two forms of induced faking in an undergraduate sample. Participants in the study were instructed to answer honestly or to fake either maximally (fake as positively as possible) or realistically (faking enough to improve one's score while still presenting a realistic profile) when completing the Agreeableness and Conscientiousness subscales from Brown's (1997) Five-Factor Model. The Z_3 and F_2 techniques were computed for all three groups to determine whether they effectively differentiated among them.

When used to detect maximal faking, neither appropriateness measurement technique proved significantly effective. Similar results were obtained when attempting to detect realistic faking. Despite the fact that those in the faking conditions did significantly increase their scores above the honest group, it was concluded that neither form of appropriateness measurement was particularly effective at detecting this faking behavior. As with Zickar and Drasgow's (1996) research, Brown and Harvey's (2003) study indicated that although appropriateness measurement shows promise for detecting faking, it is a method that requires further research and refinement before it can be considered truly effective and usable.

Harvey, Wilson, and Hansen (2005) conducted a study similar to Brown and Harvey's examination of the effectiveness of the Z_3 and F_2 indices. In this later study, state police officers completed the Responsibility subscale of the California Personality Inventory (Gough & Bradley, 1996) under two different sets of instructions. Participants were asked to answer as honestly as possible during the first testing period but to answer as if applying for a position as a state trooper during the second testing period. The latter set of instructions also included a statement indicating that faking to improve scores was an acceptable method of responding. The Z_3 and F_2 indices were then computed to determine whether they could successfully differentiate between the two conditions.

Participants' faked scores were as much as one full z-score unit higher than their honest scores, indicating that they were able to successfully engage in faking. Although F_2 index values did not differ significantly between the honest and faked conditions, Z_3 values were found to differ significantly; a higher average Z_3 score was found in the faked condition as opposed to the honest condition, an indication of possible faking. Although these results were promising, this statistically significant difference did not translate into a practically useful difference for identifying faking. This conclusion was reached due to the fact that any cutoff point created using either the Z_3 or the F_2 indices resulted in relatively equal numbers of hits and false positives.

■ WHAT MAKES A FAKER? UNDERSTANDING THE NATURE OF FAKING USING ITEM RESPONSE THEORY

Because the research discussed related to appropriateness measurement, each article was based upon the implicit assumption that the way in which people respond when faking on personality tests is different from the way they would respond when answering honestly. What most of that research fails to do, however, is to explain how the two types of respondents actually differ. The following studies attempt to come up with different item-level models for understanding the nature of the differences between faking and honest respondents. In all of these studies, the precision of IRT methods is used to better understand the nature of faking rather than simply attempting to find it.

Differential Item Functioning

Stark et al. (2001) used IRT to study faking behavior by looking for differential item functioning (DIF) and differential test functioning (DTF) in personality assessment data. When DIF or DTF is present, it is an indication that one or more items, or the scale in its entirety, are functioning differently for some participants. Specifically, DIF is present when the probability of endorsing an item varies for a subset of a sample and the remainder of the sample having the same standing on the latent trait of interest. DTF occurs when the overall test characteristic curves vary in such a fashion. Because those who fake an answer in a manner that is different from how they would answer when being honest, the presence of DIF and/ or DTF within a set of results could help to differentiate between honest and dishonest test takers.

Participants in the study of Stark et al. consisted of both job applicants and nonapplicants who completed all 16 subscales of the Sixteen Personality Factor

Questionnaire (16PF; Conn & Rieke, 1994), a commonly used general personality assessment. The job applicants completed the 16PF as part of the hiring process for a variety of different jobs, whereas the nonapplicants completed the same inventory in a research or clinical setting. All participants completed the survey under standard instructions; no faking instructions were given to any participants. The authors combined the data from both groups to conduct IRT analyses to determine if DIF and/or DTF were present. Of the 16 subscales in the 16PF, one of particular interest to the authors was the Impression Management (IM) scale. Flagging those with high IM scores is a more traditional method of detecting faking, so the authors incorporated and assessed this method by splitting the data into a high-IM group and a low-IM group for a second set of DIF/DTF analyses.

When compared across testing situations, each of the 15 non-IM personality scales contained a large proportion of items that exhibited DIF. Such results indicated that a significant number of individual items measured the underlying trait differently for applicants and nonapplicants. Furthermore, 13 of these 15 scales exhibited DTF, meaning that the entire scale functioned differently for each of these groups. The authors indicated that by dropping a handful of specific items from each scale, the DTF could often be eliminated. This meant that a certain subset of items from each scale was driving the DTF by favoring applicants over nonapplicants, or vice versa. Thus, these subsets could be used to identify test takers with varying response patterns. This showed promise for the possible use of these methods for identifying faking.

The authors' examination of the IM subscale revealed a similar but even stronger pattern of both DIF and DTF. The pattern in the IM scale indicated that although the measures were designed to tap in to impression management behaviors in both the applicant and nonapplicant situations, the items were actually measuring different underlying constructs for each group. Such results support previous research (Snell & Sydell, 1999) showing that the construct validity of IM measures can be negatively impacted when incentives or motivation factors are present. This calls into question the traditional use of IM measures for detecting faking and further establishes a case for using IRT methods to more finely differentiate among response patterns.

Zickar and Robie (1999) analyzed the same ABLE data previously analyzed by Zickar and Drasgow (1996). Instead of appropriateness measurement, though, they used DIF to better understand the differences between fakers and honest respondents. Zickar and Robie used Raju's (1988) DIF procedure, which allows for test-level DIF as well as item-level DIF. In addition, they supplemented the IRT analyses with confirmatory factor analyses that provided additional findings of interest.

Zickar and Robie (1999) found mean differences between fakers and nonfakers that replicate previous findings. One surprising finding was that the differences between faking and nonfaking conditions were minimal. That is, after accounting for the mean differences between conditions, IRFs were nearly similar for most items for both faking and nonfaking respondents. Items in general were no more discriminating. Zickar and Robie (1999) concluded that their results suggested that fakers tend to fake similarly for all items on the ABLE and that the primary difference was that fakers were less likely to answer using extremely negative options.

Another finding of note was that the confirmatory factor analysis results showed that there was an increase in the correlations between traits on different scales when people fake. In short, there is a common factor related to faking that increases the consistency of responses regardless of the content of items. When there is faking present, items will be influenced both by a scale-specific factor as well as a faking factor that is shared across different scales. Given the influence of this shared, common factor, scale-to-scale correlations are increased and, hence, the construct validity of scales is diminished. These results are consistent with previous research on faking (Schmit & Ryan, 1993) and explain the finding that faking increases the internal consistency (i.e., coefficient alpha) of tests.

Mixed-Model Item Response Theory

In this study, the authors further analyzed the ABLE data from Zickar and Drasgow (1996) and Zickar and Robie (1999), as well as data from the Personal Preferences Inventory (PPI) (Personnel Decisions International, 1997). The authors used mixed-model IRT, which combines latent class analysis with IRT. The analysis is similar to a DIF analysis except that groups are identified a posteriori instead of a priori. That is, in a DIF analysis, the researcher identifies two or more classes of respondents (e.g., fakers and honest individuals, or males and females) before the analysis and then examines IRFs to determine whether these two groups do actually differ significantly from each other. With mixed-model IRT, groups of respondents are identified in an exploratory process using a maximum likelihood procedure akin to cluster analysis. The a posteriori identified groups share similar response processes to the same items and it is the task of the researcher to identify the number of classes that best fit the data and then to determine the nature of the groups after the fact.

Zickar, Gibby, and Robie (2004) found that the experimental (PPI) data set was represented by three classes: an extreme faking class, a modest faking class, and a no faking class. By contrast, the operational (ABLE) data set was represented by two classes: a modest faking class and a no faking class. The most interesting finding was that the assignment of individuals to classes was not consistent with what should have been the logical assignment. That is, in the experimental data set, some respondents in the honest experimental condition were best fit in the modest faking data set and some respondents in the faking good experimental condition were best fit in the honest class. Similarly, in the operational data set, some applicants were best fit by the honest class and some incumbents were best fit in the modest faking class. These results are important because they suggest that rigid distinctions assumed in previous research are probably not accurate. Not all those assigned to faking conditions answer as if they are faking; similarly, not all incumbents respond honestly and not all applicants fake. These results corroborate what others have found using impression management scales (Rosse, Stecher, Miller, & Levin, 1998).

Overall, the authors concluded that mixed-model IRT was useful in identifying subpopulations within a data set that may represent faking behavior. Furthermore, mixed-model IRT appears to be able to more finely distinguish between mild and extreme forms of faking than previous non-IRT methods. Certainly, mixed-model IRT shows promise as a method for studying and identifying faking behavior both in applied settings and in future research on the subject. However, as with the previously reviewed articles, the results of Zickar et al. (2004) indicate that this method of IRT is not yet ready for deployment in practical settings. More research is necessary before we can conclude that mixed-model IRT is effective at detecting faking behavior on personality assessments.

■ COMPUTATIONAL MODELING OF THE EFFECTS OF FAKING

The previous research examined the nature of responding for respondents who were answering in an honest manner and those who were faking. The following research uses IRT to answer the question of what exactly happens when people do fake. Computational modeling is important in answering "what if" questions in scenarios in which there are a lot of unknowns. Given the secretive and uncertain nature of faking (e.g., very few people would admit to faking in actual settings), research surrounding the faking problem has many unknowns; questions are still unanswered about the nature of faking, the amount of faking that actually occurs in typical employment scenarios, and the types of individuals who fake, for instance. Computational modeling can help researchers speculate as to how a certain amount of faking that occurs will impact other outcomes. IRT is a nice framework to build computational modeling given that it provides a specific mathematical relationship between the latent trait and the probability of responding in a particular way for personality items. [The interested reader is referred to Zickar (2000) and Ilgen and Hulin (2000) for further information about computational modeling.]

The first computational modeling study of faking was conducted by Zickar (2000) and used the theta-shift model that approximated faking in the Zickar and Drasgow (1996) study. Using this IRT model, stochastic Monte Carlo studies were conducted to investigate the impact that faking had on the observed correlation between a personality test and a criterion variable. The percentage of fakers in a sample was varied from 0% to 100%, as was the magnitude of faking (i.e., the amount of the theta shift), and the true validity correlation.

Zickar (2000) found that the key variable was the percentage of fakers in a particular sample. If nearly all people in a sample were faking, there was little drop in the validity coefficient when comparing the observed correlation with the true correlation. Even in the worst scenarios though (i.e., 50% faking and 50% responding honestly and those who were faking were doing so in an extreme manner), the difference between the observed and true correlation was small (e.g., a drop of 0.10 from a true correlation of 0.30) and might be attributable to sampling error by many researchers. When ranking the top scorers, however, it was found that a disproportionate number of top scorers were faking, leading to the conclusion that fakers rise to the top. Conclusions from this research were that top-down selection was particularly vulnerable to the effects of faking and that the correlation coefficient measure was particularly insensitive to the effects of faking.

Komar, Brown, Komar, and Robie (2008) conducted a similar computational modeling investigation into faking. A Monte Carlo design was used to examine the effects of several faking-related variables on the validity of a personality assessment, specifically the NEO-FFI (Costa & McCrae, 1992) measure of conscientiousness; this measure was chosen as the focus of the article because it is generally regarded as the most important personality factor in predicting job performance (Barrick & Mount, 1991) and is often the most fakable of the personality factors (McFarland & Ryan, 2000). The authors included a total of six variables in their Monte Carlo faking investigation: variability in faking across participants, magnitude of faking, proportion of respondents faking, correlation between faking and conscientiousness, correlation between faking and performance, and selection ratio.

When the impact of these variables on the conscientiousness scale was assessed, all six variables showed at least some impact on validity, either directly or as part of an interaction. However, the authors found that four of the six variables exerted truly marked effects: faking-performance correlation (having the strongest overall relationship with validity), proportion of fakers in the sample, magnitude of faking, and faking-conscientiousness correlation. The effects were often complex, but in general, an increase in any of the four resulted in a decrease in validity. The significant effects found by the authors were strong enough that they could not be attributed to sampling error alone.

The authors point out that the results related to the faking–performance correlation have several indications for research and practices related to faking. The relationship between validity and the faking–performance correlation provides support for the idea that faking may be more detrimental when hiring for positions in which performance could be expected to be negatively impacted by faking (e.g., when the traits that allow a person to successfully fake could be harmful or undesirable in the job). Conversely, it may be less of an issue when hiring for positions that would not be impacted by faking-related behaviors. Thus, the "faking problem" may not actually *be* a problem if a person possessing qualities allowing for strong faking would be more successful.

■ LESSONS LEARNED AND FUTURE RESEARCH

The research surveyed in this chapter seemed appropriate to discuss in that each applied new psychometric techniques to try to answer existing research questions that had defied clear answers using previous techniques. Much of this research seemed disheartening, though, in that the results using sophisticated IRT methodology failed to provide much more clarity to the faking problem. These methods still seem promising in theory, but research to date has not provided sufficient support for their use in applied settings. Despite this cynicism, though, we believe that there are some important lessons to be learned from this research and some important findings that on which to build.

Lesson 1: Item Response Theory Forces Us to Focus on the Appropriate Level of Analysis

IRT provides a systematic way for researchers to think clearly and specifically about how individual respondents fake at the item level. The item is the appropriate level of analysis in that respondents must confront items individually, going through a test in a systematic, item-by-item manner. Techniques that focus on the scale level (e.g., experiments that focus only on mean scale scores across conditions) might miss much of the richness of the data that is possible at the item level.

Having said that, IRT research has, thus far, failed to advance the understanding of how individuals respond, item to item, when faking (or when responding honestly, for that matter). For example, none of the DIF studies previously discussed was able to find content features that differentiated between items that were heavily faked and those items that were resistant to faking. Future research should consider linking content features to the fakability of particular tests. There has been one study, Zickar and Ury (2002), that investigated content features of personality items and how they correlated with IRT parameter estimates, although they did not investigate the context of faking. They did find, however, that ratings of item social desirability were related to item parameters in an interactive way with transparency. There were large effects on item parameter estimates when items were transparent (i.e., their wording made the underlying construct of interest relatively easy to determine) and socially desirable. Future research, however, should pursue this idea in a faking context.

Lesson 2: People Do Not Fake in a Single Way

The study of Zickar et al. (2004) demonstrated that individuals do not use the same process when responding to a personality inventory, even if they are in the same experimental condition. Even considering applicants versus incumbents, the distinction is not as clear as previous conceptualizations of faking have assumed. The mixture-model IRT approach allowed for better investigation of the differences. Further research needs to be conducted so that we can better understand the number and nature of the different classes of respondents to personality inventories. Research conducted by McFarland and others (McFarland & Ryan, 2000, 2001; Snell, Sydell, & Lueke, 1999) on the antecedents of faking might provide some understanding of why different people belong in different classes.

Early conceptualizations of faking (e.g., Zickar, 2000) used for computational modeling were too simplistic. The idea that fakers and honest respondents use the same process except that they differ only in terms of a theta shift is inconsistent with this more current research. Further work needs to be conducted to incorporate the idea of more diversity in the styles and processes that people use when faking (and when responding honestly; see also Chapters 2, 4, and 6).

Lesson 3: To Detect Faking You Need a Good Model of Faking

The poor detection rates of appropriateness measurement are not surprising in that all of the IRT appropriateness measurement studies are based on the simple assumption that fakers respond differently than honest respondents. The findings of Zickar et al. (2004), as well as those of other researchers who have examined variations in faking on personality inventories (Rosse et al., 1998), support the idea that faking behavior is not black and white; even honest respondents do not use a single process when faking. To increase the detection of faking, researchers will need better models of faking. Appropriateness techniques such as Levine and Drasgow's (1988) optimal appropriateness measurement can be used to identify whether a particular pattern of responses better fits a profile of honest respondents or a profile of faking respondents. To do so, however, researchers will need a better and more specific model of faking.

Lesson 4: The Demands for Test Construction Need to Be Modified When Considering Faking Detection

There is a movement in testing to develop the most efficient psychological measures by reducing the number of items that are needed for a scale while maintaining acceptable levels of internal consistency. For example, Donnellan, Oswald, Baird, and Lucas (2006) came up with minimarker scales for the Big Five personality dimensions that had only four items per dimension (cut down from the usual 10). Each of the items was chosen from a broader pool of items and even though the number of items was less than half of what was originally used, each dimension had reasonable internal consistency (i.e., $\alpha > 0.60$). Other studies have focused on how to reduce scale length using sophisticated psychometric techniques (Stanton, Sinar, Balzer, & Smith, 2002). This is important as respondents have shorter attention spans while completing online questionnaires and as our research questions become increasingly more complex, there is an increased demand for multivariate investigations.

Using appropriateness measurement to detect faking, however, will require different considerations when designing personality inventories. First, the length requirements are more important for appropriateness measurement compared to developing a test only for coming up with a total score. Monte Carlo studies on the accuracy of appropriateness measurement indexes show that test length is a primary consideration (Reise & Due, 1991). Appropriateness measurement works better with scales of 20 items or more. In addition, there should be a range of items that vary in difficulty as well as fakability. There should be some items that are difficult to fake and others that would be relatively easy to fake. If all items are easy to fake, it becomes difficult to separate those who are faking a test from those who are legitimately extremely high on a particular trait. We believe that faking detection might increase if a test were designed with these considerations in mind.

■ CONCLUSIONS

To date, there has been a modest amount of research using IRT to better understand the nature of faking as well as to detect faking. Of these studies, a few have used IRT to model the effects of faking. In general, though, this research has yielded few tangible dividends that can be used to solve the "faking problem." The research does suggest, however, some avenues for future study that may prove helpful in solving this difficult problem. In this chapter, we have provided some concrete suggestions that we believe may lead future researchers to make more progress. We do not know if there is a unicorn out there, but we have done our best to provide a map to find the unicorn *if it exists!*

References

Aguilar, A., Tous, J. M., & Andrés, A. (1990). Adaptación y estudio psicométrico del EPQ-R [Adaptation and psychometric analysis of the EPQ-R]. *Anuario de Psicología, 46*, 101–118.

Barrick, M. R., & Mount, M. K. (1991). The Big Five personality dimensions and job performance: A meta-analysis. *Personnel Psychology, 44*, 1–26.

Birenbaum, M. (1986). Effect of dissimulation motivation and anxiety on response pattern appropriateness measures. *Applied Psychological Measurement, 10*, 167–174.

Brown, R. D. (1997). *The development of a computer adaptive test of the five factor model of personality: Applications and extensions.* Unpublished doctoral dissertation, Virginia Polytechnic Institute and State University.

Brown, R. D., & Harvey, R. J. (2003, April). *Detecting personality test faking with appropriateness measurement: Fact or fantasy?* Paper presented at the 2003 Annual Conference of the Society for Industrial and Organizational Psychology, Orlando.

Conn, S. R., & Rieke, M. L. (Eds.). (1994). *The 16PF fifth edition technical manual.* Champaign, IL: Institute for Personality and Ability Testing.

Costa, P. T., & McCrae, R. R. (1992). *Revised NEO Personality Inventory and NEO Five-Factor Inventory.* Odessa, FL: Psychological Assessment Resources.

Crowne, D. P., & Marlowe, D. (1960). A new scale of social desirability independent of psychopathology. *Journal of Consulting Psychology, 24*, 349–354.

DeAyala, R. J. (1993). An introduction to polytomous item response theory models. *Measurement and Evaluation in Counseling and Development, 25*, 172–189.

Donnellan, M. B., Oswald F. L., Baird B. M., & Lucas R. E. (2006). The Mini-IPIP scales: Tiny-yet-effective measures of the big five factors of personality. *Psychological Assessment, 18*, 192–203.

Drasgow, F., Levine, M. V., & McLaughlin, M. E. (1987). Detecting inappropriate test scores with optimal and practical appropriateness indices. *Applied Psychological Measurement, 11*, 59–79.

Drasgow, F., Levine, M. V., & Williams, E. A. (1985). Appropriateness measurement with polychotomous item response models and standardized indices. *British Journal of Mathematical and Statistical Psychology, 38*, 67–86.

Embretson, S. E., & Reise, S. P. (2000). *Item response theory for psychologists (Multivariate Applications Series).* New York: LEA, Inc.

Ferrando, P. J., & Chico, E. (2001). Detecting dissimulation in personality test scores: A comparison between person-fit indices and detection scales. *Educational and Psychological Measurement, 61*, 997–1012.

Gough, H. G., & Bradley. P. (1996). *CPI manual.* Palo Alto, CA: Consulting Psychologists Press.

Harvey, R. J., Wilson, M. A., & Hansen, R. L. (2005, April). *Detecting CPI faking in a police sample: A cautionary note.* Paper presented at the 2005 Annual Conference of the Society for Industrial and Organizational Psychology, Los Angeles.

Holden, R. R., & Brooks, A. S. (2009). Using hybrid Rasch-latent class modeling to improve the detection of fakers on a personality inventory. *Personality and Individual Difference, 47*, 185–190.

Ilgen, D. R., & Hulin, C. L. (2000). *Computational modeling of behavior in organizations: The third scientific discipline.* Washington, D.C.: American Psychological Association.

Komar, S., Brown, D. J., Komar, J. A., & Robie, C. (2008). Faking and the validity of conscientiousness: A Monte Carlo investigation. *Journal of Applied Psychology, 93,* 140–154.

Levine, M. V., & Drasgow, F. (1988). Optimal appropriateness measurement. *Psychometrika, 53,* 161–176.

McFarland, L. A., & Ryan, A. M. (2000). Variance in faking across noncognitive measures. *Journal of Applied Psychology, 85,* 812–821.

McFarland, L. A., & Ryan, A. M. (2001, April). *Toward an integrated model of applicant faking behavior.* Paper presented at the 2001 conference of the Society for Industrial and Organizational Psychology, San Diego, CA.

Personnel Decisions International. (1997). *Selection systems test scale manual.* Unpublished document. Minneapolis, MN: Author.

Paulhus, D. L. (1998). *Paulhus Deception Scales: The Balanced Inventory of Socially Desirable Responding-7 User's Manual.* North Tonawanda, NY: Multi-Healthy Systems Inc.

Raju, N. S. (1988). The area between two item characteristics curves. *Psychometrika, 53,* 495–502.

Reise, S. P., & Due, A. M. (1991). The influence of test characteristics on the detection of aberrant response patterns. *Applied Psychological Measurement, 15,* 217–226.

Reise, S. P., & Waller, N. G. (1990). Fitting the two-parameter model to personality data. *Applied Psychological Measurement, 14,* 45–58.

Rosse, J. G., Stecher, M. D., Miller, J. L., & Levin, R. A. (1998). The impact of response distortion on preemployment personality testing and hiring decisions. *Journal of Applied Psychology, 83,* 634–644.

Schmit, M. J., & Ryan, A. M. (1993). The Big Five in personnel selection: Factor structure in applicant and nonapplicant populations. *Journal of Applied Psychology, 78,* 966–974.

Snell, A. F., & Sydell, E. J. (1999, April). *Do impression management scores adequately measure intentional response distortion?* Paper presented at the 14th Annual Conference of the Society for Industrial and Organizational Psychology, Atlanta, GA.

Snell, A. F., Sydell, E. J., & Lueke, S. B. (1999). Towards a theory of applicant faking: Integrating studies of deception. *Human Resource Management Review, 9,* 219–242.

Stanton, J. M., Sinar, E. F., Balzer, W. K., & Smith, P. C. (2002). Issues and strategies for reducing the length of self-report scales. *Personnel Psychology, 55,* 167–194.

Stark, S., Chernyshenko, O. S., Chan, K. Y., Lee, W. C., & Drasgow, F. (2001). Effect of the testing situation on item responding: Cause for concern. *Journal of Applied Psychology, 86,* 943–953.

White, L. A., Nord, R. D., Mael, F. A., & Young, M. C. (1993). The Assessment of Background and Life Experiences (ABLE). In T. Trent & J. H. Laurence (Eds.), *Adaptability screening for the armed forces* (pp. 101–162). Washington, D.C.: Office of Assistant Secretary of Defense (Force Management and Personnel).

Young, M. C., White, L. A., & Oppler, S. H. (1991, October). Coaching effects on the Assessment of Background and Life Experiences (ABLE). *Proceedings of the 33rd annual conference of the Military Testing Association,* 446–451, San Antonio, TX.

Zickar, M. J. (1998). Modeling item-level data with item response theory. *Current Directions in Psychological Science, 7,* 104–109.

Zickar, M. J. (2000). Modeling faking on personality tests. In D. R. Ilgen & C. L. Hulin (Eds.), *Computational modeling of behavior in organizations: The third scientific discipline* (pp. 95–113). Washington, D.C.: American Psychological Association.

Zickar, M. J., & Broadfoot, A. A. (2009). The partial revival of a dead horse. Comparing classical test theory and item response theory. In C. E. Lance & R. J. Vandenberg (Eds.), *Statistical and methodological myths and urban legends: Doctrine, verity and fable in the organizational and social sciences* (pp. 37–59). New York: Routledge/Taylor & Francis.

Zickar, M. J., & Drasgow, F. (1996). Detecting faking on a personality instrument using appropriateness measurement. *Applied Psychological Measurement, 20,* 71–87.

Zickar, M. J., & Gibby, R. E. (2006). A history of faking and socially desirable responding on personality tests. In R. L. Griffith & M. H. Peterson (Eds.), *A closer examination of applicant faking behavior* (pp. 21–42). Greenwich, CT: Information Age Publishing.

Zickar, M. J., Gibby, R. E., & Robie, C. (2004). Uncovering faking sample in applicant, incumbent, and experimental data sets: An application of mixed-model item response theory. *Organizational Research, 7,* 168–190.

Zickar, M. J., & Robie, C. (1999). Modeling faking good on personality items: An item-level analysis. *Journal of Applied Psychology, 84,* 551–563.

Zickar, M. J., & Ury, K. L. (2002). Developing an interpretation of item parameters for personality items: Content correlates of parameter estimates. *Educational and Psychological Measurement, 62,* 19–31.

9 Methods for Correcting for Faking

■ MATTHEW C. REEDER AND ANN MARIE RYAN

Over the past 20 years, self-report measures of personality have regained interest from selection practitioners and researchers alike. The enthusiasm surrounding personality measurement can be attributed to a number of factors, including widespread acceptance of the five-factor model (FFM) as a potentially useful perspective on the domain of trait-based personality attributes (Tett & Christiansen, 2007), empirical evidence suggesting that personality measures have the potential to be valid predictors of performance and other organizationally relevant criteria (e.g., Barrick & Mount, 1991; Hurtz & Donovan, 2000; Ones, Dilchert, Viswesvaran, & Judge, 2007), and empirical evidence demonstrating that personality measures often evince small subgroup differences (e.g., Foldes, Duehr, & Ones, 2008; Hough, Oswald, & Ployhart, 2001) relative to other common methods in personnel selection.

Despite the resurgence of interest regarding the employment of self-report personality scales in selection settings, such measures have drawn criticism on a number of grounds. Among these criticisms is the ongoing debate regarding the extent to which socially desirable responding (SDR) or faking occurs with self-report noncognitive measures and whether its impact is deleterious to selection outcomes. Concerns about the impact of faking have been discussed in light of a number of domains, including construct validity (Barrick & Mount, 1996; Schmit & Ryan, 1993; Stark, Chernyshenko, Chan, Lee, & Drasgow, 2001), criterion-related validity (e.g., Marcus, 2006; White, Young, Hunter, & Rumsey, 2008), rank ordering of applicants and hiring decisions (Christiansen, Goffin, Johnston, & Rothstein, 1994; Mueller-Hanson, Heggestad, & Thornton, 2003), personality measure development and implementation (Haaland & Christiansen, 1998; Mueller-Hanson et al., 2003; Stark et al., 2001), and fairness and ethicality in selection practice (Hough, 1998; Morgeson, Campion, Dipboye, Hollenbeck, Murphy, & Schmitt, 2007). Chapters 2–5 in this volume address these points of debate.

In light of these potential consequences, a number of approaches have been developed or adapted to counter the effects of SDR when utilizing self-report noncognitive measures in operational settings. Such approaches can be categorized into two broad groups. *Proactive approaches* entail preventative characteristics built into the measurement process prior to administration intended to reduce the extent to which applicants fake. Examples include warnings or instructions, subtle or nontransparent items, alternative response formats and measurement methods, item selection on the basis of social desirability ratings, and item ordering. These approaches generally aim to reduce the motivation to distort, increase the difficulty of successfully distorting, or both. Chapters 12–15 in this volume describe these preventive strategies in some detail.

Reactive approaches to managing SDR include methods designed to counteract the effects of SDR after the measures have been administered and data have been collected. The first task in a reactive approach is detection, or employing measures believed to tap individual differences in SDR to identify either (1) variance in trait scores believed to be attributed to SDR, or (2) individual cases or subsets of cases that are suspected to have distorted responses. Detection techniques fall into two groups: external and internal. External approaches to detection rely on information obtained from measures administered in addition to the substantive trait measure and are employed for the sole purpose of detecting response distortion. The most prominent example of external detection approaches involves social desirability scales, which are generally designed to measure response distortion via self-report items keyed for either socially desirable and feasible responses or socially desirable and unlikely responses (Birenbaum & Montag, 1989). Table 9.1 lists several common social desirability scales with example items. Bogus item scales (e.g., Anderson, Warner, & Spencer, 1984; Pannone, 1984), another external detection approach, consist of items that require respondents to indicate the extent of their knowledge or experience with concepts, material, or equipment that appear, on the surface, to be relevant and desirable for a given job, but are nonexistent in reality (O'Connell, Kung, & Tristan, 2006; see also Chapter 10).

Internal detection approaches, or what Zickar and Drasgow (1996) refer to as internal aberrance detection techniques, use information derived from the substantive personality measure of interest (e.g., item response characteristics) in order to detect response distortion. A number of factors have contributed to the recent development of internal detection approaches, including greater utilization of computerized testing, continued advancement in psychological measurement methods, and discontent with the results observed with external detection techniques. Examples of internal detection techniques include indices derived from item response theory (IRT) and mixed-model IRT; measures of the covariance among trait personality items; response latencies, or measures of the time required by applicants to respond to personality items; and unusual, or idiosyncratic, response patterns. Methods of detection are discussed in greater depth in Chapters 7 and 8.

TABLE 9.1 *Common Social Desirability Scales and Example Items*

Scale	Example Item(s)
Balanced Inventory of Desirable Responding	My first impressions of other people are always right. (*Self-Deceptive Enhancement*) I don't gossip about other people's business. (*Impression Management*)
Edwards Social Desirability Scale	People often disappoint me.
Eysenck Personality Questionnaire: Lie Scale	Do you sometimes put off until tomorrow what you ought to do today?
Marlowe–Crowne Social Desirability Scale	I have never intensely disliked anyone.
Sackeim and Gur: Self-Deception Questionnaire and Other-Deception Questionnaire	Have you ever thought about committing suicide in order to get back at someone? (*Self-Deception*) I always apologize to others for my mistakes. (*Other-Deception*)
Unlikely Virtues Scale	Have you ever been grouchy with someone?
Wiggins Social Desirability Scale	Sometimes at elections I vote for candidates I know little about.

Once the task of detection has been carried out, there is a decision to be made as to what to do with that information. A number of options are available, ranging from simply being aware that response distortion may be present in the data to the employment of score adjustments that attempt to remove variance believed to be attributed to SDR. We define correction methods broadly as strategies employed with the intent of either (1) reducing or eliminating construct-irrelevant variance in self-report measures attributed to SDR, or (2) removing individual cases suspected to have distorted responses from the larger overall sample. Detection and correction methods are applied in tandem in an attempt to solve the problem of response distortion: Methods of detection seek to ascertain if and where the problem resides; methods of correction seek to ameliorate the problem.

The purpose of the present chapter is to review the literature on correction methodologies and to discuss issues related to their application. First, we provide an overview of ways in which SDR may relate to other variables of interest in a selection context (i.e., predictors and criteria) to provide a point from which to think about and evaluate methods of correction. Second, we review research on SDR correction strategies. The lion's share of the work in the area of correction pertains to social desirability scales; thus, we devote more space to the application of social desirability scales in correction than to discussing other methods. Finally, we conclude the chapter by discussing general issues when considering detection and correction methods. Note that the present discussion focuses on the correction of positive response bias, which has a number of labels (e.g., socially desirable responding, impression management, unlikely virtues, faking, lying). The most common label pertaining to response distortion in applied settings appears to be socially desirable responding. Thus, while acknowledging theoretical differences of degree or form, we subsume all under the label SDR or response distortion for the sake of consistency. Similarly, the literature has provided a number of labels for self-report measures designed to detect respondents who may be responding in a desirable manner (e.g., social desirability scales, response distortion scales, validity scales). We will use these terms interchangeably, as no sharp distinctions appear to have been drawn in the literature to this point.

■ STATISTICAL PERSPECTIVES ON THE EFFECTS OF SOCIALLY DESIRABLE RESPONDING

Ganster, Hennessey, and Luthans (1983) and Ones, Viswesvaran, and Reiss (1996) discuss ways in which SDR may affect relationships between substantive variables of interest, including suppression, moderation, spuriousness, and mediation. Of these, suppression and moderation are the most commonly researched perspectives relevant to selection practice and research. Thus, the present treatment focuses on these two frameworks.

The SDR-as-a-Suppressor Perspective

The view of SDR as a suppressor is a longstanding framework within the response distortion literature (e.g., Barrick & Mount, 1996; Li & Bagger, 2006; Meehl &

Hathaway, 1946). Conger (1974) viewed a suppressor as "a variable which increases the predictive validity of another variable (or set of variables) by its inclusion in a regression equation. This variable is a suppressor only for those variables whose regression weights are increased" (p. 35). For present purposes, SDR would be the suppressor variable and the substantive personality predictor of interest would be the suppressant from which nonerror, irrelevant variance (viz., response distortion) is removed by SDR.

Although suppression can take on several forms (classical, negative, reciprocal; for additional information, refer to Conger, 1974; Conger & Jackson, 1972), most often the focus in socially desirable responding is on classical suppression (e.g., Ones et al., 1996). Figure 9.1 provides an illustration of classical suppression in the context of SDR. Defined strictly, a classical suppressor is positively correlated with the substantive predictor measure and orthogonal to the criterion measure. Classical suppressors function by removing nonerror, irrelevant variance from the substantive predictor; as a result, classical suppression is observed in situations in which the standardized coefficient for the predictor is larger than its zero-order validity, while the standardized coefficient for the suppressor is negative despite the suppressor being uncorrelated with the criterion (Conger, 1974; Conger & Jackson, 1972; Lubin, 1957; Meehl, 1945). The K scale of the Minnesota Multiphasic Personality Inventory (MMPI), one of the most well-researched validity scales in the response distortion literature, was originally developed to be a suppressor variable in the classical sense (Meehl & Hathaway, 1946).

Taking this perspective, the emergence of classical suppression is dependent upon the magnitudes of the correlations between the predictor and the suppressor,

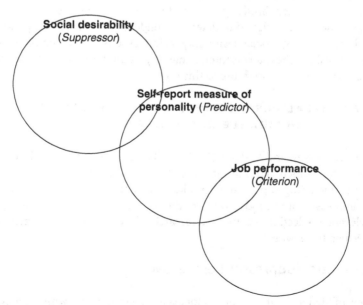

Figure 9.1 An illustration of classical suppression in the context of social desirability.

between the predictor and the criterion, and between the criterion and the suppressor (Conger & Jackson, 1972). That is, for classical suppression to occur, correlations between the predictor and both the suppressor and the criterion should be sizable in magnitude. In the event that either of these relationships (suppressor–predictor, predictor–criterion) is not strong, the weakening effects on suppression can be offset by a stronger correlation between the other set of measures (e.g., the predictor–suppressor correlation), although large increases are required.

Many researchers test the hypothesis that SDR acts as a suppressor by either computing predictor–criterion correlations after partialing out SDR via part correlation or multiple regression, or by first regressing the trait measure on the response distortion scale and then using the residualized score as a predictor. However, classical suppression is not likely to be a feasible alternative for at least two reasons: (1) correlations between personality and performance are often not large enough for suppression to have an effect; (2) correlations between response distortion and personality are also often not large enough. For a simple illustration, let us assume that the predictor–suppressor correlation reflects shared variance between personality and SDR that is completely unrelated to performance, and that the suppressor–criterion relationship is zero. Using an estimated Conscientiousness-Impression Management corrected correlation of 0.42 (Li & Bagger, 2006) and an estimated Conscientiousness-Performance corrected correlation of 0.22 (Hurtz & Donovan, 2000), the Conscientiousness-Performance correlation would be expected to increase to 0.242 after controlling for SDR, an increment of 0.022 (based on the formulas provided by Conger & Jackson, 1972). To increase the Conscientiousness-Performance correlation to 0.30, the correlation between Conscientiousness and Impression Management would have to be in the area of 0.68. This shared variance between Conscientiousness and Impression Management would also have to be entirely criterion irrelevant. For constructs demonstrating smaller predictor–criterion or predictor–suppressor relationships, the increment obtained after controlling for impression management (IM) would be smaller than that shown above. Also, we note that the liberties that we have taken here (e.g., applying corrected correlations that are larger in magnitude than the uncorrected correlations) will overestimate the increments that can be expected when partialing out SDR or adjusting scores for response distortion in operational settings.

The present example highlights two important points pertaining to methods of correction. First, we should temper our optimism in hoping for large increments in validity when applying practices stemming from a suppression perspective (e.g., trait score adjustments on the basis of scores on measures of response distortion). Except in cases in which predictor–criterion or predictor–suppressor relationships are relatively strong in magnitude, it is not reasonable to expect large gains in validity when approaches based on suppression are adopted. Second, our example assumed suppressor-criterion correlations of zero. Generally speaking, corrective methods based on SDR as a suppressor will exert diminishing gains as the suppressor–criterion correlation increases. Thus, when our aim is to use measures of SDR as suppressor variables, effort should be made to construct the response distortion measures to be as orthogonal to the criterion as possible.

The SDR-as-a-Moderator Perspective

Although a sizable body of research has adopted an SDR-as-a-suppressor perspective, SDR has also been studied as a moderator in the relationship between personality and performance (e.g., Christiansen, Robie, & Bly, 2005; Holden, 2008; Hough, 1998; Hough, Eaton, Dunnette, Kamp, & McCloy, 1990). Unlike the suppression case, the measure of SDR is not employed explicitly to remove irrelevant variance in the predictor measure; rather, the relationship between personality and performance is simply expected to vary as a function of SDR in the sample of interest. Furthermore, the extent of intercorrelation between the moderator and the predictor (or moderator and criterion) is not of central importance. Finally, Ganster and colleagues (1983) suggest that perspectives of SDR as a moderator and as a suppressor are mutually exclusive, that is, SDR may not serve as both moderator and suppressor in the same situation.

■ METHODS FOR CORRECTION OF RESPONSE DISTORTION

Defining "correction method" rather broadly, our review of the literature uncovered four strategies that have been discussed or researched in the literature. These include the following:

(1) *Residualized or rational score adjustments*: Modifications to substantive personality scores as a function of one's standing on the detection measure.
(2) *Removal of cases*: Elimination of cases from the dataset or removal of applicants from the selection process due to high standing on a detection method.
(3) *Retesting/Verification Testing*: Readministration of the personality measure to applicants flagged as potentially inflating on the first administration of the substantive personality measure.
(4) *Interpret results cautiously*: Cautious application of the results observed on the trait personality measure despite the respondent's standing on the detection measure.

Of the methods described above, the first three generally qualify as methods of correction. The fourth method, caution in interpreting results, could be viewed as corrective if scores on the detection measure are applied in some way (e.g., obtaining further data during a subsequent interview to corroborate personality scores of applicants with extreme scores on response distortion scales), but this does not seem to have been addressed extensively.

Score adjustments and the removal of cases can be distinguished by how each is believed to reduce the impact of SDR. As alluded to earlier, score adjustments imply that SDR acts as a suppressor. The intention with score adjustments is to extract or reduce nonerror components associated with response distortion from the substantive trait measure. Oftentimes, in this case, correction is done by regressing the substantive trait scale on the response distortion measure to derive corrected trait scores. The removal of applicants attempts to correct from a different perspective. Aside from suggesting a dichotomous, all-or-nothing approach (i.e., applicants either are or are not faking), this method of correction lies closer to the SDR-as-a-moderator perspective. Cases falling above some established point in the distribution of scores on the response distortion measure (e.g., cases with observed scores greater than three standard deviations above the mean on a measure of response distortion) are flagged, based on the rationale that trait measure scores for such cases may be viewed as questionable. For these flagged cases, it is assumed that relationships between the trait measure and other measures of interest (e.g., measures of job performance) are expected to differ substantially from cases that have not been flagged.

Evaluating Correction Methods

Score Adjustments

A sizable number of studies have assessed the outcomes associated with adjusting scores on substantive trait measures on the basis of response distortion scales. The majority of this research reports negligible effects on criterion-related validity for trait measures when score adjustments are made (e.g., Borkenau & Ostendorf, 1992; Christiansen et al., 1994; Dudley et al., 2005; Hough, 1998). These findings are corroborated by two meta-analyses investigating the effects of partialing SDR out of personality–performance relationships (Li & Bagger, 2006; Ones et al., 1996). In both cases, criterion-related validities for FFM constructs decreased slightly when partialing variance attributable to SDR out of the predictor–criterion correlation.

Studies addressing other outcomes of score adjustments are somewhat sparse. One area that has received attention pertains to the impact of score correction on applicant rank ordering and hiring decisions. Christiansen and colleagues (1994) found that when trait scores obtained from the Sixteen Personality Factor Questionnaire (16PF) were adjusted for response distortion, rank-order position changed for over 85% of the sample, including cases whose trait scores were not affected by the correction, but whose position shifted by virtue of other cases moving above or below them. The researchers also found that the number of discrepant selection decisions (i.e., situations in which a subject would have been selected based on their observed score, but would not have been selected based on his or her adjusted score, and vice versa) varied as a function of the selection ratio, such that there was a larger number of discrepant selection decisions at lower selection ratios. Similar findings were reported by Rosse et al. (1998), who found that the rank ordering of job applicants was far different when scores on the NEO-PI-R Conscientiousness scale were adjusted than when they were not. Thus, it appears that applying score adjustments to correct for response distortion may have some impact on hiring decisions. However, whether such decisions are necessarily more accurate than those based on observed scores has yet to be addressed extensively (although see Ellingson et al., 1999 for findings suggesting that score adjustments appear to do little to alter the proportion of correct selection decisions).

Finally, we located one study investigating the effects of correcting via score adjustments on the construct validity of trait measures in an applied setting. Ellingson and colleagues (1999) found that trait scores for those in a fake-good condition were highly correlated, resulting in a unidimensional structure, which the authors suggested reflected social desirability. Scores from an honest condition, on the other hand, resulted in a multidimensional structure that more closely resembled the hypothesized structure underlying the personality inventory employed (the ABLE). This multidimensional structure was not regained as a result of applying adjustments for response distortion to the fake-good condition scores; adjusted scores yielded a unidimensional structure similar to that of the observed scores from the fake-good condition.

In summary, although score adjustments seem likely to result in an altered rank ordering of applicants and potentially different hiring decisions compared to observed scores, they also appear to be largely ineffective in improving construct or criterion-related validity. Note that research on score adjustments based on other detection methods (e.g., IRT, response latencies) is generally lacking so their effectiveness has not been established.

Removal of Cases

Much of the research pertaining to the outcomes associated with removing cases has focused on criterion-related validity. Results in this area are somewhat inconsistent, although effects found in field settings are often rather small. Some studies report supportive findings (e.g., Pannone, 1984, White et al., 2008), while others report either mixed results or no increase in validity (e.g., Borkenau & Ostendorf, 1992; Christiansen et al., 2005; Dudley et al., 2005; Hough, 1998; Hough et al., 1990). Holden (2007, 2008) suggests that while response distortion scales may be valid indicators of faking (i.e., classifying those who fake versus those who do not), moderation effects are often not found. Holden goes on to argue this may be either because of relatively low power stemming from an imbalanced distribution of faking versus nonfaking respondents or because response distortion measures are simply not "up to the psychometric challenge of moderating validity" (p. 196). If such findings generalize to applied settings, the implication would be that while response distortion scales may accurately detect those who are faking, it may not necessarily be the case that validity, as indexed by a correlation, will be improved when such cases are removed.

Outcomes aside from criterion-related validity have also been explored. Christiansen and colleagues (2005) found that although criterion-related validity was appreciably lower for cases flagged as potentially faking versus those not flagged when an item-covariance method was used for detection ($r = -0.09$ versus $r = 0.20$, respectively), cases flagged still had higher mean job performance ratings compared with cases whose scores were identified as being valid. The difference was not, however, significant. In a simulation study, Schmitt and Oswald (2006) found that removing applicants from a selection process on the basis of faking scores had a negligible effect on both criterion-related validity and mean job performance. Hough (1998) compared the effects of removing respondents from an applicant pool on the basis of scores on the Unlikely Virtues (UV) scale in terms of hiring decisions across three samples, with highly variable results (i.e., 90%, 69% or 54% of those hired based on observed scores were also hired after removing cases on the basis of UV scores in three large samples).

Thus, research on the removal of cases as a corrective strategy has generally produced unsupportive or inconsistent findings, depending on the detection method applied and the outcome being explored (e.g., criterion-related validity, hiring decisions). In addition, concerns associated with the application of this practice yield practical complications. From a legal perspective, it may be difficult to justify the removal of applicants from a selection process solely on the basis of scoring too high on a measure of response distortion (Arthur, Woehr, & Graziano, 2001). This approach is also rendered problematic without corroborating evidence supporting the inference that someone has actually inflated his or her scores or that those exhibiting extreme scores on response distortion measures would actually be predicted to exhibit poorer job performance. Furthermore, there is little consensus on what constitutes an appropriate cut score for flagging applicants for many response distortion scales. Finally, there may be potential concerns pertaining to subgroup differences in hiring rates when applicants are removed from the selection process due to high scores on response distortion measures (e.g., Dudley et al., 2005). These issues will be addressed at greater length later in the chapter.

Retesting

We were able to locate one study that investigated the use of response distortion scales to flag applicants who may be faking with the consequence of having to retake the personality measure (Ellingson, Heggestad, & Coyne, 2007). This approach is based on the premise that informing applicants that their scores were deemed invalid triggers feelings of guilt, which should translate into more accurate responding when given a second opportunity to respond to the items. Using a laboratory sample, Ellingson and colleagues concluded that participants' retest scores were more accurate and were lower relative to their time-one scores provided under motivating circumstances, and that higher levels of state guilt were associated with more accurate time-two scores across four of the five personality traits measured.

On the surface, the retesting approach to correction appears to be beneficial in the sense that potentially hirable applicants are not simply eliminated from a selection process merely due to scoring too high on a measure of response distortion. However, one potential downside to the retesting approach is the costs incurred from having to readminister the personality measures. This approach also carries with it additional logistical questions that would need to be addressed in a practical setting (e.g., generating equated alternate forms). Furthermore, the effectiveness of this approach regarding outcomes, such as effect on criterion-related validity and rank ordering of applicants, has yet to be established. Finally, there is some evidence suggesting that multiple administrations of the same personality inventory may result in changes in scores as a function of retest or practice effects in selection contexts (e.g., Hausknecht & Howard, 2004; Kelley, Jacobs, & Farr, 1994; Reeder, Doverspike, & O'Connell, 2008). However, much of this research pertains to situations in which applicants retest due to scoring too low on an initial administration, as opposed to singling out applicants who may have inflated scores on an initial administration. As such, although retesting as a corrective technique seems potentially useful, additional research is needed.

Explaining the Ineffectiveness of Correction Methods

As might be concluded from the review of findings presented above, it is not surprising that the practice of correcting trait scores in applied selection contexts has been questioned and viewed with skepticism, particularly in regard to situations in which social desirability scales are used as the means of detection (e.g., Borkenau & Ostendorf, 1992; Christiansen et al., 1994; Goffin & Christiansen, 2003; Griffith & Peterson, 2008; Li & Bagger, 2006; Morgeson et al., 2007). We are inclined to agree with prevailing views; if someone seeks to apply an evidence-based approach toward selection practice, the application of social desirability scales to reduce the deleterious outcomes associated with response distortion cannot be advised. However, simply because extant research based largely on one method (social desirability scales) has not produced supportive findings does not mean that other methods are equally inclined to fail. To this end, we believe it may be instructive to elaborate on some of the primary reasons why correction has not been effective to date.

Construct Validity and Substance versus Style

One of the fundamental debates spanning the literature on social desirability pertains to construct validity and the structure underlying the social desirability construct. A two-factor model, comprising impression management and self-deceptive enhancement, has been the predominant view of SDR over the past 25 years, dating back largely to a review and three studies reported by Paulhus (1984). Self-deceptive enhancement (SDE) is an unconscious tendency to perceive oneself favorably as manifested by positively biased descriptions of the self that one genuinely believes to be true. IM entails the conscious act of projecting a false image, as when one purposefully distorts responses to a personality measure (Zerbe & Paulhus, 1987). IM, which may be induced by situational pressures (e.g., a high-stakes testing environment) or exist as a more stable individual-difference variable, is generally the factor that has been the primary focus among researchers and practitioners concerned with response distortion in selection contexts (Zerbe & Paulhus, 1987).

Prominent measures that distinguish between these two factors include the Balanced Inventory of Desirable Responding (Paulhus, 1998) and Sackeim and Gur's Self- and Other-Deception Questionnaires (Sackeim & Gur, 1978). In addition, factor-analytic studies (e.g., Paulhus, 1984) have demonstrated that general social desirability scales (e.g., the Edwards Social Desirability scale) tend to load on one of two factors resembling SDE and IM. Such results suggest that social desirability scales vary in the construct being measured and in the degree to which they measure it. Indeed, it is common for correlations between various response distortion scales to be rather low in magnitude, sometimes in the range of 0.10s to 0.30 (e.g., Borkenau & Ostendorf, 1992; O'Grady, 1988; Paulhus, 1984), which indicates that what is being measured by response distortion scales may be idiosyncratic to the particular scale in question.

Despite such findings, some researchers have suggested that there may be little practical utility in distinguishing between SDE and IM when evaluating the outcomes of applying response distortion measures for corrective purposes in applied contexts (Li & Bagger, 2006). However, the broader concern is understanding what a given method is measuring. That is, if detection methods are being used to alter candidates' trait scores or to remove applicants from a selection process, it is not unreasonable to suggest that we should have evidence that these methods are indeed measuring what they are designed to measure. Given that prior research has found that response distortion scales do not load on a single factor and correlations between response distortion scales are often low, the construct validity of those scales as measures of social desirability is questionable.

A related concern regarding social desirability scales is whether these measures may be tapping substantive trait variance. If this were true, the implication would be that using response distortion scales for correction via score adjustment may extract trait-relevant variance, thus leading to construct deficiency. When this situation occurs, criterion-related validities for the adjusted score may decrease relative to the measure's zero-order validity, as reported in the meta-analyses of Ones et al. (1996) and Li and Bagger (2006) discussed above. Thus, it is important to know the extent to which response distortion scales and other detection methods correlate with substantive trait measures and what this correlation implies.

In their meta-analysis, Ones and colleagues (1996) report uncorrected zero-order correlations between the FFM constructs and social desirability scales in the range of 0.00 to 0.27, with Emotional Stability and Conscientiousness showing the largest correlations with SDR (0.27 and 0.15, respectively). Similarly, Li and Bagger (2006) report meta-analytic uncorrected correlations between the FFM constructs and both IM and SDE. For IM, uncorrected correlations ranged from 0.02 to 0.33, with Conscientiousness, Agreeableness, and Emotional Stability being the strongest correlates (0.33, 0.33, and 0.27, respectively). These findings are informative insofar as they suggest some degree of shared variance between response distortion scales and trait scores. However, the question not addressed is what this shared variance constitutes. Several researchers have attempted to investigate this issue by comparing correlations between self-report trait measures and response distortion scales with observer ratings on the same trait measures and response distortion scales. The idea behind this approach is that if SDR scales are only measuring a response bias and not trait-relevant variance, scores on these measures should be uncorrelated with trait ratings provided by observers (e.g., close family, friends). However, this has often been found not to be true; numerous researchers have found SDR scales to be at least moderately correlated with observer trait ratings (e.g., McCrae & Costa, 1983). It should be noted that the majority of research examining relationships between FFM trait scores and SDR scores has focused on broad traits. Correlations at the facet level may be larger in magnitude.

Based on findings suggesting that response distortion scales tap trait-relevant variance, one might wonder whether such scales actually measure response distortion at all. Based on a meta-analytic estimate of the within-subject mean shift on social desirability scales of $d = 2.26$, Ones and Viswesvaran (1998) estimated the correlation between social desirability scales and a continuous faking outcome variable to be 0.95, leading them to conclude that response distortion scales "capture faking very well" (p. 249). However, this estimate has been disputed. Tett and

Christiansen (2007) suggested that the estimate of Ones and Viswesvaran (1998) is an overestimate given that within-subjects designs provide spuriously inflated estimates due to carryover effects. These researchers estimated the correlation between social desirability scales and a continuous faking outcome variable to be 0.32. Griffith and Peterson (2008) provided observed correlations between faking behavior on the Conscientiousness scale of the NEO-Five-Factor Inventory (NEO-FFI) and both IM and SDE of 0.12 and 0.13, respectively. Certainly, the Tett and Christiansen (2007) and Griffith and Peterson (2008) estimates of the correlation between response distortion scales and faking provide little in the way of evidence suggesting that such scales are valid indicators of faking. In summary, concerns regarding construct validity and substance versus style highlight key areas potentially underlying the ineffectiveness of SDR scales when used for correction.

Social Desirability versus Job Desirability

Kluger and Colella (1993) differentiated between social desirability (conscious distortion by presenting oneself as possessing higher levels of traits deemed desirable by society in general and lower levels of traits deemed undesirable by society in general) and job desirability (conscious distortion by presenting oneself as possessing higher levels of traits deemed desirable for the job at hand and lower levels of traits deemed undesirable for the job at hand). This distinction has been corroborated by results indicating that participants in laboratory settings produce differential patterns of scores when instructed to respond as if applying for different occupations, such as librarian or advertising executive (e.g., Furnham, 1990; Kroger & Turnbull, 1975; Mahar, Cologon, & Duck, 1995). In explaining this phenomenon, Mahar and colleagues (1995) stated that applicants may base responses on their stereotype of jobholders who occupy the position for which they are applying. Kroger and Turnbull (1975) noted that applicants undertaking such a strategy may not be merely inflating scores so as to demonstrate a good impression, but rather are applying their knowledge of the position and the social structure surrounding the job in an attempt to respond in a manner similar to role occupants while avoiding detection.

Although it has been noted by others that research on the concept of job desirability is relatively sparse (Ones et al., 1996), the distinction between job desirability and social desirability is both interesting and potentially useful, and thus may deserve additional attention for a number of reasons. First, we know little about how job desirability may operate in operational selection settings, or what proportion of variance in total response distortion it contributes when considering both dispositional and situational factors. Furthermore, given that responding in a manner deemed desirable for a given job requires knowledge that is specific to that given job and target jobholders, it is logical to assume that patterns of job desirability will differ across occupations. It also seems quite feasible that applicants may differ in their ability to respond in a desirable manner for a given job due to factors such as previous experience relevant to that job. Indeed, Mahar and colleagues (1995) concluded that applicants may not always be particularly successful at faking for certain occupations, while Kroger and Turnbull (1975) found that the ability of participants to produce responses similar to those of target jobholders varied depending on the occupation in question. Finally, one would imagine that response distortion scales might not be effective indicators of the extent to which applicants respond in a job-desirable manner, particularly when characteristics that might be desirable for the job in question might not be perceived as desirable by society at large. Hence, additional research examining the use of job desirability measures may yield some useful insights.

Item Interpretation

Questions have been raised regarding whether respondents interpret items on response distortion scales in the same way as the authors of such scales intend them to be interpreted. Borkenau and Ostendorf (1992) provide the item "I am always courteous, even to people who are disagreeable" as an example. On the one hand, Borkenau and Ostendorf suggest that authors of response distortion scales including items such as these may focus on the inconsistency or implausibility of responses to such items. On the other hand, respondents, not attending to the exact wording of such items, may endorse such items in an attempt to truthfully convey that the construct being represented (perhaps agreeableness in the example above) is characteristic of their typical behavior. Kurtz, Tarquini, and Iobst (2008) suggest that when faced with items such as these, respondents will likely choose the response option that seems most accurate, as opposed to the literally true option. In terms of the effectiveness of correction methods, the differences in interpretation of scale items meant to detect response distortion also calls into question the construct validity of SDR measures, and hence their usefulness for correction purposes.

General Concerns with Methods of Detection and Correction

There are other general concerns that may come to bear whenever detection and correction are carried out in operational selection contexts, regardless of the specific approach used. These include *assessment context, coaching, cultural variability in response tendencies, and subgroup differences and legal defensibility.*

One general issue pertains to *assessment context*. Essentially all research on faking in selection contexts approaches the problem from a large-volume hiring perspective. However, individual assessment differs from large-volume assessment in that measures are individually administered and scores from multiple measures are integrated in a clinical manner by an assessor attempting to make inferences regarding the individual's suitability in a given position (Kwaske, 2004). Correction in these contexts may be idiosyncratic to the assessor and/or inconsistent across job candidates.

In a survey of individual assessment practitioners, Robie, Tuzinski, and Bly (2006) found that assessors believed that the best indicators of faking in an individual assessment context included extreme scores on measures that are inconsistent with other information available about the respondent, high scores on a trait-based scale of impression management in conjunction with scores on the substantive scales, and a large number of extreme scores on the substantive personality scales. The top three means of remediating the effects of faking offered by the assessors included reducing the weight of the personality scores when computing competency scores, providing the resultant profile to the respondent and questioning him or her about it, and disregarding the information from the personality measures completely.

Second, *coaching* methods exist for prospective applicants who wish to learn how to inflate their scores on personality measures commonly used in selection contexts (Douglas, McDaniel, & Snell, 1996). Coaching may be used not only to aid prospective applicants in taking personality tests, but to avoid being detected by common methods for assessing response distortion. Some detection methods, such as social desirability scales and bogus items, may be more susceptible to coaching (Christiansen et al., 2005; Kuncel & Borneman, 2007), whereas other methods, such as those based on IRT, may be more difficult to coach (Zickar & Drasgow, 1996). However, comparative research investigating the efficacy of coaching methods for various detection methods is sparse.

Miller and Barrett (2001) provided short training sessions on both personality scales and lie scales to an undergraduate sample. The authors found that those receiving training on personality measures had scores elevated significantly beyond that observed in a nontrained group. For participants receiving training on lie scales, scores on a social desirability scale (a variant of the Marlowe–Crown SDS) were significantly lower than for participants who did not receive such training ($d = -0.44$). Finally, the authors rank ordered all participants across groups on a composite conscientiousness variable and assessed the percentage of participants from the separate conditions that would be selected under various selection ratios (0.01, 0.05, 0.10, and 0.20). Across all selection ratios, no participants from a nontrained condition would have been selected under any of the ratios and no participants from a nontrained condition instructed to respond as though applying for a position would have been selected until a selection ratio of 0.10 was employed. Conversely, those who received only personality training were often well overrepresented among those selected. On the basis of the results, the authors concluded that it is quite possible to coach applicants to beat personality measures and response distortion scales in selection contexts.

Robie and colleagues (2000) conducted a similar study, where coaching was directed to aiding respondents in beating response latency detection methods. In a sample of undergraduates, coaching reduced the detection ability of the response latency measures, but it also appeared to reduce the extent to which the coached group elevated their scores, which the authors suggested may have been due to the cognitive resources needed to simultaneously monitor response latencies while also inflating responses.

Another general concern pertains to *cultural variability in SDR* and related outcomes. There is little, if any, research on the application of correction methods outside of North America, although there is evidence of cross-cultural variability in response tendencies. For instance, Hui and Triandis (1989) found that Hispanics displayed a stronger tendency to use an extreme response style on five-point scales than did white participants. Members of cultures who have a stronger tendency to exhibit extreme response styles may score higher on response distortion measures computed by summing the number of extreme responses made across items (e.g., the BIDR-IM). In addition, there are several studies indicating that members of Asian cultures may be likely to score higher on measures of response distortion than other groups, including the Marlowe–Crowne (Keillor, Owens, & Pettijohn, 2001; Middleton & Jones, 2000) and the BIDR-IM (Lalwani, Shavitt, & Johnson, 2006; however, see also Heine & Lehman, 1995), leaving some to question the content of response distortion scales and whether such scales are assessing similar constructs to similar degrees across cultures (Middleton & Jones, 2000). If there are group differences on such scales due to construct-irrelevant national or cultural factors, members of some cultures may be disadvantaged if such measures are used for correction purposes in international selection projects. Furthermore, if a social desirability scale is to be used in a culturally diverse selection setting, it will need to be translated, which brings into question a number of additional issues (e.g., establishing measurement invariance, removing offensive items or items that do not have equivalent meanings). This is perhaps another area in which other means of detection and correction (specifically, internal techniques) might have a clear advantage.

Finally, when employing correction methodologies, it is important to know whether such corrections systematically affect *corrected scores and pass rates for subgroups*. If underrepresented groups score higher on measures of response distortion that are used for correction, the application of such corrections may, at the aggregate level, result in larger corrections for minority candidates, potentially translating into lower mean corrected scores and lower pass rates (Dudley et al., 2005). Evidence suggesting the existence of potential subgroup differences on social desirability scales has been provided by both primary studies (Dudley et al., 2005) and meta-analyses (Hough, Oswald, & Ployhart, 2001). In addition, subgroup differences have been found to translate into adverse outcomes in selection contexts for racioethnic minority groups relative to whites when corrections are used (Dudley et al., 2005; Hough, 1998). Aside from social desirability scales, however, research on subgroup differences on methods of detection is largely lacking.

In a related context, several authors have suggested that the practice of correcting for response distortion may be problematic from the standpoint of legal defensibility in the U.S. (Barrick & Mount, 1996; Christiansen et al., 1994; Rosse et al., 1998). As Arthur and colleagues (2001) note, it seems rather paradoxical to reject an applicant from a selection process because his or her scores were too high, especially given the standard application of linear, top-down selection models seen in practice. Conversely, Luther and Thornton (1999) suggest that the argument that faking is not a concern, given the current state of knowledge, is not likely to withstand scrutiny in a legal context. Thus, there appears to be no clear consensus regarding legal perspectives on the effects of faking. In the event that a legal challenge were to be brought, the practice of correction may be difficult to justify without clear evidence that it (1) does not increase adverse impact, (2) does not differentially affect validity across subgroups, and (3) does increase validity for the sample as a whole.

■ CONCLUSIONS

This chapter provided a review of the literature pertaining to the correction of response distortion in self-report personality measures within selection settings. The majority of this research has used social desirability scales as the means of detection; however, other detection methods and strategies introduced more recently (e.g., response latencies, appropriateness measurement) may eventually be shown to circumvent some of the drawbacks commonly associated with using social desirability scales for correction.

Our review discusses four approaches for correction: score adjustment, the removal of applicants from a selection process, retesting, and cautious interpretation of results. The first two methods, score adjustment and removal of cases, imply different perspectives on how SDR is believed to operate. Score adjustments treat SDR as a continuous suppressor variable; removal of cases, on the other hand, treats SDR as a moderator. A sizable body of research has been directed at evaluating the effectiveness of these two approaches in terms of a number of outcomes of interest in operational settings. Findings pertaining to construct validity and criterion-related validity for self-report measures following corrections have generally not been encouraging, and correction may produce change in rank order to varying degrees and may alter subsequent hiring decisions. Beyond score adjustments and removal of cases, retesting is a possible means of correcting for response distortion, but additional research is needed to determine whether the costs incurred by adopting a retesting policy are offset by the gains. In addition, our review of the literature identified a number of more general issues that researchers and practitioners may need to consider when attempting to detect and correct for response distortion, including the assessment context, coaching, cultural variability in response tendencies, and subgroup differences and legal defensibility.

From an applied perspective, a need exists for the development of methods (proactive, reactive, or likely both) to deal with response distortion in selection settings when self-report noncognitive measures are used. It is not unwarranted for organizations using self-report measures for selection purposes to want viable options for countering response distortion, just as they would want ways of dealing with cheating on other measures. Available detection and correction methodologies, representing a reactive strategy to managing response distortion, are one potential option, but they have not, as of yet, been shown to be overly effective. The use of social desirability scales has generated enough skepticism at this juncture to conclude that such scales are likely not useful for the task of detecting and correcting response distortion in operational selection settings.

A number of recent approaches to detecting response distortion have been put forth as potential alternatives to social desirability scales; however, additional research on these methods clearly needs to be done before they are put to use operationally. Similar conclusions can be drawn about newer correction strategies, such as the retesting strategy discussed by Ellingson and colleagues (2007). Thus, although we are cautiously optimistic about these recent innovations in detective and corrective approaches, it appears that we still have a ways to go.

References

Anderson, C. D., Warner, J. L., & Spencer, C. C. (1984). Inflation bias in self-assessment examinations: Implications for valid employee selection. *Journal of Applied Psychology, 69*, 574–580.

Arthur, W. Jr., Woehr, D. J., & Graziano, W. G. (2001). Personality testing in employment settings: Problems and issues in the application of typical selection practices. *Personnel Review, 30*, 657–676.

Barrick, M. R., & Mount, M. K. (1991). The big five personality dimensions and job performance: A meta-analysis. *Personnel Psychology, 44*, 1–26.

Barrick, M. R., & Mount, M. K. (1996). Effects of impression management and self-deception on the predictive validity of personality constructs. *Journal of Applied Psychology, 81*, 261–272.

Birenbaum, M., & Montag, I. (1989). Style and substance in social desirability scales. *European Journal of Personality, 3*, 47–59.

Borkenau, P., & Ostendorf, F. (1992). Social desirability scales as moderator and suppressor variables. *European Journal of Personality, 6*, 199–214.

Christiansen, N. D., Goffin, R. D., Johnston, N. G., & Rothstein, M. G. (1994). Correcting the 16PF for faking: Effects on criterion-related validity and individual hiring decisions. *Personnel Psychology, 47*, 847–860.

Christiansen, N. D., Robie, C., & Bly, P. R. (2005, April). Using covariance to detect applicant response distortion of personality measures. Paper presented in M. Zickar (Chair). *Faking research: New methods, new samples, and new questions.* Symposium conducted at the 20th annual conference of the Society for Industrial and Organizational Psychology, Los Angeles, CA.

Conger, A. J. (1974). A revised definition for suppressor variables: A guide to their identification and interpretation. *Educational and Psychological Measurement, 34*, 35–46.

Conger, A. J., & Jackson, D. N. (1972). Suppressor variables, prediction, and the interpretation of psychological relationships. *Educational and Psychological Measurement, 32*, 579–599.

Douglas, E. F., McDaniel, M. A., & Snell, A. F. (1996). *The validity of non-cognitive measures decays when applicants fake.* Cincinnati, OH: Academy of Management Proceedings.

Dudley, N. M., McFarland, L. A., Goodman, S. A., Hunt, S. T., & Sydell, E. J. (2005). Racial differences in socially desirable responding in selection contexts: Magnitude and consequences. *Journal of Personality Assessment, 85*, 50–64.

Ellingson, J. E., Heggestad, E. D., & Coyne, E. E. (2007, August). *Personality retest effects and intentional distortion: How guilty feelings lead to more honest responses.* Paper presented at the 67th annual meeting of the Academy of Management, Philadelphia, PA.

Ellingson, J. E., Sackett, P. R., & Hough, L. M. (1999). Social desirability corrections in personality measurement: Issues of applicant comparison and construct validity. *Journal of Applied Psychology, 84*, 155–166.

Foldes, H. J., Duehr, E. E., & Ones, D. S. (2008). Group differences in personality: Meta-analyses comparing five U.S. racial groups. *Personnel Psychology, 61*, 579–616.

Furnham, A. (1990). Faking personality questionnaires: Fabricating different profiles for different purposes. *Current Psychology: Research and Reviews, 9*, 46–55.

Ganster, D. C., Hennessey, H. W., & Luthans, F. (1983). Social desirability response effects: Three alternative models. *Academy of Management Journal, 26*, 321–331.

Goffin, R. D., & Christiansen, N. D. (2003). Correcting personality tests for faking: A review of popular personality tests and an initial survey of researchers. *International Journal of Selection and Assessment, 11*, 340–344.

Griffith, R. L., & Peterson, M. H. (2008). The failure of social desirability measures to capture applicant faking behavior. *Industrial and Organizational Psychology: Perspectives on Science and Practice*, *1*, 308–311.

Haaland, D., & Christiansen, N. D. (1998, June). *Departures from linearity in the relationship between applicant personality test scores and performance as evidence of response distortion*. Paper presented at the 22nd annual conference for the International Personnel Management Association Assessment Council, Chicago, IL.

Hausknecht, J. P., & Howard, M. J. (2004, August). *Effects of candidate retesting in an employment context*. Paper presented at the 64th annual meeting of the Academy of Management, New Orleans, LA.

Heine, S. J., & Lehman, D. R. (1995). Social desirability among Canadian and Japanese students. *The Journal of Social Psychology*, *135*, 777–779.

Holden, R. R. (2007). Socially desirable responding does moderate personality scale validity both in experimental and nonexperimental contexts. *Canadian Journal of Behavioural Science*, *39*, 184–201.

Holden, R. R. (2008). Underestimating the effects of faking on the validity of self-report personality scales. *Personality and Individual Differences*, *44*, 311–321.

Hough, L. M. (1998). Effects of intentional distortion in personality measurement and evaluation of suggested palliatives. *Human Performance*, *11*, 209–244.

Hough, L. M., Eaton, N. K., Dunnette, M. D., Kamp, J. D., & McCloy, R. A. (1990). Criterion-related validities of personality constructs and the effects of response distortion on those validities [Monograph]. *Journal of Applied Psychology*, *75*, 581–595.

Hough, L. M., Oswald, F. L., & Ployhart, R. E. (2001). Determinants, detection and amelioration of adverse impact in personnel selection procedures: Issues, evidence and lessons learned. *International Journal of Selection and Assessment*, *9*, 152–194.

Hui, C. H., & Triandis, H. C. (1989). Effects of culture and response format on extreme response style. *Journal of Cross-Cultural Psychology*, *20*, 296–309.

Hurtz, G. M., & Donovan, J. J. (2000). Personality and job performance: The big five revisited. *Journal of Applied Psychology*, *85*, 869–879.

Keillor, B., Owens, D., & Pettijohn, C. (2001). A cross-cultural/cross-national study of influencing factors and socially desirable response biases. *International Journal of Market Research*, *43*, 63–84.

Kelley, P. L., Jacobs, R. R., & Farr, J. L. (1994). Effects of multiple administrations of the MMPI for employment screening. *Personnel Psychology*, *47*, 575–591.

Kluger, A. N., & Colella, A. (1993). Beyond the mean bias: The effect of warning against faking on biodata item variances. *Personnel Psychology*, *46*, 763–780.

Kroger, R. O., & Turnbull, W. (1975). Invalidity of validity scales: The case of the MMPI. *Journal of Consulting and Clinical Psychology*, *43*, 48–55.

Kuncel, N. R., & Borneman, M. J. (2007). Toward a new method of detecting deliberately faked personality tests: The use of idiosyncratic item responses. *International Journal of Selection and Assessment*, *15*, 220–231.

Kurtz, J. E., Tarquini, S. J., & Iobst, E. A. (2008). Socially desirable responding in personality assessment: Still more substance than style. *Personality and Individual Differences*, *45*, 22–27.

Kwaske, I. H. (2004). Individual assessments for personnel selection: An update on a rarely researched but avidly practiced practice. *Consulting Psychology Journal: Practice and Research*, *56*, 186–195.

Lalwani, A. K., Shavitt, S., & Johnson, T. (2006). What is the relation between cultural orientation and socially desirable responding? *Journal of Personality and Social Psychology*, *90*, 165–178.

Li, A., & Bagger, J. (2006). Using the BIDR to distinguish the effects of impression management and self-deception on the criterion-related validity of personality measures: A meta-analysis. *International Journal of Selection and Assessment, 14,* 131–141.

Lubin, A. (1957). Some formulae for use with suppressor variables. *Educational and Psychological Measurement, 17,* 286–296.

Luther, N. J., & Thornton, G. C. (1999). Does faking on employment tests matter? *Employment Testing Law & Policy Reporter, 8,* 129–136.

Mahar, D., Cologon, J., & Duck, J. (1995). Response strategies when faking personality questionnaires in a vocational selection setting. *Personality and Individual Differences, 18,* 605–609.

Marcus, B. (2006). Relationships between faking, validity and decision criteria in personnel selection. *Psychology Science, 48,* 226–246.

McCrae, R. R., & Costa, P. T. Jr. (1983). Social desirability scales: More substance than style. *Journal of Consulting and Clinical Psychology, 51,* 882–888.

Meehl, P. E. (1945). A simple algebraic development of Horst's suppressor variables. *The American Journal of Psychology, 58,* 550–554.

Meehl, P. E., & Hathaway, S. R. (1946). The K factor as a suppressor variable in the Minnesota Multiphasic Personality Inventory. *Journal of Applied Psychology, 30,* 525–564.

Middleton, K. L., & Jones, J. L. (2000). Socially desirable response sets: The impact of country culture. *Psychology & Marketing, 17,* 149–163.

Miller, C. E., & Barrett, G. V. (2001). *The coachability and fakability of personality selection tests used for police selection.* Paper presented at the 25th annual conference of the International Personnel Management Association Assessment Council, Newport Beach, CA.

Morgeson, F. P., Campion, M. A., Dipboye, R. L., Hollenbeck, J. R., Murphy, K., & Schmitt, N. (2007). Reconsidering the use of personality tests in personnel selection contexts. *Personnel Psychology, 60,* 683–729.

Mueller-Hanson, R., Heggestad, E. D., & Thornton, G. C. III. (2003). Faking and selection: Considering the use of personality from select-in and select-out perspectives. *Journal of Applied Psychology, 88,* 348–355.

O'Connell, M. S., Kung, M.-C., & Tristan, E. (2006, May). Beyond impression management: Evaluating three measures of response distortion and their relationship to job performance. Paper presented in R. Griffith & Y. Yoshita (Chair), *Deceptively simple: Applicant faking behavior and prediction of job performance.* Symposium conducted at the 21st annual conference of the Society for Industrial and Organizational Psychology, Dallas, TX.

O'Grady, K. E. (1988). The Marlowe-Crowne and Edwards social desirability scales: A psychometric perspective. *Multivariate Behavioral Research, 23,* 87–101.

Ones, D. S., Dilchert, S., Viswesvaran, C., & Judge, T. A. (2007). In support of personality assessment in organizational settings. *Personnel Psychology, 60,* 995–1027.

Ones, D. S., & Viswesvaran, C. (1998). The effects of social desirability and faking on personality and integrity assessment for personnel selection. *Human Performance, 11,* 245–269.

Ones, D. S., Viswesvaran, C., & Reiss, A. D. (1996). Role of social desirability in personality testing for personnel selection: The red herring. *Journal of Applied Psychology, 81,* 660–679.

Pannone, R. D. (1984). Predicting test performance: A content valid approach to screening applicants. *Personnel Psychology, 37,* 507–514.

Paulhus, D. L. (1984). Two-component models of socially desirable responding. *Journal of Personality and Social Psychology, 46,* 598–609.

Paulhus, D. L. (1998). *Balanced Inventory of Desirable Responding (BIDR).* Toronto, Ontario, Canada: Multi-Health Systems.

Reeder, M. C., Doverspike, D., & O'Connell, M. S. (2008, April). *Temporal stability and retest effects across personnel selection methods.* Paper presented at the 23rd annual meeting of the Society for Industrial and Organizational Psychology, San Francisco, CA.

Robie, C., Curtin, P. J., Foster, T. C., Phillips, H. L., Zyblut, M., & Tetrick, L. E. (2000). The effect of coaching on the utility of response latencies in detecting fakers on a personality measure. *Canadian Journal of Behavioural Science, 32,* 226–233.

Robie, C., Tuzinski, K. A., & Bly, P. R. (2006). A survey of assessor beliefs and practices related to faking. *Journal of Managerial Psychology, 21,* 669–681.

Rosse, J. G., Stecher, M. D., Miller, J. L., & Levin, R. A. (1998). The impact of response distortion on preemployment personality testing and hiring decisions. *Journal of Applied Psychology, 83,* 634–644.

Sackeim, H. A., & Gur, R. C. (1978). Self-deception, self-confrontation, and consciousness. In G. E. Schwartz & D. Shapiro (Eds.), *Consciousness and self-regulation: Advances in research* (Vol. 2, pp. 139–197). New York: Plenum Press.

Schmit, M. J., & Ryan, A. M. (1993). The big five in personnel selection: Factor structure in applicant and nonapplicant populations. *Journal of Applied Psychology, 78,* 966–974.

Schmitt, N., & Oswald, F. L. (2006). The impact of corrections for faking on the validity of noncognitive measures in selection settings. *Journal of Applied Psychology, 91,* 613–621.

Stark, S., Chernyshenko, O. S., Chan, K.-Y., Lee, W. C., & Drasgow, F. (2001). Effects of the testing situation on item responding: Cause for concern. *Journal of Applied Psychology, 86,* 943–953.

Tett, R. P., & Christiansen, N. D. (2007). Personality tests at the crossroads: A response to Morgeson, Campion, Dipboye, Hollenbeck, Murphy, and Schmitt (2007). *Personnel Psychology, 60,* 967–993.

White, L. A., Young, M. C., Hunter, A. E., & Rumsey, M. G. (2008). Lessons learned from transitioning personality measures from research to operational settings. *Industrial and Organizational Psychology: Perspectives on Science and Practice, 1,* 291–295.

Zerbe, W. J., & Paulhus, D. L. (1987). Socially desirable responding in organizational behavior: A reconception. *Academy of Management Review, 12,* 250–264.

Zickar, M. J., & Drasgow, F. (1996). Detecting faking on a personality instrument using appropriateness measurement. *Applied Psychological Measurement, 20,* 71–87.

10 Overclaiming on Personality Questionnaires

■ DELROY L. PAULHUS

In this chapter, the term *faking* will be interpreted in the broader sense of self-presentation, that is, motivated distortion of self-reports. At the private level, self-presentation is typically labeled *self-deception* (Paulhus, 1984) or *self-enhancement* (Baumeister, 1982). At the public level, self-presentation is most commonly labeled *impression management* (Paulhus, 1984). I will treat them together because both forms of positive self-presentation constitute a threat to the validity of personality scales. Moreover both forms of positive self-presentation can be measured with the overclaiming technique (OCT).

The OCT was designed to measure knowledge exaggeration and knowledge accuracy simultaneously and independently (Paulhus, Harms, Bruce, & Lysy, 2003; Paulhus & Harms, 2004). Respondents are asked to rate their familiarity with a set of topics relevant to a content domain (e.g., academic facts, workplace items, consumer products). Critical to the technique is the inclusion of some items that do not actually exist (i.e., *foils*).

A respondent's knowledge exaggeration and accuracy are calculated from two values: (a) the proportion of real items rated as familiar and (b) the proportion of foils rated as familiar. Exaggeration is indexed by the respondent's tendency to claim familiarity with items (especially foils) whereas accuracy is indexed by the respondent's ability to distinguish real items from foils. To the extent that an audience is salient, exaggeration can be interpreted as impression management; otherwise, it is best interpreted as self-deceptive enhancement.

Details about the history, psychometrics, and applications of the OCT are fleshed out in the following sections. For illustrative purposes, Table 10.1 provides an example of the OCT format: It includes familiarity ratings provided by two hypothetical respondents.

■ HISTORY OF THE TECHNIQUE

There are several historical precedents for the notion that claiming familiarity with foils is a face-valid indicator of knowledge exaggeration. The earliest published example is a 25-item test included in the omnibus appendix of instruments developed by Raubenheimer (1925), a student of Lewis Terman. Respondents were asked to check off which books they had read. Out of 25, 10 were nonexistent. Whereas "Robinson Crusoe" was a genuine book, "The Prize-Fighters Story" was used as a foil.

TABLE 10.1 *Sample Page from the Academic Overclaiming Questionnaire (If You Are Familiar with the Item, Please Check the Box)*

Fine Arts	Respondent 1	Respondent 2
Mozart	√	√
A cappella	√	
The Pullman paintings*		
Art deco	√	√
Paul Gauguin	√	
Mona Lisa	√	√
La Neige Jaune*	√	
Mario Lanza	√	
Verdi	√	
Jan Vermeer	√	
Windermere Wild*	√	√
Grand Pooh Bah		
Botticelli	√	
Harpsichord	√	√
Dramatis personae	√	

Note: The three foils are marked with asterisks.

Although failing to acknowledge that precedent, two subsequent studies proposed and applied a similar notion (Anderson, Warner, & Spencer, 1984; Phillips & Clancy, 1972). More recently, Stanovich and West (1989) used fictitious items as a covariate for self-reports of books read. None of those studies, however, considered foil claiming as a meaningful variable in its own right.

Inspired by the Phillips and Clancy paper, my students and I launched into a comprehensive research program that began with a 1990 conference presentation by Paulhus and Bruce. About the same time, Randall and Fernandes (1991) developed a set of 10 foils for use in ethics research. Since that time, further critiques of social desirability scales have escalated the need for an alternative approach to measuring self-presentation in surveys.

■ PROBLEMS WITH PREVIOUS MEASURES

Self-presentation on questionnaires is typically referred to as *socially desirable responding* (SDR). Over the years, a host of SDR measures have been targeted specifically at the detection of faking on self-reports of personality. Currently the two most popular are the Marlowe–Crowne scale (Crowne & Marlowe, 1960) and the Balanced Inventory of Desirable Responding (BIDR) (Paulhus, 1998). Unfortunately, some researchers continue to indict the validity of self-report instruments if they show high correlations with SDR measures (e.g., Davis, Thake, & Vilhena, 2010). Other researchers continue with attempts to control faking post hoc by including SDR scales as covariates in prediction equations.

Critics of SDR scales have complained that SDR measures confound fact with fiction (e.g., Block, 1965; McCrae & Costa, 1983). After all, some people actually are blessed with an abundance of socially desirable attributes. Without faking, they can record high scores on SDR scales. To address this confounding, some research-ers turned to an approach based on departure from reality (e.g., John & Robins, 1994). Specifically designed to incorporate a criterion, it requires a contrast of self-evaluations with intrapsychic or external criteria. For example, self-reports of personality can be residualized on informant reports to provide an index of self-presentation (e.g., Paulhus & John, 1998).

To avoid the confound problem entirely, Holden and colleagues have developed a reaction-time technique (Holden, Kroner, Fekken, & Popham, 1992). That method exploits the fact that the response times of fakers exhibit a pattern distinct from those of individuals who respond honestly. For detailed examples, see Paulhus and Holden (2010).

Each category of methods entails a tradeoff of advantages and disadvantages. SDR scales offer easy administration but lack a criterion to distinguish distortion from valid personality variance. Criterion discrepancy measures tap departure from reality but are impractical in standard administration settings because they require collection of the criterion. The response-time method is objectively scored but requires an elaborate laboratory procedure.

In sum, the diagnosis of faking has been hampered by the difficulty of distin-guishing accuracy from bias. The failure to find significance with group-level sta-tistics does not rule out the possibility of some individual-level faking (Holden, 2008). On other hand, allegations of faking against individuals actually possessing positive traits would be—not merely unjust—but contrary to the goal of optimal personnel selection. Extant techniques do not seem capable of correcting person-ality scores post hoc, that is, after faking has occurred (Griffith & Peterson, 2008).

■ RATIONALE FOR THE OVERCLAIMING TECHNIQUE

The OCT was designed as an optimal compromise between earlier approaches. It captures departure from reality, but in a more practical fashion than does the cri-terion discrepancy method. Respondents are asked to rate their familiarity with a set of persons, places, items, or events. A proportion (typically 20%) of the items are foils: They do not actually exist. In Table 10.1, for example, the historical item "Paul Gauguin" refers to an actual nineteenth-century post-impressionist painter. By contrast, the item "Windermere Wild" seems as it could be genuine but, in fact, refers to a poem known only to the present author and his college girlfriend: It does not appear in a Google search.

Respondents are assigned high accuracy scores to the extent that they claim greater familiarity with real items than with foils. A high exaggeration score ensues from an overall tendency to claim items—especially foils. The intuitive appeal of this index follows from the assumption that claiming familiarity with nonexistent items is a face valid index of faking.

In short, the goal of developing the OCT was to unravel the typical inter-weaving of fact and fiction in self-descriptions. The rates of claiming real and foil items are used to create independent indexes of accuracy and exaggeration via signal detection analysis. Details of those calculations come next.

■ PSYCHOMETRICS

People are often called upon to make "yes" or "no" decisions regarding the existence of stimuli that are enveloped in noise. To model the human ability to process such information, Swets (1964) developed a framework called *signal detection analysis*. His two key performance parameters were accuracy (the ability to distinguish real stimuli from false alarms) and bias (the overall tendency to say "yes").

This signal detection framework can be applied to people's familiarity ratings of real items and foils (Paulhus & Bruce, 1990). People assign familiarity ratings on the basis of a fuzzy memory trace rather than a clear recollection. The large samples of such ratings collected on overclaiming questionnaires are summarized by two values. First is the proportion of hits (PH), that is, real items claimed. Second is the proportion of false alarms (PFA), that is, foils claimed. These two values can be analyzed with standard formulas to yield indexes of accuracy and exaggeration (Paulhus & Petrusic, 2010).

Note that in the signal detection model, accuracy and exaggeration are not opposites but are scored independently. As a result, there is no inherent cross-contamination of the OCT accuracy and exaggeration indexes. Of course, this independence does not preclude the two indexes from being correlated across individuals.

A variety of signal detection formulas are detailed by Paulhus and Petrusic (2010). Of these, the most intuitively compelling are the so called *common-sense measures*. Accuracy is simply the difference between the hit rate and the false-alarm rate (i.e., PH − PFA). Knowledge exaggeration is indexed by their mean: (PH + PFA)/2. The inclusion of PH in the latter formula is based on the assumption that those who exaggerate on the foils also exaggerate on the reals: Such respondents inflate their familiarity ratings on both sets of items. Alternatively, PFA can be used directly as an index of exaggeration: If so, then PH should be partialed out (Paulhus et al., 2003).

To illustrate, Table 10.2 presents the values calculated for the hypothetical respondents in Table 10.1. Respondent 1, for example, claimed familiarity with most of the items, including two out of three foils. As a result, this respondent received a relatively high exaggeration score of 0.80. Respondent 2 claimed only

TABLE 10.2 *Sample Calculations of the Accuracy and Exaggeration Indexes from Table 10.1 Responses*

	Respondent 1	Respondent 2
Hits (out of 12)	11	4
False alarms (out of 3)	2	1
Proportion of hits (PH)	(11/12) = 0.92	(4/12) = 0.33
Proportion of false alarms (PFA)	(2/3) = 0.67	(1/3) = 0.33
Accuracy index (PH − PFA)	0.25	0.00
Exaggeration index (PH + PFA)/2	0.80	0.33

Note: Alternatively, PFA can be used directly as an index of exaggeration. If so, PH must be partialed out.

five items (including one foil) resulting in an exaggeration index of 0.33. In fact, Respondent 1 scored higher than Respondent 2 on both accuracy and exaggeration, thereby illustrating that accuracy and bias are not polar opposites within a signal detection framework.

Users preferring more sophisticated signal detection formulas may opt for indexes such as d-prime and criterion position. A comprehensive comparison of 10 accuracy and 8 bias measures is provided by Paulhus and Petrusic (2010). Their analyses indicated that, with a few exceptions, indexes within the accuracy (or bias) category yield similar results and are relatively orthogonal to those across categories.

Reliability Assessment

A special approach to reliability assessment is required for overclaiming indexes. Because there are two types of items (reals and foils), the individual item ratings do not form meaningful responses. At least one real and one foil are required to calculate either index. Instead, the appropriate method is to calculate correlations of the accuracy scores across topics (e.g., philosophy, life sciences). The topics become the elementary units and the usual reliability indexes (e.g., alpha) can be calculated on the resulting correlation matrix. This process is then repeated to calculate the reliability of the exaggeration index.

In the studies reported here, that procedure resulted in reasonable alpha values (in the 0.70 to 0.94 range) for both accuracy and bias. Such values are not unlike those of standard personality scales: Thus it appears that two coherent individual differences are being tapped.

■ VALIDATION OF THE TWO INDEXES

Knowledge Exaggeration

The exaggeration index has been validated both as a state and a trait measure of self-presentation. Its utility as a state measure has been demonstrated by its ability to track the level of self-presentational demand across situations. In one study, participants asked to "fake good" scored significantly higher than a group asked to respond honestly (Paulhus et al. 2003, Study 2): On average, participants inflated their familiarity ratings 2.1 points on a 7-point Likert scale. Other studies have corroborated this ability of the exaggeration index to track public self-presentation demand (Roeder & Paulhus, 2009; Tracy, Cheng, Robins, & Trzeszniewski, 2009).

The exaggeration index also correlates positively with trait measures of self-presentation. These criteria include the Narcissistic Personality Inventory (Paulhus & Goldberg, 2008; Paulhus & Williams, 2002; Paulhus et al., 2003; Tracy et al., 2009), Self-Deceptive Enhancement (Paulhus et al., 2003; Randall & Fernandes, 1991), and global self-reports of knowledge (Paulhus & Bruce, 1990). These validities ranged between 0.19 and 0.46. In sum, it appears that the exaggeration index has trait-like properties. It captures meaningful individual differences when all respondents are measured in the same context.

Knowledge Accuracy

Scores on knowledge accuracy have been validated against credible alternative measures of knowledge. In one study, for example, general knowledge of psychology was measured with three formats: OCT accuracy, multiple choice, and short answer (Nathanson, Westlake, & Paulhus, 2007). After disattenuation for unreliability, the alternative methods correlated 0.66 and above with the OCT accuracy index.

When the questionnaire topics include a range of academic content, OCT accuracy scores appear to tap global cognitive ability (Paulhus & Harms, 2004). This conclusion is supported by validation against standard objective measures such as the Wonderlic IQ test, Raven's matrices, and, especially, the UBC Word test. These correlations range from 0.31 to 0.50 (Paulhus & Harms, 2004; Bertsch & Pesta, 2009). Similar associations were obtained with Chinese versions of a general over-claiming questionnaire and Chinese IQ test (Liu & Paulhus, 2009). The fact that its strongest correlate is the UBC Word test (a measure of verbal ability) suggests that the academic accuracy index taps a crystallized form of verbal intelligence (see Ackerman, 2000).

The Role of Item Content

The OCT was designed as a methodological framework rather than a fixed set of items. In their original overclaiming questionnaire (OCQ), Paulhus and Bruce (1990) included only academic content: 15 items in each of 10 categories (e.g., science, law, philosophy, history, literature, language). The primary source was the set of items compiled by Hirsch (1987): That item set was held to circumscribe the minimal cultural literacy of an educated American.

A subsequent series of studies with the academic OCQ demonstrated that the accuracy index predicted verbal IQ scores in the 0.40–0.60 range (Paulhus & Harms, 2004). The exaggeration index correlated moderately (0.25–0.38) with trait self-enhancement measures such as narcissism and self-deceptive enhancement (Paulhus et al., 2003).

Since then, a variety of other overclaiming questionnaires have been developed. One is the music OCQ, which covers 10 types (classical, jazz, country, pop, etc.). Most elaborate is the lay OCQ, which includes topics more relevant to less educated samples. It includes 25 topics ranging from sports to fashion to world leaders (Nathanson & Paulhus, 2005).

For non-academic items, the link between the exaggeration index and trait self-enhancement was more nuanced. For example, correlations with narcissism were significant only for topics that the respondent valued (Nathanson & Paulhus, 2005). It stands to reason that people do not invest their egos in knowledge about topics that are irrelevant (or in opposition) to their identities (Ackerman, 2000).

Interestingly, the accuracy index predicted IQ for virtually all of the lay topics. Across the board, high-IQ respondents seem to be able to distinguish real items from foils—even for topics in which they expressed little interest. (Of the 25 lay topics, only two accuracies yielded negative correlations with IQ: professional wrestling and monster trucks.) Our curiosity about such findings led to the laboratory research described in the next section.

The Nature of Overclaiming Behavior

What would lead individuals to claim knowledge of nonexistent foils—even under anonymous circumstances? Preliminary evidence from our laboratory suggests that cognitive, motivational, and self-presentational elements are at work (Williams, Paulhus, & Nathanson, 2002).

To evaluate the degree of automaticity involved in overclaiming, our laboratory study included a manipulation of stimulus presentation time. The presentation was either speeded (1 second) or extended (3 seconds). The substantial drop in accuracy scores confirmed that less attentional capacity was available under the speeded condition. The exaggeration scores, however, were unaffected and remained correlated with narcissism. This robust pattern suggests that the underlying exaggeration process is more automatic than controlled (Williams et al., 2002).

We also addressed the possibility that overclaiming is simply a memory bias. In other words, people may vary in knowledge exaggeration because they differ in the "feeling of knowing." For some people, everything looks familiar; for other people, the sense of familiarity with stimuli is calibrated with actual exposure to those stimuli. Both phenomena may be explained by the concept of perceptual fluency (Bernstein & Harley, 2007; Yonelinas & Jaccoby, 1996). To index individual differences in the cognitive component, we collected standard measures of memory bias. Results confirmed that individuals with high OCT exaggeration scores also showed a global memory bias. In regression analyses, however, narcissism retained its association with knowledge exaggeration after controlling for memory bias. In short, overclaiming has a motivational component (narcissism) along with a cognitive component (memory bias).

As noted earlier, exaggeration scores are subject to situational demand (Paulhus et al., 2003). However, narcissists exaggerate their knowledge even under anonymous conditions. Hence, overclaiming is not entirely a matter of conscious impression management: Compared to nonnarcissists, narcissists sense that many (even novel) items are familiar. This hindsight effect appears in narcissists even under speeded conditions, where participants cannot accurately distinguish real items from foils. In short, there remains a self-deceptive element to the narcissistic tendency to overclaim.

▪ ADVANTAGES OF THE OVERCLAIMING TECHNIQUE OVER CONVENTIONAL DETECTION METHODS

The advantages of the OCT approach include simplicity, practicality, and robustness across contexts. Its robustness encompasses several important contexts. Under fake-good instructions, for example, exaggeration scores increase but the validity of accuracy scores is sustained (Paulhus & Harms, 2004). Under warning conditions ("some items don't exist."), mean exaggeration scores decrease (Calsyn, Kelemen, Jones, & Winter, 2001; Hughes & Beer, 2010), although their validities (correlations with narcissism) are sustained (Paulhus et al., 2003). Understandably, warning about foils also introduces a correlation of exaggeration with impression management scores (Randall & Fernandes, 1991).

A singular advantage of OCT is the minimization of stress during test administration. Respondents are simply asked to rate their familiarity with items; no ability testing is implied and no time limit is imposed. Compare that framing with the stress induced by standard ability test instructions: "Get as many correct answers as you can before we stop you." The minimization of pressure also reduces the motivation to cheat. As a result, overclaiming questionnaires can be administered without supervision. We have confirmed this feature by showing valid results even when participants are allowed to complete the questionnaire at home or on the web (Paulhus et al., 2003).

In sum, the OCT offers a practical and efficient method for indexing exaggeration and accuracy in a targeted knowledge domain. It is robust across a variety of administration conditions. Finally, the method is largely nonthreatening and unobtrusive because the apparent purpose is a survey of idiosyncratic familiarities.

■ APPLICATIONS

In this section, I describe how the OCT has been applied to address questions in the domains of education, survey research, and personnel evaluation. By dint of their success, these studies also contribute to the construct validity of the two OCT indexes.

Personnel Selection

Among those most concerned with faking on personality tests are psychologists involved in personnel selection (see Griffith & Peterson, 2006). This concern is growing with accumulating evidence that personality is a useful predictor in applicant evaluations (Barrick & Mount, 1991; Hogan, Hogan, & Roberts 1996).

Because of the optimal properties detailed above, the exaggeration index has potential for use as a moderator or suppressor in application contexts. A recent study by Bing and colleagues has confirmed this promise (Bing, Kluemper, Davison, Taylor, & Novicevic, 2009). They administered the academic OCQ to 408 business students along with self-reported achievement motivation and actual GPA. Results showed a suppressor effect of the OCQ exaggeration index on the association between self-report motivation and actual GPA. In short, controlling for exaggeration improved the predictive validity of the self-report measure.

If this result holds up in future studies, the overclaiming technique may provide a valuable research tool for personnel selection. With a few exceptions (Berry, Page, & Sackett, 2007; Schmitt, Oswald, Kim, Gillespie, & Ramsay, 2003), researchers have had difficulty in establishing either suppressor or moderator effects for SDR measures. As noted earlier, the fundamental weakness in traditional SDR scales is the confounding of content and style. As Paulhus and Holden (2010) pointed out, overclaiming avoids that confound because of the objective scoring procedure. Claiming familiarity with nonexistent items is a more face-valid, concrete indicator of distortion compared to SDR scales, which simply accumulate claims to possess desirable characteristics.

Educational Contexts

In the previous section on knowledge accuracy, I noted a study that compared the validity and efficiency of three educational test item formats, namely, multiple choice, short essays, and overclaiming accuracy (Nathanson et al., 2007). These formats competed head to head in predicting the final course grades. The performance of the OCT accuracy index proved exceptional in two ways. First, it was the most efficient based on validity per unit time. Second, students reported that overclaiming induced less stress than did the other two formats. Interestingly, the OCT exaggeration index also contributed independently to the prediction of final course grades. This index may contribute by tapping a student's overall sense of confidence about expertise in the field of psychology.

A similar result was recently reported by Pesta and Poznanski (2009) who demonstrated the broader utility of the exaggeration index. Along with predicting IQ, the exaggeration index predicted several indexes of MBA student success. The authors suggested that this predictive power derives from the fact that the optimism implicit in overclaiming promotes success in business.

Finally, OCT has proved useful in tapping knowledge about mental health (Swami, Persaud, & Furnham, 2011). Their findings point to the serious consequences of assuming that the general public is sufficiently educated about important social issues.

Marketing Research

Another practical application is to the field of marketing surveys (Nathanson et al., 2007; Roeder & Paulhus, 2009). In traditional measurement of product familiarity, a survey with a list of product names is administered. But foils are rarely included. To control for overclaiming in the study by Nathanson and colleagues, we developed a consumer OCQ with 10 items for each of 12 product categories (e.g., wine, cars, fashion designers, cosmetics brands). Following the standard OCT procedure, 20% of the items in each category served as foils.

In both studies, participants responded under one of three instructional sets: honest responding, fake good, and sabotage. As expected, respondents in the fake-good condition showed the highest exaggeration scores. However, the validity of the accuracy index (i.e., its correlation with IQ scores) held up even under instructions to fake good. Validity was largely undermined in the sabotage condition.

In our more recent study (Roeder & Paulhus, 2009), we expanded the consumer OCQ to 180 items. The newer version includes more topics relevant to women's consumer interests (e.g., fashion, cosmetics). The survey package also included a measure of cynicism about advertising. Results confirmed the robustness of the accuracy measure under conditions of purposeful exaggeration. Interestingly, cynical consumers were more knowledgeable and overclaimed less than noncynics.

Together, these two studies suggest that the overclaiming technique is a promising tool for characterizing two parameters of product recognition. Although it cannot prevent sabotage, the method does help counter impression management.

■ ETHICS RESEARCH

Another domain in which it would be naive to accept self-reports is in the measurement of ethical behavior. It is not surprising, then, that the overclaiming technique has been applied to that domain (Joseph, Berry, & Deshpande, 2008; Randall & Fernandes, 1991). In self-reports of business ethics, Randall and Fernandes (1991) showed that overclaiming scores were associated with two forms of socially desirable responding, that is, both impression management and self-deceptive enhancement. That finding was recently clarified by showing that overclaiming is associated with self-reports of ethical behavior but not with reports of ethical behavior by others (Joseph et al., 2008).

■ FUTURE DIRECTIONS

Although we encourage the application of the OCT to other domains, a number of caveats should be heeded. First, the OCT is a method rather than a fixed questionnaire. The original academic version of the OCQ (Paulhus & Bruce, 1990) proved successful in research 1990s-era North American college students. That version should remain valid because there is reasonable stability in the content of a liberal education. By contrast, the lay versions of the OCQ may quickly lose validity because of instability in the content of popular culture. Researchers must revise (and, if possible, pretest) item sets to suit their sample.

In this process, the selection of foils is a vital step. In principle, researchers should perform a Google search to verify (the nonexistence of) foils immediately before administration of an overclaiming questionnaire. Whereas real items are relatively stable, the status of foils can change overnight.

Nor can the original item set be assumed to work in other cultures. Despite a shared language, the ideal item sets may differ for Scottish university students, Australian bus drivers, and Indian civil servants. Needless to say, translations to other languages require special sensitivity to linguistic issues. Although Liu and Paulhus (2009) had considerable success in comparing Mandarin and English college samples, it may well be that the technique cannot be applied to some languages.

Another recommendation is to consider the ego-relevance of the items (Ackerman, 2000). Our work with the lay OCQ, for example, showed that the exaggeration index works (i.e., correlates with trait self-enhancement) only in knowledge domains valued by the respondent. No matter how narcissistic, those who despise country music will not be inclined to exaggerate their familiarity with the topic. A failure to ensure ego-relevance may impair the detection of individual differences in exaggeration. This floor effect should not be an issue in high-stakes contexts such as scholastic testing and job interviews because all candidates value the job knowledge—at least for the duration of the interview.

A remaining challenge is to determine if the overclaiming method can be applied to *moralistic biases* as well as *egoistic biases* (see Paulhus & John, 1998; Lonnqvist, Verkasalo, & Bezmenova, 2007). Knowledge exaggeration is certainly relevant to egoistic bias—the form that distorts self-reports of agentic traits such as intelligence, power, autonomy, and creativity (see Calsyn et al., 2001). It is harder to see how knowledge overclaiming can ever capture the moralistic bias that distorts self-reports of communal traits (e.g., nurturance, cooperation, and self-sacrifice). Nonetheless, research continues on that problem.

A recent development is the use of the OCT to determine the neuropsychological processes underlying self-enhancement. Using neuropsychological methods, Hughes and Beer (2010) demonstrated the activation of the prefrontal cortex when participants are warned about the presence of foils. Presumably, such participants are actively trying to suppress their typical overclaiming tendencies. Another study found that transcranial magnetic stimulation of the prefrontal cortex tends to reduce OCT exaggeration (Kwan et al., 2007). Such studies suggest that faking is best framed as an inhibition process that can be mapped onto neurological substrates.

■ SUMMARY

The over-claiming technique (OCT) shows promise as a method of identifying fakers while simultaneously measuring their expertise in specific knowledge domains. The procedure is straightforward: Respondents are asked to rate their familiarity with a range of items relevant to the special topic (e.g., academic facts, workplace items, consumer products). Knowledge accuracy is indexed by a respondent's ability to distinguish real items from nonexistent items (foils). Exaggeration can be measured either by (1) the tendency to claim familiarity with foils or (2) the overall tendency to claim familiarity.

These OCT indexes have proved their utility in a variety of assessment contexts. The exaggeration index has been validated against trait measures of self-enhancement. It has also been shown to track self-presentational demand across situations. Thus, the utility of the OCT appears to extend to both private self-enhancement and conscious impression management.

The accuracy index has been validated against IQ scores and objective measures of knowledge. It retains its validity under varying levels of self-presentational demand. Applications of the OCT have expanded to include marketing research, educational measurement, and ethics research, as well as personnel selection.

The construct validation reviewed in this chapter suggests that the OCT is a powerful framework for self-report assessment. Although application to the faking of personality self-reports remains preliminary, the prospects are exciting.

References

Ackerman, P. L. (2000). Domain-specific knowledge as the "dark matter" of adult intelligence: Gf/Gc personality and interest correlates. *Journal of Gerontology: Psychological Sciences, 55*, 69–84.

Anderson, C. D., Warner, J. L., & Spencer, C. C. (1984). Inflation bias in self-assessment examinations: Implications for valid employee selection. *Journal of Applied Psychology*, 69, 574–580.

Barrick, M. R., & Mount, M. K. (1991). The Big Five personality dimensions and job performance: A meta-analysis. *Personnel Psychology*, 44, 1–26.

Baumeister, R. F. (1982). A self-presentational view of social phenomena. *Psychological Bulletin*, 91, 3–26.

Bernstein, D. M., & Harley, E. M. (2007). Fluency misattribution and visual hindsight bias. *Memory*, 15, 548–560.

Berry, C. M., Page, R. C., & Sackett, P. R. (2007). Effects of self-deceptive enhancement on personality-job performance relationships. *International Journal of Selection and Assessment*, 15, 94–109.

Bertsch, S., & Pesta, B. J. (2009). The Wonderlic Personnel Test and elementary cognitive tasks as predictors of religions sectarianism, scriptural acceptance, and religious questioning. *Intelligence*, 37, 231–237.

Bing, M. N., Kluemper, D. H., Davison, H. K., Taylor, S. G., & Novicevic, M. M. (2009). *A measurement of faking that enhances personality test validity: Overclaiming's suppression effect*. Academy of Management, 69th Annual Conference, Chicago, IL.

Block, J. (1965). *The challenge of response sets: Unconfounding meaning, acquiescence, and social desirability in the MMPI*. New York: Appleton-Century-Crofts.

Calsyn, R. J., Kelemen, W. L., Jones, E. T., & Winter, J. P. (2001). Reducing overclaiming in needs assessment studies: An experimental comparison. *Evaluation Review*, 25, 583–590.

Crowne, D. P., & Marlowe, D. A. (1960). A new scale of social desirability independent of psychopathology. *Journal of Consulting Psychology*, 24, 349–354.

Davis, C. G., Thake, J., & Vilhena, N. (2010). Social desirability biases in self-reported alcohol consumption and harms. *Addictive Behaviors*, 35, 302–311.

Griffith, R. L., & Peterson, M. H. (2006). *A closer examination of applicant faking behavior*. Greenwich, CT: Information Age.

Griffith, R. L., & Peterson, M. H. (2008). The failure of social desirability measures to capture applicant faking behavior. *Industrial and Organization Psychology: Perspectives on Science and Practice*, 1, 308–311.

Hirsch, E. D. (1987). *Cultural literacy*. New York: Vintage Books.

Hogan, R. T., Hogan, J., & Roberts, B. W. (1996). Personality measurement, faking, and employment selection. *Journal of Applied Psychology*, 92, 1270–1285.

Holden, R. R. (2008). Underestimating the effects of faking on the validity of self-report personality scales. *Personality and Individual Differences*, 44, 311–321.

Holden, R. R., Kroner, D. G., Fekken, G. C., & Popham, S. M. (1992). A model of personality test item response dissimulation. *Journal of Personality and Social Psychology*, 63, 272–279.

Hughes, B. L., & Beer, J. S. (2010, February). *Not so fast: Social accountability reduces evaluative bias by increasing rather than decreasing cognitive control*. Poster presented at the meeting of the Society for Personality and Social Psychology, Las Vegas.

John, O. P., & Robins, R. W. (1994). Accuracy and bias in self-perception: Individual differences in self-enhancement and the role of narcissism. *Journal of Personality and Social Psychology*, 66, 206–219.

Joseph, J., Berry, K., & Deshpande, S. P. (2008). Impact of emotional intelligence and other factors on perception of ethical behavior of peers. *Journal of Business Ethics*, 89, 539–546.

Kwan, V. S. Y., Barrios, V., Ganis, G., Gorman, J., Lange, C., Kumar, M., Shepard, A., & Keenan, J. P. (2007). Assessing the neural correlates of self-enhancement bias: A transcranial magnetic stimulation study. *Experimental Brain Research, 182*, 379–385.

Liu, C., & Paulhus, D. L. (2009). *A comparison of overclaiming tendencies among Canadian and Chinese students.* Unpublished data, University of British Columbia, Vancouver.

Lonnqvist, J. E., Verkasalo, M., & Bezmenova, I. (2007). Agentic and communal bias in socially desirable responding. *European Journal of Personality, 21*, 853–868.

McCrae, R. R., & Costa, P. T. (1983). Social desirability scales: More substance than style. *Journal of Consulting & Clinical Psychology, 51*, 882–888.

Nathanson, C., & Paulhus, D. L. (2005, June). *Accuracy and bias in lay knowledge.* Poster presented at the meeting of the Canadian Psychological Association, Calgary.

Nathanson, C., Westlake, B., & Paulhus, D. L. (2007, May). *Controlling response bias in the measurement of consumer knowledge.* Presented at the meeting of the Association for Psychological Science, Washington, D.C.

Paulhus, D. L. (1984). Two-component models of socially desirable responding. *Journal of Personality and Social Psychology, 46*, 598–609.

Paulhus, D. L. (1991). Measurement and control of response bias. In J. P. Robinson, P.R. Shaver, & L. S. Wrightsman (Eds.), *Measures of personality and social psychological attitudes* (pp. 17–59). San Diego: Academic Press.

Paulhus, D. L. (1998). *Manual for Balanced Inventory of Desirable Responding* (BIDR-7). Toronto: Multi-Health Systems.

Paulhus, D. L., & Bruce, M. N. (1990, June). *Claiming more than we can know: The Overclaiming Questionnaire.* Presented at the meeting of the Canadian Psychological Association, Ottawa.

Paulhus, D. L., & Goldberg, L. A. (2008). *Correlates of overclaiming in a community sample.* Unpublished data from the Eugene-Springfield Community Sample.

Paulhus, D. L., & Harms, P. D. (2004). Measuring cognitive ability with the overclaiming technique. *Intelligence, 32*, 297–314.

Paulhus, D. L., Harms, P. D., Bruce, M. N., & Lysy, D. C. (2003). The over-claiming technique: Measuring self-enhancement independent of ability. *Journal of Personality and Social Psychology, 84*, 681–693.

Paulhus, D. L., & Holden, R. R. (2010). Measuring self-enhancement: From self-report to concrete behavior. In C. R. Agnew, D. E. Carlston, W. G. Graziano, & J. R. Kelly (Eds.), *Then a miracle occurs: Focusing on behavior in social psychological theory and research* (pp. 227–246). New York: Oxford University Press.

Paulhus, D. L., & John, O. P. (1998). Egoistic and moralistic biases in self-perception: The interplay of self-deceptive styles with basic traits and motives. *Journal of Personality, 66*, 1025–1060.

Paulhus, D. L., & Petrusic, W. M. (2010). *Measuring individual differences with signal detection analysis: A guide to indexes based on knowledge ratings.* Unpublished manuscript.

Paulhus, D. L., & Trapnell, P. D. (2008). Self-presentation of personality: An agency-communion framework. In O. P. John, R. W. Robins, & L. A. Pervin (Eds.), *Handbook of personality: Theory and research* (3rd ed.)(pp. 492–517). New York: Guilford Press.

Paulhus, D. L., & Williams, K. M. (2002). The Dark Triad of personality: narcissism, Machiavellianism, and psychopathy. *Journal of Research in Personality, 36*, 556–563.

Pesta, B. J., & Poznanski, P. J. (2009). The inspection time and over-claiming tasks as predictors of MBA student performance. *Personality and Individual Differences, 46*, 236–240.

Phillips, D. L., & Clancy, K. J. (1972). Some effects of "Social Desirability" in survey studies. *The American Journal of Sociology, 77*, 921–940.

Randall, D. M., & Fernandes, M. F. (1991). The social desirability response bias in ethics research. *Journal of Business Ethics, 10*, 805–817.

Raubenheimer, A. S. (1925). An experimental study of some behavioral traits of the potentially delinquent boy. *Psychological Monographs, 159*, 1–107.

Roeder, S., & Paulhus, D. L. (2009, February). *Measuring consumer knowledge in the face of exaggeration and sabotage*. Poster presented at the meeting of the Society for Consumer Psychology, San Diego.

Schmitt, N., Oswald, F. L., Kim, B. H., Gillespie, M. A., & Ramsay, L. J. (2003). Impact of elaboration on socially desirable responding and the validity of biodata measures. *Journal of Applied Psychology, 88*, 979–988.

Stanovich, K. E., & West, R. F. (1989). Exposure to print and orthographic processing. *Reading Research Quarterly, 24*, 402–433.

Swami, V., Persaud, R., & Furnham, A. (2011). The recognition of mental health disorders and its association with psychiatric scepticism, knowledge of psychiatry, and the Big Five personality factors: An investigation using the overclaiming technique. *Social Psychiatry and Psychiatric Epidemiology, 46*, 181–189.

Swets, J. A. (1964). *Signal detection and recognition by human observers*. New York: Wiley.

Tracy, J. L., Cheng, J. T., Robins, R. W., & Trzesniewski, K. H. (2009). Authentic and hubristic pride: The affective core of self-esteem and narcissism. *Self and Identity, 8*, 196–213.

Williams, K. M., Paulhus, D. L., & Nathanson, C. (2002, August). *The nature of over-claiming: Personality and cognitive factors*. Poster presented at the annual meeting of the American Psychological Association, Chicago.

Yonelinas, A., & Jaccoby, L. (1996). Noncriterial recollection: Familiarity as automatic, irrelevant recollection. *Consciousness and Cognition, 5*, 131–141.

11 The Detection of Faking Through Word Use

■ MATTHEW VENTURA

Researchers have long argued that social dispositions are manifested in language (cf. Allport, 1961; Fast & Funder, 2008; Funder, 2007; Furnham, 1990; Sanford, 1942). Notably, over the past decade the systematic analysis of language has emerged as a method to identify personality and false stories (i.e., deception). Although typical assessments such as self-report have shown been to be effective by the standards of validity, they may not be telling the whole story and may be susceptible to faking due to social desirability (e.g., Viswesvaran & Ones, 1999). This chapter will review how language has been investigated in the area of personality assessment and how analysis of writing can be a method to detect faking in personality assessment. First, I will review an existing software approach to language analysis that has been studied in the context of personality assessment, namely the *Linguistic Inquiry Word Count* or LIWC (Pennebaker, Francis, & Booth, 2001). Second, LIWC will be reviewed in its use in detecting deception in writing. Finally, alternative approaches to language analysis will be reviewed and how they can be applied to personality assessment and the detection of faking.

■ MEASURING PERSONALITY THROUGH LANGUAGE USE THROUGH THE LIWC

The LIWC approach to measuring personality uses a *word count method* that involves counting a proportion of words that fall into predefined word categories of interest (e.g., negative emotion words, first person pronouns). Currently, there are 87 semantic and linguistic categories in LIWC. Table 11.1 displays some examples of word categories in LIWC. LIWC generates scores for each category by calculating the proportion of category words that occurs in each text sample. For example, if a text sample containing 100 words uses five words from the LIWC social processes category, then the text sample gets 0.05 for that category.

Fast and Funder (2008) note several reasons tools such as LIWC might be useful methods for examining the relationship between social dispositions and language. First, algorithmic methods to investigate word use may offer psychological information that is not obvious through human coding (Pennebaker, MacKenzie, Lee, & Podsakoff, 2003). Second, Fast and Funder (2008) note that the frequency of particular words used in one's lexicon reflects the degree of importance of that word to an individual (Stone, Dunphy, Smith, & Ogilvie, 1966). For example, self-interest may be important to those who use more self-references (e.g., I and me), and emotional states might be more important to those who use more emotion words (e.g., enjoy and sad; Fast & Funder, 2008). Third, the word count method may be appropriate for personality and deception research since

TABLE 11.1 *LIWC Word Categories*

Category	Examples	Words in Category
Linguistic Processes		
Word count		
Words >6 letters		
Total function words		464
Total pronouns	I, them, itself	116
Articles	A, an, the	3
[Common verbs]	Walk, went, see	383
Prepositions	To, with, above	60
Negations	No, not, never	57
Swear words	Damn, piss, fuck	53
Psychological Processes		
Social processes	Mate, talk, they, child	455
Affective processes	Happy, cried, abandon	915
Positive emotion	Love, nice, sweet	406
Negative emotion	Hurt, ugly, nasty	499
Anxiety	Worried, fearful, nervous	91
Anger	Hate, kill, annoyed	184
Sadness	Crying, grief, sad	101
Cognitive processes	Cause, know, ought	730
Tentative	Maybe, perhaps, guess	155
Certainty	Always, never	83
Perceptual processes	Observing, heard, feeling	273
Hear	Listen, hearing	51
Feel	Feels, touch	75
Biological processes	Eat, blood, pain	567
Body	Cheek, hands, spit	180
Sexual	Horny, love, incest	96
Time	End, until, season	239
Personal Concerns		
Work	Job, majors, Xerox	327
Achievement	Earn, hero, win	186
Home	Apartment, kitchen, family	93
Religion	Altar, church, mosque	159
Death	Bury, coffin, kill	62

From Pennebaker, Chung, Ireland, Gonzales, and Booth (2007).

written and spoken word use are stable across time and contexts (Fast & Funder, 2008; Mehl & Pennebaker, 2003; Pennebaker & King, 1999). Thus, this stability in language use may be bound by personality dispositions. Finally, and possibly most importantly, analysis of language to measure social dispositions may be less susceptible to faking. Typical conscious inhibition mechanisms of social desirability may not have such a strong influence on word use (Fast & Funder, 2008).

■ VALIDITY OF WORD COUNT METHODS AS PERSONALITY MEASURES

The validity of word use and personality has been investigated by evaluating the relationship between self-reports of personality and word use measure by LIWC.

Pennebaker and King (1999) analyzed language samples along 15 word categories and found weak relationships between these categories and self-reports of the Big Five personality traits. Mehl, Gosling, and Pennebaker (2006) investigated the relationship between other's ratings of personality and word use using the Electronically Activated Recorder (EAR). The EAR captured participants' word use in day-to-day conversation over 2 days. Then strangers to the participants were asked to rate the EAR participants' personalities by listening to the EAR recordings. The ratings of the Big Five personality traits were then correlated with 23 LIWC category scores. Pronouns, swear words, negative emotion words, and past tense verbs had notable correlations with personality ratings. As in past studies, however, self-reports of personality had relatively weak correlations with LIWC word use scores.

Future research on word use analysis should focus on additional word categories that are relevant to personality (Mehl et al., 2006; Pennebaker & King, 1999). Even studies that examined almost all LIWC categories (Mehl et al., 2006; Pennebaker & King, 1999) may have overlooked important word categories because of strict reliability exclusion criteria (Fast and Funder, 2008). Thus, future research should take a more exploratory approach testing new word categories consistent with the theory of the personality construct in focus. The next section will review research on language use and deception.

■ WORD COUNT METHODS AND DECEPTION

While the bulk of research using word counts has focused on the construct validity of its use as personality assessment, others have used word count methods as a means to detect deception. Being deceptive entails telling a false story and requires describing events that did not happen or attitudes that do not exist (Newman, Pennebaker, Berry, & Richards, 2003). Interest in deception and language use was sparked when Pennebaker and Francis (1996) revealed that essays that were rated more personal and honest have word use patterns different from essays that were rated more detached and distant. This suggests that deception in writing could be detected through linguistic analysis algorithms. Based on this research, at least three language dimensions have been claimed to be associated with deception: (1) fewer self-references, (2) more negative emotion words, and (3) fewer markers of cognitive complexity (Newman et al., 2003).

First, the use of the first-person singular has been claimed to implicitly indicate ownership of a statement (Newman et al., 2003). In cases of deception, individuals tend to distance themselves from this ownership to avoid taking responsibility for the statements and claims (Feldman-Barrett, Williams, & Fong, 2002). Thus, fewer first-person singular pronouns (e.g., I, me, and my) could characterized these deceptive communications.

Second, deceptive communicators may feel guilty about deception in communication (e.g., Vrij, Edward, Roberts, & Bull, 2000), and this guilt may be characterized by more words reflecting negative emotion (e.g., hate, worthless, sad; Newman et al., 2003). Diary studies of common conversational lies suggest that people feel discomfort and guilt while lying (DePaulo, Lindsay, Malone, Muhlenbruck, Charlton, & Cooper, 2003).

Finally, the process of creating a false story should consume more cognitive resources than telling the truth (Richards & Gross, 2000). A byproduct of this increased cognitive demand should lead to the use of less complex language in deceptive stories (Newman et al., 2003). Nondeceptive style writing includes distinctions and a higher number of "exclusive" words (e.g., usually, except, but, without). Conversely, deceptive stories are less complex and may focus more on simple, concrete verbs (e.g., "I worked hard") rather than evaluations and judgments (e.g., "Usually I work hard, but I was sick that day") because the former are more accessible and more easily constructed in a deceptive story (Newman et al., 2003). Thus, creating a deceptive story creates excessive cognitive demand leaving less capacity to formulate complex sentences.

Newman et al. (2003) tested these specific predictions about the linguistic features of deceptive stories using LIWC. A total of 101 undergraduates were asked to discuss both their true and false views on various topics. Newman et al. (2003) hypothesized that deceptive writing would contain fewer self-references, fewer cognitive complexity words (exclusive words, motion verbs), and more negative emotion words. They also hypothesized that a linguistic predictive model created by LIWC based on one sample would generalize to an independent sample. Human judges were asked to rate the truthfulness of the 400 communications dealing with abortion attitudes (Studies 1 through 3). The judges were asked to give a truthfulness rating about transcripts of people presenting a pro-choice or a pro-life position on the issue of abortion, and in some cases, the transcripts would be describing feelings that were truthful. Across five studies investigation of deception on multiple topics truthfulness ratings were predicted by fewer first-person singular pronouns, third-person pronouns, and exclusive words, and more negative emotion words and motion verbs. These predictors were used in a logistic regression predicting deception in all five studies combined. When all five studies were combined, the general equation explained 8% of the variance with an overall accuracy rate of 61% (i.e., better than chance).

Finally, Newman et al. (2003) investigated the ability of LIWC to identify deception relative to human judges. The human rating of truthfulness was dichotomously classified for each communication. If 50% of the judges believed a communication

TABLE 11.2 *Comparison of Human Judges' Ratings with LIWC's Prediction Equations in Three Abortion Studies*

	Predicted	
	Deceptive	Truthful
Actual instruction to participants ($n = 200$)		
LIWC		
Deceptive	68%	32%
Truthful	34%	66%
Human		
Deceptive	30%	71%
Truthful	27%	74%

From Newman et al. (2003).

to be truthful it was coded as judged truthful, while the remaining were judged false. As can be seen in Table 11.2, LIWC correctly classified 67% (i.e., average of 68% and 66%) of the abortion communications whereas the human judges correctly classified 52% (i.e., these proportions were significantly different).

In another notable study on deception and writing, Hancock, Curry, Goorha, and Woodworth (2008) investigated changes in linguistic style with LIWC across truthful and deceptive communication between individual pairs in separate rooms through a computer. Consistent with some findings from Newman et al. (2003), deceptive communication was found to contain more overall words, sensory words, and other-reference pronouns, and fewer self-references. Additionally, motivated deceptive communicators (i.e., through a manipulation) avoided causation words (e.g., because). In light of these differences in linguistic styles partners engaged in communication with deceptive communicators were unable to use this linguistic information to improve their deception detection accuracy (Hancock, et al., 2008).

In summary, there has been encouraging success in using LIWC as a tool to measure deception in communication. One criticism mentioned earlier is that LIWC does not incorporate context or phrases in its method of detecting personality deceptive information. As noted, strict word matching algorithms have limitations due to the enormous variability in language. The next section introduces a new approach to investigating personality and language through more sophisticated tools in computation linguistics.

■ LATENT SEMANTIC ANALYSIS

There are ways to detect deception in writing other than LIWC. One such tool is Latent Semantic Analysis (LSA; Landauer & Dumas, 1997). LSA is a statistical, language analysis technique that constructs relations among words on the basis of statistical properties from a large corpus of written text. The input to LSA is a set of texts that can range from a broad landscape of topics (such as an encyclopedia) to a sample of texts related to a particular topic of interest (such as the human heart, or conceptual physics). The texts are then segmented into documents. Singular value decomposition, a technique similar to factor analysis, then builds relationships between words that may not be obvious in the original texts. Specifically, LSA constructs word meanings by taking the cooccurrence of words in paragraphs over a large body of text and compressing it into a K-dimensional space. This dimension reduction serves as an induction technique that gives LSA the capability to represent semantic meaning beyond simple cooccurrence information (Landauer & Dumais, 1997). According to LSA, if two words (i.e., row vectors) are related there will be a positive relationship or correlation (i.e., cosine is used in LSA) between these words. This calculation is meaningful because words with similar meaning tend to be used over and over again in the same context of other words. For example, *doctor* and *surgeon* will typically be used in the same context of words, such as *operation, disease, hospital,* and *bed.* It is important to note that LSA does not function as a simple word cooccurrence matrix. *Doctor* and *surgeon* will be highly related not because they occur in the same documents together but because they occur with *hospital, nurse, surgery, operation, bed*, and other medical terms equally often. The process and result of singular value decomposition are far more than counting overlapping words between the two sets of texts (Landauer & Dumais, 1997). Instead, it captures and represents these co-occurrences in a vector composed of 100–500 values. One prominent example that confirms its viability is that LSA has successfully been used to grade essays with performance equal to human professionals (Foltz, Gilliam, & Kendall, 2000).

■ USING LSA TO MEASURE DECEPTION

There are several advantages to using LSA over word counts methods such as LIWC. First, LSA is not dependent on specific matches between a set of words claimed to represent a personality construct or word use by an individual. Remember that the first step in using tools such as LIWC is to determine a set of words that claimed to represent a particular personality construct. For example, a word set for extraversion could be *social, outgoing, talkative*, and *energetic*. By using LSA these words would be represented by vectors e_n as described above. Additionally, a given text by a participant [e.g., answer to a situational judgment test (SJT)] could also be represented by vectors p_n. The participant vector sets could be correlated to the extraversion vectors to detect "extraversion-like" language. This vector approach could be compared to the word overlap metrics traditionally calculated with tools such as LIWC. The efficiency of these two measures could be evaluated by calculating their unique correlation to a sample of human ratings.

Similarly, LSA can also be used to detect deception in communication. Similar to others (e.g., Hancock et al., 2008; Newman et al., 2003) who used word sets to classify deception in language, LSA can classify faking-related language by creating a faking vector set (i.e., similar to creating an extraversion vector as stated above). These faking-related words could be used to represent semantic categories that are proposed to be indicative of deception. Although creating words relevant for faking may not be as straightforward as for personality, words suggested by Newman et al. (2003) (e.g., hate, worthless, sad) could be a first step. The higher the correlation between the participant vectors and the faking vectors, the greater the likelihood the participant is not being completely truthful in his or her answer.

The next section will introduce another technique for detecting deception in language by investigating word combinations.

■ WORD COMBINATIONS AND DECEPTION

Although the LIWC is primarily focused on single word counts, there is reason to believe n-grams (word phrases) may be a useful technique to detect deviations in expected language use. N-gram analysis samples word combinations (usually bigrams) in the language and generates probabilities for individual words. For example, *boy– tree* is a low probability bigram because nouns (*boy*) never occur adjacent to other nouns (*tree*) in the English language. These probabilities are used to detect errors in grammar. Additionally, n-grams in deceptive writing may exist that could be used to train a deception detection algorithm. The general approach is to sample large sets of text from deceptive versus truthful writing. By splitting the text into n-grams (i.e., via a syntactic parser) we can see whether certain n-grams are more or less common in deceptive language versus truthful language. For example, deceptive communication might contain more bigrams related to exaggerations such as *extremely tired* or *worked really late* because these descriptions appear to give more realism to a false story. Additionally, difficult questions may be responded to by saying: "I really don't remember" or "What? Can you repeat that?" to give the responder more time to fabricate a false response. One potential source could be archived writings labeled to contain deceptive communication (e.g., fake news newspapers such as the Onion).

In summary, there are several additional techniques that should be explored measuring personality and deception in writing. The next section will outline how deception in writing can be used as a tool to detect faking in personality assessment.

■ FAKING AND DECEPTION

An obvious question arising from this chapter is how to use existing measures of deception as a tool for detecting faking in personality assessment. That is, how can we relate deceptive communication to how we might fake on a personality assessment? One possible approach would be to structure biographical questions or personal statements that cue particular personality constructs. For example, a conscientiousness constructed response question might be "Please describe your typical work day." This answer could be subject to deception since it requires the respondent to tell a story about working hard. Assuming there is a social desirability effect for working hard, we can expect the respondent will be tempted to exaggerate and distort the true story about how the respondent worked hard. Using tools such as LIWC, LSA, and n-gram analysis, we can detect the features in the language that indicate deception in the story and hence more deception dispositions for conscientiousness. Most importantly, the deception detected in the biographical story can be used as a faking indicator for a paired measure of conscientiousness such as a self-report or SJT. That is, high scores on deception from the biographical story could signal faking on a paired assessment. Moreover, the faking variance from the biographical story can then be used to identify faking variance on a paired assessment measuring the same construct. Ziegler and Buehner (2009) were successfully able to model faking variance using structural equation modeling by instructing participants to fake an assessment. This faking group displayed higher means and covariance among the traits measured. Controlling for the faking latent variable eliminated the effects of means and covariance structure in the faking group. One challenge that arises from using this approach in applied settings is to establish a method to validate faking latent variance without direct instructions to fake. Podsakoff, MacKenzie, Lee, and Podsakoff (2003) suggested using a marker variable to validate the faking latent variable. This approach can be modeled by using the deception score from a biographical story as the marker variable for the latent faking variable on the paired assessment (e.g., self-report and SJT). That is, if the latent variable is indeed modeling faking, then we should see a correlation between the latent variable and the deception score.

The faking variance can then be controlled in subsequent analysis to evaluate changes in construct and criterion-related validity.

Thus, the deception present in the biographical story about a construct (e.g., conscientiousness) could be used as a proxy for faking on another assessment (e.g., self-report) measuring the same construct. This approach can be implemented as cutoff scores or more sophisticated methods that attempt to control for the faking variance.

■ CONCLUSIONS

This chapter reviewed the work on language analysis as a tool in the assessment of personality and deception. Future work should focus on more advanced tools to understand how language use can be a useful measure of personality. LIWC appears to be a promising tool for measuring deception in writing, but because language is so variable and substitutable, using other tools such as LSA may have advantages in finding words related to constructs not explicitly stated in predefined word sets. Furthermore, biographical writing about particular behaviors (i.e., via SJTs or personal statements) may be a useful method to understand faking in personality assessment. These described behaviors indicate personality traits and are subject to social desirability effects and hence deception. Using tools such as LIWC to detect the deception about a construct can be used as a faking indicator for other assessments measuring the same construct.

References

Allport, G. (1961). *Pattern and growth in personality*. New York: Holt, Rinehart, & Winston.

DePaulo, B. M., Lindsay, J. J., Malone, B. E., Muhlenbruck, L., Charlton, K., & Cooper, H. (2003). Cues to deception. *Psychological Bulletin, 129,* 74–112.

Fast, L. A., & Funder, D. C. (2008). Personality as manifest in word use: Correlations with self-report, acquaintance report, and behavior. *Journal of Personality and Social Psychology, 94,* 334–346.

Feldman-Barrett, L., Williams, N. L., & Fong, G. (2002). Defensive verbal behavior assessment. *Personality and Social Psychology Bulletin, 28,* 776–778.

Foltz, P. W., Gilliam, S., & Kendall, S. (2000). Supporting content-based feedback in on-line writing evaluation with LSA. *Interactive Learning Environments, 8,* 111–127.

Funder, D. C. (2007). *The personality puzzle* (4th ed.). New York: Norton.

Furnham, A. (1990). Language and personality. In H. Giles & W. P. Robinson (Eds.), *Handbook of language and social psychology* (pp. 73–95). New York: Wiley.

Hancock, J. T., Curry, L., Goorha, S., & Woodworth, M. T. (2008). On lying and being lied to: A linguistic analysis of deception. *Discourse Processes, 45,* 1–23.

Landauer, T. K., & Dumais, S. T. (1997). A solution to Plato's problem: The latent semantic analysis theory of acquisition, induction, and representation of knowledge. *Psychological Review, 104,* 211–240.

Mehl, M., Gosling, S., & Pennebaker, J. (2006). Personality in its natural habitat: Manifestations and implicit folk theories of personality in daily life. *Journal of Personality and Social Psychology, 90,* 862–877.

Mehl, M., & Pennebaker, J. (2003). The sounds of social life: A psychometric analysis of students' daily social environments and natural conversations. *Journal of Personality and Social Psychology, 84*, 857–870.

Newman, M. L., Pennebaker, J. W., Berry, D. S., & Richards, J. M. (2003). Lying words: Predicting deception from linguistic style. *Personality and Social Psychology Bulletin, 29*, 665–675.

Pennebaker, J. W., Chung, C. K., Ireland, M., Gonzales, A., & Booth, R. J. (2007). The development and psychometric properties of LIWC2007. *LIWC Manual.*

Pennebaker, J. W., & Francis, M. E. (1996). Cognitive, emotional, and language processes in disclosure. *Cognition and Emotion, 10*, 601–626.

Pennebaker, J. W., Francis, M. E., & Booth, R. J. (2001). *Linguistic Inquiry and Word Count (LIWC): LIWC2001.* Mahwah, NJ: Erlbaum.

Pennebaker, J. W., & King, L. A. (1999). Linguistic styles: Language use as an individual difference. *Journal of Personality and Social Psychology, 77*, 1296–1312.

Podsakoff, P. M., MacKenzie, S. B., Lee, J. Y., & Podsakoff, N. P. (2003). Common method biases in behavioral research: A critical review of the literature and recommended remedies. *Journal of Applied Psychology, 88*, 879–903.

Richards, J. M., & Gross, J. J. (2000). Emotion regulation and memory: The cognitive costs of keeping one's cool. *Journal of Personality and Social Psychology, 79*, 410–424.

Sanford, F. (1942). Speech and personality. *Psychological Bulletin, 39*, 811–845.

Stone, P. J., Dunphy, D. C., Smith, M. S., & Ogilvie, D. M. (1966). *The general inquirer: A computer approach to content analysis.* Cambridge, MA: MIT Press.

Viswesvaran, C., & Ones, D. S. (1999). Meta-analysis of fakability estimates: Implications for personality measurement. *Educational and Psychological Measurement, 59*, 197–210.

Vrij, A., Edward, K., Roberts, K. P., & Bull, R. (2000). Detecting deceit via analysis of verbal and nonverbal behavior. *Journal of Nonverbal Behavior, 24*, 239–264.

Ziegler, M., & Buehner, M. (2009). Modeling socially desirable responding and its effects. *Educational and Psychological Measurement, 69*, 548–565.

PART FOUR

Can We Stop People from Faking?
Preventive Strategies

12 Application of Preventive Strategies

■ STEPHAN DILCHERT AND DENIZ S. ONES[1]

The primary goal of this chapter is to discuss issues surrounding preventive strategies to reduce social desirability, impression management, and faking in applied assessment settings (e.g., personnel screening and selection). In doing so, we draw upon past research that has critically evaluated these techniques in laboratory as well as applied settings.

Laboratory research is helpful in identifying techniques that do *not* work in identifying and preventing faking. After all, if a proposed strategy cannot identify individuals who are known to fake (because they have been instructed to do so), how should we identify those who may be more subtle in their impression management? Stated in another way, laboratory-based research can establish whether a faking detection or control strategy can produce a desired effect. However, such research cannot establish the *magnitudes* of such effects in real-world applications. Several scholars (e.g., McDaniel & Timm, 1990) have noted that the motivations of experimental participants to comply with experimenter requests differ from the motivations of job applicants undertaking psychological assessments as part of a personnel selection process—that is, laboratory-based experimental demand effects to fake do not approximate applicant or employee response patterns on noncognitive assessments in high-stakes testing situations (see also the discussion of the work of McDaniel and Timm by Vasilopoulos, Reilly, & Leaman, 2000). Thus, research in and information from applied settings provide the gold standard by which to evaluate the various strategies aimed at preventing faking. Unfortunately, as this chapter will show, such research in applied settings continues to be scant. Where it exists, it is limited to certain methods and points of view, and thus many of our judgments regarding the actual effectiveness of such strategies have to rely on information triangulated from laboratory experiments, applied settings, and survey studies, supplemented by our own applied experience.

In addition to providing a summary of issues relating to the application of various techniques, we will attempt to provide an overview of their prevalence in real-world testing situations. The quality of the empirical evidence on the actual prevalence of these strategies differs. Even for tools that have been developed several decades ago, no good quantitative estimates may be available. Where possible, we base this overview on survey data, and supplement it with our own experience as practicing psychologists who have encountered organizations and test users employing such approaches.

---

1. The order of authorship is arbitrary; both authors contributed equally to this chapter.

TABLE 12.1 *Classification of Strategies by Purpose and Level*

	Level	
Purpose	Identification, person level	Identification, scale/test level
	Prevention, person level	Prevention, item/scale level

Strategies against faking can be classified based on two broad dimensions, resulting in four groups, which we will use to organize our review. First, there is the distinction reflected by Sections III and IV in this book—identification versus prevention strategies. Identification strategies aim simply to identify fakers (at which point decisions of how to treat them are necessitated), whereas prevention strategies attempt to prevent the problem by making faking more difficult. There is a second distinction, which is reflected in Chapters 13, 14, and 15—person versus item level strategies. This distinction, if broadened slightly, not only applies to prevention (e.g., warning test takers versus changing the item format), but also to identification strategies (e.g., monitoring response latencies versus using an infrequency scale). Table 12.1 illustrates the framework of antifaking strategies, and we will follow this framework in discussing identification strategies at the scale and test level, identification strategies at the person level, preventive strategies at the item and scale level, and preventive strategies at the person level. The focus here is on approaches that enable decision making about particular individuals in applications (e.g., selection) and not on controlling for response sets such as social desirability in research applications.

In surveying applied issues surrounding the different strategies, three major questions need to be considered: (1) Which forms does the strategy take, i.e., what recommendations should be used in applied assessment practice? (2) To what degree do test users rely on such strategies in identifying or preventing faking and more subtle forms of impression management, i.e., what are the prevalence rates? (3) What is the effectiveness of the strategy in applied settings, i.e., does it lead to the successful identification or prevention of faking under realistic assessment conditions? Unfortunately, not all of these questions can be conclusively answered for all strategies reviewed here, at least if we rely on empirical evidence.

■ IDENTIFICATION STRATEGIES: SCALE AND TEST LEVEL

The first quadrant of Table 12.1 signifies strategies that are devoted to the identification of response distortion using scale and test level information. Social desirability scales, response inconsistency scales, infrequency scales, as well as newer item response pattern type approaches are available to applied psychologists aiming to identify various forms of response distortion.

Social Desirability Scales

Social desirability scales (e.g., Crowne & Marlowe, 1960; Paulhus, 1984; Wiggins, 1964) are among the best researched and examined strategies to identify (and eventually prevent) faking. Many standardized personality tests include scales developed to detect invalid test profiles (Paulhus, 1991). Those scales that are targeted at identifying conscious attempts of response distortion (e.g., impression management or faking) are often collectively referred to as social desirability or "lie" scales, and should be distinguished from other validity scales (e.g., those that detect carelessness, acquiescence, and other response sets, Jackson & Messick, 1961, 1969). Many test publishers recommend the use of social desirability scales to either identify active response distortion or correct scores to ameliorate the effect of response distortion (a strategy that goes beyond mere identification or prevention). Some publishers may leave the decision up to the test user, but the majority devote entire sections of their technical manuals to providing guidelines for the detection of invalid profiles using social desirability scales.

For example, on the Minnesota Multiphasic Personality Inventory (MMPI), the most widely used test of personality worldwide (Butcher, 2006, 2010), a profile should be considered invalid and uninterpretable if the "Lie" scale score is more than three standard deviations above the mean (Butcher, Graham, Ben-Porath, Tellegen, & Dahlstrom, 2001). In personnel selection settings, scores one and a half standard deviations above the mean are to be questioned on the basis of "overly positive self-presentation" (Butcher et al., 2001, p. 21). The MMPI also includes a "Correction" (K) scale to adjust scores on certain substantive personality scales for the influence of defensive test taking, resulting in "corrected" scores rather than completely invalidating personality protocols. Because measures of psychopathology such as the MMPI are commonly administered to test takers with a high motivation to distort their responses (for example, those seeking to pass a psychological evaluation after having received a conditional job offer), the use of social desirability scales (to either identify fakers or correct their scores) is often explicitly recommended by test publishers. Depending on the report or profile test users purchase, scale scores are sometimes not even generated if test takers' validity scale scores exceed a predetermined cut-off.

Many measures of normal adult personality are accompanied by similar recommendations. Users of the California Psychological Inventory (CPI) are instructed on how to differentiate test takers who "fake good" or "fake bad" from those who respond honestly and provide valid profiles. The CPI "Good Impression" scale is used to help identify individuals portraying themselves in a favorable light, and guidelines for cut-offs are reported in the technical manual (Gough & Bradley, 1996). Technical manuals for other normal personality inventories contain similarly concrete recommendations or provide tables used to convert social desirability scale raw scores to percentile ranks, which can then be used by test users to set their own (often arbitrary) cut-offs (e.g., Conn & Rieke, 1994).

Goffin and Christiansen (2003) reviewed many of the most popular personality tests (both general purpose as well as employment-specific ones) with regard to whether they included social desirability scales and what recommendations were provided regarding their use. Of the 11 inventories they compared [which included the most popular choices for all types of assessments and many of those typically used in employment settings, such as the Hogan Personality Inventory, California Psychological Inventory, Jackson Personality Inventory, NEO-Personality

Inventory–Revised (NEO-PI-R), NEO-Five-Factor Inventory (NEO-FFI), Occupational Personality Inventory, and Sixteen Personality Factor Questionnaire (16PF)], eight included at least one social desirability scale. In fact, two of those eight inventories included more than one scale targeted at identifying invalid protocols. For all of these eight tests, guidelines were provided for determining the validity of profiles based on social desirability scores. Additionally, three of the eight tests included corrections of substantive personality scale scores based on social desirability scale scores.

Although the use of social desirability scale scores appears to be encouraged by many test publishers, it is not always clear whether this is out of a conviction that these scales are efficient in detecting or ameliorating the effects of response distortion, or simply in response to common test user concerns over test takers' impression management. Goffin and Christiansen (2003) surveyed 67 researchers active in personality testing regarding their use of social desirability scales. It is noteworthy that although the participants surveyed were researchers, the survey specifically asked respondents to report on social desirability scale use for *applied purposes* such as "personnel selection" and "assessment center evaluations" (p. 341). Of the 36 psychologists who responded, 56% indicated that they typically use social desirability or lie scales to correct scores on personality measures. An additional 14% indicated that they did not use such corrections, but would do so if they were available in the personality tests they typically use.

It is worrisome that such high regard for social desirability scales and their purported ability to identify fakers is encountered even among the most educated of test users (e.g., scholars surveyed about their applied test use by Goffin and Christiansen, other well-respected personality or assessment researchers, and reviewers whose comments we and our colleagues have received in the course of journal peer reviews). Longstanding empirical evidence has shown traditional social desirability scales to be ineffective in addressing the issue of faking and impression management in applied settings. Whether "faking" actually occurs or not, studies have repeatedly and conclusively shown that social desirability scales contain more "substance than style" (McCrae & Costa, 1983), meaning they capture true variance in emotional stability, agreeableness, and, to a lesser degree, conscientiousness (Ones, Viswesvaran, & Reiss, 1996). Using them to disqualify "fakers" thus often eliminates desirable test takers. Additionally, applying corrections based on social desirability scale scores neither approximates individuals' honest responses (Ellingson, Sackett, & Hough, 1999) nor improves the criterion-related validity of personality measures in applied settings (Christiansen, Goffin, Johnston, & Rothstein, 1994; Hough, 1998; Ones et al., 1996).

Some conceptual arguments have been presented for why scores on social desirability scales could relate to performance-relevant on-the-job behaviors (e.g., Marcus, 2003; Nicholson & Hogan, 1990). Hypothetically, if social desirability scales measure (at least in part) the ability to identify and endorse desirable traits and behaviors, scores on such scales might also relate to displaying such desirable behaviors on the job (e.g., in interpersonal interactions, see Hogan, Barrett, & Hogan, 2007). However, the empirical evidence is clear that social desirability scales do not predict job performance (including overall, task performance, or avoidance of counterproductive work behaviors, see Ones et al., 1996). For jobs that have a large interpersonal component, meta-analytic and large sample research thus far has also failed to uncover useful relationships with performance-related work behaviors and outcomes [e.g., managerial job performance, promotion potential, and organizational level (Viswesvaran, Ones, & Hough, 2001) as well as job performance and its facets among expatriates (Foldes, Ones, & Sinangil, 2006)].

There has been much hypothesizing that if two aspects of social desirability (impression management and self-deception) were to be measured separately, these could provide a more fruitful way to assess and therefore control for response distortion. In a meta-analytic investigation, however, Li and Bagger (2006) demonstrated that the same drawbacks of social desirability scales are mimicked at the impression management and self-deception subscale level. Both self-deception and impression management scales are related to substantive personality scales; for self-deception scales, relationships with emotional stability and conscientiousness appear to be considerably stronger ($\rho = 0.54$ and 0.42, respectively) than with other Big Five personality dimensions, whereas impression management scales correlate most notably with agreeableness ($\rho = 0.42$), conscientiousness ($\rho = 0.42$), and, to a lesser degree, with emotional stability ($\rho = 0.35$). Both impression management and self-deception scales have small unreliability corrected correlations with job performance ($\rho = 0.12$ and 0.10, respectively) and thus by themselves are not particularly useful in the prediction of work performance. Finally, controlling for either of the two facets of social desirability in Big Five personality scales does not appreciably improve prediction of job performance (Li & Bagger, 2006). The empirically based conclusions regarding the (lack of) usefulness of social desirability scales are the same for impression management and self-deception scales. Overall, the practice of correcting scores or challenging the validity of test results based solely on high social desirability scale scores is questionable on many other grounds (see the reviews by Dilchert, Ones, Viswesvaran, & Deller, 2006; Nederhof, 1985), only one of which is the "fakability" of these scales themselves (Baer & Sekirnjak, 1997; Hurtz & Alliger, 2002; Pauls & Crost, 2004).

Those readers who are not yet convinced of the harm done by such scales may consider the following anecdotal, yet entirely true and thus frightening evidence: A recent discussion (November 2009) held on the listserv of the International Personnel Assessment Council (IPAC), the leading professional organization of applied human resources selection and assessment professionals, illustrates how social desirability scales are often used to decide on the careers of individuals. In this case, a consultant described a promotional process among law enforcement job incumbents that included a standardized personality test. Based on the social desirability scale, two candidates were judged to have provided "invalid profiles" and were asked to retake the test. The process resulted in one of the candidates complaining about being "unfairly treated," other candidates suggesting that he should be failed for the relevant portion of the promotional process, and at least two Civil Service hearings after which the consultant was asked to recommend substitute procedures. This example does not pertain to an isolated incident—readers should note that many of the strategies here are commonly used in applied settings. Moreover, as in this example, these strategies are not only used when assessing job *applicants* in traditional hiring scenarios. Job *incumbents* and other test takers who are being assessed for a variety of purposes are also subjected to many questionable practices. It is clear that such practices have a real impact on individuals' work lives—even if we often do not have reliable survey data available to illustrate the full extent of their use in applied settings. The incident described above also illustrates another important issue: Ethical implications are rarely discussed. One of the first replies in the discussion postulated that in cases in which noncognitive tools are used to make personnel decision, the typical test instructions (e.g., "there are no right or wrong answers on this test") are really not true (or ethical) when strategies are used to identify fakers.

Response Inconsistency Scales

Response inconsistency scales were developed as a remedy to existing response distortion scales such as those described above, which were almost exclusively all confounded with true psychological construct variance (Tellegen, 1982). The Differential Personality Questionnaire (now the MPQ, see Tellegen & Waller, 2008) included three such scales, which inspired the development of similar indicators for other inventories (see Butcher et al., 2001). Response inconsistency scales employ the simple principle that certain response patterns to particular item *pairs* consisting of different yet similar (or directly opposing) items are inconsistent if the respective items are carefully matched. Thus, these scales come in varieties such as desirable, true, and variable response inconsistency, depending on which inconsistent answer pattern they are trying to detect. They are distinct from social desirability scales, because they do not necessarily reflect particular item content or desirable or undesirable responses. For example, an item pair on a (true) response inconsistency scale could be "I never remember my dreams" and "My dreams don't have an elaborate or detailed plot." Answering "true" (or strongly agreeing) as a response to both statements would indicate inconsistency in responding.

Although the general principles are the same, different types of response inconsistency scales can detect different response sets and fulfill different purposes. For example, if scores on these scales are interpreted in conjunction with traditional validity scales measuring defensiveness, it may be possible to differentiate between response sets such as carelessness, nonacquiescence, faking bad, or positive impression management (see the detailed treatment in Butcher et al., 2001).

For the purpose of this chapter, desirable inconsistency scales are of most relevance. They consist of pairs of similar yet slightly different items measuring desirable personality traits. The underlying rationale is that an individual who does not exhibit a high level of a given trait and is instead trying to actively manage a positive impression ("fake" a high trait level) would provide answers to these item pairs that are more inconsistent than those of a person with a true high trait level. Of course, the difficulty with response inconsistency scales is that they require a large number of item pairs to assess response inconsistency reliably and avoid false-positive identification of "fakers" due to inconsistent responses (which can be a function of item idiosyncratic variance, rather than a conscious faking attempt). As such, they are typically embedded only in clinical personality inventories that can afford a much larger number of items (and item redundancy) than those inventories used for other practical applications, including preemployment testing. For example, the True Response Inconsistency scale of the MMPI-2 includes 23 item *pairs*, whereas the Variable Response Inconsistency scale contains 49 unique item pairs. Given that item pairs often appear redundant in content, such scales require a large item pool, especially in tests that are targeted as assessing more than just a few traits.

Interestingly, inconsistency scales work in a way that is anticipated by test takers whether such scales are actually present on a test or not. In fact, test takers typically misinterpret normal personality items as checking on the consistency of their responses. Interview studies (e.g., Weijters, Geuens, & Schillewaert, 2009, see below) reveal that similarly worded items are often perceived to function as checks on response consistency even though their actual purpose is solely to increase the reliability of substantive scales. This is because some test developers attempt to increase the internal consistency of scales by including items that are only slight modifications of one another. Although this approach increases internal consistency, it compromises construct coverage and thus criterion-related validity for complex criteria such as overall job performance. It also results in negative test-taker reactions, and may ultimately lower the usefulness of true response consistency scales, which is why we strongly recommend not using inventories that employ such practices. However, well-constructed response consistency scales will be less impacted by these problems, as they depend on item pairs that stem from different content areas and thus do not trigger as much suspicion on behalf of test takers (e.g., "I enjoy being part of a loud crowd" and "I seek quiet").

It is our opinion that response inconsistency scales as part of normal personality inventories are understudied and underutilized. We see a potential for a resurgence of such scales in applied settings, especially in light of computerized testing. The number of item pairs necessary to assess response inconsistencies reliably may be significantly reduced in computerized assessments, where test takers are not allowed to revisit or change their responses to earlier items. Thus, response inconsistency scales may have a place in normal personality assessment after all. Another advantage of these scales will be that more objective cut-offs can be established to identify those individuals providing inconsistent answers. We encourage test publishers to investigate such scales among the large datasets of test takers available to them so as to include empirically established guidelines in technical manuals. For example, at a minimum, cut-off scores should be provided for inconsistency scales to identify groups of test takers among which the factor structure of scores departs from that in the development sample. Similarly, criterion-related validity investigations should be conducted for different groups of test takers based on inconsistency scores. Until such large-scale data are made available, the applied use of inconsistency scales will be very limited.

Infrequency Scales

Infrequency scales rely on the principle that certain answers to certain items (e.g., "I cut others to pieces") are simply so infrequent in the normal (honestly responding) population of test takers that an accumulation of such answer patterns is an indication of a response set. Infrequency scales can be very useful for detecting conscious attempts to fake bad, as well as to detect random or careless response patterns. If designed to measure positive impression management or faking, these scales sum responses across rarely endorsed options of positively scored items (e.g., "I never shirk my duties"). Hence, they present the same problem as traditional social desirability scales: They identify, at least in part, honest test takers with high trait levels on desirable traits. Also, they often require the same arbitrary judgment as social desirability scales in identifying fakers (i.e., above which percentile score on the infrequency scales do we regard a response pattern as too implausible to be the result of an honest response?). Although guidelines could certainly be established empirically, the applied usefulness of such scales will be limited: If cut-offs are set in ways that reduce the number of false positives (misidentifying high-scoring honest test takers as fakers), the number of fakers that will be identified will be very small as well. One way around this issue might be the construction of infrequency scales using items measuring traits that are not part of the predictor battery utilized for decision making. However, another problem with this approach is that it would unnecessarily lengthen the test or inventory, which is often of concern in applied settings, as many organizations are not willing to administer personality inventories consisting of more than 300 items (which is typically the number required for a reliable yet comprehensive assessment that includes both factor and facet scales).

Building Trait-Free Faking Indicators

Scales designed to assess social desirability and related constructs such as impression management are typically fakable themselves, and capture true personality trait variance (see above). In attempts to overcome these shortcomings, new approaches are being proposed, although few have made it into the peer reviewed literature. One such approach is a covariance index based on the premise that strong response sets function like method variance, spuriously increasing the covariance between responses that might otherwise be relatively independent (see Jones & Christiansen, 2004). We should note that approaches that statistically remove method variance from normative inventory scores (e.g., because they assume that the first principal component represents self-presentation bias) result in (biased) scale intercorrelations that can resemble those obtained under ipsative measurement (Dunlap & Cornwell, 1994; Kemery & Dunlap, 1986; see below for a discussion on ipsativity in noncognitive measurement). Here, we review a recently developed strategy to construct an indicator of faking that appears to be conceptually sound and empirically supported, at least as evidenced in laboratory studies.

Indicators Using Idiosyncratic Item Response Pattern Scoring

Recently, Kuncel and Tellegen (2009) demonstrated that social desirability resides at the item response level. That is, response options presented for each item can be scaled in terms of their rated desirabilities, and a plethora of nonlinear models can be used to explain the desirability of response endorsement levels. Individuals asked to present themselves in a favorable light do not necessarily gravitate to the most extreme item response option based on the desirability of the *trait* being assessed. Rather, individuals appear to weigh a number of factors to select the *response option* they believe would be the most desirable in a given situation. This results in idiosyncratic item response patterns, especially when individuals are trying to present a favorable view of themselves. In other words, in responding to personality items, more of a given trait may or may not be deemed desirable by test takers. At least with regard to individuals' intuitive perceptions, for some items the most desirable response options may be at the intermediate level (e.g., some might believe that an average or moderate level of detail orientation is more desirable in work settings, out of fear of appearing too pedantic). Based on this premise, Kuncel and Borneman (2007) developed two scoring schemes that successfully identified faked protocols with an extremely low false-positive rate and negligible correlations with individual differences measures (personality traits and cognitive ability). Now that Kuncel and colleagues have demonstrated that the social desirability of traits, test items, individual response options, and the setting or purpose for which assessment is taking place are interdependent, field research will need to be undertaken to establish the utility of indicators using idiosyncratic item response pattern scoring when personality test scores are used in organizational decision making. A key follow-up question for such research will be what happens to those individuals who are deemed to be responding in an overly desirable way (see the section on person level prevention strategies below). We next turn our attention to strategies that are aimed at identifying response distortion at the person level without relying on response distortion scales of any kind.

■ IDENTIFICATION STRATEGIES: PERSON LEVEL

Response Latencies

The most widely recognized identification strategy on the person level is the utilization of response latencies. It has been hypothesized that the amount of time it takes an individual to respond to personality items can be taken as an indicator of faking. There are three models that have been proposed that make conflicting predictions about the amount of time it should take individuals to respond if they are engaging in dissimulation. First, the Self Schema model suggests that lying should take longer as respondents attempt to provide answers discordant with their self schema (McDaniel & Timm, 1990). Second, the Semantic Exercise model proposes that impression management should lead to faster response times, because semantic evaluations are cognitively less demanding and less complex than self-referenced evaluations (Rogers, Kuiper, & Kirker, 1977). Third, the

Adopted Schema Model (Holden, 1998; Holden & Hibbs, 1995) hypothesizes that fakers respond to personality items faster when they are responding in a manner consistent with their schemas. However, fakers are slower when their responses are inconsistent with their faking schemas. The Adopted Schema Model provides a potentially valuable insight into the processes that result in responding one way or another to personality items. Detailed discussions of these models and the conceptual basis for using respondent response latencies for assessing impression management among job applicants have been presented by Vasilopoulos et al. (2000).

Empirical evidence to date has been mixed in supporting the usefulness of response latency measures in *identifying* fakers (Robie et al., 2000). Also, limiting response times on personality measures does not *avert* faking behavior. As Holden, Wood, and Tomashewski (2001) indicate, the amount of time it takes for individuals to respond to a personality item is a function of several interacting individual and contextual variables. Although the influence of relevant variables such as reading speed and general intelligence is typically taken into account in obtaining response latency indices, there can be a host of unexamined effects on response time (e.g., socially skilled individuals attempting to manage impressions appear to be faster, Walczyk et al., 2005). These are relevant issues based on the Adopted Schema Model, as they can interact with schema-relevant items and/or the respondent's relevant schema.

With regard to practical applications, particularly in computerized and Internet-based testing for personality (the modus operandi for most organizations using such measures), faking-irrelevant contextual factors can and would be expected to influence response times and interact with respondent schemas. In addition, sampling error and unreliability of measurement can have deleterious effects on the final response latency estimate for a given test taker if the pool of items used is small. In addition to these difficulties, response latency measures appear to be easily coachable (Robie et al., 2000).

Demonstrating the usefulness of response latency measures in applied settings remains difficult. This is well illustrated by a study that compared the usefulness of response latencies to detect faking among university students and U.S. border patrol agent applicants. In that study, Vasilopoulos et al. (2000) reported that among university students participating in a laboratory study, when test takers were familiar with the job for which they were applying, faster responses were indicative of impression management. However, when test takers were less familiar with the job, slower responses indicated response distortion. (Although the results of the field study among applicants were congruent with the university student sample, the response distortion among job applicants was operationalized by scores on a social desirability scale; see our earlier section on the true nature of such scales.) Finally, whether response latency indices can be used to enhance criterion-related validity has also been investigated. Stricker and Alderton (1999) reported that among Navy recruits completing a biodata inventory, latency scores did not moderate the validity for a 6-month retention criterion. Latency scores did not function as a suppressor variable in improving validity either. All in all then, although response latency measures have generated much conceptual interest as well as empirical studies aimed at determining their efficacy, there is at present no compelling data supporting their widespread use in noncognitive assessments.

■ PREVENTION STRATEGIES: ITEM AND TEST LEVEL

Alternative Formats

Item Placement

Standardized tests require a decision about the order in which items are presented—either grouped by construct, scrambled, or randomized. Conscious decisions to order items so that proximal items load on different scales are typically used to make faking on noncognitive measures more difficult, especially if items were developed using a theory-driven approach and scales are constructed to be homogeneous (rather than empirically keyed). The assumptions are that faking will be more difficult if test takers cannot identify the constructs being assessed, and that such identification will be more difficult if items are not grouped by scales. Indirect empirical support for these assumptions has been presented by McFarland, Ryan, and Ellis (2002), who administered NEO-PI-R items to undergraduates in either grouped or randomized order under different response instructions (honest and fake good, honest and respond like an applicant). In both formats, both the fake-good and the applicant instructions elicited responses that resulted in higher mean scores on scales measuring desirable traits (conscientiousness and emotional stability). However, the differences between scores in the respective response distortion conditions and honest responses were larger in grouped format. If confidence intervals around the various d values presented by McFarland et al. were computed, the intervals would overlap. Nonetheless it is reasonable to assume that grouping of items by constructs resulted in higher scores under instructions to fake because test takers were better able to identify the traits being assessed. Recent evidence provided by Weijters et al. (2009) provides direct support for this assumption. They interviewed 36 respondents who completed a questionnaire assessing personality-based consumer attitudes. Interviews revealed that test takers actively look for relationships between items, and that these relationships can be more precisely established the more proximal the items are on the questionnaire. However, quantitative analyses revealed that proximity results in stronger correlations only for non-reversed items measuring the same characteristics.

Both sets of results have wide-ranging implications for psychometric properties of noncognitive measures. In principle, grouping items by constructs will result in increased internal consistency and stronger factors representing individual traits. Given that these effects seem to hold only for negatively worded items, the precise effect on measurement properties of individual scales that incorporate both types of items (positively and negatively worded) is hard to predict. Given that most traits are assessed using items of both types, grouping items by traits may result in undesirable properties overall (e.g., general factors that overrepresent variance from negatively worded items). Until these implications are fully explored, our recommendation with regard to preventing response distortion is to space items measuring the same trait at reasonable and equal intervals, rather than grouping them or randomizing their order.

Subtle versus Obvious Items

In noncognitive assessment, the distinction between subtle and obvious items describes an item property that could also be described as transparency. Item transparency is often confused with face validity. However, item transparency only refers to whether test takers can develop reasonably accurate hypotheses about what trait an item is targeted at. Item transparency does not include test taker perceptions of a trait's validity for a given criterion or purpose. Subtle items are often found on criterion-keyed scales. Disguised purpose, personality-based integrity tests are another example of assessments that frequently use subtle items (Ones, Viswesvaran, & Schmidt, 2003).

The relationship between subtle items and the psychological characteristics they are measuring can be difficult or impossible to detect for laypeople. As such, the rationale supporting the development of such items is the same as that underlying distal item spacing: Making it difficult to identify the underlying characteristics should prevent faking to a certain degree. Subtle items may sometimes be perceived as peculiar (e.g., "I like to stand during the national anthem," "I love flowers," "I make a lot of noise"). It should be noted that the items themselves may not invasive, but some test takers might nonetheless consider questions that bear no immediately obvious relationship to relevant criteria as inappropriate.

With regard to potential faking on personality tests, empirically or criterion keyed items and scales certainly provide an advantage, at least if fakability is measured in terms of mean-score increases from honest to fake-good and respond-like-an-applicant instructions. Empirically keyed scales tend to display smaller increases when test takers are given a motivation to perform well. However, empirically keyed scales often suffer from low face validity, and by design display lower internal consistency reliabilities. Depending on the circumstances and assessment purpose, organizations may be more than willing to trade face validity for fake resistance, and may value validity of scores derived from a well-developed empirically keyed scale more than unidimensionality. Additionally, while the frame-of-reference literature argues for contextualizing items (and thus against empirical keying) to obtain higher criterion-related validity for certain jobs, research provides evidence for the higher long-term validity of subtle items (White, Young, Hunter, & Rumsey, 2008). Because of their advantageous properties regarding fakability as well as their long-term predictive power (and because some of the most successful personality measures such as the California Psychological Inventory and the MMPI use subtle items), we urge researchers and test publishers to continue to explore this avenue as a means of reducing the potential for faking despite some face validity concerns, at least until it can be conclusively shown that negative applicant reactions to subtle items have any real-world consequences.

Forced-Choice Formats

Rather than presenting a single personality item, forced-choice item formats present more than one stimuli to test takers and force them to choose the response option they regard as most (or sometimes least) descriptive of themselves (see Chapter 14). Early forms of forced-choice formats often used adjectival stimuli, but personality items in the form of longer statements can also be used. Variations of the forced-choice format are paired comparisons (providing combinations of exactly two response options) and ranking formats (which ask test takers to rank order several stimuli, rather than choosing the most descriptive one). The general principle by which these formats attempt to prevent faking is matching response options in terms of their purported social desirability, making it more difficult for test takers to identify and select the more desirable option, a strategy that is hoped will result in more accurate self-descriptions.

The first issue surrounding this preventive strategy is that it alters the meaning of faking. In applied settings, faking on a test that uses a forced-choice response format becomes a game of guessing which of the response options represents the more desirable trait in terms of job-relatedness, not social desirability. Thus, in constructing such tests, it becomes imperative to scale response options in terms of their perceived desirability in terms of job relatedness among true job applicant samples, not simply based on their social desirability. Because the desirability of noncognitive traits from a societal point of view may not be the same as those that are perceived as relevant in personnel staffing settings (and, moreover, the traits that are perceived in high-stakes settings such as personnel selection may also depend on the job for which individuals are applying), it is imperative that the appropriate samples are used to calibrate and match response options—an approach that few if any test developers have taken to date. If response options are matched for how socially desirable they appear to a population of test takers (most often individuals from the general population or student samples), it may still be possible for job applicants to identify and endorse the options that they think will be more relevant to the job in question. Similarly, the efficacy of forced-choice formats in preventing faking may be compromised if the desirability of response options and the resulting stimulus pairings specific to one setting do not generalize to other situations.

These conceptual concerns are echoed in the empirical literature that has so far not produced persuasive evidence for the elimination of faking among motivated test takers when forced-choice formats are used. Although some studies have attempted to address this issue and are often cited to this effect (e.g., Martin, Bowen, & Hunt, 2002), results are far from conclusive. As Meade (2004) has cogently shown, measures of faking used in many investigations do not make it possible to draw unequivocal conclusions about nonfakability of forced-choice measures. In the case of Martin et al., for example, not only were objective measures of respondents' personality not available, but the measure used to judge whether respondents faked had to result in the erroneous conclusion that the forced-choice measure was less fakable by design (see the discussion in Meade,

2004). More recent investigations using innovative forced-choice formats that provide fair comparisons of fakability (i.e., a clear standard of score elevation) point to the fact that these measures are fakable (Heggestad, Morrison, Reeve, & McCloy, 2006), even though the magnitudes of the effects are inconsistent across studies.

In addition to their conceptual difficulties and hitherto unproven efficacy in eliminating faking, there are other issues that lead us to raise questions about the applied usefulness of this strategy. Formats such as forced-choice, paired comparison and rank ordering often result in scores with ipsative properties. Although ipsative measurement has been a hotly debated topic in the psychometric literature (as well as applied psychology) over the last half-century, a recent resurgence of forced-choice formats requires revisiting some of the basic problems underlying such scores. Although some innovative solutions have been offered for addressing the shortcomings of ipsative measurement (Chernyshenko et al., 2009; Stark, Chernyshenko, & Drasgow, 2005), the majority of problems remain unresolved, preventing forced-choice tests from being a viable strategy to prevent faking. Most of these issues are caused by the fact that "ipsative scales, because of their mathematical interdependence, tend to force negative correlations in the data" (Saville & Willson, 1991, p. 222).

When responding to forced-choice, paired comparisons, and ranking formats, test takers can lower their score on one scale simply by selecting another, unrelated stimulus paired with it that they perceive as more descriptive. When response options representative of two different traits are frequently paired together, a high score on one scale will automatically result in a low score on the other, regardless of the test taker's true trait level. Test scores will typically have purely ipsative properties if test takers have to rank all response options per item, all paired comparisons are taken into account in scoring a test, or response options representing all variables are presented to test takers (Hicks, 1970). Hicks' seminal article also outlined the conditions under which scores maintain only partially ipsative properties. These are (1) when different scales have varying numbers of items, (2) when some response options are not scored, (3) when differential weights are applied in scoring response options, (4) when different scoring keys are applied to different test takers, based on some characteristic not assessed by the test, (5) when in rank-ordering options, test takers have to rank only some response alternatives, (6) when in analyzing ipsative data, some scales are dropped from predictor sets, and (7) when there are normative sections of the assessment instrument.

The scale interdependence of purely ipsative, and to a lesser degree, partially ipsative scores is problematic in several respects. When scale scores for an individual are dependent, even in part, on their scores on other variables assessed by the test, this results in person-centered scale scores (distributed about an individual's mean score across scales) that renders them meaningless at worst or makes interindividual comparisons difficult at best (Guilford, 1954). Proponents of ipsative measurement and forced-choice formats often claim that this problem can be avoided by increasing the number of scales on a test. It is true that the average scale intercorrelations that result from the forced dependency of ipsative scale scores is reduced as the number of scales increases. It has long been known that the average scale intercorrelations in ipsative measures can be predicted from the number of scales (Clemans, 1966). Johnson, Wood, and Blinkhorn (1988) provided a persuasive, empirical demonstration of this fact by using data from the normative samples of several purely and partially ipsative personality tests. However, it is a common misconception that the problems associated with ipsative measurement are resolved if a test includes enough scales not to result in artificially high dependencies between scale scores (i.e., when the scale interdependencies approach zero). Artificially low scale interdependence is just as problematic in interpreting the construct meaning of scores as artificially high scale interdependence. For example, as we know well from normative measurement, personality traits (both facet measures in the same domain, but also different, broad personality domains such as the Big Five, for example) are far from orthogonal (Ones et al., 2005). Forcing scale intercorrelations to be zero by increasing the total number of scales creates an unhealthy illusion of trait independence that is incongruent with the true nature of interrelationships among constructs or data obtained from more appropriate, absolute measurement.

There are other psychometric problems caused by an artifactual dependence among scales due to ipsative measurement. One such issue is the inflation of reliability coefficients computed in the traditional manner, particularly those estimating internal consistency of test scores. Tenopyr (1988) has shown that true reliability in one scale on an ipsative test can result in artifactual reliabilities in other scales even when responses on those scales are random. She cautions that this can lead to false confidence in interpreting the substantive, construct meaning of ipsative scale scores, and also warns against using coefficients of stability as estimates of ipsative score reliability, as these can also be subjected to scale interdependence effects. Similarly, Johnson et al. (1988) convincingly argued that the most common forms of reliability estimates (internal consistency, test–retest, alternate form) are not appropriate to ipsative measures as they all "share a common theoretical justification and this justification does not apply to ipsative tests" thus rendering computations of reliability in the ordinary way "merely an exercise in arithmetic with not significance for practice."

Another issue caused by score interdependence occurs when subjecting ipsative scores to traditional factor analysis. In the extreme case of purely ipsative scores, factor analytic results obtained from ipsative scores are uninterpretable (Dunlap & Cornwell, 1994). But even if scores are only partially ipsative and artificial scale interdependencies are low, results most often do not resemble those obtained from normative measurement. This particularly vexing problem has even been acknowledged by the most ardent proponents of ipsative measurement; Baron (1996) concluded that the number of ipsative scales needed to produce factor analytic results equivalent to those obtained from normative data is incredibly large and not in the realm of what is typically administered on a single questionnaire. Hence, in her opinion, "there is little chance of ipsative data being useful to understand the underlying structure of constructs" (p. 8). With regard to construct interpretation and validity, in addition to internal structure, the pattern of correlations with external variables is also a concern. At least two studies have shown that when employing a forced-choice format, the cognitive load of certain noncognitive measures increases (Christiansen, Burns, & Montgomery, 2005; Vasilopoulos, Cucina, Dyomina, Morewitz, & Reilly, 2006).

Finally, and perhaps most importantly in terms of applied implications, forced-choice formats that result in ipsative scores are not a good means of preventing faking because they do not result in higher criterion-related validity. Although some may argue that preventing faking is a goal in and of itself, in the absence of evidence that forced-choice formats actually prevent faking (see above), the criterion for evaluating their usefulness will need to be whether they improve the prediction of valued behaviors and outcomes. Clemans (1956) has shown that in predicting external criteria, even though rare exceptions might exist, "the maximum multiple correlation of a set of ipsative predictors with a particular criterion is equal or less than the multiple correlation of the same predictors measured using absolute measurement." In a similar vein, Johnson et al. (1988) provided details on why the sum of covariances of (purely) ipsative scale scores with a criterion is zero; when variances are equal (as in the case of standardized measures), the sum of ipsative validities for a given criterion will always sum to zero. These methodological arguments are underscored by the fact that after half a century of research on forced-choice measures, there is no conclusive evidence that shows that ipsative measures predict a set of criteria better than equivalent normative forms of the measure. Even ardent supporters of ipsative personality tests reported equal levels of predictive efficiency (Saville & Wilson, 1991). The only way to address this issue in favor of ipsative assessment seems to be to offer validity evidence for every scale on a test that is based on a different criterion measure, and to neglect the full correlational pattern for all predictor scales and criterion measures.

Much effort is currently being invested in finding remedies for the psychometric problems associated with traditional forced-choice methods (Chernyshenko et al., 2009; Stark et al., 2005). These innovative item response theory (IRT)-based approaches constitute a departure from the status quo in ipsative measurement that for too long has focused simply on reducing artificial scale interdependencies while neglecting construct validity of scores. However, we need to ask ourselves whether these efforts (even if they prove fruitful) will be worthwhile unless they improve either criterion-related validity or eliminate response distortion without altering the meaning of the constructs being assessed. These questions are particularly relevant when considering that test takers also are less accepting of forced-choice formats (Martin et al., 2002). In 1970, Hicks, in his influential article on ipsative measurement, stated that the justifications for using ipsative scores (individuals fake, faking reduces validity, and ipsative formats reduce faking and increase validity) had not yet been met. Fifteen years ago, Bartram (1996) concluded "to the best of my knowledge, that is still true today" (p. 38). It seems that Bartram's evaluation of Hicks' criteria is still an accurate portrayal of forced-choice response formats.

■ PREVENTION STRATEGIES: PERSON LEVEL

Warnings

Even though statements that caution test takers against response distortions are found on some of the earliest noncognitive assessment tools (most notably personality inventories), Dwight and Donovan (2003) rightfully point out that assumptions of their efficacy have long been based on common wisdom rather than systematic research. Of course it is intuitively appealing that if warned against untruthful responding, individuals in high-stakes settings (e.g., job applicants) should try to engage in less (or less obvious) response distortion. Such effects should be observable in terms of mean-score differences across groups (those who have been warned versus those who have not). Intraindividual differences across conditions should also be observed: An individual test taker should display less elevated scores after having been warned compared to when no warning was issued; however, this situation is likely to occur more frequently in laboratory studies than in real-world assessment scenarios.

In their small-scale meta-analysis, Dwight and Donovan (2003) attempted to investigate whether warnings not to fake actually reduce faking. At the time their analysis was conducted, however, research on the efficacy of this preventive strategy was still in its infancy. Hence, they had to pool results across qualitatively different studies, which resulted in a cumulative summary that is not easily interpretable. First, due to the dearth of primary studies, Dwight and Donovan had to combine studies across several different types of noncognitive assessment tools (biodata and personality measures) and could also not separate effects based on the trait assessed (a crucial issue, as those who fake will likely attempt to fake only traits or scales that they perceive as most relevant to the assessment purpose). In addition, because the field had not yet developed a comprehensive taxonomy of warning types (see below) and had not investigated a sufficient number of different types of warnings, an overall analysis had to be conducted that combined all studies into one analysis. Finally, their meta-analysis combined data from laboratory and applied settings, as well as between-subject and within-subject designs, a distinction that is crucial in the domain of faking research (Viswesvaran & Ones, 1999). Hence, the modest effect size for warnings they obtained was associated with unexplained variability in observed effects, providing little if any insight into the efficacy of warnings as a preventive strategy. Their ensuing primary study, however, showed that a certain type of warning (telling test takers that faking could be detected and would have consequences) reduced mean scores in a between-subjects, laboratory design using a sample of undergraduate students. The cautious conclusion from their research is that warnings of identification alone are unlikely to reduce mean scores in motivated test takers, but that warnings of identifications with negative consequences in case of detection will lead to small or moderate reductions in personality scale mean scores.

As a preventive strategy, warnings against faking are intriguing. Warnings themselves can be implemented at no cost and without much effort, and it would certainly be encouraging if a simple statement that faking could be detected (and would have negative consequences, whether true or not) would result in a reduction of its prevalence. A real contribution to the field was made by Pace and Borman (2006) who provided a taxonomy of warning types that can be used to systematically study the effects of warnings on response distortion on noncognitive measures.

Warning Type 1: Detection

First, the simplest type is the warning of identification or detection previously discussed. Such warnings let test takers know that within the assessment (typically a standardized personality test, but the same principles apply to other noncognitive assessment methods, such as interviews or biodata inventories), mechanisms that detect dishonest responding are embedded. Such warnings can differ in their specificity, ranging from simple claims that such methods exist to explaining what such methods entail (e.g., lie scales, inconsistency or infrequency scales). Variations of such warnings may warn test takers that their responses will be verified using external sources; such warnings are rare on traditional personality tests but do occur occasionally in other assessment methods such as interviews or application blanks (especially in high-stakes assessment settings). The goal of identification or detection warnings is to reduce test takers' belief in their own ability to fake without being detected.

Warning Type 2: Consequential

The second type of warning is a warning of the consequence of faking, indicating to test takers what will happen should response distortion be detected. Of course, the severity (and thus potential efficacy) of such warnings depends on the actual consequences that are being presented, which can range from mild (e.g., retesting) to severe (e.g., exclusion from the applicant pool). Test takers' intentions to fake are expected to decrease as a result of such warnings, as test takers are trying to avoid these negative consequences.

Warning Type 3: Appeal to Reason

The third type of warning appeals to test takers' reasoning and self-interest: Here, it is claimed that honest responding will result in a more accurate portrayal of their personal characteristics, and that such an accurate portrayal will result in positive consequences such as a good fit or matching to an appropriate job. This type of warning is expected to alter individuals' beliefs about the desirability of faking, and its efficacy is built on the assumption that test takers place trust in warnings of this nature.

Here, it is important to consider that all types of warnings presented so far rely to a certain degree on test takers' trust in the warning itself. Even when we warn of detection and negative consequences, it is not guaranteed that test takers will believe these warnings and act accordingly. Especially in the case of detection warnings, it is doubtful that test takers can be made to believe that *all* attempts to fake will be detected with perfect accuracy (the question of whether this would be ethical, especially in light of shortcomings of common lie detection scales, is yet another issue). Moreover, a question that has not received much consideration is whether the effects of different types of warnings (especially those of specific negative consequences) differ across time and setting. For example, it is likely that the supply and demand of applicants in the labor market would moderate the efficacy of warnings about consequences of faking. To complicate matters further, these issues may interact with individual difference characteristics of test takers (e.g., applicants who possess characteristics that typically make them a desirable candidate may be aware of this, and thus be less concerned about negative consequences such as retesting or disqualification).

Warning Type 4: Educational

The fourth type of warning is of an educational nature: These statements try to elaborate on the nature and purpose of the assessment, and clearly explain that if assessments yield accurate results, they are beneficial from the perspective of the organization (or test administrator). For example, such warnings could state that fair and accurate personnel selection can occur only if it is based on truthful test results. As such, the route through which these warnings attempt to prevent faking is by making test takers believe that faking would have negative consequences overall or on an institutional level.

Warning Type 5: Appeal to Moral Principles

Finally, in a similar vein, another type of warning appeals to the moral conviction as well as self-perception of test takers as moral beings. The underlying principle is to inform test takers that as moral and honest individuals, they should have no motivation to fake, and that faking is not an appropriate behavior. By trying to portray faking as immoral test taking behavior and the test takers themselves as moral, these types of warnings enforce honesty by appealing to positive self-perceptions of test takers.

As discussed above and evidenced in Dwight and Donovan's (2003) quantitative summary, there are only a few empirical studies that have investigated the effect of warnings against faking on scores derived from noncognitive assessments. More importantly, there are very few studies that pit two types of warnings (or combinations thereof) against each other. Moreover, the fact that the available studies differ in terms of experimental design and setting makes comparisons of the efficacy of warnings as a method to prevent faking very difficult. Because of the relative ease with which these studies can be conducted, we are optimistic that our field will eventually be able to provide better advice regarding warnings on noncognitive assessments in applied settings. For this purpose, we strongly urge researchers to conduct systematic investigations using Pace and Borman's (2006) taxonomy outlined above. However, in doing so, the common pitfalls of faking research must be avoided (e.g., overreliance on laboratory studies and unrealistic experimental conditions that fail to simulate real-world incentives to distort). Finally, it will be important to investigate the consequences of warnings that go beyond changes in assessment mean scores. Especially with regard to construct validity, correlations with external variables as well as convergent validity need to be investigated under different warning conditions. Important preliminary evidence suggests that warnings increase the cognitive load of some personality scales (Vasilopoulos, Cucina, & McElreath, 2005), and that convergent validities among scales designed to assess the same traits may suffer (Robson, Jones, & Abraham, 2008). Nonetheless, should certain types of warnings also prove consistently effective in discouraging individuals from faking (that means discourage everyone from faking, not just certain subgroups of test takers), the relative ease and cost efficiency with which they can be implemented certainly justify increased exploration of this preventive strategy.

■ DISCUSSION

In this chapter, we aimed to provide an overview of item and person level strategies that are being used or discussed to either identify response distortion or to prevent it. It is reasonable to ask what palliatives are available once test takers who manage impressions on noncognitive assessments have been identified. The responses to this question range from (1) nothing, to (2) making corrections to substantive scale scores, to (3) asking respondents to retake the personality test, and (4) removing "faking" individuals from the applicant pool. Validity problems and false positives associated with the use of most faking indicators need to be carefully weighed before such measures are utilized in practice (the discussion of a recent case using a lie scale illustrates this dilemma; see above). The option of "correcting" substantive scale scores using social desirability scales alters the meaning of scores on such scales and does not improve criterion-related validity (although the lists of individuals comprising the very top end of score distributions appear to change after corrections). Even with the best mouse traps (which are yet to be designed), the question of how to treat individuals who display varying degrees of impression management is a vexing one. Allowing individuals who trigger faking indices on personality tests to remain in the applicant pool may cause moral discomfort. However, the same concerns should exist regarding individuals who distort their responses on other noncognitive assessments (such as interviews, for example), and thus advance in a selection process to the disadvantage of potentially more honest candidates. It seems that many organizations are more concerned with the criterion-related validity of their noncognitive assessments in the entire applicant pool than with the response behavior of those who have been selected. And this concern may be justified if looking through a utilitarian lens that focuses on the excellent psychometric properties and very good criterion-related validities of noncognitive measures that have been shown to exist, at least for personality measures, despite the potential effects of response distortion among real job applicant samples (see Ones, Dilchert, Viswesvaran, & Judge, 2007).

In personnel selection settings, personality measures have shown indisputable and useful levels of criterion-related validity. Impression management pervades all interpersonal interactions as individuals constantly negotiate and renegotiate their reputations. All non-performance based measures, including interviews, biodata inventories, situational judgment tests, and the like, are subject to such impression management. Perhaps a simple and humble approach to ensuring that noncognitive measures continue to be useful in personnel decision making is to rely on job applicant pools in test construction and to use applicant norms in evaluating scale scores. Interestingly, in the domain of personality assessment, there are few commercially available tests that have been built using job applicant samples, and there are very few personality inventories that rely on job applicant normative data in providing results to test users.

Despite the vast amount of research dedicated to designing detection and preventive strategies, it is our evaluation that no method exists that in applied settings can reliably distinguish "fakers" from those engaging in acceptable (or even expected) forms of guardedness on the variety of available noncognitive measures with acceptable false-positive rates. The two detection and preventive strategies that have received the most attention so far do not present viable solutions. Over 40 years ago, Dunnette (1966) defined fads as "those practices and concepts characterized by capricious and intense, but short lived interest" (p. 343) and listed social desirability (and forced-choice measures) as one example. Some fads, unfortunately, continue and most other palliatives offered so far have turned out to be either fashions or folderol.

References

Baer, R. A., & Sekirnjak, G. (1997). Detection of underreporting on the MMPI-2 in a clinical population: Effects of information about validity scales. *Journal of Personality Assessment, 69*, 555–567.

Baron, H. (1996). Strengths and limitations of ipsative measurement. *Journal of Occupational and Organizational Psychology, 69*, 49–56.

Bartram, D. (1996). The relationship between ipsatized and normative measures of personality. *Journal of Occupational and Organizational Psychology, 69*, 25–39.

Butcher, J. N. (Ed.). (2006). *MMPI-2: A practitioner's guide.* Washington, D.C.: American Psychological Association.

Butcher, J. N. (2010). Personality assessment from the nineteenth to the early twenty-first century: Past achievements and contemporary challenges. *Annual Review of Clinical Psychology, 6*, 1–20.

Butcher, J. N., Graham, J. R., Ben-Porath, Y. S., Tellegen, A., & Dahlstrom, W. G. (2001). *MMPI-2 (Minnesota Multiphasic Personality Inventory-2). Manual for administration, scoring, and interpretation* (rev. ed.). Minneapolis: University of Minnesota Press.

Chernyshenko, O. S., Stark, S., Prewett, M. S., Gray, A. A., Stilson, F. R., & Tuttle, M. D. (2009). Normative scoring of multidimensional pairwise preference personality scales using IRT: Empirical comparisons with other formats. *Human Performance, 22*, 105–127.

Christiansen, N. D., Burns, G. N., & Montgomery, G. E. (2005). Reconsidering forced-choice item formats for applicant personality assessment. *Human Performance, 18*, 267–307.

Christiansen, N. D., Goffin, R. D., Johnston, N. G., & Rothstein, M. G. (1994). Correcting the 16PF for faking: Effects on criterion-related validity and individual hiring decisions. *Personnel Psychology, 47*, 847–860.

Clemans, W. V. (1956). *An analytical and empirical investigation of some properties of ipsative measures.* Unpublished doctoral dissertation, University of Washington.

Clemans, W. V. (1966). An analytical and empirical examination of some properties of ipsative measures. *Psychometric Monographs, 14*.

Conn, S. R., & Rieke, M. L. (1994). *The 16PF fifth edition technical manual.* Champaign, IL: Institute for Personality and Ability Testing.

Crowne, D. P., & Marlowe, D. (1960). A new scale of social desirability independent of psychopathology. *Journal of Consulting Psychology, 24,* 349–354.

Dilchert, S., Ones, D. S., Viswesvaran, C., & Deller, J. (2006). Response distortion in personality measurement: Born to deceive, yet capable of providing valid self-assessments? *Psychology Science, 48,* 209–225.

Dunlap, W. P., & Cornwell, J. M. (1994). Factor analysis of ipsative measures. *Multivariate Behavioral Research, 29,* 115–126.

Dunnette, M. D. (1966). Fads, fashions, and folderol in psychology. *American Psychologist, 21,* 343–352.

Dwight, S. A., & Donovan, J. J. (2003). Do warnings not to fake reduce faking? *Human Performance, 16,* 1–23.

Ellingson, J. E., Sackett, P. R., & Hough, L. M. (1999). Social desirability corrections in personality measurement: Issues of applicant comparison and construct validity. *Journal of Applied Psychology, 84,* 155–166.

Foldes, H. J., Ones, D. S., & Sinangil, H. K. (2006). Neither here, nor there: Impression management does not predict expatriate adjustment and job performance. *Psychology Science, 48,* 357–368.

Goffin, R. D., & Christiansen, N. D. (2003). Correcting personality tests for faking: A review of popular personality tests and an initial survey of researchers. *International Journal of Selection and Assessment, 11,* 340–344.

Gough, H. G., & Bradley, P. (1996). *Manual for the California Psychological Inventory.* Palo Alto, CA: Consulting Psychologists Press.

Guilford, J. P. (1954). *Psychometric methods* (2nd ed.). New York: McGraw-Hill.

Heggestad, E. D., Morrison, M., Reeve, C. L., & McCloy, R. A. (2006). Forced-choice assessments of personality for selection: Evaluating issues of normative assessment and faking resistance. *Journal of Applied Psychology, 91,* 9–24.

Hicks, L. E. (1970). Some properties of ipsative, normative, and forced-choice normative measures. *Psychological Bulletin, 74,* 167–184.

Hogan, J., Barrett, P., & Hogan, R. (2007). Personality measurement, faking, and employment selection. *Journal of Applied Psychology, 92,* 1270–1285.

Holden, R. R. (1998). Detecting fakers on a personnel test: Response latencies versus a standard validity scale. *Journal of Social Behavior & Personality, 13,* 387–398.

Holden, R. R., & Hibbs, N. (1995). Incremental validity of response latencies for detecting fakers on a personality test. *Journal of Research in Personality, 29,* 362–372.

Holden, R. R., Wood, L. L., & Tomashewski, L. (2001). Do response time limitations counteract the effect of faking on personality inventory validity? *Journal of Personality and Social Psychology, 81,* 160–169.

Hough, L. M. (1998). Effects of intentional distortion in personality measurement and evaluation of suggested palliatives. *Human Performance, 11,* 209–244.

Hurtz, G. M., & Alliger, G. M. (2002). Influence of coaching on integrity test performance and unlikely virtues scale scores. *Human Performance, 15,* 255–273.

Jackson, D. N., & Messick, S. (1961). Acquiescence and desirability as response determinants on the MMPI. *Educational and Psychological Measurement, 21,* 771–790.

Jackson, D. N., & Messick, S. (1969). A distinction between judgments of frequency and of desirability as determinants of response. *Educational and Psychological Measurement, 29,* 273–293.

Johnson, C. E., Wood, R., & Blinkhorn, S. F. (1988). Spuriouser and spuriouser: The use of ipsative personality tests. *Journal of Occupational Psychology, 61,* 153–162.

Kemery, E. R., & Dunlap, W. P. (1986). Partialling factor scores does not control method variance: A reply to Podsakoff and Todor. *Journal of Management, 12,* 525–530.

Kuncel, N. R., & Borneman, M. J. (2007). Toward a new method of detecting deliberately faked personality tests: The use of idiosyncratic item responses. *International Journal of Selection and Assessment, 15,* 220–231.

Kuncel, N. R., & Tellegen, A. (2009). A conceptual and empirical reexamination of the measurement of the social desirability of items: Implications for detecting desirable response style and scale development. *Personnel Psychology, 62,* 201–228.

Li, A., & Bagger, J. (2006). Using the BIDR to distinguish the effects of impression management and self-deception on the criterion validity of personality measures: A meta-analysis. *International Journal of Selection and Assessment, 14,* 131–141.

Marcus, B. (2003). Persönlichkeitstests in der Personalauswahl: Sind "sozial erwünschte" Antworten wirklich nicht wünschenswert? [Personality testing in personnel selection: Is "socially desirable" responding really undesirable?]. *Zeitschrift für Psychologie, 211,* 138–148.

Martin, B. A., Bowen, C. C., & Hunt, S. T. (2002). How effective are people at faking on personality questionnaires? *Personality and Individual Differences, 32,* 247–256.

McCrae, R. R., & Costa, P. T. (1983). Social desirability scales: More substance than style. *Journal of Consulting and Clinical Psychology, 51,* 882–888.

McDaniel, M. A., & Timm, H. (1990). *Lying takes time: Predicting deception in biodata using response latencies.* Poster presented at the annual conference of the American Psychological Association, Boston, MA.

McFarland, L. A., Ryan, A. M., & Ellis, A. (2002). Item placement on a personality measure: Effects on faking behavior and test measurement properties. *Journal of Personality Assessment, 78,* 348–369.

Meade, A. W. (2004). Psychometric problems and issues involved with creating and using ipsative measures for selection. *Journal of Occupational and Organizational Psychology, 77,* 531–552.

Nederhof, A. J. (1985). Methods of coping with social desirability bias: A review. *European Journal of Social Psychology, 15,* 263–280.

Nicholson, R. A., & Hogan, R. (1990). The construct validity of social desirability. *American Psychologist, 45,* 290–292.

Ones, D. S., Dilchert, S., Viswesvaran, C., & Judge, T. A. (2007). In support of personality assessment in organizational settings. *Personnel Psychology, 60,* 995–1027.

Ones, D. S., Viswesvaran, C., & Reiss, A. D. (1996). Role of social desirability in personality testing for personnel selection: The red herring. *Journal of Applied Psychology, 81,* 660–679.

Ones, D. S., Viswesvaran, C., & Dilchert, S. (2005). Personality at work: Raising awareness and correcting misconceptions. *Human Performance, 18,* 389–404.

Ones, D. S., Viswesvaran, C., & Schmidt, F. L. (2003). Personality and absenteeism: A meta-analysis of integrity tests. *European Journal of Personality, 17,* S19–S38.

Pace, V. L., & Borman, W. C. (2006). The use of warnings to discourage faking on noncognitive inventories. In D. Svyantek, R. L. Griffith, & M. H. Peterson (Eds.), *A closer examination of applicant faking behavior* (pp. 283–301). Greenwich, CT: Information Age.

Paulhus, D. L. (1984). Two-component models of socially desirable responding. *Journal of Personality and Social Psychology, 46,* 598–609.

Paulhus, D. L. (1991). Measurement and control of response bias. In J. P. Robinson, P. R. Shaver, & L. S. Wrightsman (Eds.), *Measures of personality and social psychological attitudes.* (pp. 17–59). San Diego: Academic Press.

Pauls, C. A., & Crost, N. W. (2004). Effects of faking on self-deception and impression management scales. *Personality and Individual Differences, 37,* 1137–1151.

Robie, C., Curtin, P. J., Foster, T. C., Phillips, H. L., Zbylut, M., & Tetrick, L. E. (2000). The effects of coaching on the utility of response latencies in detecting fakers on a personality measure. *Canadian Journal of Behavioural Science, 32*, 226–233.

Robson, S. M., Jones, A., & Abraham, J. (2008). Personality, faking, and convergent validity: A warning concerning warning statements. *Human Performance, 21*, 89–106.

Rogers, T. B., Kuiper, N. A., & Kirker, W. S. (1977). Self-reference and the encoding of personal information. *Journal of Personality and Social Psychology, 35*, 677–688.

Saville, P., & Willson, E. (1991). The reliability and validity of normative and ipsative approaches in the measurement of personality. *Journal of Occupational Psychology, 64*, 219–238.

Stark, S., Chernyshenko, O. S., & Drasgow, F. (2005). An IRT approach to constructing and scoring pairwise preference items involving stimuli on different dimensions: The multi-unidimensional pairwise-preference model. *Applied Psychological Measurement, 29*, 184–203.

Stricker, L. J., & Alderton, D. L. (1999). Using response latency measures for biographical inventory. *Military Psychology, 11*, 169–188.

Tellegen, A. (1982). *Brief manual for the Differential Personality Questionnaire.* Unpublished manuscript, Minneapolis, MN.

Tellegen, A., & Waller, N. G. (2008). Exploring personality through test construction: Development of the Multidimensional Personality Questionnaire: *The SAGE handbook of personality theory and assessment* (Vol. 2: *Personality measurement and testing*, pp. 261–292). Thousand Oaks, CA: Sage.

Tenopyr, M. L. (1988). Artifactual reliability of forced-choice scales. *Journal of Applied Psychology, 73*, 749–751.

Vasilopoulos, N. L., Cucina, J. M., Dyomina, N. V., Morewitz, C. L., & Reilly, R. R. (2006). Forced-choice personality tests: A measure of personality and cognitive ability? *Human Performance, 19*, 175–199.

Vasilopoulos, N. L., Cucina, J. M., & McElreath, J. M. (2005). Do warnings of response verification moderate the relationship between personality and cognitive ability? *Journal of Applied Psychology, 90*, 306–322.

Vasilopoulos, N. L., Reilly, R. R., & Leaman, J. A. (2000). The influence of job familiarity and impression management on self-report measure scale scores and response latencies. *Journal of Applied Psychology, 85*, 50–64.

Viswesvaran, C., & Ones, D. S. (1999). Meta-analyses of fakability estimates: Implications for personality measurement. *Educational and Psychological Measurement, 59*, 197–210.

Viswesvaran, C., Ones, D. S., & Hough, L. M. (2001). Do impression management scales in personality inventories predict managerial job performance ratings? *International Journal of Selection and Assessment, 9*, 277–289.

Walczyk, J. J., Schwartz, J. P., Clifton, R., Adams, B., Wei, M., & Zha, P. (2005). Lying person-to-person about life events: A cognitive framework for lie detection. *Personnel Psychology, 58*, 141–170.

Weijters, B., Geuens, M., & Schillewaert, N. (2009). The proximity effect: The role of inter-item distance on reverse-item bias. *International Journal of Research in Marketing, 26*, 2–12.

White, L. A., Young, M. C., Hunter, A. E., & Rumsey, M. G. (2008). Lessons learned in transitioning personality measures from research to operational settings. *Industrial and Organizational Psychology, 1*, 291–295.

Wiggins, J. S. (1964). Convergences among stylistic response measures from objective personality tests. *Educational and Psychological Measurement, 24*, 551–562.

13 Social Desirability in Personality Assessment

Outline of a Model to Explain Individual Differences

■ MARTIN BÄCKSTRÖM, FREDRIK BJÖRKLUND,
AND MAGNUS R. LARSSON

■ INTRODUCTION

From a psychometric point of view social desirability constitutes a problem when investigating the relationship between the dimensions of the Five-Factor Model (FFM; e.g., Costa & McCrae, 1992) and other personality factors or valued criteria, since whether the predictive validity of the FFM inventory should be attributed to personality or to social desirability (or both) is always a question. Hence there are good reasons to develop techniques to methodologically control for the possible influence of social desirability in studies using the FFM. In this chapter we present a new technique with the primary aim of reducing social desirability in personality inventories. Simply put, the valence of an existing item is changed by rephrasing it in a way that makes the item more neutral. Positive items are framed less positively, whereas negative items are framed less negatively, making all items relatively more neutral. Below we will summarize the literature concerning social desirability and its relationship to personality traits. This will be followed by a presentation of our suggested technique and some data supporting it. Finally, we will reflect upon some issues regarding the relation between personality traits and evaluative items in personality inventories.

■ SOCIAL DESIRABILITY AND THE BIG FIVE

Studies have shown that social desirability seems to relate to personality traits in a predictable way. In inventories based on the FFM, the general trend seems to be that participants scoring high on social desirability also score higher on Extraversion, Agreeableness, Conscientiousness, Openness, and Emotional Stability. This pattern suggests that social desirability consists of one general and overarching evaluative factor. Such a model gained empirical support in early research (Edwards; 1957; Goldberg, 1993; Hendriks, Hofstee, & de Raad, 2002) and also more recently in studies conducted by Musek (2007) and Bäckström (2007). This general factor has been a problem when empirically validating the FFM (Block, 1995) since it creates correlations between factors. Although the typical definition of the five-factor model suggests that each factor is independent of all the other factors, structural tests of the model have often revealed correlations between scales measuring the factors. Bäckström, Björklund, and Larsson (2009) showed that one general factor explained most of the correlations between scales in three different FFM inventories and that the scales measuring the FFM were almost independent (orthogonal) after controlling for the general factor. In other words, these results suggest that the correlation between factors in inventories measuring the FFM can be explained by a single general evaluative factor.

■ TWO-FACTOR MODELS OF SOCIAL DESIRABILITY

The one-factor model of social desirability has been challenged by two-factor models suggesting that the concept consists of two different but related factors. Paulhus (1984; Paulhus & John, 1998) has repeatedly presented empirical evidence supporting the view that social desirability consists of two factors labeled impression management and self-deception. It is generally found that impression management is related to Conscientiousness and Agreeableness, whereas self-deception is related to Emotional Stability, Extraversion, and Openness. Paulhus and John (1998) suggest that socially desirable responding consists of two general self-favoring tendencies or self-deceptive styles. The first tendency, called alpha, is an egoistic tendency to see oneself as an exceptionally talented and socially prominent member of society. The second tendency, called gamma, is a moralistic tendency to view oneself as an exceptionally good member of society. Later Paulhus (2002) suggested that the alpha and the gamma factor differ as regards personality content and that both vary in level of consciousness, e.g., that both can be influenced by self-deception and/or impression management. Paulhus (2002) based his model on the residuals from self-ratings regressed on peer-ratings. In this conception alpha is related to Openness and Extraversion and gamma to Conscientiousness and Agreeableness. Emotional stability is primarily related to the alpha factor, but also has a rather strong relation to gamma (Paulhus & John, 1998).

Paulhus' two-factor model has some resemblance to a model proposed by Digman (1997). Digman defined two general factors to the FFM, the alpha factor, related to Conscientiousness, Agreeableness, and Emotional Stability, and the beta factor, related to Extraversion and Openness. Digman did not suggest that his factors were caused by socially desirable responding; instead he defined them as two overarching personality factors to the FFM. The alpha factor was suggested to be a general socialization factor, whereas the beta factor was suggested to be related to personal growth. A direct comparison of the models presented by Paulhus (1984) and Digman (1997) reveals that they do not overlap perfectly. Paulhus' alpha and Digman's beta are similar as they both include Extraversion and Openness. Paulhus' alpha is, however, related to Emotional stability (Paulhus & John, 1998) whereas Digman's beta is not. Paulhus' gamma and Digman's alpha are similar since they share Agreeableness and Conscientiousness, but while Digman's alpha clearly includes Emotional Stability, Paulhus' gamma has a comparatively weak relation to this factor. It seems then that Digman's model is a rotational variant of Paulhus' model. Digman's two-factor model has been corroborated by new research by DeYoung, Peterson, and Higgins (2002), who suggested a modification to the FFM where Digman's factors form specific sub-factors, facets to the FFM. In their model each factor of the FFM has two sub-factors, one related to the alpha and one to the gamma factor. They changed the name of alpha and gamma to plasticity and stability, and found relationships between this model and Gray's (e.g., Gray & McNaughton, 2000) BIS/BAS model of personality.

Both Paulhus and Digman argue for two-factor models and they both refer to a large number of other two-factor models (e.g., Bakan, 1966; Digman, 1997). Both argue for models that have the FFM as personality content factors, but suggest there are two higher order factors. Another alternative, which we argue for in this chapter, is a model with only one higher order factor. Such a model was delineated by Edwards (1957) and refined by Peabody (1967, 1984) and Saucier (1994). Because higher order factors in this context are based on common variance (correlation) between personality factors, proponents of two-factor models have to show that two factors are necessary to explain the patterns of correlation between scales. Using Confirmatory Factor Analysis, Bäckström (2007) and Bäckström et al. (2009) found, in a number of personality inventories, that a single factor accounted for almost all of the common variance between factor scales.

∎ CONTEXTUAL FACTORS INFLUENCE SOCIALLY DESIRABLE RESPONDING

Psychologists describe social desirability not only as a moderating (individual difference) variable but also as a mediating (process) variable influenced by contextual factors that affect the extent to which we portray ourselves in a socially desirable way. Framed this way, the effect that different contextual factors have on the level of desirability in self-ratings is primarily attributed to the level of social desirability motivation that they trigger. Commentators, including Holden, Kroner, Fekken, and Popham (1992) and Holtgraves (2004), have provided more detailed accounts regarding which particular mechanisms mediate these effects, but the findings diverge, e.g., concerning the role of automaticity and control in socially desirable responding, as measured by response times. It is fairly obvious that contexts that are associated with instrumental motivation (such as applying for a job) may trigger increased socially desirable responding. But other contextual factors are more subtle. We propose that the framing of the items themselves may trigger social desirability. Items may be phrased in such a way that they elicit a motivation for socially desirable responding (see Buss, 1959, for a similar approach). In this case social desirability acts as a mediator of the effect that the framing of an item has on the rating of the relevant trait. Several different contextual factors could have additive effects on the ratings. For example, if a person has a contextually activated instrumental goal, and if the items of the inventory are phrased in such an apparently positive or negative way that they themselves elicit the motivation to respond desirably, the risk of a biased measurement should be greater.

∎ SOCIAL DESIRABILITY IN PERSONALITY ASSESSMENT

According to McCrae and Costa (1983), social desirability is not much of a problem in personality measurement. One reason for this is that the predictive validity of personality measures is not affected much when the influence from social desirability is removed. For example, in a recent meta-analysis (Li & Bagger, 2006) the reduction in correlation was small and was suggested by the authors to be negligible, a conclusion to which some may of course disagree. Others have suggested methods for taking care of desirability bias in self-report measures of personality. Paulhus and Vazire (2007) suggest that methods of controlling social desirability can be organized under three different headings: (1) *rational techniques,* (2) *demand reduction techniques,* and (3) *covariate techniques.* Rational techniques prevent the respondent from answering in a desirable way. Demand reduction is all about convincing the participant that it is safe to endorse undesirable responses. The covariate techniques use an inventory of social desirability to statistically control for socially desirable responses. The method presented below rests on a combination of rational techniques and covariate techniques. It is based on a reduction of the evaluative aspect of items and it is expected that less evaluative items will activate less social desirability. The method is based on the rational technique in the sense that the items are constructed (or changed) so as not to activate social desirability concerns, and it is based on the covariate technique since the change in items is dependent on a deliberate attempt to retain the personality-related content of the original item while at the same time getting rid of the variance related to social desirability.

As for related ideas, Peabody (1967) proposed a method that focuses on the separation of evaluative and descriptive aspects, which are usually confounded in personality items. A similar idea has been put forward by Konstabel, Aavik, and Allik (2006), who suggest that social desirability is related to the participants' reaction to the evaluative content of an item, in contrast to their reaction to the descriptive content. We find these to be psychometrically appealing analyses of the role of social desirability in personality measurement. The more obvious the valence of an item is, the greater the risk of a socially desirable response. In Peabody's model each factor is measured by packets of four different versions of each trait descriptor: One that describes a high level of the trait (e.g., Extraversion) and positive valence (e.g., bold), one that describes a high level of the trait and negative valence (e.g., rash), one that describes a low level of the trait and positive valence (e.g., cautious), and one that describes a low level of the trait and negative valence (e.g., timid). This method allows for separation of the descriptive and the evaluative component, as the evaluative influence from positive and negative trait descriptors cancel each other out when added together. Although there have been successful attempts to reduce social desirability using the method (e.g., Saucier, Ostendorf, & Peabody, 2001), it appears rather difficult to implement. In addition, it has been difficult to find combinations of trait descriptors for all personality factors, which could be one reason why a model with only two content factors has been proposed on the basis of research with this method (as in Saucier et al., 2001). In other words, the method may be less appealing for the kind of self-report measures that are supposed to provide a global view of the personality, such as measures of the FFM (but see Saucier, 2002, for a personality marker test of the FFM). However, the method appears very suitable for the separation of the desirability component from the content component in attitude measurement, or in measurement of aspects of personality that may be particularly desirable.

■ A SUGGESTED METHOD: EVALUATIVE NEUTRALIZATION

The methodology that we propose is close to the one proposed by Peabody (1967), but differs in how the reduction of social desirability is achieved. Socially desirable responding tends to be stronger on socially desirable (or clearly undesirable) items and weaker on more neutral items. In our method the valence of an existing item is changed simply by rephrasing it so as to make it more neutral (evaluative neutralization). Positive items (in the direction of the five factors) are framed less positively, whereas negative items are framed less negatively, making all items relatively more neutral. Of course the reasoning is that the responses to the items are altered to the extent that the phrasing of the items is altered. Because the new version of the inventory has a rephrased version of each item from the original inventory, with similar semantic content, the risk of changing the empirical structure of the inventory is reduced. This technique, resting on creating neutral items, is probably as old as the self-rating method itself, since it seems safe to assume that nobody wants to generate items that activate social desirability. What is new is simply the systematic reduction of social desirability in preexisting items, thereby making use of items that have proven to be efficient in measuring a model of personality (e.g., the FFM). The guiding principle is to find a phrasing of each item that reduces its desirability. For example, the item "*Make plans and stick to them*" was reformulated as "*Avoid departing from a plan once I have made one.*" The difference between the two items may seem subtle. Here is how they differ: The first item focuses on the ability to guide oneself in the direction of one's goal. This is probably experienced as a desirable trait. The second item focuses on the unwillingness to change plans. This is probably a less desirable trait. However, both items portray Conscientiousness and should operate as measures of this factor. If you are a conscientious person you will tend to rate both of these items as describing you well, but the second one will be less attractive. Therefore participants high in social desirability will find it less appealing. How about items that are negative in relation to the direction of the scale? Take the item: "*Feel little concern for others*" for example. This is an item that should measure low Agreeableness. According to the present hypothesis such items also trigger socially desirable responses, but in a direction opposite from the "positive" item above. People high in social desirability will disagree with these items since they describe unattractive traits. The item, "*Believe it is better if everyone cares for himself or herself*" frames the same kind of descriptor in a more neutral tone; accordingly, persons high in social desirability will not think of the item as equally undesirable.

To make the original items less evaluative we aimed at getting the ratings closer to the middle of the scale. If the general population rates in the middle of the scale then the item is probably neither desirable nor undesirable. Different techniques were used (see Table 13.1). Sometimes the level (such as the intensity or frequency of the trait-related content) of the item was changed upward, either making the item less negative, such as when "*Get upset easily*" was reframed as "*Sometimes react strongly to things that happen*" or making a positive item depict a person with an exaggerated level of the trait, such as when the item "*Am exacting in my work*" was reframed as "*Continue working with a task so that every small detail is right.*" Sometimes an intention or goal was added making a positive item more neutral,

TABLE 13.1 *Examples of How Original Items Were Made Evaluatively More Neutral*

Original	Neutral	FFM Scale	Technique
Am the life of the party	Prefer to be the central figure at a party	Extraversion	Intentions or goal (rated lower and more neutral)
Get upset easily	Sometimes react strongly to things that happen	Emotional stability (–)	Level (rated higher and more neutral)
Am exacting in my work	Continue working with a task so that every small detail is right	Conscientiousness	Level (exaggerated, rated lower and more neutral)
Spend time reflecting on things	Can sit around and think about things for a long time	Openness	Level (exaggerated, rated lower and more neutral)
Inquire about others' well-being	Really want to know how other people are doing	Agreeableness	Intentions or goal (rated lower and more neutral)

Note: Minus sign = reversed item.

such as when *"Am the life of the party"* was changed to *"Prefer to be the central figure at a party."* It simply does not sound as attractive to be striving for something as just being it, and this was a frequently used technique. Although it would, of course, have been possible to make positive items more neutral by using a more neutral descriptor of the trait (Peabody, 1967), there were only a few examples of this technique in the neutral inventory.

■ CURRENT EVIDENCE IN SUPPORT OF THE MODEL

We have conducted a number of studies to compare neutralized items with original items. In one of them (Bäckström, Björklund, & Larsson, 2009) we created 92 new items based on a 100 item FFM inventory from the International Personality Item Pool (IPIP). To determine whether we succeeded in our attempt to create more neutral items we asked a group of students ($N = 55$) to rate the social desirability of the items. We found a very large difference in social desirability ratings for almost all items; mean Cohen $d = 0.76$. When a large group of Internet users made self-ratings it was found that our neutralized items, compared with the original, were rated closer to the mean of the scale, but with somewhat lower SD (the mean SD on the item level being 0.70 for the original and 0.60 for the neutralized, on a Likert scale ranging from 1 to 5). Additionally, it was shown, using Confirmatory Factor Analysis, that the factor structure of the neutralized items was comparable with regard to the size of the loadings on all five factors, after controlling for a higher order factor. The correlations were high with the original inventory (E = 0.79; A = 0.81; C = 0.78; Es = 0.83; O = 0.70) and the correlation between the neutralized inventory and social desirability as captured by an aggregate variable of the responses to the IPIP equivalents of Paulhus' Impression Management and Self-Deception scales (E = 0.14; A = 0.16; C = 0.23; Es = 0.38; O = 0.07) was lower compared with the same correlation for the original inventory (E = 0.36; A = 0.38; C = 0.31; Es = 0.52; O = 0.29).

We have also conducted two further studies in which context was experimentally manipulated to vary the amount of social desirability. In the first study there were only two contexts: job seeking and control. In the other there were four contexts: fake bad, job seeking, fake good, and control. Generally it was found that neutralized items were somewhat less influenced by the context, although the difference was small. The results showed that a job-seeking context increased the ratings of, for example, Conscientiousness in both the neutralized and the original inventory. This indicates that participants are well aware of the personality content of the item and also know which personality dimensions are most desired in the workplace. In another study we attempted to demonstrate the ease with which "neutral" test items can be created from evaluative items, and tested whether undergraduate psychology students provided with a very short description of the method would succeed in creating neutral items. Each participant was presented with 10 items from one of the original FFM scales and asked to create new ones. They had approximately 15 minutes at their disposal, and in spite of the limited time they succeeded in creating items that independent raters clearly regarded as less desirable. When successful items (new items having a lower social desirability index) were used to create a new inventory it still had the factorial structure of the FFM and the scales correlated highly with the original IPIP inventory scales.

One explicit aim in creating the neutral inventory was that factor intercorrelation should be reduced. In a large ($N = 2011$) nonpublished dataset the mean correlation between the scales of the neutral inventory was lower ($M = 0.02$; $SD = 0.11$; ranging from -0.18 to 0.14) compared to the mean correlation for the original inventory ($M = 0.31$; $SD = 0.09$; ranging from 0.09 to 0.46). Because the common variance was low and some of the correlations were negative, the common variance between the factors of the neutral inventory could not have been used to create higher order factors (e.g., Digman's alpha and beta; see Bäckström et al., 2009, for a more elaborated argument). From these data it is possible to hypothesize that higher order factors are not a real problem for the FFM, but rather a problem with the measurement of the FFM, since the evaluatively neutral inventory has five orthogonal factor scales (five independent dimensions of personality). However, there seems to be at least one additional factor in many personality inventories, which consists of either personality content or variability related to response style (e.g., social desirability).

■ SOCIAL DESIRABILITY AS A PERSONALITY VARIABLE AND ITS RELATION TO NONEVALUATIVE ITEMS

Evaluative neutralization of items may be useful in other areas of personality measurement. One is in the identification of personality traits such as "repressive coping style" and "self-enhancement." The repressive coping style was defined by Weinberger, Schwartz, and Davidson (1979) as individuals scoring low on measures of trait anxiety (i.e., Neuroticism) and high on measures of social desirability. The underlying theoretical assumption regarding individuals with a repressive coping style is that they have a high degree of ego defense protecting them from subjective distress and empirical evidence has been presented showing that repressors have an inclination toward amplifying characteristics such as trait emotional intelligence, self-estimated IQ, and functional impulsivity (Furnham, Petrides, Sisterson, & Baluch, 2003) and also to report higher self-esteem, higher life-satisfaction, and the use of more "healthy coping-styles" than nonrepressors (Furnham, Petrides, & Spencer-Bowdage, 2002). Self-enhancement is a tendency to have an unrealistically positive view of oneself, to have an exaggerated perception of personal control, and/or being unrealistically optimistic (e.g., Taylor & Brown, 1988). In comparison to a repressive coping style self-enhancement seems to be more general in relation to personality traits (i.e., it is related to several personality traits, not only anxiety) and people high in self-enhancement seem to have an overall view of themselves as good, whereas people with a repressive coping style do not like to view themselves as anxious. It has been suggested that the self-deception facet of the Paulhus (1984) scale could be used to distinguish repressors from nonrepressors (see, e.g., Ashley & Holtgraves, 2003). In addition, empirical evidence also suggests that impulsivity, self-estimated intelligence, and trait emotional intelligence can be used to differentiate repressors from nonrepressors (Furnham et al., 2002)

Using non-evaluative items offers a new way to investigate the tendency to rate in a socially desirable direction. For example, when it comes to repressors, it would be possible to use the evaluative neutralization method instead of measuring anxiety and social desirability as two unique variables. If repressors really react to the social desirability content of items it would be possible to compare responses to anxiety items with an obvious valence (e.g., "I am nervous") to items with a less obvious valence (e.g., a more neutral item, such as "I am sensitive to threats in my proximity"). The expected outcome from this comparison would be that repressors respond to the latter item with a higher rating than on the former item.

■ SOCIAL DESIRABILITY IN FFM SELF-RATINGS: ONE OR TWO FACTORS?

In sum, Paulhus' (1984) very influential model of Social Desirability suggests that there are two social desirability factors. This model is partly corroborated by Digman's two-factor model since his model explains correlations between FFM scales with two general factors. Alternative to these models are the models suggesting that one single higher order factor explains correlations between personality ratings, i.e., a general evaluative factor. It is not possible to judge from our data which model is the best, but in spite of that, we will present a speculative argument for a model where one social desirability factor is sufficient to explain correlations between scales from different domains of the FFM. This argument rests on the fact that it is necessary to show correlations between scales to introduce a method factor such as social desirability or a general factor such as Digman's alpha; if there is no correlation then there is nothing to explain. There can be "method factors" on a more specific level, of course, for example, if the measure of a specific trait, say Emotional Stability, is specifically influenced by some unknown factor, say more cautious ratings, and this specific factor is not influencing the measure of other traits. Our argument will not include this kind of specific factor; we are concerned only with factors influencing personality inventories in general.

TABLE 13.2 *Hierarchical Regression Analysis on the Prediction of the Difference between the Original and the Neutral Items*

	SD alone	IM alone	SD and IM together			
			SD	IM	R^2 change adding IM	R^2 change adding SD
E Diff	−0.390	−0.229	−0.354	−0.080	0.005*	0.103*
A Diff	−0.287	−0.120	−0.287	−0.001	0.000	0.068*
C Diff	−0.368	−0.307	−0.290	−0.184	0.028*	0.069*
Es Diff	−0.351	−0.232	−0.290	−0.109	0.010*	0.069*
O Diff	−0.338	−0.278	−0.268	−0.165	0.022*	0.059*

Note: $N = 2011$. All predictors are defined as the difference between the original and the neutral inventory scales; SD = Self-deception; IM = Impression Management, E = Extraversion, A = Agreeableness, C = Conscientiousness, Es = Emotional stability, O = Openness.
*$p < 0.001$.

We examined whether the difference between ratings of the original and the neutralized items (DIFF-ON) was related to ratings of social desirability. Table 13.2 displays the results of several regression analyses predicting the difference between the original and the neutral items of each scale. The first two columns show the standardized coefficients for Self-deception and Impression Management alone, where Self-deception had generally stronger relations than Impression management (all differences are statistically significant). The last two columns show the R^2 change of adding Impression Management and Self-deception as a second predictor.[1] For Impression Management the unique contribution is close to zero for three of the scales and low for Conscientiousness and Openness. The unique contribution of Self-deception is larger for all scales.

The result that Self-deception is related to the evaluative content of the personality items, whereas Impression Management made a meager contribution, lends some support to Paulhus' Social Desirability model, or more cautiously, there seems to be at least one social desirability factor. The result also suggests that Social Desirability, as it is defined here, as the difference in ratings between the original and the neutralized items, is a factor that is independent of the Big Five traits. Even so, the pattern of correlations of Self-deception with Extraversion and Emotional Stability, and of Impression Management with Agreeableness and Conscientiousness, requires explanation. The suggested method to neutralize the evaluative factor in the items reduced the amount of variance related to Self-deception in the personality inventory. In our data the difference in ratings between the original and the neutralized items (DIFF-ON) was strongly related to Self-deception, but also moderately related to Emotional Stability (all other correlations were weak). From these two correlations it is not possible to determine if the DIFF-ON should be attributed to social desirability (e.g., Self-deception) or if it should be attributed to a personality factor (e.g., Emotional Stability), or both. Piedmont, McCrae, Riemann, and Angleitner (2000) have suggested that many

1. The neutral inventory used in these analyses was an optimized version based on 50 items from the 92 items presented in Bäckström et al. (2009), 10 items in each FFM scale.

validity scales (e.g., social desirability) are contaminated with content variance, that is, variance from the proper personality traits.

If the correlations between social desirability (i.e., DIFF-ON) and the neutral content scales had all been zero and not revealed a moderate correlation to emotional stability, then it would have been more straightforward to argue that Social Desirability is a separate factor from the FFM. Our conclusion must be that we do not know whether Social Desirability is an entirely independent dimension or is partly related to one or several of the five factors. In a very preliminary analysis, probing for an answer, we made an exploratory factor analysis (PCA and Varimax rotation; $N = 2011$) of the neutralized items (aggregated in parcels consisting of three or four items each) together with the five DIFF-ON variables. The DIFF-ON variables formed a separate factor, which was independent of the other five factors.

Bäckström (2007; see also Bäckström, Björklund, & Larsson, 2009) has shown that a single higher order factor explains most of the covariation between factors in a number of FFM inventories. In light of this result it is also interesting to note that in the dataset referred to in this chapter ($N = 2011$) the first principal component of the items from the original inventory, a variable closely related to the higher order factor, correlated about 0.7 with the DIFF-ON. The DIFF-ON correlated positively with Self-deception and Impression Management (0.49 and 0.34, respectively), but the partial correlation controlling for the first principal component of the original items was 0.02 and –0.01, respectively, both insignificant. In other words the common variance for social desirability and DIFF-ON could be attributed to a general factor in the original inventory. A viable explanation for this result is that participants' responses to the evaluative content in items create the common factor (Konstabel, Aavik, & Allik, 2006). Based on our previously reported results, the common factor is closely related to the Self-deception factor described by Paulhus (1984).

Is the common factor a personality factor? We speculatively suggest that the common factor is strongly related to Self-enhancement. Usually self-enhancement is measured either with self-ratings alone, e.g., with measures of social desirability, or as a contrast using self-ratings and peer-ratings of the same subject or, alternatively, ratings of self and ratings of peers. Kwan, John, Robins, and Kuang (2008) suggest a more elaborate model using self-ratings and peer-ratings where the self-enhancement factor is extracted by partialling out other factors. Paulhus and Holden (2010) discuss different problems with measures of self-enhancement, e.g., that if it is measured with Self-deception the concept is not independent of other personality factors since Self-deception is often related to Emotional stability, Extraversion, and Openness. They also criticize the method of using self-ratings and peer-ratings and instead suggest that self-enhancement should be estimated by a measure of exaggerations or with response time techniques. These methods may, however, be difficult to use in applied settings, e.g., it is difficult to get hold of peers, it is somewhat awkward to rate a peer if you are applying for a job, and when applying for a job you are supposed to be allowed to exaggerate somewhat. A viable, but untested, alternative operationalization would be to use the evaluative factor (DIFF-ON) as an indicator of Self-enhancement, suggesting that self-enhancers are especially sensitive to the evaluative content in the personality items.

■ TOWARD A NONEVALUATIVE INVENTORY MEASURING THE FFM AND ITS RELATION TO INDIVIDUAL DIFFERENCES

Saucier (2002), among others, has called for nonevaluative scales for measuring personality. We think an inventory with neutral items is a step in that direction. The instrument is not ready yet; several psychometric studies have to be conducted before the scales can be used as a measure of the FFM in any research or applied context. The items have to be optimized for reliability and structural validity. The preliminary items used in Bäckström et al. (2009) had lower reliability than the original scales, possibly due to the fact that the evaluative factor was reduced. The evaluative factor tends to inflate the reliability in a scale since it increases the correlation among items. In addition, the variance in the neutral items was somewhat lower. Because reliability (alpha) is down to about 0.8 in the neutral scales, from about 0.9 in the original test, better or more items are needed to create a psychometrically comparable scale. Naturally, these new items must not compromise the factorial structure of the inventory.

The most important evaluation of the neutral item inventory is its criterion-related validity (predictive or concurrent). The first and perhaps most obvious study is a validation of self-ratings against peer-ratings, where the inventory must reveal correlations comparable to the original inventory controlled for social desirability. The problem here is that the original scale includes the evaluative dimension (i.e., good vs. bad), and this dimension can contaminate the criteria, the peer-ratings. If a person is believed to have positive or negative qualities, a general positive versus negative rating, maybe due to a halo effect, will be possible.

Finally, a comment on the cross-cultural generalization of neutral items: Because social desirability is related to cultural norms (Lalwani, Shrum, & Chiu, 2009), neutral items cannot simply be translated from one language to another.

■ CONCLUDING THOUGHTS

From a psychometric perspective, the separate measurement of social desirability and personality would be ideal. But the odds of succeeding with this may not be very high, particularly if restricted to methods that require self-ratings. These measures have strong advantages when it comes to measuring personality. In just a few moments and with little effort on the part of the participant a relatively clear picture of the personality can be achieved. But it may be harder to capture the evaluative factor with self-ratings. The problem is that the evaluative factor, which is closely related to social desirability, intrudes on all kinds of self-ratings, and that measures of social desirability seem to be influenced by other personality factors. Because it appears to be difficult to capture the evaluative factor with self-ratings, other methods have to be developed. The strongest advantage with evaluatively neutral personality items is the reduction of factor complexity in the scales of personality inventories, e.g., that the validity and reliability of the FFM factor scales can be attributed with higher confidence to the personality content of the scales, and not to social desirability stemming from the evaluative content of the scales. If neutral and evaluative items are combined in the same inventory, then it is possible to extract a measure of the evaluative factor (see also Borkenau & Ostendorf, 1989, and Saucier, Ostendorf, & Peabody, 2002 for alternative models). This factor, free from the influence of other content factors of the FFM, is perhaps best portrayed as an independent personality factor with a suitable name that will distinguish it from the method factor Social desirability.

References

Ashley, A., & Holtgraves, T. (2003). Repressors and memory: Effects of self-deception, impression management, and mood. *Journal of Research in Personality, 37,* 284–296.

Bäckström, M. (2007). Higher-order factors in a five-factor personality inventory and its relation to social desirability. *European Journal of Psychological Assessment, 23,* 63–70.

Bäckström, M., Björklund, F., & Larsson, M. R. (2009). Five-factor inventories have a major higher order factor related to social desirability which can be reduced by framing items neutrally. *Journal of Research in Personality, 43,* 335–344.

Bakan, D. (1966). *The duality of human existence: Isolation and communion in Western man.* Boston: Beacon Press.

Block, J. (1995). A contrarian view of the five-factor approach to personality description. *Psychological Bulletin, 117,* 187–215.

Borkenau, P., & Ostendorf, F. (1989). Descriptive consistency and social desirability in self- and peer reports. *European Journal of Personality, 3,* 31–45.

Buss, A. H. (1959). The effect of item style on social desirability and frequency of endorsement. *Journal of Consulting Psychology, 23,* 510–513.

Costa, P. T., & McCrae, R. R. (1992). *Revised NEO personality inventory (NEO-PI-R) and NEO five-factor inventory (NEO-FFI) professional manual.* Odessa, FL: Psychological Assessment Resources.

DeYoung, C. G., Peterson, J. B., & Higgins, D. M. (2002). Higher-order factors of the Big Five predict conformity: Are there neuroses of health? *Personality and Individual Differences, 33,* 533–552.

Digman, J. M. (1997). Higher-order factors of the big five. *Journal of Personality and Social Psychology, 73,* 1246–1256.

Edwards, A. L. (1957). *The social desirability variable in personality assessment and research.* New York: Dryden Press.

Furnham, A., Petrides, K. V., Sisterson, G., & Baluch, B. (2003). Repressive coping style and positive self-presentation. *British Journal of Health Psychology, 8,* 223–249.

Furnham, A., Petrides, K. V., & Spencer-Bowdage, S. (2002). The effects of different types of social desirability on the identification of repressors. *Personality and Individual Differences, 33,* 119–130.

Goldberg, L. R. (1993). The structure of phenotypic personality traits. *American Psychologist, 48,* 26–34.

Gray, J. A., & McNaughton, N. (2000). *The neuropsychology of anxiety: An enquiry into the functions of the septo-hippocampal system.* New York: Oxford University Press.

Hendriks, A. A. J., Hofstee, W. K. B., & de Raad, B. D. (2002). *The five-factor personality inventory: Assessing the big five by means of brief and concrete statements.* Ashland, OH: Hogrefe & Huber Publishers.

Holden, R. R., Kroner, D. G., Fekken, C. G., & Popham, S. M. (1992). A model of personality test item response dissimulation. *Journal of Personality and Social Psychology, 63,* 272–279.

Holtgraves, T. (2004). Social desirability and self-reports: Testing models of socially desirable responding. *Personality and Social Psychology Bulletin, 30,* 161–172.

Konstabel, K., Aavik, T., & Allik, J. (2006). Social desirability and consensual validity of personality traits. *European Journal of Personality, 20,* 549–566.

Kwan, V. S. Y., John, O. P., Robins, R. W., & Kuang, L. L. (2008). Conceptualizing and assessing self-enhancement bias: A componential approach. *Journal of Personality and Social Psychology, 94,* 1062–1077.

Lalwani, A. K., Shrum, L. J., & Chiu, C. (2009). Motivated response styles: The role of cultural values, regulatory focus, and self-consciousness in socially desirable responding. *Journal of Personality and Social Psychology, 96,* 870–882.

Li, A., & Bagger, J. (2006). Using the BIDR to distinguish the effects of impression management and self-deception on the criterion validity of personality measures: A meta-analysis. *International Journal of Selection and Assessment, 14,* 131–141.

McCrae, R. R., & Costa, P. T. (1983). Social desirability scales: More substance than style. *Journal of Consulting and Clinical Psychology, 51,* 882–888.

Musek, J. (2007). A general factor of personality: Evidence for the big one in the five-factor model. *Journal of Research in Personality, 41,* 1213–1233.

Paulhus, D. L. (1984). Two-component models of socially desirable responding. *Journal of Personality and Social Psychology, 46,* 598–609.

Paulhus, D. L. (2002). Socially desirable responding: The evolution of a construct. In H. I. Braun, D. N. Jackson, & D. E. Wiley (Eds.), *The role of constructs in psychological and educational measurement* (pp. 49–69). Mahwah, NJ: Lawrence Erlbaum Associates.

Paulhus, D. L., & Holden, R. R. (2010). Measuring self-enhancement: From self-report to concrete behavior. In C. R. Agnew, D. E. Carlston, W. G. Graziano, & J. R. Kelly (Eds.), *Then a miracle occurs: Focusing on behavior in social psychological theory and research* (pp. 227–246). New York: Oxford University Press.

Paulhus, D. L., & John, O. P. (1998). Egoistic and moralistic biases in self-perception: The interplay of self-deceptive styles with basic traits and motives. *Journal of Personality, 66,* 1025–1060.

Paulhus, D. L., & Vazire, S. (2007). The self-report method. In R. W. Robins, R. C. Fraley, & R. F. Krueger (Eds.), *Handbook of research methods in personality psychology* (pp. 224–237). New York: Guilford Press.

Peabody, D. (1967). Trait inferences: Evaluative and descriptive aspects. *Journal of Personality and Social Psychology, 7,* 1–18.

Peabody, D. (1984). Personality dimensions through trait inferences. *Journal of Personality and Social Psychology, 46,* 384–403.

Piedmont, R. L., McCrae, R. R., Riemann, R., & Angleitner, A. (2000). On the invalidity of validity scales: Evidence from self-reports and observer ratings in volunteer samples. *Journal of Personality and Social Psychology, 78,* 582–593.

Saucier, G. (1994). Separating description and evaluation in the structure of personality attributes. *Journal of Personality and Social Psychology, 66,* 141–154.

Saucier, G. (2002). Orthogonal markers for orthogonal factors: The case of the Big Five. *Journal of Research in Personality, 36,* 1–31.

Saucier, G., Ostendorf, F., & Peabody, D. (2001). The non-evaluative circumplex of personality adjectives. *Journal of Personality, 69,* 537–582.

Taylor, S. E., & Brown, J. D. (1988). Illusion and well-being: A social psychological perspective on mental health. *Psychological Bulletin, 103,* 193–210.

Weinberger, A. D., Schwartz, E. G., & Davidson, J. R. (1979). Low-anxious, high-anxious, and repressive coping styles: Psychometric patterns and behavioral and physiological responses to stress. *Journal of Abnormal Psychology, 88,* 369–380.

14 Constructing Fake-Resistant Personality Tests Using Item Response Theory

High-Stakes Personality Testing with
Multidimensional Pairwise Preferences

■ STEPHEN STARK, OLEKSANDR S.
CHERNYSHENKO, AND FRITZ DRASGOW

Personality factors comprise some of the most important individual difference variables for describing, understanding, and predicting human behavior. Personality test scores have been shown to predict a diverse array of outcomes such as college GPA (Noftle & Robins, 2007), health and risk-taking behaviors (Booth-Kewley & Vickers, 1994), organizational citizenship performance (Hogan, Rybicki, Motowidlo, & Borman, 1998), individual and organizational deviance (Berry, Ones, & Sackett, 2007), and turnover intentions and attrition (Timmerman, 2006). Clinical, counseling, and organizational development professionals have embraced these findings and incorporated personality test scores into their diagnostic systems and developmental interventions. Yet, despite the fecundity of criteria personality measures predict, large-scale testing programs have seemingly overlooked these assessments as sources of information for high-stakes decision making. Undergraduate, graduate, and professional school admissions committees, human resource departments, and, until recently, even military selection commands have relied mainly on cognitive tests and biographical data to evaluate the suitability of applicants for admission, employment, or service. Why might this be the case?

One obvious explanation is concern for the well-documented effects of "faking good" (Rosse, Stecher, Miller, & Levin, 1998; Stark, Chernyshenko, Chan, Lee, & Drasgow, 2001). Applicants for jobs or college admissions might answer in a socially desirable way in an effort to improve their scores and ultimately their chances of being selected. Highly motivated examinees might also turn to professional coaching organizations to gain insights about test composition, use, and strategies for score enhancement. When the number of examinees is very large and tests are clearly tied to high-stakes outcomes, examinees might even conspire to "break" a test by memorizing blocks of items and exposing their content on the Internet. Thus, for personality measures to be considered as viable selection tools, methods are needed that can accurately detect and correct for faking. Or tests must be made more resistant to response distortion and utilize features that make cheating more difficult, such as large item banks and adaptive item selection (Guo, Tay, & Drasgow, 2009).

In this chapter, we briefly review methods that have been explored to handle response distortion in applied personality assessment. We cite some key findings that have moved the field from a detection and correction to a prevention focus. We then explain why multidimensional forced choice (MFC) tests are now of high interest in selection environments, and review a relatively new item response theory (IRT) method for creating fake-resistant tests involving multidimensional pairwise preference (MDPP) items. The efficacy of this method of test construction and scoring is demonstrated using simulation evidence involving tests of high dimensionality, as well as empirical findings from ongoing laboratory and field studies showing the stability of trait scores across testing situations. We then discuss the benefits and challenges of MDPP and, more generally MFC, testing and provide suggestions for future research.

■ WHAT TO DO ABOUT FAKING?

Although some of the earliest personality inventories attempted to control for response distortion by selecting and scoring opaque items through empirical keying [e.g., the Minnesota Multiphasic Personality Inventory (MMPI); Butcher, Dahlstrom, Graham, Tellegen, & Kaemmer, 1989], concerns about construct and face validity moved personality assessment toward rationally based tests containing positive and negative statements describing typical thoughts, feelings, and behaviors that can be grouped into short, homogeneous scales of 10–15 items. Such scales are relatively easy to construct, they are well received by respondents, and they show good construct and criterion-related validities in settings in which examinees can be presumed to answer honestly. Unfortunately, when there are strong incentives to fake, score inflation as high as 1.5 standard deviations has been observed (Hough, Eaton, Dunnette, Kamp, & McCloy, 1990; Stark et al., 2001). For these reasons, scales designed to detect socially desirable responding or impression management are usually administered in conjunction with content scales and are used for score adjustments or flagging examinees for possible retesting. Research on the effectiveness of these scales has been equivocal at best, however (Ellingson, Sackett, & Hough, 1999; Ones, Viswesvaran, & Reiss, 1996; Schmitt & Oswald, 2006; Stark et al., 2001; Zickar & Drasgow, 1996), and it has even been argued that score adjustments may reduce test validity by partialling out variance that is related to performance (Ellingson et al., 1999; Kriedt & Dawson, 1961).

IRT aberrance detection methods, which were designed originally to detect cheating on cognitive tests (Drasgow & Levine, 1986; Meijer, 2004), have also been explored for screening personality scale response patterns. Essentially, person fit statistics are used to identify unusual strings of responses (Meijer, 2003), or the likelihoods of responses given hypothesized normal and aberrant response models are compared via likelihood ratio tests (Levine & Drasgow, 1988). Although these methods have been shown to be somewhat effective, technical complexity and concerns about power relative to false positive rates, particularly with computerized adaptive tests, have precluded widespread application (Drasgow, Levine, & Zickar, 1996; Meijer, 2004). Moreover, just as with social desirability and impression management scales, practical questions remain as to what to do about examinees who are identified as aberrant. In the absence of perfect detection, which is certainly unattainable, questions can always be raised by individual examinees who claim that they were misclassified as fakers and denied opportunities as a result. And this could lead to legal scrutiny that would offset whatever utility gains were associated with using the tests. Consequently, research with rationally constructed personality scales has gravitated toward preventing faking, rather than detecting and correcting for it.

An intuitive way of reducing faking is through the use of warnings that are presented along with test instructions. For example, benign warnings try to convince examinees that responding honestly is in their best interest. Respondents may be told that test scores will be used to match them with jobs in which they are likely to succeed and that fit their interpersonal styles. Coercive warnings, in contrast, threaten examinees with punitive action if dissimulation is detected (Dwight & Donovan, 2003). In our view, research is needed to evaluate the effectiveness of both of these strategies in operational settings before these approaches can be advocated. Benign warnings may be effective with examinees who value long-term person–environment congruence, and coercive warnings may be effective in reducing score inflation in laboratory experiments. Yet, whether either of these approaches works as intended in real-world settings remains to be seen (Dwight & Donovan, 2003; Robson, Jones, & Abraham, 2008). When stakes are high, vague arguments about future unhappiness or threats of disqualification from an application process may be less salient than the immediate denial of highly valued opportunities. Consequently applicants may be motivated to respond in ways they believe will maximize their outcomes and hence "fake good." Warnings could also have important ramifications for recruitment and hiring. Aggressive warnings could not only evoke response sets in characteristically honest respondents, but also deter them from continuing with the application process or divert them toward organizations that take an adulatory approach to recruitment, particularly when the numbers of available positions exceed the number of well-qualified applicants. Threats of punitive action could also expose organizations to legal action if applicants perceive they are disqualified based on assumptions about behavior that cannot be conclusively supported by psychometric or behavioral evidence. Thus, pending more extensive research into the benefits and risks of using warnings in high-stakes environments, caution is recommended.

Another approach to reducing faking is to change the format in which personality statements are presented. Instead of presenting statements individually and asking examinees to indicate their levels of agreement, groups of statements can be organized into blocks and administered to examinees with instructions telling them to choose the statement(s) that are most and/or least descriptive of them. Variations of this theme currently dominate the research literature in applied psychology, as researchers are exploring formats ranging from pairwise preferences to tetrads (Christiansen, Burns, & Montgomery, 2005; Heggestad, Morrison, Reeve, & McCloy, 2006; Jackson, Wrobleski, & Ashton, 2000; McCloy, Heggestad, & Reeve, 2005; Stark, 2002a; Stark, Chernyshenko, & Drasgow, 2005; Vasilopoulos, Cucina, Dyomina, Morewitz, & Reilly, 2006; White & Young, 1998). Measures administered in such formats are collectively known as **forced choice** tests. Although the methods of test construction, the underlying psychometric models, and details such as dimensionality and the number of answers required per block differ across implementations, a common feature of these multidimensional forced choice tests is that the statements composing each block are matched in terms of social desirability so that respondents have a difficult time discerning which answers are better, and thus faking is less effective. Unless respondents know which dimensions are being used for selection, unless they are able to discern which statements measure those dimensions, and unless they can keep track of their answers on several dimensions simultaneously and provide consistent patterns of responses across blocks, then respondents should not be able to increase scores on selection dimensions as easily as when traditional, single-statement measures are used.

To date empirical support for this notion has been mixed (see Dilchert, Ones, Viswesvaran, & Deller, 2006), with some studies showing that MFC measures reduce score inflation and maintain criterion-related validities in situations in which examinees are motivated to fake (Bowen, Martin, & Hunt, 2002; Christiansen et al., 2005; White & Young, 1998), and others showing considerable score inflation, especially for conscientiousness (Heggestad et al., 2006). Because these studies differed appreciably in how the MFC measures were constructed and scored, it is difficult to determine whether design features or uncontrolled situational factors led to the conflicting results. Experimental research is clearly needed to uncover the sources of discrepancies and identify optimal ways of composing forced choice items and tests.

In addition to being potentially more difficult to fake, MFC tests are particularly well suited for large-volume high-stakes testing environments because the numbers of possible items are very large. In principle, any statement can appear with any other(s) in a block, and therefore even small numbers of statements representing each dimension can yield thousands of items. For example, a pool of 500 statements measuring, say, 10 personality dimensions can potentially produce as many as $500 \times 499/2 = 124{,}750$ pairwise preference items. Constraints for matching on social desirability certainly reduce the number of possibilities, but when many dimensions are assessed simultaneously, the numbers of items available for test construction are still vast. This gives test designers tremendous flexibility when creating forms and it enhances test security, especially when combined with adaptive item selection procedures that dynamically tailor items to the trait levels of examinees, subject, of course, to high-level content specifications that ensure comparability across administrations. In contrast, with traditional single statement tests, the number of items available for administration is always less than or equal to the number of statements in the pool. And this undoubtedly limits the ability to construct alternate forms and offsets advantages that computer adaptive tests (CATs) may provide in terms of exposure control and test security.

■ CLASSIC APPROACHES TO CONSTRUCTING AND SCORING MFC MEASURES

Early attempts to construct MFC measures focused on multidimensional pairwise preference items (Edwards, 1954; Rounds, Henly, Dawis, Lofquist, & Weiss, 1981)

218 ■ New Perspectives on Faking in Personality Assessment

that required a respondent to choose the statement in each pair that is "more like me." Statements chosen by respondents were assigned scores of 1 and those not selected were assigned scores of 0. Scores for the statements representing their respective dimensions were then summed to obtain a set of scale scores for each respondent. The resulting scores had ipsative properties, however, meaning that they reflected only respondents' relative standings on the dimensions assessed. This is because ipsative scale scores for each respondent sum to a constant equal to the number of paired comparisons. This feature introduces dependencies among scale scores that results in negative correlations between dimensions and precludes interindividual comparisons, which are important for selection applications.

In an effort to address ipsativity problems, researchers have since experimented with ways of capturing between-person variance with MFC test scores. One approach adds a small number of single statement items representing each dimension in an attempt to anchor the metric (Böckenholt, 2004; Rounds et al., 1981). Another approach includes statements from "distractor" dimensions that are essentially ignored when computing scores (Christiansen et al., 2005). Perhaps the most popular approach, however, is to form tetrads involving two positively keyed statements and two negatively keyed statements. For each tetrad, a respondent must choose one statement that is "most like me" and one statement that is "least like me." If a negatively keyed statement is selected as "least like me" or a positively keyed statement is selected as "most like me" a score of 1 is assigned to the statement; a score of –1 is assigned if the reverse is true, and the unselected statements are assigned 0s. Scale scores are then computed as the sum across the statements assessing each dimension. An example of an MFC tetrad is shown in Figure 14.1. Overall, strategies such as these seem to mitigate the ipsativity problems that have historically beleaguered MFC measures (Stark, 2002a; Stark et al., 2005; Heggestad et al., 2006; Hicks, 1970; Meade, 2004; White & Young, 1998). Studies showing the construct and criterion-related validities of these new MFC tests are beginning to mount (Bowen et al., 2002; Chernyshenko et al., 2009; Christiansen et al., 2005; Dilchert et al., 2006; Jackson et al., 2000; Villanova, Bernardin, Johnson, & Dahmus, 1994; White & Young, 1998), but questions remain about how to adapt these methods for use in large-scale operational testing environments.

For each group of statements that follow, choose one that is *most like you (M) and one that is least like you (L) and indicate your answers as shown in the example below.*

M | L

O | O   I sometimes turn in my assignments late. (–C)
● | O   I generally perform well under pressure. (+Em)
O | ●   I tend to say things that hurt others' feelings. (–A)
O | O   I enjoy learning about other cultures. (+O)

Figure 14.1 A multidimensional tetrad involving positively (+) and negatively (–) keyed statements representing Conscientiousness (C), Emotional Stability (Em), Agreeableness (A), and Openness to Experience (O). The content codes and valences of the statements are shown for illustration purposes only on the right-hand side.

The main limitation of classic methods is that they do not utilize a formal psychometric model for the preferential choice process. Both classical test theory (CTT) and IRT models have been used to analyze MFC data (Christiansen et al., 2005; Drasgow, Lee, Stark, & Chernyshenko, 2001; Heggestad et al., 2006), but the "response patterns" that were actually scored in those studies were reconstructed from MFC judgments by disassembling the pairs or tetrads, coding all statements as if they were explicitly answered, and then grouping the coded responses to the statements representing the respective dimensions for scoring. The response data were therefore analyzed as if a series of single statement unidimensional scales had been administered. Importantly, such approaches to unwrapping and repackaging MFC responses (e.g., Christiansen et al., 2005; Vasilopoulos et al., 2006; White & Young, 1998) do not seem to negate test validities. Yet, because there is no direct connection between latent trait scores and the process of evaluating the statements that compose MFC items, it is difficult to envision how endorsement probabilities and item information can be readily computed to select items dynamically in CAT applications or to construct parallel test forms.

■ IRT MODELING OF MULTIDIMENSIONAL PAIRWISE PREFERENCES

Multistatement formats, such as tetrads and pentads, that require multiple responses from examinees arguably require more complex psychometric models than single statement items. Multidimensionality further complicates calibration and scoring. It is therefore no surprise that the very few IRT models that have been developed for MFC judgments have utilized the simplest format, namely the multidimensional pairwise preference (MDPP) judgment. MDPP items require respondents simply to indicate which of two personality statements in a pair more accurately describes them. An example item involving Well Being and Order statements is presented below:

_____ I like order.
_____ I am very optimistic about my future.

If one assumes that a respondent's levels of, say, Well Being and Order are the only traits influencing his or her choice of statements in a pair and an IRT model is specified to calculate preferential choice probabilities, then trait scores can be estimated directly from dichotomously coded pairwise preference responses via methods such as maximum likelihood or Bayes modal estimation.

With this idea in mind, Stark (2002a) proposed the Multi-Unidimensional Pairwise Preference (MUPP) model and a sequential approach to test construction and scoring involving multidimensional and unidimensional pairwise preference items. He examined the efficacy of a Bayes modal scoring algorithm (Stark, 2002b) with one- and two-dimensional tests of various lengths using a Monte Carlo simulation, and found that the scoring method was able to estimate trait scores with good relative and absolute accuracy, thus paving the way for future research involving tests of higher dimensionality and adaptive item selection. Although a thorough description of the model and estimation methods is beyond the scope of this presentation, readers are referred to the Appendix for a technical summary of the model and Stark et al. (2005a) for more details.

The sequential approach to MDPP test construction and scoring, mentioned above, proceeds as follows. First, researchers must write large numbers of personality statements representing each dimension of interest and administer them individually to large groups of respondents. A unidimensional IRT model, which adequately fits the data,[1] is then used to estimate parameters for the statements representing each dimension separately to assess their discriminating power and extremity; at this point, statements exhibiting poor psychometric properties may be discarded or revised. Social desirability ratings are then obtained for the remaining personality statements, either by asking respondents to judge their desirability in a hypothetical selection situation, or by instructing respondents to fake good and using the item means as indicators of social desirability. Although we have found that these strategies yield similar results, we prefer using the fake-good approach as it is easier to implement and it seems to exert less cognitive strain on the respondents. Ideally, all respondents used to estimate statement parameters should belong to the population for which the MDPP test is designed.

Once all necessary parameters have been estimated, nonadaptive MDPP tests can be created by pairing statements subject to content and psychometric considerations. Usually, items are formed by matching statements assessing different dimensions but having similar social desirability estimates, but location and discrimination parameters may also be considered. A small number of unidimensional pairings should be included as well to anchor the metric and ensure that normative information is produced (Stark et al., 2005a). The only real difference between nonadaptive and adaptive test construction is that CAT identifies items that are nearly optimal in terms of reducing the error in a respondent's estimated trait scores at any point during a test. Additionally, if at any point during a test an item meeting content or information constraints cannot be found, those constraints can be relaxed systematically until a suitable item is chosen, thus allowing testing to continue until the desired number of items has been administered.

■ EVALUATING NONADAPTIVE MULTIDIMENSIONAL PAIRWISE PREFERENCE TESTS IN SIMULATION AND EMPIRICAL SETTINGS

Since the proposal of this methodology in 2002, a number of simulation and empirical studies have been conducted to assess its feasibility for operational testing. Simulation studies make it possible to examine how test characteristics, such as length, dimensionality, percentages of unidimensional pairings, and correlations

---

1. In principle, any unidimensional IRT model can be used for estimating statement parameters. However, the multi-unidimensional scoring (MUPP) model algorithm developed by Stark (2002a) utilized the generalized graded unfolding model (GGUM; Roberts, Donoghue, & Laughlin, 2000), because it was found to provide a good fit for a wide range of personality items (see Chernyshenko, Stark, Chan, Drasgow, & Williams, 2001; Chernyshenko, Stark, Drasgow, & Roberts, 2007a; Stark, Chernyshenko, Drasgow, & Williams, 2006).

among generating trait scores, influence the relative and absolute accuracy of trait score estimates. By emulating conditions likely to be encountered in practice, it is possible to obtain realistic assessments of MDPP test construction and scoring approaches prior to launching a test in the field. Yet, empirical studies are always needed to determine whether the test scores actually predict important organizational outcomes; simulation studies are unable to identify inappropriateness of the psychometric model for a particular population, improperly specified constraints on item formation, a poor choice of dimensions for predicting performance, or problems with the content or wording of the specific statements chosen to measure each dimension. In addition, empirical studies are needed to demonstrate that MDPP scores are comparable to those obtained using traditional single-statement formats under normal testing conditions and that both nonadaptive and adaptive MDPP tests are resistant to pronounced score inflation in high-stakes contexts. The next section of this chapter presents simulation and empirical results concerning the proposed MDPP methodology and sets the stage for a discussion of its application in the Tailored Adaptive Personality Assessment System (Drasgow, Stark, & Chernyshenko, 2011; Stark, Drasgow, & Chernyshenko, 2008).

Simulation Research

Stark (2002a) and Stark et al. (2005a) conducted simulation studies examining the viability of MDPP test construction and scoring for two-dimensional tests of 20, 40, and 80 pairwise preference items. By sampling large numbers of trait scores from designated distributions, simulating the process of test administration and scoring, and examining the correspondence between the estimated trait scores and the known or generating values, it was shown that the Bayes modal algorithm could score response patterns with a high degree of accuracy. Absolute bias statistics were small, except at unusual combinations of extreme trait levels (very high on one dimension and very low on the other), and the average correlations between known and estimated trait scores ranged from 0.77 to 0.96 across conditions. Importantly, it was shown that test length, rather than the percentage of unidimensional pairings, was of primary importance to estimation accuracy (i.e., as expected, shorter tests yielded less accurate trait estimates). This finding supported the viability of the proposed approach for reducing the effects of faking in personality testing and it paved the way for research involving MDPP tests of higher dimensionality.

In a follow-up study, Stark, Chernyshenko, and Drasgow (2005b) investigated the effect of increasing dimensionality on MDPP trait score recovery using nonadaptive, fixed-length tests. Approximately 200 personality statements, measuring five lower-order facets of the Big Five (Order, Traditionalism, Responsibility, Energy, and Dominance), were used to construct three-dimensional and five-dimensional non-adaptive MDPP tests; Generalized Graded Unfolding Model (GGUM) parameters were taken from previous investigations involving student samples (Chernyshenko, Stark, Drasgow, & Roberts, 2007a; Chernyshenko, Stark, Prewett, Gray, Stilson, & Tuttle, 2009). The key question was whether accurate MDPP scoring required that tests include items representing all possible combinations of facets (a *complete* design), or would a minimal or *circular* linking design (e.g., pairing dimensions 1–2, 2–3, 3–4, 4–5, 5–1) be equally effective?

To answer this question, a simulation study was conducted to compare trait score recovery in conditions involving combinations of four factors: (1) Linking design (complete, circular), (2) Dimensionality (3-D and 5-D), (3) Test length (30 items, 60 items), and (4) Percentage of unidimensional pairings (10%, 20%). After constructing tests to meet the design specifications in each condition, trait scores for 5000 simulees were sampled for the respective numbers of facets from independent standard normal distributions, and item responses were generated according to the MUPP model. The quality of normative score recovery in each condition was then assessed using the correlation between the estimated and known latent trait values. To obtain a single index of recovery for each condition, the correlations were averaged across dimensions.

Table 14.1 presents the correlations between known and estimated trait scores across each personality facet and test type. For example, the 0.95 in the first row of the last column represents the correlation between the estimated and known trait scores for the facet of Order, as measured by the 100 item 5-D test having 20% unidimensional pairings. As can be seen, there was little, if any, effect for the percentage of unidimensional pairings, which suggests that 10% is enough when all combinations of dimensions are present. In addition, the correlations between estimated and known trait scores were high even for the short tests in each condition (0.88), and they improved with increased test length. Interestingly, the accuracy of score estimation in the circular linking conditions was almost identical to the accuracy in the complete linking conditions. In fact, the average correlations in the corresponding conditions were identical. This result is extremely important because it indicates that circular linking is sufficient for accurate trait score recovery with the MDPP procedure. Therefore, complete linking is unnecessary and linking requirements do not pose serious constraints on the development of tests with higher dimensionality.

Building on the encouraging results of this nonadaptive test simulation, a fixed-length adaptive testing algorithm was developed, and a simulation study was conducted to see how much scoring accuracy could be improved through CAT item selection for assessments of varying dimensionality (Stark & Chernyshenko, 2007). The first step in this CAT algorithm was to specify initial content requirements for the sequence of pairwise preference items to be administered to each simulee. These initial content codes were then randomly ordered and items were chosen adaptively for presentation, subject to constraints on content, social desirability, and statement parameters, and item information at the simulee's estimated trait scores, until the desired number of items was administered. Trait scores were updated after the presentation of each item using the Bayes modal scoring algorithm discussed previously.

A Visual Basic.NET program was used to compare the efficacy of the adaptive algorithm described above with nonadaptive tests of the same length and dimensionality. Estimation accuracy was examined using a fully crossed design involving varying numbers of dimensions (5, 7, 10), test lengths (5, 10, 20 items "per dimension"), and percentage of unidimensional pairings (5 and 10) needed to identify the latent metric.

TABLE 14.1 Correlations between Estimated and Known Trait Scores for 3-D and 5-D Tests in the Complete and Circular Linking Simulation Conditions

| | 3-D Tests with Complete Linking | | | | 5-D Tests with Complete Linking | | | | 5-D Tests with Circular Linking | | | |
| | 30 items | | 60 items | | 50 items | | 100 items | | 50 items | | 100 items | |
Personality Facet	10%	20%	10%	20%	10%	20%	10%	20%	10%	20%	10%	20%
Order	0.91	0.91	0.95	0.95	0.91	0.91	0.95	0.95	0.91	0.92	0.96	0.95
Traditionalism	0.89	0.90	0.93	0.94	0.89	0.89	0.94	0.94	0.89	0.89	0.93	0.94
Energy	0.86	0.85	0.92	0.92	0.85	0.85	0.92	0.92	0.87	0.86	0.92	0.92
Responsibility	*	*	*	*	0.86	0.85	0.92	0.92	0.86	0.85	0.93	0.92
Dominance	*	*	*	*	0.90	0.90	0.95	0.95	0.89	0.89	0.95	0.95
Average	0.89	0.89	0.93	0.94	0.88	0.88	0.94	0.94	0.88	0.88	0.94	0.94

Note: *Data not simulated for this facet; 10% = 10 percent of pairings were unidimensional; 20% = 20 percent of pairings were unidimensional.

In each condition, data were generated by sampling 1000 latent trait scores (θs) from independent standard normal distributions, and trait score recovery was assessed using correlations and error statistics computed with respect to the known values. To increase realism and the generalizability of the findings, parameters and social desirability ratings for actual personality statements were used to generate pairwise preference responses.

Table 14.2 presents the correlations and absolute bias statistics for the simulation described above. In the table, the first column shows the percentage of unidimensional items used to identify the metric. The second column indicates the number of items per dimension; for example, a 5-D test involving 5 items per dimension would involve 25 items. The remaining columns show the results for the nonadaptive and adaptive conditions, respectively. In each case, the value shown in a cell represents the average across dimensions.

As can be seen in Table 14.2, the average correlations between estimated and known trait scores increased as test length increased from 5 to 20 items per dimension, and there was little to no effect for the percentage of unidimensional pairings, which is consistent with previous simulations involving nonadaptive MDPP tests. Importantly, note the striking gains in efficiency that were obtained by going from nonadaptive to adaptive item selection. Adaptive tests yielded almost the same correlations as nonadaptive tests that were nearly twice as long, a finding that is consistent with a multitude of studies involving unidimensional cognitive ability CATs. The absolute bias results showed that the estimated trait scores were not only good in terms of rank order, but also in terms of accuracy—even with 10-D tests. For example, the average absolute bias (i.e., the absolute value of the difference between the estimated and known trait score) was just 0.27 with 10-D tests involving 100 items, only 5 of which were unidimensional, and the corresponding correlation between generating and estimated trait scores was 0.93. Moreover,

TABLE 14.2 *Comparison of Correlations and Absolute Bias Statistics for Estimated and Known Trait Scores for Nonadaptive and Adaptive MDPP Tests*

% Unidim.	Items per Dimension		Nonadaptive			Adaptive		
			5-D	7-D	10-D	5-D	7-D	10-D
	5	Corr	0.72	0.76	0.76	0.85	0.86	0.87
		AbsBias	0.53	0.51	0.49	0.39	0.38	0.37
5	10	Corr	0.87	0.87	0.86	0.93	0.93	0.93
		AbsBias	0.39	0.38	0.38	0.28	0.27	0.27
	20	Corr	0.93	0.93	0.94	0.96	0.96	0.96
		AbsBias	0.29	0.39	0.27	0.21	0.21	0.21
	5	Corr	0.74	0.75	0.75	0.87	0.85	0.88
		AbsBias	0.52	0.51	0.50	0.38	0.39	0.36
10	10	Corr	0.85	0.86	0.87	0.93	0.93	0.93
		AbsBias	0.40	0.39	0.38	0.28	0.27	0.27
	20	Corr	0.93	0.94	0.94	0.96	0.96	0.96
		AbsBias	0.29	0.28	0.27	0.21	0.20	0.20

Note: % Unidim., percentage of unidimensional pairings; Corr, correlation between estimated and known trait scores, averaged across dimensions; AbsBias, mean absolute value of the difference between the estimated and known trait scores, averaged across dimensions.

recent simulations involving adaptive tests with as many as 25 dimensions have shown similar results with generating trait scores correlated 0 to 0.3, and only slight decreases in accuracy were observed when generating scores were correlated as high as 0.5 (Stark, Chernyshenko, & Dragsow, 2010). In tandem, these findings clearly indicate the viability of adaptive testing with this MDPP approach.

Laboratory Research

Chernyshenko et al. (2009) conducted a laboratory experiment to examine the equivalence of personality test scores obtained using three response formats under "honest" conditions. First, personality statements representing Order, Self-Control, and Sociability were compiled and groups of subject matter experts were asked to rate the extremity and social desirability of each statement on a scale of 1 to 7. Next single-statement (SS), unidimensional pairwise preference (UPP), and multidimensional pairwise preference (MDPP) tests were created and administered, along with scales measuring study and health behavior criteria, to 602 participants in a university setting who were instructed to answer all questions honestly. By design, the personality measures had comparable lengths (36 items assessing three personality dimensions). In the SS conditions, respondents were asked to indicate their level of agreement with 36 personality statements (12 per dimension) using a 4-option Likert format (1 = Strongly Disagree, 2 = Disagree, 3 = Agree, 4 = Strongly Agree). In the pairwise preference conditions, respondents were asked to indicate which statement in each of the 36 pairs better described them. Each UPP measure was created by pairing statements from the same dimension that differed between 1.0 and 4.0 units in location on a scale of −3 to +3, as per the recommendations of Stark and Dragsow (2002). The MDPP measure was created by combining 30 multidimensional items with six unidimensional items. The multidimensional items were formed by pairing statements from different dimensions that had similar social desirability and location ratings. The unidimensional items (two per trait) were created by pairing statements from the same dimension that were similar in desirability but differed in their locations on the trait continuum. There was no statement overlap between the MDPP, UPP, and SS measures.

Responses to the SS measures were analyzed using the GGUM2000 computer program (Roberts, Donoghue, & Lauglin, 2000), which computes statement parameters via marginal maximum likelihood (MML) estimation and person parameters by expected a posteriori (EAP) estimation. The UPP measures were scored using Stark's (2006) ZG-EAP program for the Zinnes and Griggs (1974) IRT model. Finally, the MDPP measure was scored using Stark's (2002b) program for dichotomous multi-unidimensional pairwise preference responses. Marginal reliabilities, trait score intercorrelations, and validities for predicting behavioral criteria were also computed. These findings are summarized in Table 14.3.

The first nine rows of Table 14.3 present the correlations among Order, Self-Control, and Sociability scores obtained using the SS, UPP, and MDPP formats. The values appearing on the main diagaonal are marginal reliabilities. The monotrait-heteromethod (Campbell & Fiske, 1959) correlations (shown in bold print) are nearly identical to the respective marginal reliabilities, indicating good

TABLE 14.3 Correlations for Single Statement, Unidimensional Pairwise Preference, and Multidimensional Pairwise Preference Scales Measuring Order, Self-Control, and Sociability

		Response Format								
		SS			UPP			MDPP		
Format	Scale Name	Order	Self-Control	Sociability	Order	Self- Control	Sociability	Order	Self-Control	Sociability
SS	Order	0.79								
	Self-Control	0.39	0.56							
	Sociability	-0.06	-0.34	0.59						
UPP	Order	**0.78**	0.50	-0.17	0.81					
	Self-Control	0.39	**0.62**	-0.26	0.48	0.58				
	Sociability	-0.10	-0.32	**0.84**	-0.14	-0.27	0.75			
MDPP	Order	**0.78**	0.43	-0.15	**0.82**	0.40	-0.18	0.79		
	Self-Control	0.29	**0.64**	-0.32	0.39	**0.66**	-0.36	0.38	0.71	
	Sociability	-0.09	-0.28	**0.82**	-0.17	-0.26	**0.75**	-0.12	-0.30	0.77
Checklist	Substance Avoidance	0.12	0.20	-0.18	0.14	0.28	-0.18	0.17	0.30	-0.18
Checklist	Study Behaviors	0.36	0.22	0.02	0.38	0.28	0.00	0.38	0.27	0.01

Note: SS, single statement; UPP, unidimensional pairwise preference; MDPP, multidimensional pairwise preference. Bold values indicate monotrait heteromethod correlations.

convergent validity across formats. Moreover, similar intercorrelations and criterion-related validities were observed across formats, indicating that the MDPP, UPP, and SS measures yielded higly comparable scores. The observed correlation between Substance Avoidance and Sociability, for example, was −0.18 across all three formats. Importantly, the correlations between Order and Self-Control (both facets of the Big Five factor, Conscientiousness) were positive and similar in magnitude (about 0.38) across formats. Thus, in contrast to historical findings of negative intercorrelations among scores derived from MFC measures due to ipsativity (Meade, 2004), both IRT methods for constructing and scoring pairwise preference tests yielded results that were essentially equivalent to those obtained with SS personality tests.

In general, this study provided clear empirical support for the IRT-based pairwise preference test construction and scoring approaches. The previous simulation studies showed accurate recovery of trait scores under a wide range of conditions, but questions remained as to whether violations of model assumptions would adversely affect the accuracy or relational equivalence of trait score estimates for real examinees. This investigation showed unequivocally that they did not. In fact, the findings support the use of both MDPP and UPP methods as alternatives to traditional single-statement personality measures when examinees can reasonably be expected to answer honestly.

Because the assumption of honest responding is open to question in many applied settings, our belief is that MDPP methods will be more effective than their UPP counterparts for self-report personality applications in high-stakes settings. We therefore recommend that research focus on identifying better ways to construct fake-resistant MDPP and, more broadly, MFC assessments. The next section describes initial efforts to explore MDPP testing in Army field research and, ultimately, in a high-stakes selection environment.

Field Research

One of the first field applications of MDPP testing was in the U.S. Army Expanded Enlistment Eligibility Metrics (EEEM) research project conducted by the Army Research Institute (ARI) in 2007–2009. The objective of the EEEM research was to evaluate several noncognitive instruments that could be used during preenlistment processing to identify applicants who are motivated to perform well and are capable of successful service in the Army. Several thousand soldiers from six military occupational specialties (MOS) were followed through basic training and administered a variety of criterion measures, including job-specific knowledge tests, fitness tests, and job satisfaction and career intentions scales. Soldiers were also evaluated by their peers and supervisors on several performance rating scales.

Before starting their basic training, soldiers completed a 95-item MDPP measure, called TAPAS-95s, which assessed 12 dimensions of personality that were believed to be important for predicting performance and attrition. The measure was developed using procedures described above, based on social desirability ratings and statement parameters estimated using data collected from Army recruits. Items constructed for TAPAS-95s were randomly ordered and a paper questionnaire was created by placing five items on each page of a test booklet, preceded by an information sheet showing respondents a sample item and illustrating how to properly record their answers to the "questions" that followed. Respondents were specifically instructed to choose the statement in each pair that was "more like me" and were told that they must make a choice even if they found it difficult to do so. Item responses were coded dichotomously and scored using an updated version of Stark's (2002b) computer program for MUPP trait estimation.

Table 14.4 shows means, standard deviations, and intercorrelations of TAPAS-95s and Armed Forces Qualification Test (AFQT) scores for 2422 active duty soldiers. (AFQT is a cognitive ability composite formed from Armed Services Vocational Aptitude Battery subtest scores.) Overall, the TAPAS-95s showed construct validity. Intellectual Efficiency and Curiosity, for example, showed moderate positive correlations with AFQT and correlations of 0.35 with each other. This was expected, given that both facets tap the intellectance aspects of the Big Five factor, Openness to Experience, as were the positive, but smaller, correlations with Tolerance, another facet of Openness reflecting comfortableness around others having different customs, values, or beliefs (Chernyshenko, Stark, Woo, & Conz, 2008). Even Tempered and Optimism, both facets of Emotional Stability, also correlated 0.22 with each other, whereas the Achievement and Order facets of Conscientiousness showed a smaller than expected, but still positive, correlation of 0.17. Finally, Excitement Seeking and Nondelinquency correlated –0.36, as expected, given that persons who take risks and engage in thrill-seeking behaviors are more apt to have disciplinary incidents.

Overall, the correlations among the facets shown in Table 14.4 are somewhat lower than those typically found in studies using single statement response formats. On the one hand, this may be attributable to the use of independent normal distributions as priors during trait estimation. On the other hand, the MDPP format could have reduced social desirability response bias in the same way that UPP questionnaires have been found to reduce rater bias in performance appraisal studies (Borman, Buck, Hanson, Motowidlo, Stark, & Drasgow, 2001). At this point, it is just too early to determine whether the low correlations among facets are more reflective of scoring model assumptions or the distinctiveness among traits when controlling for biasing effects. What is clear, however, is that provided the facets show reasonable zero-order correlations with Army criteria, the low correlations with AFQT scores should result in noteworthy incremental validities.

Although validation of TAPAS-95s with respect to Army performance and attrition criteria is ongoing, preliminary results suggest incremental validity over AFQT. For example, based on a sample of several hundred, the multiple correlation increased by 0.35 for the prediction of physical fitness, by 0.20 for the prediction of disciplinary incidents, and by 0.11 for the prediction of 6-month attrition, when personality scores were added into the regression analysis. Interestingly, none of these criteria was predicted well by AFQT alone (validities were below 0.10). These results suggest that MDPP personality scores can be useful predictors of military outcomes and, for the first time in many years, serious consideration should be given to the widespread implementation of personality testing in an operational military environment.

TABLE 14.4 *Descriptive Statistics and Intercorrelations for TAPAS-95s and Armed Forces Qualification Test (AFQT) Scores in Army Expanded Enlistment Eligibility Metrics (EEEM) Research*

Scale	Mean	SD	1	2	3	4	5	6	7	8	9	10	11	12
1 Achievement	0.17	0.64												
2 Curiosity	-0.08	0.79	0.21											
3 Nondelinquency	0.09	0.65	0.15	0.12										
4 Dominance	-0.15	0.61	0.15	0.17	0.01									
5 Even tempered	-0.46	0.77	0.06	0.24	0.11	-0.04								
6 Excitement seeking	-0.14	0.79	-0.11	-0.11	-0.36	0.14	-0.14							
7 Intellectual efficiency	-0.19	0.64	0.16	0.34	0.01	0.14	0.14	-0.06						
8 Order	-0.04	0.64	0.17	0.03	0.14	0.07	-0.03	-0.07	0.07					
9 Physical conditioning	0.12	0.71	0.20	0.04	-0.09	0.08	-0.02	0.10	0.02	0.04				
10 Tolerance	-0.42	0.67	0.07	0.24	0.03	0.10	0.07	0.00	0.17	0.05	0.03			
11 Trust	-0.30	0.86	0.03	-0.06	0.17	0.14	0.07	-0.02	-0.08	0.02	-0.14	-0.01		
12 Optimism	-0.07	0.59	0.08	0.11	0.04	0.07	0.22	-0.04	0.18	0.02	0.05	0.10	0.09	
13 AFQT score	57.24	19.51	0.06	0.21	0.03	0.03	0.11	-0.04	0.38	-0.04	-0.03	0.05	-0.04	0.16

Note: Correlations are for the Active Duty Army Sample (*N* = 2422). AFQT, Armed Forces Qualification Test.

Based on the EEEM research and the Monte Carlo results showing the efficacy of trait score recovery with CATs of high dimensionality, approval was granted in 2009 to conduct an initial operational testing and evaluation of a 30-minute TAPAS CAT in military entrance processing stations (MEPS). Fifteen personality facets were selected for tryout on rational and empirical grounds with the aim of predicting job performance and attrition over the term of enlistment. Eleven facets were retained from the TAPAS-95s measure (Curiosity was dropped) and four additional TAPAS facets (Generosity, Self-Control, Adjustment, and Sociability) were added to increase the coverage of Agreeableness, Extraversion, and Conscientiousness. [For details on the TAPAS personality trait taxonomy, see Chernyshenko, Stark, and Drasgow (2011) or Chernyshenko et al., (2007b).] Over 800 statements formed the initial pool for the TAPAS application, which is more than sufficient to generate thousands of pairwise preference items tailored to the trait levels of individual examinees. Statement parameters were estimated in 2006–2008 using large samples of Army recruits. Adaptive item selection was implemented via an algorithm similar to the one used in the simulations described above.

At this time, a longitudinal field experiment is underway in the MEPS with U.S. Army and Air Force applicants taking the TAPAS CAT under different instruction sets (selection in the Army vs. research only in the Air Force) to gauge its susceptibility to score inflation, as well as to examine its predictive validity for performance and attrition criteria over the course of enlistment. Data for this 15-dimensional assessment are being collected and analyzed on a continuing basis, with sample sizes already well into the tens of thousands. Thus far, the scores appear to be fairly consistent across the two test administration contexts, with none of the mean differences exceeding 0.20 SD and most falling in the 0.05 to 0.08 SD range. Importantly, correlations among TAPAS facets and the relationships with AFQT scores appear very similar to those in the previous EEEM research involving job incumbents. This is the strongest evidence we have to date for the viability of MDPP personality testing in high-stakes environments.

■ DISCUSSION

Personality traits are among the most widely used individual difference variables for explaining and predicting human behavior. Conscientiousness scores, for example, have been found to correlate positively with long-term career success (Judge, Higgins, Thoresen, & Barrick, 1999), college retention (Tross, Harper, Osher, & Kneidinger; 2000), marital stability (Tucker, Kressin, Spiro, & Ruscio, 1998), healthy lifestyle behaviors (Bogg & Roberts, 2004), and job performance (Barrick, Mount, & Judge, 2001). Moreover, because personality facets generally exhibit low to moderate correlations with each other and with cognitive ability measures, composites formed by adding scores on several personality facets can substantially enhance the prediction of organizational criteria without increasing adverse impact (Hough, Oswald, & Ployhart, 2001). Overall, racial group differences on various personality scales are small and the directions vary, so that mean differences in facet scores tend to offset each other when forming composites (Foldes, Duehr, & Ones, 2008).

These potential benefits notwithstanding, the likelihood that single-statement personality tests will be used for decision making in high-stakes settings remains small. Scientists may continue to debate the extent to which faking is a problem (Ones et al., 1996), whether one can reliably detect fakers (Zickar & Drasgow, 1996), whether it is possible to correct suspected response patterns post hoc to improve the quality of selection decisions (Ellingson et al., 1999; Stark et al., 2001), and whether warnings and scare tactics can be effectively used to reduce faking (Dwight & Donovan, 2003). However, there is clearly more interest at this time in alternative formats for administering items. Simply put, there are only so many unique ways to craft rationally based statements describing how someone typically thinks, feels, or acts. And even with adaptive item selection and exposure control methods in place, it would not take long for an item bank to be exposed and examinees to develop heuristics for "beating a test," and those heuristics would be simple and few in number.

In contrast, with MFC formats, the range of potential items and test forms is tremendously expanded. Although pentad- and tetrad-based methods have been examined in a number of studies (e.g., Christiansen et al., 2005; Heggestad et al., 2006; McCloy et al., 2005; Vasilopoulos et al., 2006; White & Young, 1998), our focus has been on MDPP testing because we believe this format can reduce faking, and it is tractable in a mathematical sense. Unidimensional pairwise preference methods have already been shown to reduce various types of rater bias (Borman et al., 2001), and we suspect that MDPP tests will be more effective in this regard for personality assessment. It is just harder to present yourself consistently in a positive light when faced with multidimensional combinations of statements representing large numbers of dimensions. Balancing on social desirability and identifying dimensions that should never be paired ("enemy dimensions") can make it even harder for a respondent to elevate all of his or her scores, even if what the individual statements measure is somewhat obvious. Moreover, because testing companies never disclose the details of their regression composites and, of course, different composites and norms can be created for different applications, general rules for beating a test could be so complex that very few examinees would be able to manage them effectively.

This chapter admittedly presents only limited information with regard to the resistance of MDPP methods to faking in high-stakes environments, because the field research examining this issue is still in its early stages. What we have shown, however, indicates that substantial progress has been made since the idea of MFC testing emerged almost 70 years ago. Concerns about ipsativity dominated early research and impeded widespread application of MFC methods despite their intuitive appeal. The simulation evidence shown earlier for tests of high dimensionality clearly indicates that the two-step approach to scaling statements and persons, in connection with minimal linking procedures in test construction, provides an effective way of deriving normative information from MDPP tests for organizational decision making (Stark et al., 2005a). The laboratory study that followed (Chernyshenko et al., 2009) provided convincing evidence that MDPP and traditional single-statement measures produce similar scores and patterns of validity under honest testing conditions. The empirical comparisons involving the TAPAS-95s measure in the Army EEEM research (Stark, Chernyshenko, &

Drasgow, 2008) demonstrate that composites of personality facets measured using MDPP tests can provide incremental validity with respect to cognitive ability scores in field settings. And the preliminary results from the longitudinal operational testing and evaluation of the TAPAS CAT in military entrance processing stations have been promising, with scores for Army and Air Force applicants being very similar despite applicants taking the test under very different instruction sets.

Despite this stream of positive results, it is nevertheless necessary to ask how MDPP, and more generally, MFC testing can be improved. In our view, research is needed to determine the best ways to construct items and tests. Must a minimum number of dimensions be involved to make a test fake resistant? Should context-specific social desirability ratings be used to form pairs or tetrads? Would MFC test scores be more resistant to response sets if benign or coercive warnings accompanied test instructions? Can scoring be improved if multidimensional models are used for scaling statement parameters or facet covariances are accounted for explicitly in trait estimation? How applicable are current multidimensional linking and equating methods to MFC data? Can aberrance detection methods be adapted for effective use with MFC models, and would their use be empirically and legally justifiable in high-stakes settings? These are some of the questions that we are exploring, and we hope this chapter provides a springboard for further research and discussion.

■ ACKNOWLEDGMENTS

We would like to thank the U.S. Army Research Institute for the Behavioral and Social Sciences, which supported the development of the TAPAS CAT via a SBIR grant (A04-29) to Drasgow Consulting Group. All statements expressed in this document are those of the authors and do not necessarily reflect the official opinions or policies of the U.S. Army Research Institute, the U.S. Army, the U.S. Air Force, or the Department of Defense.

Stephen Stark is currently an associate professor of Psychology at the University of South Florida. His research focuses on the development and application of item response theory methods to practical problems in organizations with an emphasis on noncognitive assessment, computerized adaptive testing, and the detection of differential item functioning.

Oleksandr S. Chernyshenko is currently an associate professor at Nanyang Technological University School of Business. His research focuses on applications of psychometric methods in the areas of personality and job attitudes, and he teaches graduate level courses including advanced industrial organizational psychology, research methods, human resource management, performance management, and organizational development.

Fritz Drasgow is currently a professor of Psychology and of Labor and Employment Relations at the University of Illinois at Urbana-Champaign. His research focuses on psychological measurement. He has conducted research designed to identify individuals mismeasured by tests, used multimedia computer technology to assess social and interpersonal skills not easily measured by paper-and-pencil tests, and explored psychometric models for noncognitive assessment.

References

Andrich, D. (1995). Hyperbolic cosine latent trait models for unfolding direct responses and pairwise preferences. *Applied Psychological Measurement, 19*, 269–290.

Barrick, M., Mount, M. K, & Judge, T. A. (2001). Personality and performance at the beginning of the new millennium: What do we know and where do we go next?. *International Journal of Selection & Assessment, 9*, 9–30.

Berry, C. M., Ones, D. S., & Sackett, P. R. (2007). Interpersonal deviance, organizational deviance, and their common correlates: A review and meta-analysis. *Journal of Applied Psychology, 92*, 410–424.

Birnbaum, A. (1968). Some latent trait models and their use in inferring an examinee's ability. In F. M. Lord & M. R. Novick (Eds.), *Statistical theories of mental test scores* (pp. 397–472). Reading, MA: Addison-Wesley.

Böckenholt, U. (2004). Comparative judgments as an alternative to ratings: Identifying the scale origin. *Psychological Methods, 9*, 453–465.

Bogg, T., & Roberts, B. W. (2004). Conscientiousness and health behaviors: A meta-analysis. *Psychological Bulletin, 130*, 887–919.

Booth-Kewley, S., & Vickers, R. R., Jr. (1994). Associations between major domains of personality and health behavior. *Journal of Personality, 62*, 281–298.

Borman, W. C., Buck, D., Hanson, M. A., Motowidlo, S. J., Stark, S., & Drasgow, F. (2001). An examination of the comparative reliability, validity, and accuracy of performance ratings made using computerized adaptive rating scales. *Journal of Applied Psychology, 86*, 965–973.

Bowen, C., Martin, B. A., & Hunt, S. T. (2002). A comparison of ipsative and normative approaches for the ability to control faking in personality questionnaires. *International Journal of Organizational Analysis, 10*, 240–259.

Butcher, J. N., Dahlstrom, W. G., Graham, I. R., Tellegen, A., & Kaemmer, B. (1989). *MMPI-2: Minnesota Multiphasic Personality Inventory-2: Manual for administration and scoring.* Minneapolis: University of Minnesota Press.

Campbell, D. T., & Fiske, D. W. (1959). Convergent and discriminant validation by the multitrait-multimethod matrix. *Psychological Bulletin, 56*, 81–105.

Chernyshenko, O. S., Stark, S., Chan, K. Y., Drasgow, F., & Williams, B. A. (2001). Fitting item response theory models to personality data. *Multivariate Behavioral Research, 36*, 523–562.

Chernyshenko, O. S., Stark, S., & Drasgow, F. (2011). Individual differences, their measurement, and validity. In S. Zedeck (Ed.), *Handbook of industrial and organizational psychology.* Washington, D.C.: American Psychological Association.

Chernyshenko, O. S., Stark, S., Drasgow, F., & Roberts, B. W. (2007a). Constructing personality scales under the assumptions of an ideal point response process: Toward increasing the flexibility of personality measures. *Psychological Assessment, 19*, 88–106.

Chernyshenko, O. S., Stark, S., Drasgow, F., Hulin, C. L., & Lopez-Rivas, G. E. (2007b). *Behavioral domains assessed by TAPAS.* Technical Report No. 2007-009. Urbana, IL: Drasgow Consulting Group.

Chernyshenko, O. S., Stark, S., Prewett, M. S., Gray, A. A., Stilson, F. R., & Tuttle, M. D. (2009). Normative scoring of multidimensional pairwise preference personality scales using IRT: Empirical comparisons with other formats. *Human Performance, 22*, 1–23.

Chernyshenko, O. S., Stark, S., Woo, S. E., & Conz, G. (2008). *Openness to experience: Its facet structure, measurement, and usefulness in predicting important organizational outcomes.* Paper presented at the 23rd annual conference for the Society of Industrial and Organizational Psychology, San Francisco, CA.

Christiansen, N. D., Burns, G. N., & Montgomery, G. E. (2005). Reconsidering forced-choice item formats for applicant personality assessment. *Human Performance, 18,* 267–307.

Dilchert, S., Ones, D. S., Viswesvaran, C., & Deller, J. (2006). Response distortion in personality measurement: Born to deceive, yet capable of providing valid self-assessments? *Psychological Science, 48,* 209–225.

Dragsow, F., Lee, W. C., Stark, S., & Chernyshenko, O.S. (Spring, 2001). *Alternative methodologies for predicting attrition in the Army: The new AIM scales.* (Report to HUMMRO.) Alexandria, VA.

Dragsow, F., & Levine, M. V. (1986). Optimal detection of certain forms of inappropriate test scores. *Applied Psychological Measurement, 10,* 59–67.

Dragsow, F., Levine, M. V., & Zickar, M. J. (1996). Optimal identification of mismeasured individuals. *Applied Measurement in Education (Special Issue on Appropriateness Measurement), 9,* 47–64.

Dragsow, F., Stark, S., & Chernyshenko, O.S. (2011). *Tailored Adaptive Personality Assessment System (TAPAS) prediction of soldier performance.* Paper presented at the 26th annual conference for the Society of Industrial and Organizational Psychology. Chicago, IL.

Dwight, S. A., & Donovan, J. J. (2003). Do warnings not to fake reduce faking? *Human Performance, 16,* 1–23.

Edwards, A. L. (1954). *Personal preference schedule.* New York: Psychological Corporation.

Ellingson, J. E., Sackett, P. R., & Hough, L. M. (1999). Social desirability corrections in personality measurement: Issues of applicant comparison and construct validity. *Journal of Applied Psychology, 84,* 155–166.

Foldes, H., Duehr, E. E., & Ones, D. S. (2008). Group difference in personality: Meta-analyses comparing five US racial groups. *Personnel Psychology, 61,* 579–616.

Guo, J., Tay, L., & Dragsow, F. (2009). Conspiracies and test compromise: An evaluation of the resistance of test systems to small-scale cheating. *International Journal of Testing, 9,* 283–309.

Heggestad, E. D., Morrison, M., Reeve, C. L., & McCloy, R. A. (2006). Forced-choice assessments of personality for selection: Evaluating issues of normative assessment and faking resistance. *Journal of Applied Psychology, 91,* 9–24.

Hicks, L. E. (1970). Some properties of ipsative, normative, and forced-choice normative measures. *Psychological Bulletin, 74,* 167–184.

Hogan, J., Rybicki, S. L., Motowidlo, S. J., & Borman, W. C. (1998). Relations between contextual performance, personality, and occupational advancement. *Human Performance, 11,* 189–207.

Hough, L. M., Eaton, N. K., Dunnette, M. D., Kamp, J. D., & McCloy, R. A. (1990). Criterion-related validities of personality constructs and the effect of response distortion on those validities. *Journal of Applied Psychology, 75,* 95–108.

Hough, L. M., Oswald, F. L., & Ployhart, R. E. (2001). Determinants, detection and amelioration of adverse impact in personnel selection procedures: Issues, evidence, and lessons learned. *International Journal of Selection and Assessment, 9,* 152–194.

Jackson, D. N., Wrobleski, V. R., & Ashton, M. C. (2000). The impact of faking on employment tests: Does forced-choice offer a solution? *Human Performance, 13,* 371–388.

Judge, T. A., Higgins, C. A., Thoresen, C. J., & Barrick, M. R. (1999). The big five personality traits, general mental ability, and career success across the life span. *Personnel Psychology, 52,* 621–652.

Kriedt, P. H., & Dawson, R. I. (1961). Response set and the prediction of clerical job performance. *Journal of Applied Psychology, 45,* 175–178.

Levine, M. V., & Dragsow, F. (1988). Optimal appropriateness measurement. *Psychometrika, 53,* 161–176.

McCloy, R. A., Heggestad, E. D., & Reeve, C. L. (2005). A silk purse from the sow's ear: Retrieving normative information from multidimensional forced-choice items. *Organizational Research Methods, 8*, 222–248.

Meade, A. W. (2004). Psychometric problems and issues involved with creating and using ipsative measures for selection. *Journal of Occupational and Organizational Psychology, 77*, 531–552.

Meijer, R. R. (2003). Diagnosing item score patterns on a test using IRT based person-fit statistics. *Psychological Methods, 8*, 72–87.

Meijer, R. R. (2004). Using patterns of summed scores in paper-and-pencil tests and CAT to detect misfitting item score patterns. *Journal of Educational Measurement, 41*, 119–136.

Noftle, E. E., & Robins, R. W. (2007). Personality predictors of academic outcomes: Big five correlates of GPA and SAT scores. *Journal of Personality and Social Psychology, 93*, 116–130.

Ones, D. S., Viswesvaran, C., & Reiss, A. D. (1996). Role of social desirability in personality testing for personnel selection: The red herring. *Journal of Applied Psychology, 81*, 660–679.

Roberts, J. S., Donoghue, J. R., & Laughlin, J. E. (2000). A general item response theory model for unfolding unidimensional polytomous responses. *Applied Psychological Measurement, 24*, 3–32.

Robson, S. M., Jones, A., & Abraham, J. (2008). Personality, faking, and convergent validity: A warning concerning warning statements. *Human Performance, 21*, 89–106.

Rosse, J. G., Stecher, M., Miller, J. L., & Levin, R. A. (1998). The impact of response distortion on preemployment personality testing and hiring decisions. *Journal of Applied Psychology, 83*, 634–644.

Rounds, J. B., Henly, G. A., Dawis, R. V., Lofquist, L. H., & Weiss, D. J. (1981). *Manual for the Minnesota Importance Questionnaire*. Minneapolis: University of Minnesota, Vocational Psychology Research.

Schmitt, N., & Oswald, F. L. (2006). The impact of corrections for faking on the validity of noncognitive measures in selection settings. *Journal of Applied Psychology, 91*, 613–621.

Stark, S. (2002a). *A new IRT approach to test construction and scoring designed to reduce the effects of faking in personality assessment*. Doctoral dissertation. University of Illinois at Urbana-Champaign.

Stark, S. (2002b). *Computer program for scoring multi-unidimensional pairwise preference (MUPP) tests*. Unpublished manuscript. University of Illinois at Urbana-Champaign.

Stark, S. (2006). ZG-EAP: A computer program for EAP scoring with the Zinnes-Griggs model. Unpublished manuscript. University of South Florida.

Stark, S., & Chernyshenko, O. S. (June, 2007). *Adaptive testing with the multi-unidimensional pairwise preference (MUPP) model*. Proceedings of the 2007 Graduate Management Admissions Council conference on computerized adaptive testing, Minneapolis, MN.

Stark, S., Chernyshenko, O. S., Chan, K. Y., Lee, W. C., & Drasgow, F. (2001). Effects of the testing situation on item responding: Cause for concern. *Journal of Applied Psychology, 86*, 943–953.

Stark, S., Chernyshenko, O. S., & Drasgow, F. (2005a). An IRT approach to constructing and scoring pairwise preference items involving stimuli on different dimensions: An application to the problem of faking in personality assessment. *Applied Psychological Measurement, 29*, 184–201.

Stark, S., Chernyshenko, O. S., & Drasgow, F. (2005b). *Examining the recovery of normative scores with three- and five- dimensional nonadaptive multidimensional forced choice tests*. Paper presented at the 47th annual conference of the International Military Testing Association. Singapore.

Stark, S., Chernyshenko, O. S., Drasgow, F., White, L. A., Heffner, T., & Hunter, A. (2008). *Using multidimensional pairwise preference personality tests in military contexts: Development and evaluation of the TAPAS-95s.* Paper presented at the 50th annual conference of the International Military Testing Association. Amsterdam, The Netherlands.

Stark, S., Chernyshenko, O. S., & Drasgow, F. (2010). *Update on Tailored Adaptive Personality Assessment System (TAPAS): Results and ideas to meet the challenges of high stakes testing.* Paper presented at the 52nd annual conference of the International Military Testing Association. Lucerne, Switzerland.

Stark, S., Chernyshenko, O. S., Drasgow, F., & Williams, B. A. (2006). Item responding in personality assessment: Should ideal point methods be considered for scale development and scoring? *Journal of Applied Psychology, 91,* 25–39.

Stark, S., & Drasgow, F. (2002). An EM approach to parameter estimation for the Zinnes and Griggs paired comparison IRT model. *Applied Psychological Measurement, 26,* 208–227.

Stark, S., Drasgow, F., & Chernyshenko, O. S. (October 2008). *Update on the Tailored Adaptive Personality Assessment System (TAPAS): The next generation of personality assessment systems to support personnel selection and classification decisions.* Paper presented at the 50th annual conference of the International Military Testing Association, Amsterdam, The Netherlands.

Timmerman, T. A. (2006). Predicting turnover with broad and narrow personality traits. *International Journal of Selection and Assessment, 14,* 392–399.

Tross, S. A., Harper, J. P., Osher, L. W., & Kneidinger, L. M. (2000). Not just the usual cast of characteristics: Using personality to predict college performance and retention. *Journal of College Student Development, 41,* 323–334.

Tucker, J. S., Kressin, N. R., Spiro, A., & Ruscio, J. (1998). Intrapersonal characteristics and the timing of divorce: A prospective investigation. *Journal of Social and Personal Relationships, 15,* 211–225.

Vasilopoulos, N. L., Cucina, J. M., Dyomina, N. V., Morewitz, C. L., & Reilly, R. R. (2006). Forced-choice personality tests: A measure of personality and cognitive ability? *Human Performance, 19,* 175–199.

Villanova, P., Bernardin, H. J., Johnson, D. L., & Dahmus, S. A. (1994). The validity of a measure of job compatibility in the prediction of job performance and turnover of motion picture theater personnel. *Personnel Psychology, 47,* 73–90.

White, L. A., & Young, M. C. (1998). *Development and validation of the Assessment of Individual Motivation (AIM).* Paper presented at the Annual Meeting of the American Psychological Association, San Francisco, CA.

Zickar, M. J., & Drasgow, F. (1996). Detecting faking on a personality instrument using appropriateness measurement. *Applied Psychological Measurement, 20,* 71–87.

Zinnes, J. L., & Griggs, R. A. (1974). Probabilistic, multidimensional unfolding analysis. *Psychometrika, 39,* 327–350.

The Multi-Unidimensional Pairwise Preference (MUPP)
Model and an Illustrative Item Response Surface

Stark (2002a) proposed a model that can be used with both multidimensional and unidimensional pairwise preference items [the Multi-Unidimensional Pairwise Preference model (MUPP)]. In essence, the MUPP model assumes that when a respondent is presented with a pair of stimuli (e.g., personality statements), denoted *s* and *t*, and is asked to indicate a preference, he or she first evaluates each statement in terms of how well it describes himself or herself and then selects the more descriptive statement in the pair (i.e., the one with the higher probability of endorsement). If the endorsement probabilities are equal for both statements, then the respondent reevaluates them independently until a preference is reached. [This assumption is similar to that underlying Andrich's (1995) hyperbolic cosine model for unidimensional pairwise preferences.] The probability of preferring personality statement *s* to personality statement *t* can therefore be written as

$$P_{(s>t)_i}(\theta_{d_s}, \theta_{d_t}) = \frac{P_{st}\{1,0\}}{P_{st}\{1,0\} + P_{st}\{0,1\}} \approx \frac{P_s\{1\}P_t\{0\}}{P_s\{1\}P_t\{0\} + P_s\{0\}P_t\{1\}}, \tag{1}$$

where

i = index for items, $i = 1$ to I (note that an *item* is defined as a pair of statements),

d = index for dimensions, $d = 1,\dots, D$,

s,t = indices for first and second statements, respectively, in an item,

$\theta_{d_s}, \theta_{d_t}$ = latent trait values for a respondent on dimensions d_s and d_t, respectively,

$P_s\{1\}, P_s\{0\}$ = probability of endorsing/not endorsing statement *s* at θ_{d_s},

$P_t\{1\}, P_t\{0\}$ = probability of endorsing/not endorsing statement *t* at θ_{d_t},

$P_{st}\{0,1\}$ = joint probability of endorsing statement *s* and not endorsing statement *t* at $\left(\theta_{d_s}, \theta_{d_t}\right)$,

$P_{st}\{0,1\}$ = joint probability of not endorsing statement *s* and endorsing statement *t* at $\left(\theta_{d_s}, \theta_{d_t}\right)$, and

$P_{(s>t)i}\left(\theta_{d_s}, \theta_{d_t}\right) =$ probability of a respondent preferring statement s to statement t in item i, given his or her standing on the respective personality dimensions.

A preference for each item is thus represented by the joint outcome {Agree (1), Disagree (0)} or {Disagree (0), Agree (1)}. An outcome of {1,0} indicates that statement s was preferred to statement t, and is considered a positive item response; an outcome of {0,1} indicates that statement t was preferred to statement s and is considered a negative item response. To compute endorsement probabilities for each statement in a pair, Stark (2002a) used the dichotomous case of the Generalized Graded Unfolding Model (GGUM; Roberts, Donoghue, & Laughlin, 2000), which was shown to provide good fit to single-statement personality data in a series of studies (Chernyshenko, Stark, Chan, Drasgow, & Williams, 2001; Chernyshenko, Stark, Drasgow, & Roberts, 2007a; Stark, Chernyshenko, Drasgow, & Williams, 2006). However, other IRT models for single statement personality data can also be used toward that end.

To better understand Equation 1, it is useful to plot the probabilities of preferring statement s to statement t at levels of θ_{d_s} and θ_{d_t} for a hypothetical item. Because multidimensional pairwise preference items involve statements representing different personality dimensions, the relationship between trait levels and endorsement probabilities cannot be represented by a single trace line; instead, a three-dimensional response surface is required. For example, an item response surface involving personality statements representing Attention Seeking ("I tend to be loud and lively at social events") and Adjustment ("I don't dwell on mistakes for very long") might resemble the one shown in Figure 14A.1, where values along the vertical axis indicate the probability of preferring the Attention Seeking statement (i.e., stimulus s) to the Adjustment statement (i.e., stimulus t) given a respondent's

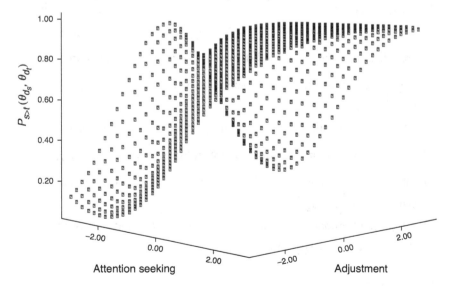

Figure 14A.1 Item response surface for a multidimensional pairwise preference item measuring attention seeking and adjustment.

standing on the respective dimensions and each statement's GGUM parameters. Unlike item response functions for single-statement models, such as the two-parameter logistic model (Birnbaum, 1968) or the GGUM, response surfaces for MDPP items exhibit complex shapes because of the interplay between trait levels and the discrimination and location parameters of each of the two statements. Clearly, peaks and valleys on the response surfaces can make it difficult to know in advance which items will be informative for which examinees just by inspecting the statement parameters. However, the availability of an item response theory (IRT) model for pairwise preference judgments makes it possible to compute item information at specific trait scores, which means that items can be constructed and chosen dynamically via computer adaptive test (CAT) principles to produce shorter, more efficient tests. [For details on MUPP item response and item information surfaces, see Stark et al. (2005a).]

15 Is Faking Inevitable?

Person-Level Strategies for Reducing Faking[1]

■ BRIAN LUKOFF

■ INTRODUCTION

In some sense, it is impossible to develop an instrument that can never be faked. An instrument is administered because there is something that is not known about the respondent; as a result, keen respondents will know that unless there are logical contradictions in their response patterns, it is impossible to say with certainty whether a particular set of responses arose naturally or due to faking. To take some clichéd examples: How can you be certain that particular respondents are faking when they say that they would *never* run a red light in the middle of the night when no one is around, or that they would *never* pick their nose in private? Such model human beings, without any flaw or indulged temptation, may indeed exist. Thus, a respondent may always choose to fake with impunity, knowing that there is no way to be certain of the falsehood of his or her responses.

In practice, of course, there are many suggested ways to detect, correct for, and prevent faking. Detection and correction are expanded on at length elsewhere (see especially Chapters 7–11 of this volume), and Chapters 13 and 14 of this volume examine the various ways item response formats can be used to combat faking. This chapter focuses on preventing faking at the person level. In particular, is it possible to change the way personality data is collected from respondents so that the data collected are less susceptible to faking? Or can the test situation be actively manipulated so that respondents are less likely to fake?

The methods examined here turn the traditional paradigm for noncognitive assessments on its head by changing the way these questions are asked (verifiable biodata and situational judgment tests), the person to whom they are asked (third-party ratings), or the instructions that accompany the assessment itself (warning respondents not to fake). The chapter will conclude by proposing a new method that combines a real-time faking detection algorithm with warnings based on the results of the algorithm, which can potentially harness the power of warnings while avoiding some of their pitfalls.

■ RATINGS BY A THIRD PARTY

A sensible solution to the problem of faked responses by an applicant is simply to not get the responses from the applicant and instead to get those same ratings

1. Part of this research was completed while the author was a graduate student intern in the Center for New Constructs at the Educational Testing Service.

from a third party. Ratings by third parties can be more useful for measurement than self-reported ratings (Atkins & Wood, 2002), although the ratings given to the applicant can depend on the relationship of the rater to the applicant (Fletcher & Baldry, 2000).

Third-party ratings were used by the Educational Testing Service in developing the Personal Potential Index (ETS PPI), a system currently offered by ETS to help graduate schools assess noncognitive attributes of their applicants through faculty members' ratings. The ETS PPI system is still relatively new, but it has been used operationally to select ETS graduate student interns. In this setting, useful correlations have been found between ratings given by professors through the PPI and a criterion measure consisting of the final ratings by the student interns' research supervisors at ETS (Kyllonen, 2008).

Using third-party ratings as a faking-free measure of some underlying respondent construct is conceptually clean, but is not always a useful technique for a given noncognitive assessment situation because it depends on the existence of a knowledgeable third party. In the case of the PPI, such a third party is readily available (faculty at the students' home institutions), but this is often not the case for job applicant selection or other similar procedures because there may be no known third party that can be counted on to be relatively unbiased. Furthermore, it is not necessarily true that faking is eliminated even if a suitable third party is available: When Liu, Minsky, Ling, and Kyllomen (2009) studied an earlier version of the PPI (the Standardized Letter of Recommendation used to select graduate student interns), they found that interns were rated more positively by their professors (the third party providing the ratings used for selection) than their ETS mentors (research supervisors). Although this does not necessarily indicate faking, it does serve as a reminder that third parties are not always completely impartial. Furthermore, human ratings are subject to biases even when the raters are impartial, such as the well-known halo effect (Nisbett & Wilson, 1977).

Kyllonen (2008) suggests a number of methods that could ameliorate some of the issues that come with third-party ratings. He notes that post hoc adjustments could be made to ratings based either on the overall severity of the rater or the degree to which that rater's ratings tend to be predictive of applicants' eventual achievements. He also proposes implementing a mechanism to give real-time feedback to raters (e.g., about the severity of the current ratings in relation to their previous ratings) while they are completing the PPI.

■ VERIFIABLE BIODATA MEASURES

In a typical noncognitive assessment, respondents are asked for a single data point, typically a rating of how well a broad statement might apply to them. One reason faking might be such a concern in these types of items is because it is so easy: "Who will know if I am really a 1, 3, or a 5 on this item?" the respondent may think. There is typically no verification of the ratings (the "facts" that the respondent provides), and the respondent knows it. Several studies have shown that lack of verifiability of the responses is associated with higher levels of faking (Becker & Colquitt, 1992; McManus & Masztal, 1999).

In the verifiable biodata technique, questions are asked that require respondents to back up their assertion with specific facts that could potentially be verified (Mael, 1991). Examples of verifiable biodata items include "how many software packages have you used to analyze data? . . . indicate the software programs and the nature of the data analysis briefly" (Schmitt & Kunce, 2002) and "how many times did you lead class discussions during your senior year in high school? . . . list the classes and discussion topics you led" (Schmitt et al., 2003). Requiring elaboration on these biodata items has been found to reduce the degree of faking, and there is some evidence that criterion validity in the form of correlations with GPA remain unchanged when participants are asked to elaborate on their item responses (Schmitt & Kunce, 2002; Schmitt et al., 2003).

Just as with third-party ratings, verifiable biodata offers a promising way to reduce faking, but with some limitations. Verifiable biodata items are necessarily limited to those constructs that can be measured by eliciting facts that can be independently verified. In other words, if the underlying trait to be measured is private in nature, then this technique may not be appropriate. However, there are many traits that can be measured through the elicitation of verifiable facts; for example, in personality assessment it is possible to develop items that elicit concrete manifestations of the underlying personality dimension [e.g., using Schmitt & Kunce's (2002) "how often have you rearranged files . . . to make them more efficient in the last year" to measure conscientiousness]. Unfortunately, adapting an existing assessment by rewriting the items to request verifiable data from participants introduces another source of error that must be studied and kept under control, as even the performance of nonfaking participants on the new items will not be perfectly correlated with their performance on the original items.

A final tantalizing result is that sprinkling some verifiable biodata items among a set of standard items for which elaboration is not required *may* reduce faking on the nonbiodata items. Not surprisingly, the reduction in faking for the nonverifiable items is not as large as the reduction in faking for the biodata items. This result suggests that converting even a subset of items on a noncognitive assessment to request verifiable data may reduce faking on all of the items; however, a caveat is that this halo-like effect for faking reduction has not been found consistently across studies (Schmitt & Kunce, 2002; Schmitt et al., 2003).

■ SITUATIONAL JUDGMENT TESTS

Situational judgment tests (SJTs) differ from traditional noncognitive assessments in that they present a series of "what would you do if . . ." questions to respondents based on real-world situations. Although there has been a surge in recent research on SJTs (see Lievens, Peeters, & Schollaert, 2008 for an overview), the concept is nothing new; the format (also known as a "low-fidelity simulation" since it can present the simulated situations in as low-fidelity a format as paper) has been around since at least the 1940s and has validity for employee performance prediction (Motowidlo, Dunnette, & Carter, 1990).

However, some forms of SJTs may be no more immune to faking than standard assessment formats, yielding to standard coaching procedures (Cullen, Sackett,

& Lievens, 2006) and with possible faking effects of up to nearly a standard deviation (Peeters & Lievens, 2005). Nguyen, Biderman, and McDaniel (2005) make the distinction between "behavioral" SJTs—where respondents are asked to select which action they would take in the situation—and "knowledge" SJTs—where respondents are asked which of the possible situational outcomes is the best. They found that faking is more of an issue with the former than with the latter, perhaps because the latter type of SJT starts to resemble a traditional cognitive assessment.

One promising method for preventing faking on SJTs is reminiscent of a technique from the verifiable biodata procedure described above: asking respondents for further elaboration on their responses, rather than simply for an answer. Lievens and Peeters (2008) found that on items that are "familiar" to the respondent (i.e., items for which respondents can draw on personal experience to say what they have done in the past rather than simply anticipate what they might do in the future), asking respondents for elaboration substantially reduced faking on an SJT measuring college success. Faking was reduced by simply asking respondents to provide justifications for their selections; unlike verifiable biodata, where respondents know that their elaborations can be cross-checked against factual data, the elaborations in the Lievens and Peeters study need not have contained any verifiable data at all. Therefore, it appears that simply asking respondents to do more than just choose an answer choice may reduce faking on SJTs, at least for items that are familiar—elaboration had no effect on faking for nonfamiliar items.

Today's SJTs have little resemblance to the "low-fidelity simulations" of the 1940s and 1950s. Modern SJTs often include video questions that provide a higher fidelity than the traditional pencil-and-paper versions, although the format may change the psychometric properties of the assessments (Chan & Schmitt, 1997; Lievens & Sackett, 2006). Kyllonen (2008) argues that the final word on faking may be yet to come on SJTs; innovation in delivery methods, response formats, etc. may substantially alter the fakability (not to mention the other psychometric properties) of SJTs. Existing research should certainly not be considered definitive as innovation is ongoing.

■ WARNINGS NOT TO FAKE

Another technique for preventing faking—orthogonal to, and not necessarily exclusive of, the methods previously discussed—is to simply warn respondents not to fake. Dwight and Donovan (2003) performed a meta-analysis of research that studied the relationship between warnings and faking behavior. They distinguish between *identification* warnings (a warning to the respondent that the test scorer will be able to detect any dishonesty in their responses) and *consequences* warnings (a warning that indicates what the consequences will be if the respondent is dishonest). Their meta-analysis showed that only consequences warnings made a difference in faking. However, their subsequent experimental work found that both types of warnings together were necessary to effect a statistically significant result.

Pace and Borman (2006) introduce three additional types of warnings that they hypothesize may reduce faking. Two of the warning types are similar in that they appeal to the applicant's sense of logic and understanding about the test itself. In *reasoning* warnings, the warning attempts to reduce applicant/test tension by suggesting that responding honestly will help match the applicant with an appropriate job; similarly, in *educational* warnings, the warning informs respondents why they are being tested in the hopes that by convincing them of the test's validity (or face validity) they will respond more honestly. A third type of warning, *moral conviction* warnings, appeals directly to the conscience of the respondent by adopting a moral tone to try to convince him or her of the ethical pitfalls of dishonest responding.

Pace and Borman cite an earlier study (Pace, Xu, Penney, Borman, & Bearden, 2005) that found promising results when using reasoning warnings, but note that reasoning warnings are of somewhat limited applicability—they do not apply when the selection procedure is a zero-sum game of acceptance or rejection. In fact, reasoning warnings are already in widespread use in one context—college applications, where admissions officers exhort applicants not to fake in their application materials. But as college admissions is a zero-sum game, such warnings can ring hollow to applicants, who quickly realize that responding more honestly on their application for one college will not help them gain acceptance to another. For this reason, it is to be expected that reasoning warnings would be more effective in a placement situation, where applicants send materials to a central authority who then places them in one of several programs.

Pace and Borman note that further work is needed on whether these three new types of warnings will function better than the traditional identification or consequences warnings. But they argue that these more positive types of warnings may cause respondents to view the organization testing them in a better light and may lead them to view the testing procedure as more fair, resulting in more honest responding than might have otherwise occurred. They advocate for increased frequency of these more positive warnings throughout the administration of the assessment, to continually reinforce more positive conceptions of the test.

An important area of related research is in the area of neuropsychology, where researchers in that field have been investigating malingering (faking) on self-reports of health problems (see, for example, Chapter 16 in this volume). Sullivan and Richer (2002) examined whether warning helped to reduce faking on the Neuropsychological Symptoms Checklist, a commonly used self-report measure of this type; they found a small numerical difference but were unable to show statistical (nor practical) significance.

One important discovery in this field is that warnings before the administration of neuropsychological measures may simply result in faking that is more "sophisticated," in the sense that the respondents that want to fake still do so, but in a way that becomes more difficult to detect (Youngjohn, Lees-Haley, & Binder, 1999). This is a worrisome finding for personality researchers, even for multiple-choice assessments: When the difference between fakers and nonfakers is reduced [as Dwight & Donovan (2003) found in their meta-analysis], does that mean that faking was actually reduced when respondents were warned? Or does it instead mean that when warned, potential fakers decided to be less extreme in their responses or throw in a few "wrong" answers to seem more honest? In one sense this can be the same thing, since the effect (lowered scores for fakers) is the same. In another sense, though, it suggests that warnings may not substantially alter the mechanism by which people fake, which in turn implies that warnings are not addressing the root of the problem.

Another issue with the traditional method of warnings is that respondents are often simply given blanket warnings. Warnings themselves are not without effects. Respondents may alter their responses in a way that makes them appear to be more honest but that in reality simply lowers their scores, lowering test validity (Dwight & Donovan, 2003). This is the same effect that we see in everyday life: witness the traffic jam on the highway caused by cars all excessively reducing their speed when approaching a waiting police car. This is a potentially orthogonal issue to the sophistication problem: For those who were planning to fake, warnings may result in more sophisticated faking behavior, but for those who were planning to respond honestly, warnings may simply scare respondents into distorting their responses in a way that is actually dishonest. Luckily, warnings do not appear to substantially alter how respondents' perceive the test to be a fair measurement of their abilities (McFarland, 2003). But the potential issues necessitate that warnings should be kept to a minimum, and that it is not ideal to warn respondents unnecessarily.

■ INTELLIGENT, DATA-DRIVEN WARNINGS

A potential solution to the problem of blanket warnings inappropriately affecting honest responders is to somehow deliver the warning only to those whose intend to fake. At first, one might want to administer a separate assessment that measures respondents' intentions to fake on the target assessment of interest. But this is not really feasible, because it is to be expected that the respondent will fake on the intention-measuring assessment just as much as they would fake on the target assessment. One solution is to use the very beginning of the target assessment as a device to detect faking and, if faking is detected, to warn the respondent during the test based on the evidence collected (Lukoff, 2006). This eliminates the second problem of using warnings to reduce faking, where honest respondents distort their answers to appear "more honest" and the validity of the assessment is reduced. If the faking detection mechanism has a high level of accuracy, then all (or most) fakers are identified and warned, whereas no (or only a small number of) honest respondents are unnecessarily warned. These warnings are in "real time" because they occur immediately after a small number of items have been administered but immediately before the remainder of the assessment.

The types of faking detection methods that are useful in this scenario may be unlike traditional types of faking detection schemes. Traditionally, one might administer a long lie (or candidness) scale, which gives the test developer the luxury to explore candidness from different angles. However, such scales can take a significant amount of time for respondents to complete. As a result, they are not ideal for providing real-time warnings, because each extra candidness item administered detracts from the overall testing time. The presence of a long lie scale will usually mean that the assessment of the actual construct under study must be shorter (and thus both less informative and less reliable).

There is also a reason why it is not necessary to administer a complete lie scale to respondents in this scenario. When using traditional faking detection methods to invalidate scores, the accuracy of the method is (rightly) a key concern; because of the potential consequences for respondents identified as faking, it is extremely undesirable to mistakenly call out honest respondents for faking, and only somewhat less undesirable not to detect faking when it actually occurs. In contrast, for real-time detection, we are not as concerned about accuracy, because the only action that will be taken upon detecting faking is the delivery of a warning. Thus, the most desirable faking detection methods for real-time warning of respondents will be simple and fast, but perhaps not as accurate as traditional methods.

Machine learning techniques—algorithms that aim to discern simple patterns from complex data sets—provide a potential solution to the problem of quickly and systematically detecting faking. There are a large number of what are essentially "meta-algorithms": algorithms that, given a set of training data, produce a procedure for either classifying new data into categories or scoring new data along some dimension. The training data—a large number of data points already categorized or scored—are used to allow the system to "learn" how to classify a new data point for which the score or category is unknown. This is known as *supervised learning*, since the system is provided with a set of training data that is already correctly scored or categorized. *Unsupervised learning* systems, in contrast, simply attempt to discern patterns from a large data set, without any prescored or precategorized training data to from which to learn.

What both types of learning have in common is a training data set with a large number of data points. For each data point, a number of "features" are known, and the machine learning algorithm is designed to utilize these features to predict how each data point is to be scored or categorized. Medical diagnosis is a typical application of machine learning: A large data set of patients is available, and for each patient the data set records his or her vital signs (blood pressure, heart rate, etc.) as well as the symptoms they present (cough, fever, etc.). If supervised learning were to be used, then the goal would be to have the system use these symptoms and vital signs to predict the correct diagnosis for each patient. The system would first be presented with a training set consisting of a number of patients with known diagnoses. The system would then be asked to develop a model for diagnosis and to use this model to diagnose a new set of patients. If unsupervised learning were to be used, then the outcome would not be a system for automatic diagnosis per se but instead simply a model of how patients relate to each other (e.g., a clustering of patients based on their symptoms and vital signs).

Supervised learning is the more relevant of the two types of machine learning algorithms when it comes to quickly detecting faking, as there is a specific outcome variable (whether the respondent is faking) that we want to predict. Conceptually, we would train a machine learning classifier by providing it with a large training database of respondents, some of whom were known to have faked and some of whom were known to have responded honestly. In practice, such a training set may not truly exist in the faking context (because we really never know whether respondents were faking, even in experimental studies), but there are several ways to construct a training set for operational use. One possibility is to use

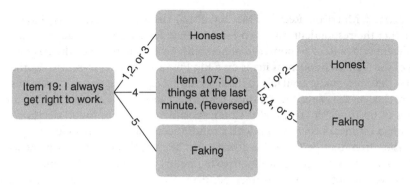

Figure 15.1 A decision tree for predicting whether a respondent is faking or honest on the International Personality Item Pool (IPIP).

experimental data where some respondents are told to fake and others are told to respond honestly; another is to use a nonexperimental data set that contains a lie scale.

There are a large number of supervised learning algorithms available; however, most algorithms unfortunately produce complex, "black box" models in the sense that the model provides little insight into the underlying structure of the problem domain. This is undesirable in general but particularly problematic for a system that will detect faking, since transparency enhances the face validity of the system for the organizations or individuals that use it, and makes use of the system more palatable to respondents. One technique in particular stands out in the simplicity of its models: *Decision trees* are a method for generating flowcharts that help the user make decisions based on the available features. The benefit of decision trees in general is that they are easy to apply and provide meaningful insight into the domain. They are particularly useful for detecting faking because of the face validity of the models they produce. Figure 15.1 shows an example that uses a respondent's responses to two International Personality Item Pool (IPIP) items to predict whether they are faking or responding honestly. Using this decision tree, one would predict that a respondent who selected 5 on the scale for Item 19 ("I always get right to work") is faking, regardless of what his or her response to Item 107 was. Similarly, one would predict honest responding if 1, 2, or 3 was selected for Item 19. However, if a respondent selected 4 for Item 19, his or her response to Item 107 ("Do things at the last minute") would come into play; a response of 1 or 2 here would be indicative of honest responding, and a response of 3, 4, or 5 would suggest faking. This decision tree was generated by a machine learning algorithm that used the training data to attempt to choose a decision tree that would have the best performance.

The decision tree technique has been applied to the faking problem in several studies that used decision trees to detect faking (Lukoff, 2006; Lukoff, Heggestad, Kyllonen, & Roberts, 2006). In two nonexperimental studies, decision trees were built to predict the score a respondent would have received had they been administered a full-length lie scale. In an experimental study (reanalyzing data from

Heggestad, Morrison, Reeve, & McCloy, 2006), decision trees were used to predict whether the respondent was in an experimental faking group. In all three studies, different sets of item responses to noncognitive assessments (e.g., the responses to all of the Conscientiousness items on a Big Five assessment) were used as the features that were made available to the algorithm. Depending on which sets of items were chosen, the experimental study found decision trees with estimated accuracy rates of up to about 70%, and the nonexperimental studies found decision trees that had estimated correlations with a candidness scale of up to about $r = 0.6$. The decision trees that performed well were also often fairly compact, utilizing as few as two items (and more typically six to ten items) to make a prediction.

However, not all decision trees performed equally well; performance varied greatly depending on the particular data set and features used. For example, using items on an Assertiveness scale (from the KeyPoint Job Fit Assessment) yielded a decision tree that had an estimated correlation of only 0.26 with a lie scale score, but using items from the Achievement Striving, Dependability, or Stress Tolerance scales yielded estimated correlations above 0.50. This suggests that some sets of items are simply more indicative of faking than others. Intuitively, one might expect applicants to be less likely to fake Assertiveness—where it is less obvious to the applicant what a "good" response is—than a scale with clearer "right" answers such as Dependability or Stress Tolerance.

Also of note is the fact that when comparing the two nonexperimental studies, the applicant data set (where respondents were actually applicants for a job) resulted in generally better-performing decision trees than the nonapplicant data set. This may be because the applicants had clearer patterns of faking than the nonapplicants. The fact that the results vary dramatically means that using this technique takes some care and experimentation. The variation in results also points to the need for the use of statistical methods to prevent data "snooping" and overfitting (Russell & Norvig, 2003), which these results are not completely free of due to the exploratory design of these studies. In addition, further validation work in the future is needed to examine more closely the types of faking that this method can (and cannot) detect. For example, it would be useful to determine whether a decision tree can still cleanly separate faking respondents from honest respondents in an experimental study in which one group is told to respond honestly, a second group is told to fake, and a third group is told to fake but in a way that would avoid detection.

Even the best decision trees failed to detect faking at the level of accuracy that would be required to invalidate scores in a high-stakes applicant selection situation. The most accurate classification tree (that aimed to predict which experimental group a respondent was in—faking or honest/control) still had an estimated false-positive rate of 25%, much too high to say with confidence that a respondent predicted by the decision tree to be faking is actually faking, and of course too high to take decisive action that would punish the respondent by invalidating his or her score.

However, the detection quality achieved by the decision trees may be good enough to use in a real-time warning situation. To do this, the items on the assessment should be reordered so that the ones used by the decision tree come first; this is done so that only a minimal number of items is administered before having enough information to decide whether it is necessary to issue a warning. After administering the first few items of the assessment, the decision tree would be applied to the responses from those first few items before the respondent proceeds further. If the decision tree predicts that the respondent is faking, the respondent would be warned at this point and then allowed to continue (perhaps disregarding the first set of items when computing their score). By contrast, if the decision tree predicts that the respondent is responding honestly, then no action would be taken and the respondent would proceed as usual.

If the assessment is administered on a computer, then this can be done instantaneously after the respondent finishes answering the items needed by the decision tree. The respondent who does not receive a warning would not notice anything amiss. Depending on the complexity of the decision tree, this technique is possible even if the assessment is administered on paper: The first page would contain the items used by the decision tree, and the respondent would have to turn in the first page to a proctor to receive the rest of the test. The proctor could easily memorize a simple decision tree and tell at a glance whether the responses to the first page of items are indicative of faking. If the proctor sees item responses that indicate faking, then along with the second part of the assessment the proctor might hand the respondent a paper with a warning. Respondents who are responding honestly would receive the second part of the test but no warning.

More work is needed before this technique can be used operationally. Field research is needed to determine whether these data-driven warnings help to provide the potential positive effects of warnings (the reduction in faking for those that are actually faking) while mitigating the potential negative effects (honest respondents who are unnecessarily warned and then respond dishonestly). Because the consequences of being labeled as faking do not extend beyond a simple warning, it is not necessary for the decision trees to be highly accurate. However, it is not clear what level of accuracy is necessary for the technique to be useful. Finally, altering the assessment by reordering the items may also alter the psychometric properties of the assessment (McFarland, Ryan, & Ellis, 2002), and thus assessments used in this way must be reevaluated from a psychometric perspective.

■ SUMMARY AND CONCLUSIONS

This chapter began by surveying a number of methods for reducing faking by changing the nature of questions that are asked or the person to whom they are asked. Each may potentially reduce faking but is not always broadly applicable. Asking a third party to rate an applicant instead of asking questions of applicants themselves works because the applicant no longer has direct control over the responses to the questions. Of course, the third party may decide to fake on behalf of the applicant. More importantly, though, this technique has limited applicability to many applicant and selection situations in which an impartial third party is not readily available. The verifiable biodata technique is another method that provides a conceptually clean method for reducing or even preventing faking, but it is limited to assessments in which verifiable data exist. Such assessments are less applicable when the dimensions to be measured are more abstract and less tied to facts in the respondent's background. Situational judgment tests also provide a way of framing an assessment that can be less fakable, but it can be expensive and time-consuming to design (or redesign) an assessment in that format. Certainly, when creating a noncognitive assessment, a test developer should carefully consider each of these three formats to determine if any can be adapted to the needs of the particular test under development.

Warnings are applicable to any kind of noncognitive assessment in which item response data are available, and have been shown to be somewhat effective in reducing faking, although they have negative consequences that make it inadvisable to always warn respondents. An alternative solution is to use a robust method for quickly detecting faking on the first few items in an assessment and then warn only those respondents who are suspected of faking. Decision trees built using historical item response data can create simple procedures for detecting, with reasonable accuracy and using only a small number of items, whether a respondent is faking. The simplicity of the method allows the test maker to take action in real time that is customized to the individual respondent. Furthermore, the decision tree method for determining when to warn a respondent in real time can even be combined with other faking reduction methods described in this chapter. For example, they could be applied to faculty members' ratings in the PPI to warn raters who might be faking, or to responses on a situational judgment test to warn respondents who start to exhibit behavior consistent with faking.

None of the methods proposed here is foolproof, and none alters the observation that all noncognitive assessments can, at least in principle, be faked. This fact should not prevent us from seeking to reduce faking, though, and the methods discussed here can be valuable tools to use towards this end. This is important business: Reducing faking is not simply an academic exercise; it has practical consequences for real people. Failing to address faking results in undeserved benefits for those who fake and get away with it as well as missed opportunities for honest respondents. Rewarding faking with a job or a promotion sends the message that such behavior is not just condoned but encouraged, and that it is acceptable to do whatever it takes to win, even if "what it takes" involves misrepresentation or outright lying. Putting even a small number of people that believe this into a position of power—cf. Ken Lay or Bernie Madoff—can be (and has been) disastrous.

Furthermore, by rewarding faking we may fail to find those applicants whose honesty would result in the kinds of business or government leaders that we need. An autoworker from General Motors who had tried to advance into management from the factory floor (based upon the recommendation of the foreman) but failed the noncognitive assessment needed to get there told a *New York Times* reporter that "I guess I could have given them the answers they wanted, but that's just not me. . . . I'm going to be honest—I'm going to put down how I would do the job, and if that doesn't line up with what you like, then that's cool, I don't take offense at that" (Mahler, 2009). Did the applicant who did get the management job answer honestly as well? Perhaps, but perhaps not, given what we know about the fakability of noncognitive assessments. Coincidentally, GM filed for bankruptcy, billions have been lost to Madoff's Ponzi scheme, and many Enron employees lost their life's savings when the company folded due to their executives' malfeasance. There is clearly an incentive for a society to reward honesty and punish dishonesty, and when high-stakes testing is involved it is particularly important to ensure that we do both—and not mistakenly do the opposite by allowing faking on important assessments.

References

Atkins, P. W. B., & Wood, R. E. (2002). Self versus others' ratings as predictors of assessment center ratings: Validation evidence for 360-degree feedback programs. *Personnel Psychology, 55*, 871–904.

Becker, T. E., & Colquitt, A. L. (1992). Potential versus actual faking of a biodata form: An analysis along several dimensions of item type. *Personnel Psychology, 45*, 389–406.

Chan, D., & Schmitt, N. (1997). Video-based versus paper-and-pencil method of assessment in situational judgment tests: Subgroup differences in test performance and face validity perceptions. *Journal of Applied Psychology, 82*, 143–159.

Cullen, M. J., Sackett, P. R., & Lievens, F. (2006). Threats to the operational use of situational judgment tests in the college admission process. *International Journal of Selection and Assessment, 14*, 142–155.

Dwight, S. A., & Donovan, J. J. (2003). Do warnings not to fake reduce faking? *Human Performance, 16*, 1–23.

Fletcher, C., & Baldry, C. (2000). A study of individual differences and self-awareness in the context of multi-source feedback. *Journal of Occupational and Organizational Psychology, 73*, 303–319.

Heggestad, E. D., Morrison, M., Reeve, C. L., & McCloy, R. A. (2006). Forced-choice assessments of personality for selection: Evaluating issues of normative assessment and faking resistance. *Journal of Applied Psychology, 91*(1), 9–24.

Kyllonen, P. C. (2008). *The research behind the ETS Personal Potential Index (PPI)*. Princeton, NJ: Educational Testing Service.

Lievens, F., & Peeters, H. (2008). Impact of elaboration on responding to situational judgment test items. *International Journal of Selection and Assessment, 16*, 345–355.

Lievens, F., Peeters, H., & Schollaert, E. (2008). Situational judgment tests: A review of recent research. *Personnel Review, 37*, 426–441.

Lievens, F., & Sackett, P. R. (2006). Video-based versus written situational judgment tests: A comparison in terms of predictive validity. *Journal of Applied Psychology, 91*, 1181.

Liu, O. L., Minsky, J., Ling, G., & Kyllonen, P. (2009). Using the standardized letters of recommendation in selection: Results from a multidimensional Rasch model. *Educational and Psychological Measurement, 69*(3), 475–492.

Lukoff, B. (2006). Detecting faking on noncognitive assessments using decision trees. In R. D. Roberts, R. Schulze, & P. C. Kyllonen (Chairs), Technical Advisory Committee on Faking on Noncognitive Assessments. Princeton, NJ.

Lukoff, B., Heggestad, E., Kyllonen, P., & Roberts, R. (2006). *Detecting faking on noncognitive assessments using decision trees*. Unpublished manuscript.

Mael, F. A. (1991). A conceptual rationale for the domain and attributes of biodata items. *Personnel Psychology, 44*, 763–792.

Mahler, J. (2009, June 28). G. M., Detroit, and the Fall of the Black Middle Class. *The New York Times*. Retrieved June 29, 2009, from http://www.nytimes.com/2009/06/28/magazine/28detroit-t.html?_r=1.

McFarland, L. A. (2003). Warning against faking on a personality test: Effects on applicant reactions and personality test scores. *International Journal of Selection and Assessment, 11,* 265–276.

McFarland, L. A., Ryan, A. M., & Ellis, A. (2002). Item placement on a personality measure: Effects on faking behavior and test measurement properties. *Journal of Personality Assessment, 78,* 348–369.

McManus, M. A., & Masztal, J. J. (1999). The impact of biodata item attributes on validity and socially desirable responding. *Journal of Business and Psychology, 13,* 437–446.

Motowidlo, S. J., Dunnette, M. D., & Carter, G. W. (1990). An alternative selection procedure: The low-fidelity simulation. *Journal of Applied Psychology, 75,* 640–647.

Nguyen, N. T., Biderman, M. D., & McDaniel, M. A. (2005). Effects of response instructions on faking a situational judgment test. *International Journal of Selection and Assessment, 13,* 250–260.

Nisbett, R. E., & Wilson, T. D. (1977). The halo effect: Evidence for unconscious alteration of judgments. *Journal of Personality and Social Psychology, 35,* 250–256.

Pace, V. L., & Borman, W. C. (2006). The use of warnings to discourage faking on noncognitive inventories. In R. L. Griffith & M. H. Peterson (Eds.), *A closer examination of applicant faking behavior* (pp. 283–304). Greenwich, CT: Information Age Publishing.

Pace, V. L., Xu, X., Penney, L. M., Borman, W. C., & Bearden, R. M. (2005). Using warnings to discourage personality test faking: An empirical study. Paper presented at the Society for Industrial and Organizational Psychology annual conference, Los Angeles, CA.

Peeters, H., & Lievens, F. (2005). Situational judgment tests and their predictiveness of college students' success: The influence of faking. *Educational and Psychological Measurement, 65,* 70–89.

Russell, S. J., & Norvig, P. (2003). *Artificial intelligence: A modern approach* (2nd ed.). New York: Prentice Hall.

Schmitt, N., & Kunce, C. (2002). The effects of required elaboration of answers to biodata questions. *Personnel Psychology, 55,* 569–587.

Schmitt, N., Oswald, F. L., Kim, B. H., Gillespie, M. A., Ramsay, L. J., & Yoo, T. Y. (2003). Impact of elaboration on socially desirable responding and the validity of biodata measures. *Journal of Applied Psychology, 88,* 979–988.

Sullivan, K., & Richer, C. (2002). Malingering on subjective complaint tasks: An exploration of the deterrent effects of warning. *Archives of Clinical Neuropsychology, 17,* 691–708.

Youngjohn, J. R., Lees-Haley, P. R., & Binder, L. M. (1999). Comment: Warning malingerers produces more sophisticated malingering. *Archives of Clinical Neuropsychology, 14,* 511–515.

PART FIVE

Is Faking a Consequential Issue Outside a Job Selection Context?

Current Applications and Future Directions in Clinical and Educational Settings

16 Plaintiffs Who Malinger

Impact of Litigation on Fake Testimony

■ RYAN C. W. HALL AND RICHARD C. W. HALL

■ INTRODUCTION

Malingering includes both the fabrication of clinical symptoms and/or diagnoses and the gross exaggeration of symptoms for the purpose of obtaining a specific secondary gain, often in a legal context (e.g., financial, to avoid duty or responsibility, or to avoid a negative outcome). Depending on the population studied, reported rates of malingering/exaggeration on psychometric testing range from 5% to 70% (Lees-Haley & Fox, 2004; Mittenberg, Patton, Canyock, & Condit, 2002; Rüsseler, Brett, Klaue, Sailer, & Münte, 2008). Clinicians who rely on psychometric testing as a source of data have to address this issue with ever increasing frequency (Table 16.1). Not only is malingering more prevalent because of societal change (e.g., increasing divorce rates leading to more potential issues of custody or alimony payments for feigned injuries, workplace instability leading to claims of improper termination due to disability, issues with obtaining disability benefits, and increasing legal claims of dubious merit), but the sophistication of malingering attempts is increasing due to expanded access to information [i.e., symptom constellations for posttraumatic stress disorder (PTSD), head injury, reflex sympathetic dystrophy, etc.] and the *Diagnostic and Statistical Manual of Mental Disorders, Fourth Edition* (DSM-IV) diagnostic criteria on the Internet.

The culture as a whole seems to be more accepting and almost tolerant of exaggeration, if not outright fabrication. Some individuals, who present themselves as doctors, have made a living running malingering seminars (e.g., "sick schools") and have written books on how to malinger, such as *The Malingerer's Manual* ("Malingering Manual," 2009). In addition, lawyers frequently prepare their clients for independent medical evaluations (IMEs) and refer them to physicians and others who make and support diagnoses based on subjective symptoms. In this environment, psychometric testing provides a valuable independent tool for clinicians, helping them to differentiate bonafide patients from "sham patients" (i.e., individuals who are malingering illness or deficits for personal gain). Testing is also useful to differentiate the legitimate plaintiff (e.g., personal injury, child custody, or disability) from fakers/manipulators. In addition, psychometric testing helps to separate and understand patients who are accurately reporting perceived symptoms from those who are exaggerating symptoms either consciously (e.g., concerned others will minimize their suffering, factious disorder, malingerers) or unconsciously (e.g., conversion disorder, somatization disorder).

TABLE 16.1 *Common Tests Used for Clinical Evaluations and/or Detection of Malingering*

Millon Clinical Multiaxial Inventory (MCMI-II or III)
Minnesota Multiphasic Personality Inventory (MMPI-2)
Neuroticism-Extroversion-Openness Personality Inventory (NEO-PI-R)
Personality Assessment Inventory (PAI)
Test of Memory Malingering (TOMM)
The Rey 15-Item Memory Test

In a survey done by Mittenberg et al. (2002) of the American Board of Clinical Neuropsychology, it was estimated that the prevalence of malingering was geographically consistent across America. Malingering was suspected in approximately 30% of personal injury cases, 30% of disability claims, 19% of criminal evaluations, and 8% of clinical/medical cases. Approximately 40% of people suffering from head injury, 35% of people with fibromyalgia/chronic fatigue, 31% of chronic pain patients, 27% of neurotoxic syndromes, and 22% of electrical injury claims were suspected of malingering. The fact that other DSM-IV diagnostic disorders were not included in the list does not indicate that they were not also malingered at a similar rate. Many psychiatric conditions may be successfully faked (i.e., PTSD, depression, postconcussive disorder) and therefore go unrecognized (Hall & Hall, 2001, 2006, 2007; Hall, Hall, & Chapman, 2005; Resnick, 1993, 2005). Some are more readily detectable on initial clinical observation as malingered (i.e., schizophrenia) and are thus not referred for testing.

In the survey by Mittenberg et al. (2002), a diagnosis/suspicion of malingering was based on several indicators, with the factors most likely to raise suspicion being an excessive severity of claimed symptoms, 65% of cases; patterns of inconsistent cognitive impairment, 64% of cases; scores below empiric cutoffs on forced choice tests, 57% of cases; discrepancies among reports of deficits, 56% of cases; inconsistent test scores across repeated examination, 45% of cases; and validity scale scores outside of normal ranges on objective personality tests, 38% of cases. Because the percentages of indictors of malingering exceeded 100%, it is obvious that in most cases the evaluators noted multiple indicators in each malingerer. Mittenberg's study highlights how widespread malingering on psychometric testing has become and that it can occur in any given population.

■ FACTORS TO BE CONSIDERED WHEN EVALUATING MALINGERING IN A CLINICAL SETTING

When psychometric testing is used in the clinical context, it is usually assumed that the results are valid due to the patient/client's desire to honestly participate in the evaluation process to obtain maximum therapeutic benefit (Kertzman et al., 2006). This assumption is in fact often erroneous. Eight percent of medical patients in the Mittenberg survey were suspected of malingering, with no clear secondary gain being identified (Mittenberg et al., 2002).

TABLE 16.2 *Types of Malingering Categorizations That Can Have Clinical Implications (More Than One May Apply)*

Faking good
Faking bad
Sophisticated (selective symptom endorsement showing knowledge of symptoms patterns/profiles)
Unsophisticated (endorses most severe symptoms in a nonsubtle way)
Coached
Uncoached
Seeking immediate specific short-term benefit (i.e., short-term disability, avoiding criminal responsibility, obtaining drugs)
Seeking long-term benefit (i.e., settlement, lawsuit, permanent disability)
Financial derived motivation
Personally derived motivation (e.g., maintaining a behavior)
Justification for malingering (entitled, correcting previous wrong, "everyone does it")

When malingering is detected, the type of malingering engaged in should be identified (e.g., faking good or faking bad; unsophisticated attempt versus subtle manipulation) and the possible reasons for the misrepresentations examined (Table 16.2). The examination of malingered or exaggerated responses may provide valuable insights about the examinee, his or her motivation, and/or likely future course in therapy.

Malingers may fake bad in one of three ways. They may (1) exaggerate symptoms that are actually occurring or attribute real symptoms to a factitious cause; (2) report that symptoms are still occurring, which have in fact remitted; or (3) totally fabricate symptoms that have never occurred (Boone & Lu, 2003; Hall et al., 2005; Hall & Hall, 2006, 2007; Resnick, 1993, 2005). Individuals who are fabricating symptoms that have resolved or who are exaggerating symptoms that are still occurring are the most difficult to detect because their clinical presentation is similar to what would be expected if their reports were true (Hall & Hall, 2006, 2007; Resnick, 2005; Vanderploeg & Curtiss, 2001). For example, people who have experienced hallucinations or flashbacks will be less likely to describe the events in an unrealistic manner since they have actually experienced these phenomena. As Vanderploeg and Curtiss (2001, p. 245) warn when assessing patients with mild traumatic brain injury, "validity assessment is difficult and at times ambiguous in part because real and feigned deficits are not mutually exclusive. In some clinical situations, the most that can be said about an invalid performance is that it is not indicative of the true neurobehavioral capabilities of the person being evaluated, and is not consistent with the presumed etiologic event." Even so, psychometric testing can still be beneficial in detecting malingering in patients with real disease. Malingered symptoms are often dramatic to ensure their presence is recognized, that they are severe enough to be disabling, and warrant compensation (Bianchini, Curtis, & Greve, 2006; Fox, Gerson, & Lees-Haley, 1995). The malingerers' need to overdramatize their injury is often the element best detected on psychometric testing. For example, a study by Vickery et al. (2004) found that individuals who had suffered an actual head injury, who were instructed to malinger, were just as likely to be identified by established cutoff scores on motivational tests and other neuropsychological examinations as those individuals instructed to malinger who had no history of head injury.

When assessing individuals who are faking bad, one may see different patterns, depending on whether the testing was done in a criminal or civil legal context (Resnick, 2005; Wygant, Sellbom, Ben-Porath, Stafford, Freeman, & Heilbronner, 2007). People trying to malinger to gain admission to a hospital or who are in criminal jeopardy are more likely to malinger symptoms of a psychosis or severe depression with suicidal ideation. Individuals involved in civil or disability litigation are more likely to malinger cognitive deficits, somatic problems related to an injury, moderate to severe depression without extreme suicidal ideation, anxiety symptoms, or symptoms of PTSD. The differences in presentation relate to the differences in the secondary gain being sought.

In criminal situations, malingerers often feign psychiatric illnesses that will, if accepted, cause them to be removed from a prison or jail and transferred to a hospital setting. Civil litigants often malinger illnesses that emphasize symptoms that result in them being seen as unable to work, but not symptoms that are so severe that hospitalization or a loss of freedom is necessary. In both settings, malingerers engage in drug-seeking behavior by emphasizing or exaggerating their pain or disability complaints. The different types of malingering that occur in institutions versus outpatient settings are shown in Table 16.3.

Research by Wygant et al. (2007) found that criminal malingerers often had elevations in global scales of pathology and the somatic scales of the Minnesota Multiphasic Personality Inventory (MMPI-2). Individuals in civil litigation generally evidenced elevations of somatic symptoms. The overall conclusion of Wygant et al. was that the Fake Bad scale of the MMPI-2 was useful in detecting malingering in both criminal and civil populations, whereas different scales were more predictive in specific populations. The Infrequency-Psychopathology (F_p) scale was more predictive of malingering in examinees involved in criminal prosecutions than in civil litigants (Table 16.4).

■ FAKING GOOD IN CLINICAL SETTINGS

Often, when the topic of malingering is discussed, the focus of the conversation is on detecting people who are trying to fake being ill. However, clinicians often encounter patients who are trying to appear normal when they are in fact impaired.

TABLE 16.3 *Common Types of Disease States Malingered Based on Location*

Outpatient	Institutionalized setting (hospital/jail)
Acute/chronic pain	Acute/chronic pain
Attention Deficit Hyperactivity Disorder (ADHD)	Amnesia/memory disorder
Amnesia/memory disorder	Any Axis I diagnosis with suicidal ideation
Anxiety disorders	Cognitive deficits
Cognitive deficits	Psychosis
Mild to moderate depression	
Posttraumatic Stress Disorder (PTSD)	

TABLE 16.4 *Minnesota Multiphasic Personality Inventory (MMPI) Scales and Subscales That May Be Helpful for the Detection of Malingering*

1. Cannot Say (? Or CS): number left unanswered or answered as both true and false
2. Correction or Defensiveness (K): attempts to portray oneself favorably, but more subtle than L
3. Deceptive Subtle (DS): subset of the subtle questions noted for high face validity, but minimal predictive value for pathology
4. Ego Strength (ES): original indicated prognosis for psychotherapy, extremely low (ES with normal mental status suggests overreporting psychopathology)
5. Fake Bad (FBS): designed to detect simulated emotional stress in personal injury claimants, obvious items endorsed versus more subtle items not listed
6. Back F (FB): infrequently endorsed items, indicating extreme pathology, cry for help, symptom exaggeration (questions 280 on)
7. F-FB: consistency of answers for first half of test and second half
8. Gough Dissimulation Index (F-K): high scores correlate with overreporting, low scores correlate with underreporting
9. Gough Dissimulation Scale for the MMPI-2 (Ds2): infrequently endorsed affective items
10. Infrequency (F): infrequently endorsed items, indicating extreme pathology, cry for help, symptom exaggeration (first 361 questions)
11. Infrequency–Psychopathology (Fp): infrequent responses in a psychiatric population
12. Infrequency–Posttraumatic Stress Disorder (Fptsd): infrequently endorsed responses in a sample of veterans diagnosed with PTSD
13. Lie (L): unsophisticated attempt to portray favorable impression
14. Obvious Items (Ob): selections with high face value of pathology
15. Obvious Minus Subtle (OS): index of symptom exaggeration
16. Other Subtle (Os): subset of subtle questions more predictive of pathology
17. Subtle items (Su): 100-question subscale
18. Superlative Self-Presentation (S): test of defensiveness for people presenting self in highly virtuous manner
19. Total Obvious (OT): obvious symptoms associated with pathology reported
20. Variable Response Inconsistency (VRIN): sum of inconsistent responses

This type of presentation, especially in the British literature, has been referred to as dissimulation (Mohíno-Justes et al., 2004). These patients may not raise their clinicians' suspicions of malingering because they strive to appear normal. If the extent of their impairment is not recognized, their secondary gain is also frequently missed.

In contrast to faking bad, attempts to fake good are usually perceived as noble due to the romanticized notion that the patients' deceptions are brought about by their sense of duty to their work or comrades. However, this romantic notion is frequently wrong since patients most often fake good for more selfish motives. Individuals trying to fake good lie about and conceal symptoms because they have enough insight to realize that if they admit their impairment, they will lose something tangible and important to them, such as their job/identity (e.g., classic examples are a pilot lying to a flight surgeon or a physician to a hospital board), security clearance, marriage, or a behavior they do not want to give up (e.g., alcohol or drug use) (Caruso, Benedek, Auble, & Bernet, 2003). Individuals will also commonly fake good to avoid being stigmatized with an illness, as sometimes occurs in court-ordered proceedings (Caruso et al., 2003).

The desire to fake good may also be due to symptoms of a mental illness such as schizophrenia (i.e., paranoia with command hallucinations) (Caruso et al., 2003). The authors have participated in a court-ordered evaluation of a paranoid schizophrenic defendant who believed the judge wanted him committed to a mental hospital so the judge could sodomize him. The defendant initially denied psychotic symptoms, but later explained that he did so because he felt safer in jail where he would be protected from the judge. Ironically, individuals who intentionally fake good are often believed to have poor insight (i.e., acute mania) or are in denial (i.e., alcoholics). Although the motivation for deception may be initially unknown, the evaluator must ultimately determine if the deception is intentionally perpetrated for secondary gain versus an ego defense. The diagnoses of malingering versus pathological denial versus cognitive impairment with poor insight are not mutually exclusive. For example, alcoholics may deny the medical consequences of their condition while minimizing cognitive impairment and malingering fake good to diminish any responsibility for an accident.

When patients are forced into therapy by family, they may present themselves, as one patient put it, as "the most 'involuntary' voluntary patient possible." This frank honesty did raise the suspicion that the individual was faking good after being "forced" into treatment by his family. He later admitted that he was trying to appear as honest and forthcoming as possible so that later questionable statements would be believed by the therapist. Outpatients who fake good often engage in therapy under the duress of their spouse/family, boss, or court. Personality tests show they often report behaviors/symptoms at a rate below that found in the general population (i.e., answering questions such as "I never get mad" in the affirmative manner). Analysis of their profiles often shows a high level of defensiveness, narcissism, and/or potentially hypomanic symptoms. These symptom response patterns are due to patients endorsing what they perceive to be "normal or idealized" answers to hide their pathology.

■ SUGGESTIONS FOR INTERPRETING MALINGERING IN CLINICAL TESTING SITUATIONS

Psychometric testing should never be applied in a vacuum (Lanyon, Almer, & Curran, 1993). When the clinical picture and test results do not match, a careful review of data is in order as information is likely to be either inaccurate or missing (Vanderploeg & Curtiss, 2001). There are several reasons that psychometric testing may suggest malingering, and not all are nefarious. Potential causes range from a cry for help, ordinary therapeutic occurrences such as resistance, denial, a desire to appear socially desirable, or a desire to please the therapist (e.g., not to appear ill for fear of abandonment or to appear more ill to warrant attention) to overt situational concerns such as how the testing might affect employment, the ability to maintain custody of children, disability status, or pending civil or criminal litigation (Deshields, Tait, Gfeller, & Chibnall, 1995; Goetz, 2007).

Unexpected test results can also occur due to poor effort associated with fatigue, old age, low IQ, diminished cognitive ability, hypochondriasis, test taking anxiety, an error in how the test was given or scored, or to an initially erroneous clinical perception of the patient by the therapist (e.g., sicker than first appeared, needed information that is not available) (Boone, 2008a, 2008b; Dean Victor, Boone, & Arnold, 2008b; Dean, Victor, Boone, Philpott, & Hess, 2008c; Frazier, Youngstrom,

Naugle, Haggerty, & Busch, 2007; Locke, Smigielski, Powell, & Stevens, 2008; Loring, Lee, & Meador, 2005; Marshall & Happe, 2007; Rankin, Gilner, Gfeller, & Katz, 1994). For example, in a sample of people with low IQ, who were not involved in litigation or seeking disability benefits, Dean et al. (2008b) found that 60% of individuals with an IQ of 50–59, 44% with IQs of 60–69, and 17% with IQs of 70–79 failed multiple parts of a malingering examination that included nine different tests that measured effort. Every individual with an IQ below 70 failed at least one measure even though there was no obvious reason for them to intentionally exaggerate their symptoms or limitations.

Whenever clinicians use psychometric tests, it is crucial for them to not only be familiar with the instruments they are using (e.g., the presence or absence of validity scales and what form of pathology, trait, or deficit is being measured), but also to be aware of the potential patterns of a malingered response, gender, and ethnic/cultural effects (Boone, Victor, Wen, Razani, & Pontón, 2007; Gasquoine, 2001; Kennepohl, Shore, Nabors, & Hanks, 2004). In addition to being familiar with patterns of malingering, it is important to be familiar with patterns consistent with psychological illness, such as the Conversion V on the MMPI-2 [e.g., a higher elevation of the hypochondriasis (Scale 1) and hysteria (Scale 3) scales compared to an elevated depression scale (Scale 2)], which may be mistaken for malingering or a factitious disorder (Boone, 2007; Boone & Lu, 1999; Finset, Anke, Hofft, Roaldsen, Pillgram-Larsen, & Stanghelle, 1999).

Elevation of validity scales by itself does not imply malingering, nor does lack of elevation indicate that malingering is not occurring. In a study by Tsushima and Tsushima (2001) looking at five commonly used validity scales on the MMPI-2 in personal injury litigants, clinic patients not involved in a lawsuit, and normal controls, significant elevations were found for both clinic patients and litigants on the Infrequency scale (F), Back Infrequency scale (F_B), Dissimulation scale-2 (Ds2), and the Fake Bad Scale (FBS) of the MMPI-2 compared to controls. Only the FBS scale of the MMPI-2 separated the injury litigants from the clinical patients, indicating that the FBS was a "useful index of symptom magnification when employed within a comprehensive assessment of malingering in personal injury plaintiffs." What is significant is not that the FBS was successful, but that (at least in this study) the three other validity scales (F, F_B, Ds2) were not, since elevations occurred in both groups of patients compared to controls.

Similar results were found in a study by Larrabee (2003). In his study, individuals involved in litigation, who were initially determined to be malingering using the Slick, Sherman, and Iverson criteria for definite and probable malingering of neurocognitive deficits caused by head injury, were better detected using elevations of the MMPI-2 FBS scale than by the more traditional validity scales of F_P, F, and F_B. Larrabee also noted that the litigant group scored higher on the MMPI-2 scales of Hypochondriasis (Scale 1), Hysteria (Scale 3), and Psychasthenia (Scale 7) compared to various nonlitigating control groups with physical ailments such as head injury, multiple sclerosis, spinal cord injury, chronic pain, and depression. He concluded that individuals trying to fake physical or psychiatric complaints showed elevations on different validity scales than on the traditional F_P, F, and F_B scales. This again highlights the need to not blindly interpret scale elevations or the lack of elevations as indications of malingering, but to integrate such elevations with the pertinent clinical presentation of the case.

Clinicians who suspect malingering also need to be aware that additional data to support the conclusion of malingering can be further obtained from subset analysis of the raw data. For example, individuals faking memory loss usually do so by suppressing performance on tasks that involve recall as well as recognition memory where true patients will often perform better on one type of task than another (Bernard, 1990; Bernard, Houston, & Natoli, 1993). Malingerers also often overestimate the extent of deficits that exist in head trauma patients. This results in malingerers performing significantly worse than genuinely injured patients on both difficult and easier memory tasks or tasks involving different types of memory, such as acquisitional and procedural memory. Malingerers characteristically experience difficulty knowing and maintaining impaired patterns of memory function. Suhr (2002) noted that malingerers did worse on the serial position effect test (tendency to remember words at the beginning of a list and end of a list, also known as primacy and recency effect) than did both controls and patients with head injuries. This is the basis for the "Pattern of Performance Theory" for detecting malingering, which holds that people simulating malingering do poorly on both obvious and subtle tasks compared to people with verified brain damage and other mental disabilities. Due to the difficulty malingerers have of internally tracking obvious performance (e.g., overall number recalled) and subtle differences (number from beginning, middle, and end of a list recalled), they are often unable to keep track of all the variables, even when well coached (Bernard, McGrath, & Houston, 1996). This does not mean that it is impossible to successfully malinger, just that it is difficult. When an individual successfully malingers one portion of a battery of tests, but is detected by a different portion, it may suggest that the examinee is a sophisticated malingerer, who is able to function at a very high level. In their attempt to deceive, such patients are often demonstrating the abilities they claim are impaired.

Although studies have indicated that racial/ethnic differences occur on some psychometric tests, several studies show that their specific malingering scales are not significantly affected by race or ethnicity (Boone et al., 2007; Dean et al., 2008a; DuAlba & Scott, 1993; Gasquoine, 2001; Kennepohl et al., 2004; Tsushima & Tsushima, 2009). Tsushima and Tsushima (2009) found no significant racial differences between white and Asian compensation-seeking litigants for the MMPI-2 validity scales of the F scale, the $F_{(B)}$, the Symptom Validity Scale, the $F_{(P)}$ scale, and the Dissimulation Scale. A study by Dean et al. (2008a) found no ethnic differences for the FBS scale scores when comparing white, African-American, and Hispanic outpatients separated into controls and patients involved in litigation or disability claims. Thus, it appears that standardization of the malingering scales has been partially, if not fully, effective in limiting the effects of racial or ethnical differences (Boone et al., 2007; Dean et al., 2008a; DuAlba & Scott, 1993; Tsushima & Tsushima, 2009). When evaluating testing, clinicians need to be aware that race may affect the results, but for large, widely normed psychometric tests, the effect may be minimal.

The study by Dean et al. (2008a) did find some differences in responses based on gender. They encouraged that if the FBS scale was used, clinicians apply gender-specific cutoff scores to address the issue. Many of the potential gender differences in psychometric testing have been studied and are addressed or minimized by using different scale norms based on gender-normed studies (Lees-Haley & Fox, 2004). It is a good idea for clinicians to check to see if appropriate norms are being used for the tests they perform, especially when results are unexpected.

■ ELEVATED SCORES: MALINGERING OR STRESS

The stress experienced by the examinee at the time of testing can elevate scores in such a way as to suggest malingering. Litigation and employment screens are both situations in which stress and a desire to be believed may result in scale elevations that may or may not be due to a "gross" intention to fabricate (Lees-Haley, 1997). Even if clinicians do not perceive that their testing will be used in litigation or hiring, the psychometric results can be affected. Legal cases are adversarial in nature and can take years to resolve. The stress they cause, the potential of having to repeat and justify symptoms, and the obvious notion that others may not believe the accusations being made or are against the examinee, can result in the litigant's need to maintain the initial severity of symptoms or to report them more dramatically (i.e., a condition we call litigation stress/litigation distortion/compensation neurosis) (Boone, 2007; Lees-Haley, 1997).

In addition, the stress of litigation itself may produce symptoms that can often be confused with those caused by a specific medical/mental illness, toxic syndrome, or head injury. In a study by Lees-Haley and Brown (1993) looking at personal injury claimants with no history of brain injury, toxic exposure, or documented neuropsychological impairment, the litigants reported high rates of symptoms that are often seen following central nervous system (CNS) trauma, concussion, and in individuals suffering from psychiatric disorders. Lees-Haley and Brown found that 93% of these claimants reported anxiety or nervousness, 92% reported sleep problems, 89% reported depression, 88% headaches, 79% fatigue, 78% concentration problems, 77% irritability, 65% impatience, 61% feeling disorganized, 59% confusion, 56% loss of efficiency performing everyday tasks, 53% memory problems, 44% dizziness, 39% numbness, and 34% word-finding problems. Whether these symptoms were all due to the stress of litigation or were due to results of malingering is unclear, but the high rates of occurrence suggest that litigation stress/compensation neurosis is a powerful potential etiological factor. Lees-Haley and Brown cautioned that further research is needed to determine the base rate of symptoms associated with litigation stress to better differentiate clients who are intentionally malingering impairment from those who are primarily reacting to the stress of the litigation itself.

Individuals involved in litigation are also more prone to demonstrate a response bias. They report past functioning at a level higher than actually existed (Lees-Haley, Williams, & English, 1996; Lees-Haley, Williams, Zasler, Marguilies, English, & Stevens, 1997). The increased number of newly reported symptoms may result in an elevation of validity scales. The clinician must use his or her experience and judgment to decide if the symptom reports and subsequent scale elevations are mild to moderate exaggerations related to an ongoing lawsuit; the effects of the patient's medical condition, such as mild traumatic brain injury; somatization related to the stress from another cause (e.g., marital issues unrelated to a lawsuit); or if the individual is grossly exaggerating/malingering to obtain a secondary gain, such as increased compensation in a lawsuit (Dunn, Lees-Haley, Brown, Williams, & English, 1995; Lees-Haley, 1997; Lees-Haley & Fox, 1990; Leininger, Kreutzer, & Hill, 1991).

Clinicians also need to recognize that the secondary gain sought by malingerers may not be the traditional type that the therapist expects (e.g., money from litigation) or even initially be recognized by the therapist as a secondary gain. For example, in the late 1990s, many families brought their adolescent children in with specific requests that they be diagnosed with attention deficit disorder (ADD). Many of these children clearly did not display behaviors suggestive of attention deficit disorder nor did they have histories suggestive of the condition. When the parents were informed that their children did not have ADD, they continued to push for the diagnosis. It was later learned that the families wanted the diagnosis of ADD so they could get untimed college admission tests for their children. Although it was initially assumed that the families would have wanted to avoid the stigma of having their children labeled as "learning disabled," these particular families felt the condition was an advantage in the college admissions process and were willing to misrepresent their child's actual performance and condition to obtain the diagnosis.

It is important for clinicians to remember that psychometric testing needs to be evaluated in the context in which it was obtained and that it can be reevaluated if questions arise. The tests are only as good as the data provided, the effort the patient puts forth, and the clinician's understanding of the issues involved. The more suggestive the data regarding malingering, the greater the likelihood that malingering is truly occurring (Cato, Brewster, Ryan, & Giuliano, 2002; King, Sweet, Sherer, Curtiss, & Vanderploeg, 2002; Larrabee, 2008; Lynch, 2004; Van Gorp et al., 1999; Victor, Boone, Serpa, Buehler, & Ziegler, 2009). Larrabee (2008) found that a base rate assumption of malingering of between 0.1 and 0.9 resulted in a probability findings of malingering of 35.7 to 97.8% for failure of one symptom validity test (SVT), 73.5 to 99.6 for failure of two SVTs, and 93.3% to 99.9% for failure of three SVTs. Larrabee's study helps demonstrate that regardless of the base rate, failure on multiple instruments increases the probability of detecting malingering.

■ WHEN TO CLINICALLY OBTAIN PSYCHOMETRIC TESTING AND HOW TO ASSESS PREVIOUS TESTING

Psychometric testing can be administered in many different settings (i.e., therapist's office, school, military, or hospital settings). In addition, psychometric testing can be used in settings that are not traditionally considered to be clinical, such as court, clinics, or in jails. Wherever administered, psychometric testing can help clarify diagnosis, reveal important deficits (e.g., IQ limitations/lateralization of injuries), and also provide important information to be explored in therapy. Tests also provide baseline data concerning a patient's current level of functioning, which can be used to document improvement or deterioration in the patient's cognitive and emotional function. The question then becomes what tests to obtain and when. Once testing is ordered, this issue is further complicated if the testing is ordered as a routine part of treatment or ordered to specifically address whether someone is malingering. Shotgun approaches to testing often produce conflicting bits of core information, which may make determination of the subject's response validity and reliability difficult. For example, is an individual malingering a memory impairment, embellishing actual symptoms, legitimately fatigued after completing earlier tests, having cognitive difficulties due to currently prescribed medications, or feigning symptoms after being coached? We must also remember that in various clinical settings, opportunities to fake are not restricted to just questionnaires and psychometric testing.

In a strictly clinical setting, the decision to obtain testing depends on the style of the therapist and how the therapist plans to incorporate the testing into illness/impairment documentation and/or treatment planning. In general, clinical testing is ordered to evaluate individuals who have a suspected deficit (e.g., IQ, executive function following mild traumatic brain injury), to provide a baseline to monitor a known impairment (e.g., memory related to head trauma), or to help investigate a patient's specific personality make-up and how that may be influencing his or her behavior or is influenced by a mental/medical illness or other condition [e.g., effects on concentration of sleep apnea treated with Constant Positive Airway Pressure (CPAP) in pilots]. Some therapists obtain testing only if a patient seems "stuck in psychotherapy," is not improving despite treatment with medications, or to further substantiate or clarify diagnosis. The latter usage of testing is becoming more common due to increasing financial pressures by insurance companies to limit the duration of therapy. Where there are a limited number of sessions available, testing may help identify personality features that may have taken multiple sessions to fully uncover and appreciate in the past. Other reasons that therapists may routinely order psychometric testing are to help the patient engage in treatment, confirm or suggest a potential diagnosis, provide a second opinion for both the patient's and the therapist's benefit, objectively confirm personality characteristics, and potentially to provide additional documentation in difficult or high-risk cases to reduce malpractice risk.

■ USING VALIDITY SCALES TO GAUGE MALINGERING ON PSYCHOMETRIC TESTS

Often if tests such as the MMPI-2, Millon Clinical Multiaxial Inventory (MCMI-III), Personality Assessment Inventory (PAI), or NEO-Personality Inventory–Revised (NEO-PI-R) (all with validity scales) are obtained for therapy purposes, they will be the only test administered due to cost and time constraints (Bagby, Nicholson, Bacchiochi, Ryder, & Bury, 2002; Morasco, Gfeller, & Elder, 2007; Sellbom & Bagby, 2008). In these situations, clinicians should remember that a single test, although potentially helpful for therapy, may not be sufficient to provide an adequate assessment for degree of exaggeration, consistency of exaggeration, or scope of symptoms exaggerated.

Validity scales on psychometric tests provide a structured and impersonal way to address issues of personality disorder and/or potential exaggeration/malingering. A therapist can use an elevated validity scale to address the issue of potential malingering or character pathology in a nonconfrontational manner with a patient without the need to directly say, "I think you are not telling the truth" or "I think you are narcissistic or antisocial." If the elevations are due to therapeutic concerns such as denial, then the therapist can begin to address them directly and in a timely manner; if they are malingered symptoms, their disproportionate or inconsistent quality can be addressed.

Validity scales can help identify malingering, but short of a direct confession from the individual that they are intentionally lying and why, the diagnosis of malingering cannot be made with 100% certainty from just a test (e.g., it can suggest high probability but does not confirm with certainty as it cannot speak to motive). Few people will admit to malingering when directly challenged or confronted. A nonconfrontational approach using psychometric test results and clinical information is often more effective in obtaining the truth. For example, "The test results show you may be overreporting your symptoms. This can occur for a lot of reasons, such as the need to convince people you are really sick, your own fear of illness, a cry for help, or because of the stress of litigation. What do you believe is the cause?" Another approach is to recognize the temptation to malinger and to have the therapist potentially downplay the negative aspects with a statement such as "Many people feel pressure to indicate they are sicker then they really are for many different reasons. I am concerned this may have happened here and we should talk about it." The best way to therapeutically uncover and address the issue of malingering is to allow the patient a face-saving way to admit to the exaggeration if possible (Hall & Hall, 2001, 2006, 2007; Resnick, 2005). These approaches define the problem, permit a better understanding of the patient, and maintain some form of therapeutic alliance.

Mental health practitioners, who are not expert in interpreting psychometric testing, may obtain reports on tests such as the MMPI-2 or the MCMI-III through large testing corporations that can score and provide detailed computer-generated interpretations in a timely manner, often with reference to specific populations (e.g., forensic, clinical). The advantage of such reports is that they remove any potential for personal/professional bias and reduce the risk that the evaluator will be seen as a "hired gun" working for a lawyer to provide a biased opinion. After all, if the report is generated by an individual or a computer program that never met the patient, it cannot be influenced by the patient's appearance, demeanor, in-office statements, attorney affiliation, or history. These tests can be very helpful in detecting malingering and adding an additional degree of objectivity to the clinical evaluation.

For clinical evaluations, integrating test data with a thorough clinical evaluation and detailed review of records provides an important advantage (Table 16.5). The clinician knows the patient has developed a defined relationship and may be

TABLE 16.5 *Possible Indications during an Interview for Fabrication Based on Response Style Assuming Change from Baseline*

Blinks eyes frequently
Frequent "slips of the tongues"
Grammatical errors
Hedging statements
Hesitant answers
High-pitched tone
Inconsistent symptoms
Irrelevant statements (different from providing more detail than needed,
    which may indicate truthfulness)
May or may not be able to maintain eye contact
Negative statements
Overgeneralizations
Perceived as "thrusting forth symptoms"
Repetitive gestures (e.g., rubbing hands)
Short answers
Symptoms feel "rehearsed"
Use of passive voices
Vague statements

better able to apply test results due to having a longitudinal view of the patient (Lanyon et al., 1993). Scores suggesting either faking good or faking bad may help the therapist identify transference or countertransference issues. Also, the therapist's relationship with the patient may help to identify potential elevations due to errors in completing the test. For example, an MCMI-III for therapeutic purposes on an individual with anxiety and social phobia whose test results from an out-of-office rating service indicated the patient had antisocial traits and was trying to fake good was obtained. Prior to the testing, the individual had been perceived as highly motivated for improvement, voluntarily seeking treatment, highly conscientious, suffering from obsessive-compulsive traits/disorder, and wanting to please the therapist. When the raw score sheet was reviewed, it was noticed that the patient had bubbled in one of the reasons for seeking treatment as being due to "antisocial concerns" when he meant to indicate he was seeking treatment for "social phobic" concerns. The individual had also noticed an improvement in his social anxiety since starting a medication, but was not sure if he should answer questions about how he felt when he first sought treatment or at the time when he was beginning to feel better. This problem with knowing how to answer was compounded by his obsessive–compulsive disorder. He also believed that the optimism that he experienced when he took the test due to beginning to feel better and his desire to please the therapist may have caused him to be viewed as trying to fake good, as there was significant discordance in many of his responses.

■ PSYCHOMETRIC TESTING AND MALINGERING IN A LEGAL CONTEXT

If a clinician is later asked to comment on or use previously obtained therapeutic test results, such as in a forensic case, it is crucial that the clinician understands the context in which the original tests were obtained (e.g., therapy versus forensic evaluation). Unexpected inconsistencies between earlier and later tests, with no significant intervening event, raise a question of malingering either in the past or currently. If testing is compared, individuals comparing the testing need to ensure that they are comparing similar data and versions of the examination and, if possible, are evaluating the raw data, not simply a previous interpretation. Just as patients and lawyers may be tempted to skew a patient's presentation, it is also possible for psychologists, intentionally or unintentionally, to interpret psychometric results in different ways (i.e., previous report bias, desire to please the individual who referred the case, or preconceived ideas about the effect of a particular illness) (Bauer & McCaffrey, 2006; Mittenberg et al., 2002).

The amount of forensic work currently being done by neuropsychologists is growing, with approximately 95% of neuropsychologists reporting that at least some portion of their practice is forensic in 2001, up from 68% in 1991. Lawyers are the third most common referral source for neuropsychologists after neurologists and psychiatrists. Seventy-five percent of lawyers report they choose neuropsychologists to be involved in their cases based on recommendations from other lawyers (Essig, Mittenberg, Petersen, Strauman, & Cooper, 2001). This puts considerable pressure on the neuropsychologist to please the referring lawyer in order to maintain or grow an ever-important source of revenue and may lead to a conscious or unconscious desire to skew the interpretation of data.

■ WHAT TESTING TO OBTAIN

If psychometric testing is used to evaluate malingering, it is important that the test has validity scales or is specifically designed to look for malingering and/or poor effort. Psychometric tests that generally do well in this capacity are multiple-question tests, such as the MMPI-2 or MCMI-III, which have several scales to assess consistency and validity. In addition, the MMPI-2 also has scales, such as the Back-Page Infrequency scale (F_B), Variable Response Inconsistency (VRIN) scale, and True Response Inconsistency (TRIN) scale, that evaluate variance suggesting fatigue or a bubbling error versus a pattern more suggestive of overt malingering (Hall & Hall, 2007). Also, the MMPI-2 has a cutoff if a certain number of questions are not answered, which can be a not-so-subtle way to avoid defining symptoms or to invalidate the test, making it difficult for the evaluator to draw conclusions (Hall & Hall, 2007).

Also beneficial are forced choice tests of memory or ability. Forced choice tests are not "yes/no" rating scales but are tests that require an examinee to "make a choice" between two stimuli, one of which is correct and one of which is false. These tests in general operate on the principle that a score of 50% indicates random guessing, better than 50% indicates some degree of effort, and scores less than 50% indicate that individuals are intentionally trying to mislead, since they are scoring less than chance. Forced choice tests are also effective because malingerers often do not understand that even people with severe deficits (i.e., head trauma or traumatic amnesia) will score better than chance (Bernard et al., 1996; Jelicic, Merckelbach, Candel, & Geraerts, 2007; Leng & Parkin, 1995; Suhr, 2002). Examples of forced choice tests include the Test of Memory Malingering (TOMM) and the

Victoria Symptom Validity Test (VSVT) (Slick, Tan, Strauss, Mateer, Harnadek, & Sherman, 2003; Tan, Slick, Strauss, & Hultsch, 2002).

In general, forced choice tests do best at predicting people who are unsophisticated malingerers. In a study by Tan et al. (2002) that evaluated strategies used by untrained malingerers (e.g., not coached), most individuals instructed to fake head trauma on the TOMM, VSVT, and Word Memory Test (WMT) attempted to do so by feigning memory loss. All of the uncoached individuals instructed to feign head injury were detected. Individuals who have a basic understanding of the concept of these tests may be able to successfully malinger. In a study by DenBoer and Hall (2007), 40% of individuals coached about the TOMM were able to successfully avoid detection (e.g., indicated adequate effort), whereas only 20% of uncoached individuals were able to avoid detection. Of note, the individuals who were simulators, who displayed adequate effort, still generally scored lower than controls who had traumatic brain injury. A study by Powell, Gfeller, Hendricks, and Sharland (2004) found that the TOMM was harder to successfully malinger than the Denboer and Hall study found, with the TOMM correctly categorizing normal controls, traumatic brain injury patients, and coached simulators 96% of the time. The study by Powell et al. did, however, find that the TOMM best detected simulators coached about illness symptoms, but was less effective detecting individuals coached about the principle/theory of the test.

Another category of test is the simple memory test. This is an instrument that when initially presented looks complicated and difficult for the evaluee to remember, but in actuality is not. Malingerers often perform very poorly on this type of instrument due to their naivety about the simplicity of the task. An example of such an instrument is the Rey 15-Item Test that requires an individual to remember 15 objects, a task that initially seems to be difficult, but in fact is simpler than it appears due to the grouping of objects (Reznek, 2005).

Studies have shown that individuals who are able to avoid detection by validity scales have higher IQs (Pelfrey, 2004; Steffan, Kroner, & Morgan, 2007). They are better able to understand validity assessment measures, have the concentration necessary to keep track of past responses, and appreciate how two seemingly different questions may measure a similar concept. Although it takes effort to successfully malinger on psychometric tests, it is possible to do, particularly when only a single test is administered. In a review of tests that are effort based in a population suffering from traumatic brain injury, Lynch (2004) recommended that if malingering or poor effort is suspected, then at least two measures should be used to verify such concerns. In a survey of the members of the National Association of Neuropsychologists (NAN), the five most common measures used to assess effort or response bias were the TOMM, MMPI-2 F-K ratio, MMPI-2 FBS, Rey 15-Item Test, and California Verbal Learning Test (Sharland & Gfeller 2007). Clinicians must remember that a normal test result does not rule out malingering or exaggeration, it just does not provide evidence to support that it is occurring.

Although, in general, psychometric testing can be beneficial in detecting patients who are malingering symptoms of illness, not all forms of "psychometric testing" will aid in this function. For example, some screening tests/instruments/tools can actually make it easier for people to malinger an illness. These tests use checklists with cutoff scores, but have no or questionable internal validity scales (Elhai et al., 2005; Etcoff & Kampfer, 1996; Hall & Hall, 2006, 2007; Lees-Haley & Dunn, 1994; Rosen, Sawchuk, Atkins, Brown, Price, & Lees-Haley, 2006). Lees-Haley and Dunn(1994) found that the diagnoses of major depression, posttraumatic stress disorder, generalized anxiety disorder, and mild traumatic brain injury could be readily malingered by naive simulators when screened with checklist-type instruments. In their study, 97% of the simulators were able to successfully malinger depression, 97% generalized anxiety, 86% PTSD, and 63% mild head injury.

The well-known forensic psychiatrist, Dr. Philip Resnick, who has done extensive work in the field of malingering, often tells a story in his malingering workshops about how checklist screening tests can aid or be abused by a malingerer (Resnick, 2005). In the 1980s, a Veterans Administration hospital in the northwestern United States ran an advertisement listing the symptoms of PTSD in the local newspaper. The purpose of the advertisement was to encourage veterans with symptoms of PTSD to come to the hospital to be evaluated for treatment and eligibility for disability payments. More than 200 Vietnam veterans came to be assessed. Four of the veterans arrived with their "Vietnam quilts," which they presented as a sign of their PTSD. It turned out that there was a typo in the original newspaper advertisement soliciting participation. Instead of "survivor's guilt" being listed as a symptom, it read "survivor's quilt." If symptom checklist screens are used, they should be considered solely for diagnostic purposes and should not be considered as a reliable tool for detecting malingering in a clinical setting.

In addition to classic psychometric testing, there are also standardized interviews that combine the clinical interview with a scoring sheet. The standardized interviews are helpful in that they include a direct clinical component and provide an ability to perform interrater consistency testing and reliability assessments based on a standardized scoring system. Examples of this type of testing include the Clinician-Administered PTSD Scale (CAPS) and the Structured Interview of Reported Symptoms (SIRS) (Hall & Hall, 2006, 2007).

■ INFORMING ABOUT VALIDITY SCALES AND THE ISSUES OF COACHING

Before administering psychometric testing in a clinical situation, it is important to inform the patient why the tests are being obtained for both clinical reasons as well as to meet ethical requirements for valid informed consent (Iverson, 2006; Johnson & Lesniak-Karpiak, 1997; Sullivan, Keane, & Deffenti, 2001). It may not be enough to just tell the patient that it is a "routine" part of a clinician's practice or that it is required for a thorough evaluation. The patient needs to be informed that the test is to help clarify diagnosis, obtain insight into treatment, and identify strengths/weaknesses or personality response styles. During this discussion, a difficult ethical question for clinicians may arise: Should clinicians in general inform the patient that validity scales are present on many psychometric examinations (Iverson, 2006)? Some clinicians do, citing ethical concerns such as informed consent, and some clinicians do not, citing ethical reasons relating to test integrity

(Iverson, 2006; Johnson & Lesniak-Karpiak, 1997; Sullivan et al., 2001; Youngjohn, Lees-Haley, & Binder, 1999).

It is clear that being informed about validity scales can change the response patterns of individuals who have been instructed to malinger (Johnson & Lesniak-Karpiak, 1997; Youngjohn et al., 1999). Suhr and Gunstad (2000) found that simply warning simulated malingerers that some of the tests being given had validity scales effected the degree to which the warned malingering group performed and reduced their detection rate. Although the group, which was warned that some of the psychometric tests that they were to be given detected malingering, did worse than controls with head trauma, the warned malingerers did better than another group of malingerers that was not warned. On the particular forced choice test used, with cutoff scores designed for maximum specificity, 31.6% of the uncoached malingerers were detected whereas only 6.5% of the warned malingerers were detected. Suhr and Gunstad concluded that warning examinees about malingering allows them to be better malingerers (i.e., better able to avoid detection). However, a study by King and Sullivan (2009) found that individuals who were instructed to malinger on a personality inventory test and who were informed that the test can assess for malingering were found to fake bad less often and frequently approximated responses given by the normal control group. King and Sullivan concluded that warning about a test's ability to detect malingering "complement[ed] existing malingering detection methods." Further research is needed on how deterrence theory affects malingering, on what the optimal warning for reduction of malingering should be, and on the types of tests for which warnings are most appropriate and effective (Sullivan & Richer, 2002).

Youngjohn et al. (1999), in a commentary on warning about validity scales, advocate taking a very limited approach to direct warnings. They encourage testers, whether in a forensic or treatment situation, to ask only "if there is anything limiting [the evaluee's] ability to answer all questions accurately to the best of their knowledge, or anything besides their injury limiting their ability to put forth their best effort on performance tests." Youngjohn et al. also encourage testers to encourage evaluees only to "put forth their best effort" if there is a question of malingering or poor effort during the examination. Even if warnings do diminish the temptation to malinger, Youngjohn et al. believe that this will interfere with the purpose of the evaluations, especially in forensic or disability settings. Their rationale is that the malingerers have often already malingered in front of other evaluators before the testing or will malinger to other evaluators after the testing, so even if deterrence theory does work and diminishes malingering on the psychometric testing, the "valid testing" will then be used to justify the accuracy of the malingered behavior demonstrated elsewhere.

A survey of neuropsychologists who perform neuropsychological testing of litigants in lawsuits found that it was common for them, 79% of the time, to include at least one test to assess malingering, such as the Rey 15-Item Test or the Test of Memory Malingering, as well as referring to validity scales from "standard neuropsychological tests" (Slick, Tan, Strauss, & Hultsch, 2004). Of the individuals surveyed, only 50% routinely gave warnings prior to performing testing that "suboptimal performance may be detected." However, if suboptimal performance were suspected, approximately 50% would encourage evaluees to put forth a "good effort." Less than 25% of the neuropsychologists would directly confront or warn the evaluees who they thought were malingering or would terminate the examination early due to concerns of malingering. What may be surprising for clinicians who are not familiar with how psychometric tests are given in a legal context was that even when malingering was strongly suspected, that term was rarely used in the official report. Twelve percent of neuropsychologists reported that they never use the term "malingering" in any legal reports. Although almost all reports had some indication of malingering or diminished effort, this was usually addressed by commenting about whether the "test results were valid or invalid," pointing out inconsistencies of symptoms compared to the severity of the injury or that there were "indications of exaggeration." The reluctance to directly suggest that an individual is malingering might be better understood from the fact that making a claim of malingering opens up the neuropsychologist to malpractice claims, since a claim of malingering implies a specific intent, which may or may not be clearly elucidated from just testing.

Although there is debate about whether general warnings about validity measures are ethical, it is clearly unethical to describe the way these scales work to individuals who are going to be tested. The ethical and legal violation is clear in the sense that many of these instruments are copyrighted and protected intellectual properties. There are ethical guidelines established by professional organizations such as the American Psychological Association (APA), which identify this behavior as a clear ethical violation (Axelrod et al., 2000). For clinicians to give the test, they enter into an agreement with the developer not to release the content of questions or reveal the intent of questions. This is done to maintain the integrity of the tests both as a clinical tool and to diminish the chances of successful malingering. The APA and other professional organizations are concerned that if individuals are able to successfully malinger when tested, then the public will perceive the field to be flawed, that resources for the legitimately ill will become unavailable, and that the integrity of research and diagnostic criteria will be called into question.

■ TEST INTEGRITY

Maintaining test integrity has become harder in the digital age. Information about these tests is readily available to the general public on the Internet (Bauer & McCaffrey, 2006; Hall & Hall, 2006, 2007). Bootleg computer copies of the test and interpretation programs can be obtained on the Internet (e.g., chat room connections, file transfer programs). Books that discuss most aspects regarding psychometric testing, which previously were readily available or used only by professionals, can now be purchased at online bookstores by anyone.

Support groups are another source of information about various diseases and the findings encountered on neuropsychological testing. At best, support groups are organizations that may be unwittingly helping individuals malinger while they fulfill their mission of providing valuable services to individuals who are legitimately suffering. At worst, there are groups whose sub-rosa purpose is to provide malingerers with information about symptom clusters/presentations and information about how to "beat" tests and obtain compensation (Bohr, 1995; Youngjohn et al., 1999). Unfortunately, this ease of availability of information, whether from the Internet or old-fashioned person-to-person communication, makes it difficult to maintain the integrity of many tests and also increases the cost of testing since new versions of the test need to be created sooner than otherwise needed to maintain test validity.

Although concerns about the integrity of validity scales may sound academic, many studies have shown that the most successful way to malinger on psychometric tests is not necessarily to have large amounts of clinical information about an illness, but rather to have a better technical understanding of how a test works (Brennan, Meyer, David, Pella, Hill, & Gouvier, 2009; Powell et al., 2004; Rogers, Bagby, & Chakraborty,1993; Rüsseler et al., 2008; Storm & Graham, 2000). In a study by Brennan et al. (2009) looking at tests that measured effort, seven of the 14 tests were susceptible to being successfully malingered by coaching. A study by Rüsseler et al. (2008) found, it was relatively easy to detect individuals who had been coached with symptom information because they frequently reported more symptoms at greater severity than was commonly seen. The group that was hardest to detect involved individuals who were coached on detection methods because they did not report as many severe symptoms and were less likely to inappropriately answer easy questions. Similar results were found in a study by Storm and Graham (2000), where malingerers were coached on strategies to avoid detection by validity scales. The result was that the coached malingerers scored lower on the MMPI-2 F scale than the uncoached malingerers, but still had higher F_p scores compared to actual patients.

In addition to information provided to patients, clinicians must be circumspect about providing information to other professionals, particularly lawyers and paralegals (Axelrod et al., 2000; Essig et al., 2001; Hall & Hall, 2007; Lees-Haley & Courtney, 2000; Wetter & Corrigan, 1995). The American Psychological Association's Code of Ethics sections, on General Principles (Principle A: Beneficence and Nonmaleficence), section 1.01 (Misuse of Psychologists' Work) and section 9.11 (Maintaining Test Security) proscribes participation in activities in which the psychologist's skills will be misused by others and requires "Psychologists [to] make reasonable efforts to maintain the integrity and security of test materials and other assessment techniques" (Ethical principles of psychologists and code of conduct, 2003). In a survey by Essig et al. (2001), lawyers reported they typically spend about an hour preparing their clients for neuropsychological evaluations and commonly covered test content, detection of malingering strategies, and symptoms associated with the claimed illness during that time. In a survey of lawyers by Wetter and Corrigan (1995), most lawyers believed that it was appropriate to provide clients with at least a moderate amount of information about the psychometric testing they might undergo and some believed, it was appropriate to provide as much information as possible about the specific psychometric testing. At best, many lawyers believe that providing information may help prevent individuals from attempting to engage in unneeded/harmful attempts to exaggerate. At worst, lawyers may be "coaching clients" about how to take the tests (Essig et al., 2001; Hall & Hall, 2007; Lees-Haley & Courtney, 2000; Rüsseler et al., 2008. Wetter & Corrigan, 1995; Youngjohn et al., 1999).

The legal profession operates under a different code of ethics than do healthcare professionals. This statement is not meant to impugn lawyers' character, but simply to define the fact that the legal code of ethics is predicated on an adversarial system in which advancing a position or "theory" to improve the clients' best interest [e.g., American Bar association Model Rules of Professional Conduct (2009) "As advocate, a lawyer zealously asserts the client's position under the rules of the adversary system"] may take precedent over elements of "truth" (Group for the Advancement of Psychiatry. Report 131). The ethics of healthcare providers, although also representing the patient, are also responsive to society at large, as evident from the development of obligations to third parties such as Tarasoff warnings, child abuse reporting, and infectious disease reporting requirements (Hall & Resnick, 2008). It is this ethical obligation to society at large, which restricts healthcare professionals from breaching the security of various instruments. Lawyers do not have the legal, societal, or moral obligation to maintain the integrity of psychological tests, as it is the clinician who has the licensing agreement with the test originator, not the lawyer.

In general, it is our belief that it is ethical and proper to inform examinees that some psychological tests include methods to detect exaggeration or malingering. This may prevent individuals who are truly seeking treatment from exaggerating deficits in order to be believed. It may also help prevent honest patients from minimizing illness to avert some loss or cover some defect. As for the issue of deterrence theory in forensic practice, in our experience there is a high likelihood that individuals intending to malinger will already be aware of validity and other scales due to interactions with their lawyers, "support groups," or their own research on the Internet or elsewhere about these tests. Therefore, giving a general warning is not likely to greatly change the behavior of an individual who already plans to malinger. Warnings may, however, help discourage litigants, who because of anxiety and/or the stress of the legal process are tempted to exaggerate.

■ CONCLUSIONS

Unfortunately, there is no easy, readily available answer for the clinician trying to decide about and reconcile often-conflicting information regarding malingering as it applies to an examinee seated before him or her. With the forthcoming DSM-5 scheduled to be published in 2013, this task is likely to become more difficult. The DSM-5 promises to use new diagnostic schemes and dimensions to assess and categorize illnesses, as well as becoming a "living document" that will continuously update and redefine diagnostic criteria every 2 years. These changes will further complicate psychometric validity and illness research and make comparing new and old test data more difficult.

The best advice for clinicians and other evaluators is to treat or assess the total individual, not simply their numbers. As the famous neurologist, Charcot, warned his students in the 1800s, "to learn how to unveil simulation in such cases (neurological symptoms that did not seem to correspond to normal patterns), at the very least, one must have completely studied the real condition in the greatest and most serious detail . . . and to know it in all its various forms" (Goetz, 2007) (Table 16.6). Although psychometric testing can be helpful in determining if an individual is malingering, it is important to remember that the instruments never make the diagnosis of malingering. What testing can provide is tangible results and probabilities that are highly suggestive of malingering. Psychometric testing can indicate that an individual is responding in a way that suggests that they are trying to appear sicker or better than they actually are, but the scales cannot tell the clinician what the motivations of the individual are. In the end, the diagnosis of malingering has to be made by the clinician based on multiple sources of information (e.g., clinical interview, substantiated history, situation in which

TABLE 16.6 *Commonly Seen Presentations Suggestive for Malingering of Common Conditions*

General—Displays symptoms of illness more at the beginning of the interview than as the interview progresses; Calls attention to symptoms or "thrusts forward" symptoms with explanation of causes; No improvement in severity of symptoms over time; Lists multiple problems but does not endorse impotency (exception is lawsuit involving loss of consortium); Recreational activities are not affected; History of unstable employment; History of multiple past lawsuits; Given history of performance or abilities does not match past records such as school or work reports

Amnesia/memory—Only provided examples related to case; Involves recollection, recall, and procedural memory; Able to provide specific examples of times when he or she was not able to remember specific information; Does not believe clues will be helpful for recall; Memory is poorer when it is stated that memory is being tested; Forgets overlearned information such as the colors in the American flag

Concentration—Reports being easily distracted but is able to focus during the interview; Concentration is worse at beginning of the interview and better at the end; Performs noticeably worse when he or she believes concentration is being judged or assessed; Concentration is impaired only for certain nonspecific tasks

Chronic Pain—Nothing alleviates pain symptoms, even temporarily; No position alleviates pain, even temporarily; Pain never changes in character or severity at any time; Reports pain prevents certain activities such as sitting at work but does not affect other similar activities such as long car trips

Delusions—Abrupt onset of delusion; abrupt resolution of delusions when treated; Calls attention to delusions; Conduct not consistent with delusions (e.g., worried he or she is going to be poisoned but does not change eating habits); Bizarre or unusual content without disorganized thoughts

Depression—Does not display distressed facial expressions (e.g., furrowed brow); Frequently focuses on extreme dysphoria, anhedonia, and suicidal thoughts but does not report more subtle symptoms such as diurnal variation in mood, multiple awaking, insomnia, or psychomotor retardation; Objective changes such as psychomotor retardation and weight changes are not observed or recorded in records

Psychosis—Reports continuous symptoms such as hallucinations; Auditory hallucinations are reported as vague or inaudible, blocked by putting things in ears; Hallucinations are not associated with a delusion; No strategies to diminish hallucinations; Not able to describe details of hallucinations such as male voice or female voice; Black and white visual hallucinations; Reports positive symptoms but lacking in terms of negative symptoms reported or observed; Reports severe cognitive deficits related to psychosis; In general, malingerers report visual hallucinations more than auditory hallucinations when feigning psychosis

Posttraumatic Stress Disorder—Describes flashbacks as seeing an event occurring as portrayed in Hollywood rather than feeling it is occurring again; Reports having the exact same dream every night; Frequently reports avoidance symptoms but does not report numbing symptoms; Exaggerates role in initial trauma (e.g., hero of event); Reports extreme symptoms but denies any potential psychotic symptoms the client is seen). Psychometric testing is but one source of this critical mass of information.

Psychometricians will face multiple upcoming challenges in the years to come as they try to maintain the integrity of their tests. New mandates and prohibitions (i.e., HIPAA, electronic medical records) will require that more information be shared with other professionals, including physicians, lawyers, regulators, patients, insurance companies, national databases, and the military, as well as with information obtained by freedom of information suits, and perhaps even the general public (e.g., websites and articles published). It is advisable for clinicians to consider how they should ethically and practically respond to such inquires and interactions before they occur.

References

Axelrod, B., Heilbronner, R., Barth, J., Larrabee, G., Faust, D., Pliskin, N., Fisher, J., & Silver C (2000). Planning and Policy Committee, National Academy of Neuropsychology Test Security: Official position statement of the National Academy of Neuropsychology. Approved 10/5/99. *Archives of Clinical Neuropsychology, 15*, 383–386.

Bagby, R. M., Nicholson, R. A., Bacchiochi, J. R., Ryder, A. G., & Bury, A. S. (2002). The predictive capacity of the MMPI-2 and PAI validity scales and indexes to detect coached and uncoached feigning. *Journal of Personality Assessment, 78*, 69–86.

Bauer, L., & McCaffrey, R. J. (2006). Coverage of the Test of Memory Malingering, Victoria Symptom Validity Test, and Word Memory Test on the Internet: Is test security threatened? *Archives of Clinical Neuropsychology, 21*, 121–126.

Bernard, L. C. (1990). Prospects for faking believable memory deficits on neuropsychological tests and the use of incentives in simulation research. *Journal of Clinical and Experimental Neuropsychology, 12*, 715–728.

Bernard, L. C., Houston, W., & Natoli, L. (1993). Malingering on neuropsychological memory tests: Potential objective indicators. *Journal of Clinical Psychology, 49*, 45–53.

Bernard, L. C., McGrath, M. J., & Houston, W. (1996). The differential effects of simulating malingering, closed head injury, and other CNS pathology on the Wisconsin Card Sorting Test: Support for the "pattern of performance" hypothesis. *Archives of Clinical Neuropsychology, 11*, 231–245.

Bianchini, K. J., Curtis, K. L., & Greve, K. W. (2006). Compensation and malingering in traumatic brain injury: A dose-response relationship? *The Clinical Neuropsychologist, 20*, 831–847.

Bohr, T. W. (1995). Fibromyalgia syndrome and myofascial pain syndrome. Do they exist? *Neurologic Clinics, 13*, 365–384.

Boone, K. B. (2007). Commentary on "Cogniform disorder and cogniform condition: proposed diagnoses for excessive cognitive symptoms" by Dean C. Delis and Spencer R. Wetter. *Archives of Clinical Neuropsychology, 22*, 675–679.

Boone, K. B. (2008a). Fixed belief in cognitive dysfunction despite normal neuropsychological scores: Neurocognitive hypochondriasis? *The Clinical Neuropsychologist, 16*, 1–21.

Boone, K. B. (2008b). The need for continuous and comprehensive sampling of effort/response bias during neuropsychological examinations. *The Clinical Neuropsychologist, 22*, 1–13.

Boone, K. B., & Lu, P. H. (1999). Impact of somatoform symptomatology on credibility of cognitive performance. *The Clinical Neuropsychologist, 13*, 414–419.

Boone, K. B., & Lu, P. (2003). Noncredible cognitive performance in the context of severe brain injury. *The Clinical Neuropsychologist, 17*, 244–254.

Boone, K. B., Victor, T. L., Wen, J., Razani, J., & Pontón, M. (2007). The association between neuropsychological scores and ethnicity, language, and acculturation variables in a large patient population. *Archives of Clinical Neuropsychology, 22*, 355–365.

Brennan, A. M., Meyer, S., David, E., Pella, R., Hill, B. D., & Gouvier, W. D. (2009). The vulnerability to coaching across measures of effort. *The Clinical Neuropsychologist, 23*, 314–328.

Caruso, K. A., Benedek, D. M., Auble, P. M., & Bernet, W. (2003). Concealment of psychopathology in forensic evaluations: A pilot study of intentional and uninsightful dissimulators. *The Journal of the American Academy of Psychiatry and the Law, 31*, 444–450.

Cato, M. A., Brewster, J., Ryan, T., & Giuliano, A. J. (2002). Coaching and the ability to simulate mild traumatic brain injury symptoms. *The Clinical Neuropsychologist, 16*, 524–535.

Dean, A. C., Boone, K. B., Kim, M. S., Curiel, A. R., Martin, D. J., Victor, T. L., Zeller, M. A., & Lang, Y. K. (2008a). Examination of the impact of ethnicity on the Minnesota Multiphasic Personality Inventory-2 (MMPI-2) Fake Bad Scale. *The Clinical Neuropsychologist, 22*, 1054–1060.

Dean, A. C., Victor, T. L., Boone, K. B., & Arnold, G. (2008b). The relationship of IQ to effort test performance. *The Clinical Neuropsychologist, 22*, 705–722.

Dean, A. C., Victor, T. L., Boone, K. B., Philpott, L. M., & Hess, R. A. (2008c). Dementia and effort test performance. *The Clinical Neuropsychologist, 8*, 1–20.

DenBoer, J. W., & Hall, S. (2007). Neuropsychological test performance of successful brain injury simulators. *The Clinical Neuropsychologist, 21*, 943–955.

Deshields, T. L., Tait, R. C., Gfeller, J. D., & Chibnall, J. T. (1995). Relationship between social desirability and self-report in chronic pain patients. *The Clinical Journal of Pain, 11*, 189–193.

DuAlba, L., & Scott, R. L. (1993). Somatization and malingering for workers' compensation applicants: A cross-cultural MMPI study. *Journal of Clinical Psychology, 49*, 913–917.

Dunn, J. T., Lees-Haley, P. R., Brown, R. S., Williams, C. W., & English, L. T. (1995). Neurotoxic complaint base rates of personal injury claimants: Implications for neuropsychological assessment. *Journal of Clinical Psychology, 51*, 577–584.

Elhai, J. D., Gray, M. J., Naifeh, J. A., Butcher, J. J., Davis, J. L., Falsetti, S. A., & Best, C. L. (2005). Utility of the trauma symptom inventory's atypical response scale in detecting malingered post-traumatic stress disorder. *Assessment, 12*, 210–219.

Essig, S. M., Mittenberg, W., Petersen, R. S., Strauman, S., & Cooper, J. T. (2001). Practices in forensic neuropsychology: Perspectives of neuropsychologists and trial attorneys. *Archives of Clinical Neuropsychology, 16*, 271–291.

Etcoff, L. M., & Kampfer, K. M. (1996). Practical guidelines in the use of symptom validity and other psychological tests to measure malingering and symptom exaggeration in traumatic brain injury cases. *Neuropsychology Review, 6*, 171–201.

Ethical principles of psychologists and code of conduct. American Psychological Association, Effective date June 1, 2003. Retrieved on April 28, 2009, from http://www.apa.org/ethics/code2002.html#1_01.

Finset, A., Anke, A. W., Hofft, E., Roaldsen, K. S., Pillgram-Larsen, J., & Stanghelle, J. K. (1999). Cognitive performance in multiple trauma patients 3 years after injury. *Psychosomatic Medicine, 61*, 576–583.

Fox, D. D., Gerson, A., & Lees-Haley, P. R. (1995). Interrelationship of MMPI-2 validity scales in personal injury claims. *Journal of Clinical Psychology, 51*, 42–47.

Frazier, T. W., Youngstrom, E. A., Naugle, R. I., Haggerty, K. A., & Busch, R. M. (2007). The latent structure of cognitive symptom exaggeration on the Victoria Symptom Validity Test. *Archives of Clinical Neuropsychology, 22*, 197–211.

Gasquoine, P. G. (2001). Research in clinical neuropsychology with Hispanic American participants: A review. *The Clinical Neuropsychologist, 15*, 2–12.

Goetz, C. G. (2007). Charcot and simulated neurologic disease: Attitudes and diagnostic strategies. *Neurology, 69*, 103–109.

Group for the Advancement of Psychiatry. Report 131. (1991). *The mental health professional and the legal system: Chapter 2: The Law and the legal process* (pp. 7–16). Washington, D.C.: American Psychiatric Press.

Hall, R. C., & Hall, R. C. (2001). False allegations: The role of the forensic psychiatrist. *Journal of Psychiatric Practice, 7*, 343–346.

Hall, R. C., & Hall, R. C. (2006). Malingering of PTSD: Forensic and diagnostic considerations, characteristics of malingerers and clinical presentations. *General Hospital Psychiatry, 28*, 525–535.

Hall, R. C., & Hall, R. C. (2007). Detection of malingered PTSD: An overview of clinical, psychometric, and physiological assessment: Where do we stand? *Journal of Forensic Sciences, 52*, 717–725.

Hall, R. C., Hall, R. C., & Chapman, M. J. (2005). Definition, diagnosis, and forensic implications of postconcussional syndrome. *Psychosomatics, 46*, 195–202.

Hall, R. C., & Resnick P. J. (2008). Psychotherapy malpractice: New pitfalls. *Journal of Psychiatric Practice, 14*, 119–121.

Iverson, G. L. (2006). Ethical issues associated with the assessment of exaggeration, poor effort, and malingering. *Applied Neuropsychology, 13*, 77–90.

Jelicic, M., Merckelbach, H., Candel, I., & Geraerts, E. (2007). Detection of feigned cognitive dysfunction using special malinger tests: A simulation study in naïve and coached malingerers. *International Journal of Neuroscience, 117*, 1185–1192.

Johnson, J. L., & Lesniak-Karpiak, K. (1997). The effect of warning on malingering on memory and motor tasks in college samples. *Archives of Clinical Neuropsychology, 12*, 231–238.

Kennepohl, S., Shore, D., Nabors, N., & Hanks, R. (2004). African American acculturation and neuropsychological test performance following traumatic brain injury. *Journal of the International Neuropsychological Society, 10*, 566–577.

Kertzman, S., Reznik, I., Grinspan, H., Shliapnicov, N., Birger, M., Weizman, A., & Kotler, M. (2006). The role of real-time computerized neuropsychological examination in forensic psychiatry practice. *The Israel Journal of Psychiatry and Related Sciences, 43*, 174–180.

King, J., & Sullivan, K. A. (2009). Deterring malingered psychopathology: The effect of warning simulating malingerers. *Behavioral Sciences and the Law, 27*, 35–49.

King, J. H., Sweet, J. J., Sherer, M., Curtiss, G., & Vanderploeg, R. D. (2002). Validity indicators within the Wisconsin Card Sorting Test: Application of new and previously researched multivariate procedures in multiple traumatic brain injury samples. *The Clinical Neuropsychologist, 16*, 506–523.

Lanyon, R. I., Almer, E. R., & Curran, P. J. (1993). Use of biographical and case history data in the assessment of malingering during examination for disability. *Bulletin of the American Academy of Psychiatry and the Law, 21*, 495–503.

Larrabee, G. J. (2003). Exaggerated MMPI-2 symptom report in personal injury litigants with malingered neurocognitive deficit. *Archives of Clinical Neuropsychology, 18*, 673–686.

Larrabee, G. J. (2008). Aggregation across multiple indicators improves the detection of malingering: Relationship to likelihood ratios. *The Clinical Neuropsychologist, 22,* 666–679.

Lees-Haley, P. R. (1997). MMPI-2 base rates for 492 personal injury plaintiffs: Implications and challenges for forensic assessment. *Journal of Clinical Psychology, 53,* 745–755.

Lees-Haley, P. R., & Brown, R. S. (1993). Neuropsychological complaint base rates of 170 personal injury claimants. *Archives of Clinical Neuropsychology, 8,* 203–209.

Lees-Haley, P. R., & Courtney, J. C. (2000). Disclosure of tests and raw test data to the courts: A need for reform. *Neuropsychology Review, 10,* 169–174.

Lees-Haley, P. R., & Dunn, J. T. (1994). The ability of naive subjects to report symptoms of mild brain injury, post-traumatic stress disorder, major depression, and generalized anxiety disorder. *Journal of Clinical Psychology, 50,* 252–256.

Lees-Haley, P. R., & Fox, D. D. (1990). Neuropsychological false positives in litigation: Trail making test findings. *Perceptual and Motor Skills, 70,* 1379–1382.

Lees-Haley, P. R., & Fox, D. D. (2004). Commentary on Butcher, Arbisi, Atlis, and McNulty (2003) on the Fake Bad Scale. *Archives of Clinical Neuropsychology, 19,* 333–336.

Lees-Haley, P. R., Williams, C. W., & English, L. T. (1996). Response bias in self-reported history of plaintiffs compared with nonlitigating patients. *Psychological Reports, 79,* 811–818.

Lees-Haley, P. R., Williams, C. W., Zasler, N. D., Marguilies, S., English, L. T., & Stevens, K. B. (1997). Response bias in plaintiffs' histories. *Brain Injury, 11,* 791–799.

Leininger, B. E., Kreutzer, J. S., & Hill, M. R. (1991). Comparison of minor and severe head injury emotional sequelae using the MMPI. *Brain Injury, 5,* 199–205.

Leng, N. R., & Parkin, A. J. (1995). The detection of exaggerated or simulated memory disorder by neuropsychological methods. *Journal of Psychosomatic Research, 39,* 767–776.

Locke, D. E., Smigielski, J. S., Powell, M. R., & Stevens, S. R. (2008). Effort issues in post-acute outpatient acquired brain injury rehabilitation seekers. *NeuroRehabilitation, 23,* 273–281.

Loring, D. W., Lee, G. P., & Meador, K. J. (2005). Victoria Symptom Validity Test performance in non-litigating epilepsy surgery candidates. *Journal of Clinical and Experimental Neuropsychology, 27,* 610–617.

Lynch, W. J. (2004). Determination of effort level, exaggeration, and malingering in neurocognitive assessment. *The Journal of Head Trauma Rehabilitation, 19,* 277–283.

Malingering Manual. (2009). Retrieved April 20, 2009, from http://www.malingerersmanual.com/index2.asp.

Marshall, P., & Happe, M. (2007). The performance of individuals with mental retardation on cognitive tests assessing effort and motivation. *The Clinical Neuropsychologist, 21,* 826–840.

Mittenberg, W., Patton, C., Canyock, E. M., & Condit, D. C. (2002). Base rates of malingering and symptom exaggeration. *Journal of Clinical and Experimental Neuropsychology, 24,* 1094–1102.

Model Rules of Professional Conduct: Preamble and Scope, American Bar Association Center for Professional Responsibility. Retrieved April 28, 2009, from http://www.abanet.org/cpr/mrpc/mrpc_toc.html.

Mohíno-Justes, S., Dolado-Cuello, J., Arimany-Manso, J., Ortega-Monasterio, L., Cuquerella-Fuentes, A., Vilardell-Molas, J., & Planchat-Teruel L. M. (2004). Relationship between malingered psychometric profiles and personality styles in prisoners. *Actas Españolas de Psiquiatría, 32,* 264–268.

Morasco, B. J., Gfeller, J. D., & Elder, K. A. (2007). The utility of the NEO-PI-R validity scales to detect response distortion: A comparison with the MMPI-2. *Journal of Personality Assessment, 88*, 276–283.

Pelfrey, W. V., Jr. (2004). The relationship between malingerers' intelligence and MMPI-2 knowledge and their ability to avoid detection. *International Journal of Offender Therapy and Comparative Criminology, 48*, 649–663.

Powell, M. R., Gfeller, J. D., Hendricks, B. L., & Sharland, M. (2004). Detecting symptom- and test-coached simulators with the test of memory malingering. *Archives of Clinical Neuropsychology, 19*, 693–702.

Rankin, E. J., Gilner, F. H., Gfeller, J. D., & Katz, B. M. (1994). Anxiety states and sustained attention in a cognitively intact elderly sample: Preliminary results. *Psychological Reports, 75*, 1176–1178.

Resnick, P. J. (1993). Defrocking the fraud: The detection of malingering. *The Israel Journal of Psychiatry and Related Sciences, 30*, 93–101.

Resnick P. J. (2005). *The detection of malingered mental illness.* Presented at the American Psychiatric Association's 159th Annual Meeting, Toronto, Canada, May 23.

Reznek, L. (2005). The Rey 15-item memory test for malingering: A meta-analysis. *Brain Injury, 19*, 539–43.

Rogers, R., Bagby, R. M., & Chakraborty, D. (1993). Feigning schizophrenic disorders on the MMPI-2: Detection of coached simulators. *Journal of Personality Assessment, 60*, 215–226.

Rosen, G. M., Sawchuk, C. N., Atkins, D. C., Brown, M., Price, J. R., & Lees-Haley, P. R. (2006). Risk of false positives when identifying malingered profiles using the trauma symptom inventory. *Journal of Personality Assessment, 86*, 329–333.

Rüsseler, J., Brett, A., Klaue, U., Sailer, M., & Münte, T. F. (2008). The effect of coaching on the simulated malingering of memory impairment. *BMC Neurology, 7*, 1–14.

Sellbom, M., & Bagby, R. M. (2008). The validity and utility of the positive presentation management and negative presentation management scales for the Revised NEO Personality Inventory. *Assessment, 15*, 165–176.

Sharland, M. J., & Gfeller, J. D. (2007). A survey of neuropsychologists' beliefs and practices with respect to the assessment of effort. *Archives of Clinical Neuropsychology, 22*, 213–223.

Slick, D. J., Tan, J. E., Strauss, E. H., & Hultsch, D. F. (2004). Detecting malingering: A survey of experts' practices. *Archives of Clinical Neuropsychology, 19*, 465–473.

Slick, D. J., Tan, J. E., Strauss, E., Mateer, C. A., Harnadek, M., & Sherman, E. M. (2003). Victoria Symptom Validity Test scores of patients with profound memory impairment: Nonlitigants case studies. *The Clinical Neuropsychologist, 17*, 390–394.

Steffan, J. S., Kroner, D. G., & Morgan, R. D. (2007). Effect of symptom information and intelligence in dissimulation: An examination of faking response styles by inmates on the Basic Personality Inventory. *Assessment, 14*, 22–34.

Storm, J., & Graham, J. R. (2000). Detection of coached general malingering on the MMPI-2. *Psychological Assessment, 12*, 158–165.

Suhr, J. A. (2002). Malingering, coaching, and the serial position effect. *Archives of Clinical Neuropsychology, 17*, 69–77.

Suhr, J. A., & Gunstad, J. (2000). The effects of coaching on the sensitivity and specificity of malingering measures. *Archives of Clinical Neuropsychology, 15*, 415–424.

Sullivan, K., Keane, B., & Deffenti, C. (2001). Malingering on the RAVLT. Part I. Deterrence strategies. *Archives of Clinical Neuropsychology, 16*, 627–641.

Sullivan, K., & Richer, C. (2002). Malingering on subjective complaint tasks: An exploration of the deterrent effects of warning. *Archives of Clinical Neuropsychology, 17*, 691–708.

Tan, J. E., Slick, D. J., Strauss, E., & Hultsch, D. F. (2002). How'd they do it? Malingering strategies on symptom validity tests. *The Clinical Neuropsychologist, 16*, 495–505.

Tsushima, W. T., & Tsushima, V. G. (2001). Comparison of the Fake Bad Scale and other MMPI-2 validity scales with personal injury litigants. *Assessment, 8*, 205–212.

Tsushima, W. T., & Tsushima, V. G. (2009). Comparison of MMPI-2 validity scales among compensation-seeking Caucasian and Asian American medical patients. *Assessment, 16*, 159–164.

Vanderploeg, R. D., & Curtiss, G. (2001). Malingering assessment: Evaluation of validity of performance. *NeuroRehabilitation, 16*, 245–251.

Van Gorp, W. G., Humphrey, L. A., Kalechstein, A. L., Brumm, V. L., McMullen, W. J., Stoddard, M. A., & Pachana, N. A. (1999). How well do standard clinical neuropsychological tests identify malingering? A preliminary analysis. *Journal of Clinical and Experimental Neuropsychology, 21*, 245–250.

Vickery, C. D., Berry, D. T., Dearth, C. S., Vagnini, V. L., Baser, R. E., Cragar, D. E., & Orey S. A. (2004). Head injury and the ability to feign neuropsychological deficits. *Archives of Clinical Neuropsychology, 19*, 37–48.

Victor, T. L., Boone, K. B., Serpa, J. G., Buehler, J., & Ziegler, E. A. (2009). Interpreting the meaning of multiple symptom validity test failure. *The Clinical Neuropsychologist, 23*, 297–313.

Wetter, M., & Corrigan, S. (1995). Providing information to clients about psychological tests: A survey of attorneys' and law students' attitudes. *Professional Psychology, Research and Practice, 26*, 474–477.

Wygant, D. B., Sellbom, M., Ben-Porath, Y. S., Stafford, K. P., Freeman, D. B., & Heilbronner, R. L. (2007). The relation between symptom validity testing and MMPI-2 scores as a function of forensic evaluation context. *Archives of Clinical Neuropsychology, 22*, 89–99.

Youngjohn, J. R., Lees-Haley, P. R., & Binder, L. M. (1999). Comment: Warning malingerers produces more sophisticated malingering. *Archives of Clinical Neuropsychology, 14*, 511–515.

17 Intentional and Unintentional Faking in Education[1]

■ JEREMY BURRUS, BOBBY D. NAEMI,
AND PATRICK C. KYLLONEN

Adam Wheeler enjoyed a distinguished career as a student at Harvard. His accomplishments included winning a research grant, the Hoopes Prize for outstanding scholarly work, and the Winthrop Sargent Prize in English (Guzzardo, 2010). He was also awarded nearly $50,000 in scholarships and other financial aid while at Harvard. Ordinarily, this would be an impressive list of accomplishments. The problem, however, is that each was a product of faking. In fact, faking also led to his acceptance to Harvard as a transfer student in 2007 (Steinberg & Zezima, 2010). Wheeler plagiarized work from university professors, falsified transcript grades and SAT scores, and incorrectly claimed that he had previously attended MIT rather than the institution he actually attended, Bowdoin College in Maine (where he was suspended due to academic dishonesty).

We would not be surprised if "Wheeleresque" faking plots become more common in education in the near future. The increasing pressure to be accepted to top colleges and universities provides a high incentive to fake credentials as a student. Additionally, the recent emphasis on the importance of noncognitive skills in education provides even greater incentive, and more opportunities, for faking. We define faking according to *Dictionary.com's* second definition of faking, "*to conceal the defects of or make appear more attractive, interesting, valuable, etc., usually in order to deceive*" (Dictionary.com, 2010). The first half of this definition is consistent with definitions provided in other chapters in this book. We chose this particular definition, however, because the second half of the definition uses the wording, "*usually* in order to deceive." That is, we believe that if the ultimate goal of countering faking is to more accurately identify someone's true score, then researchers should consider the possibility that scores that appear faked may be artificially inflated for reasons other than intentional faking. Psychological principles of human judgment dictate that self-estimates will often be inflated through *unintentional* faking—especially in the case of noncognitive assessments. As such, in these circumstances, countermeasures against intentional faking, that do not take into account the possibility that faking may be unintentional, may at times be of little use in bringing researchers closer to identifying someone's true score.

In this chapter we first briefly discuss the importance of noncognitive skills in education, skills that are perhaps easier to fake than other information commonly gathered from students and teachers. The remainder of the chapter is essentially

---

1. The views expressed here are those of the authors and do not reflect the views of the Educational Testing Service.

divided into two major topics: intentional faking and unintentional faking. The intentional faking section focuses on techniques for countering intentional faking in education and some ways in which these techniques are being used in applied settings. Finally, the chapter concludes with a discussion of unintentional faking, when it may occur, and ways in which it may be minimized.

■ NONCOGNITIVE SKILLS IN EDUCATION

As the importance of measuring 21st century skills becomes clearer, the need to develop faking-resistant assessments of these skills will become necessary. The Partnership for 21st Century Skills, a U.S.-based organization composed of leading corporations and research institutions, identifies numerous abilities and skills that will be required of students in the 21st century and beyond, a number of which (e.g., collaboration, flexibility, initiative, social skills, leadership) are noncognitive skills. These noncognitive skills have typically been measured through self-report assessments in other fields such as social, personality, and industrial and organizational psychology. As these assessments are applied to students in school and university settings (for example, in selection contexts for higher education), faking will begin to represent an increasing concern for the field of education. There is no doubt that noncognitive skills play an important role in predicting achievement in both school and the workplace, and a large body of literature attests to the impact of noncognitive skills in education and workforce readiness research.

In terms of existing research, several meta-analyses have demonstrated the predictive validity of noncognitive skills (e.g., personality and attitudes) on educational outcomes such as grades, absenteeism, and adjustment (e.g., Crede & Kuncel, 2008; Lafontaine & Monseur, 2007; Noftle & Robins, 2007; Poropat, 2009). Because the scope of the literature on noncognitive constructs in education is too large to thoroughly review in this chapter, we provide just a few notable examples. They are listed in Table 17.1.

For example, *Are They Really Ready to Work?*, a report published by The Conference Board, Partnership for 21st Century Skills, Society for Human Resource Management, and Corporate Voices for Working Families, identified skills that are important and/or will be increasing in importance over the next 5 years as critical to workplace success based on responses from 400+ surveys and 12 interviews with human resources professionals and executives in the business community (Conference Board, 2006). Teamwork was listed as one of the most important personal skills for success in the workplace in the 21st century. Interestingly, this skill was rated more important than skills traditionally taught and assessed by high schools and colleges. That is, teamwork was rated as more important than writing, reading comprehension, English, and math.

Given the large body of evidence supporting the importance of noncognitive variables in education and workforce readiness, assessments of 21st century skills will need to account for potential problems in the assessment of noncognitive skills as a result of faking. Below we briefly discuss self-report methods for assessing noncognitive skills. Next, we discuss several possibilities for countering intentional faking of noncognitive skills.

TABLE 17.1 *Example Findings from Research Investigating the Relation of Noncognitive Constructs to Academic Achievement*

Construct	Example Findings
Agreeableness	Predicts grades at primary education levels (e.g., Poropat, 2009)
Conscientiousness	Predicts grades at all education levels (e.g., Poropat, 2009)
Openness	Predicts grades at primary education levels (e.g., Poropat, 2009)
	Correlated with measures of cognitive ability (e.g., Ackerman and Heggestad, 1997)
Neuroticism	Predicts test scores (e.g., Seipp, 1991)
	Anxiety and impulsiveness facets of Neuroticism are especially predictive of academic performance (e.g., Kuncel et al., 2005).
Study habits	Predicts cumulative GPA and individual course grades in college, controlling for high school grades and standardized test scores (e.g., Crede & Kuncel, 2008)
Study skills	Predicts cumulative GPA and individual course grades in college, controlling for high school grades and standardized test scores (e.g., Crede & Kuncel, 2008)
	Predicts college retention (e.g., Robbins, Lauver, Le, Davis, Langley, & Carlstrom, 2004)
Study motivation	Predicts cumulative GPA and individual course grades in college, controlling for high school grades and standardized test scores (e.g., Crede & Kuncel, 2008)
Academic motivation	Predicts cumulative GPA in college (e.g., Robbins et al., 2004)
Academic goals	Predicts college retention (e.g., Robbins et al., 2004)
Self-efficacy	Predicts college retention (e.g., Robbins et al., 2004)
	Predicts cumulative GPA in college (e.g., Robbins et al., 2004)

■ METHODS OF MEASURING NONCOGNITIVE SKILLS

Self-Report Assessments

Self-assessments are the most widely used approach for capturing students' noncognitive characteristics. Self-assessments typically ask individuals to describe themselves by answering a series of standardized questions. The answer format is often a Likert-type rating scale, but other formats may also be used (such as Yes–No or open answer). Typically, questions assessing the same construct are aggregated; this aggregated score serves as an indicator of the relevant noncognitive attribute.

Many issues need to be taken into account when developing a psychometrically sound questionnaire, and there is a large literature on such issues (e.g., number of points on a scale, scale point labels, neutral point, alternative ordering; see Krosnick, Judd, & Wittenbrink, 2005). Faking, however, represents a particular concern for self-report assessments, and respondents have the potential to fake their responses to appear more attractive for a variety of reasons (e.g., Griffith, Chmielowski, & Yoshita, 2007; Viswesvaran & Ones, 1999), resulting in decreased validity (Pauls & Crost, 2005).

Despite the obvious pitfalls regarding the use of self-assessments in educational measures of noncognitive skills, there are several promising methods for collecting self-assessments that may account for faking. These methods include using a multidimensional forced choice format (Stark, Chernyshenko, & Drasgow, 2005), using estimates of how others will respond (Prelec, 2004), using vignettes to anchor the self-assessment (King, Murray, Salomon, & Tandon, 2004), using biographical data (e.g., Mumford & Owens, 1987), situational judgment tests (McDaniel, Morgesen, Finnegan, Campion, & Braverman, 2001), conditional reasoning tests (James, 1998), and other-report ratings. Each of these methods is briefly discussed in the sections that follow, with the caveat that a complete review of each of these topics is outside the scope of this chapter.

Forced Choice

One approach to reducing faking and other response styles is to change the format in which self-assessment statements are presented. Instead of presenting statements individually and asking examinees to indicate their levels of agreement, groups of statements can be organized into blocks. These are then administered to examinees with instructions telling them to choose the statement(s) that are most and/or least descriptive of them. Variations of this theme currently dominate the literature, as researchers explore formats ranging from pairwise preferences to tetrads (e.g., Christiansen, Burns, & Montgomery, 2005; Heggestad, Morrison, Reeve, & McCloy, 2006; Stark et al., 2005).

A common feature of forced choice tests is that the statements composing each block are matched in terms of social desirability so that respondents have a difficult time discerning which answers are better, making faking less effective. A variety of item response theory (IRT) models have also been developed for scoring these items (see Stark, Chernyshenko, & Drasgow, 2010).

Forced choice approaches have been applied in numerous personality assessments in industrial and organizational psychology, and the technique could easily be applied to noncognitive assessments in education. Measuring important 21st century skills such as work ethic and teamwork that might be susceptible to faking with a forced choice approach could be a promising avenue for further assessment development in education.

Bayesian Truth Serum

The Bayesian Truth Serum (BTS) approach is a method that has been proposed to reduce faking and to reward truth-telling (Prelec, 2004). BTS is based on experimental evidence of the false consensus effect in social psychology. The false consensus effect refers to a well-replicated finding that people are likely to overestimate the number of people who share their beliefs. The BTS technique incorporates this phenomenon into a scoring mechanism that rewards those who respond honestly when answering multiple-choice questions about their personal characteristics or opinions. The method requires the respondent to provide not only a personal answer to every question, but also to estimate in percentage terms how other respondents will answer that same question.

The BTS method thus requires that respondents report their own preferences in terms of item choices (e.g., choosing "I work well with teams" over "I work hard") and also asks respondents to estimate the larger population's preferences (e.g., estimating that 70% of the overall population would choose "I work well with teams" over "I work hard" to describe themselves). Prelec argues that respondents who answer questions honestly will tend to overestimate the percentage of other people who agree with them.

Using the previous example, a person who is actually high on teamwork would report that more people prefer to choose the item "I work well with teams" over the item "I work hard" to describe themselves, whereas a person who is faking a high level of teamwork will report less people choosing the "I work well with teams" item than the truthful respondent. By accounting for this discrepancy, the BTS algorithm thus produces an "information" score that penalizes respondents who underestimate those that agree with them.

Prelec and Weaver (2006) provide experimental evidence supporting these claims. For example, one study, simulating lying about gender by changing gender in the data file for some respondents (but keeping other responses intact), showed reduced BTS scores for those respondents. Prelec and Weaver (2006) also demonstrated that BTS information scores were related to more honest responding in a sample of students tested for claiming knowledge and that BTS scores could not be exploited when respondents were instructed to fake.

Prelec (2004) used the following formula to calculate the BTS score for an individual item:

$$\sum_k x_k^r \log \frac{\overline{x}_k}{y_k} + a \sum_k \overline{x}_k \log \frac{y_k^r}{x_k}, 0 < a.$$

This equation represents the score for respondent r, which is the sum of their information score plus the prediction score. As stated by Prelec, the best prediction score is 0, which is when the prediction by the respondent exactly matches reality. For a complete explanation of this equation, see Prelec (2004).

Although the BTS approach has primarily been used in marketing studies, the technique could easily be applied to noncognitive assessments in education. Forced choice assessments that incorporate the BTS approach could be used to measure specific 21st century skills that are susceptible to faking, such as work ethic. In this way, the BTS approach represents a potentially promising avenue for controlling faking in educational research and practice.

Anchoring Vignettes

Anchoring vignettes typically involve brief descriptions of a hypothetical person or scenario, which are presented to the respondent before completing assessment ratings. The vignette serves as a concrete exemplar that respondents can use to "anchor" their own self-assessments of the concept being measured onto the same scale, based on each of several hypothetical individuals described in the anchoring vignettes (King et al., 2004). In this way, anchoring vignettes are used to control for any bias effects that occur when respondents interpret an item or question in a different or unanticipated way.

An example of a series of vignettes describing a hypothetical mathematics teacher appears in Table 17.2. In this example, the respondent is a mathematics

TABLE 17.2 *Vignettes Describing a Hypothetical Mathematics Teacher*

	Not Very Interested	Not Interested	Neutral	Interested	Very Interested
a. Mr. <name> regularly assigns mathematics homework but does not get the homework back on time for review before examinations. He encourages his students to pursue a career in mathematics, but does not always know the answers to questions. He is often late to class. How interested is Ms. <name> in getting his students to work hard?	☐	☐	☐	☐	☐
b. Ms. <name> assigns mathematics homework only once a week but always gets the answers back on time for review before examinations. She encourages her students to pursue a career in mathematics and always knows the answers to questions. She always arrives at class 5 minutes early. How interested is Ms. <name> in getting her students to work hard?	☐	☐	☐	☐	☐
c. Mr. <name> assigns mathematics homework once a week but does not get the homework back on time for review before examinations. He shows no interest in getting his students to pursue a career in mathematics and seldom knows the answers to questions. He is often late to class. How interested is Mr. <name> in getting his students to work hard?	☐	☐	☐	☐	☐
How interested are you as a mathematics teacher in getting students to work hard?	☐	☐	☐	☐	☐

teacher who rates the performance of a series of hypothetical mathematics teachers, and then makes a self-assessment of his or her own performance as a mathematics teacher that presumably incorporates the information learned from the anchoring vignettes.

In the preceding example, respondents should thus use the vignettes as a basis for determining the appropriate ratings for the teacher's own self-rating.

The technique has gained momentum in policy research, and appears to address problems concerning cultural comparability. Buckley (2008) warns, however, of some important factors that need to be considered in item design (e.g., randomization of the vignettes, not always having the self-assessment come first). Its use, thus far, in education has been limited (see, however, Buckley, 2008).

Biodata

Biographical data (biodata) are typically obtained by asking standardized questions about individuals' past behaviors, activities, or experiences. Respondents are given multiple-choice answer options or are requested to answer in an open format (e.g., frequency). Measures of biodata have been found to be incrementally valid beyond SAT and the Big Five in predicting student performance (e.g., Oswald, Schmitt, Kim, Ramsay, & Gillespie, 2004).

Obviously, biodata can be faked, but there are several ways to minimize faking (e.g., Schmitt, Oswald, Kim, Gillespie, & Ramsay, 2003). Asking students to verify with details, for example, can minimize faking (Schmitt & Kuncel, 2002). In an educational context, biodata can be used to gather supplemental information that validates student or teacher self-reports of noncognitive skills.

Situational Judgment Tests

A situational judgment test (SJT) is one in which participants are asked how best to, or how they might typically deal with some situation. Situations can be described in words, audiotaped, or videotaped, and response types used can include multiple choice, constructed response, and ratings (how good would this response be?), among others (McDaniel et al., 2001).

SJTs may be developed to reflect more subtle and complex judgment processes than are possible with conventional tests. The methodology enables the measurement of many relevant attributes of individuals, including leadership, teamwork, achievement orientation, self-reliance, dependability, sociability, emotion management, and conscientiousness (e.g., Kyllonen & Lee, 2005; MacCann & Roberts, 2008; Oswald et al., 2004; Wang, MacCann, Zhuang, Liu, & Roberts, 2009).

SJTs have been shown to predict many different criteria such as academic success (Lievens & Coestsier, 2002; Oswald et al., 2004), leadership (Legree, 1995), and managerial performance (Howard & Choi, 2000). Though applications in education have been more limited, there is emerging evidence that they are effective predictors in educational domains (Lievens, Buyse, & Sackett, 2005; MacCann & Roberts, 2008; Oswald et al., 2004; Sternberg et al., 2000; Wang et al., 2009). Hooper, Cullen, and Sackett (2006) also review evidence that SJTs are less prone to faking than self-report assessments, pointing to the promise of SJTs as a method of addressing faking issues in education.

Conditional Reasoning Tests

Conditional Reasoning Tests (CRTs) are multiple-choice tests consisting of items that appear to be logical reasoning items, but actually measure world view, personality, biases, and motives (James, 1998; LeBreton, Barksdale, & Robin, 2007). Following a passage and a question, the CRT presents two or three logically incorrect alternatives and two logically correct alternatives that reflect different world views. Participants are asked to state which of the alternatives seems to be most reasonable based on the information given in the text. Thus, respondents believe that they can solve a problem by reasoning about it, not realizing that there are two correct answers, and that their selection is guided by implicit assumptions underlying answer alternatives. To illustrate this idea consider the example adapted from James (1998) below.

Studies of the stress-related causes of heart attacks led to the identification of the Type A personality. Type A persons are motivated to achieve, involved in their schoolwork and education, competitive to the point of being aggressive, and eager, wanting things completed quickly. Interestingly, these same characteristics are often used to describe the successful person. It would appear that people who wish to strive to be a success should consider that they will be increasing their risk for a heart attack.

Which of the following would most weaken the prediction that striving for success increases the likelihood of having a heart attack?

(A) Recent research has shown that it is aggressiveness and impatience, rather than achievement motivation and educational involvement, that are that primary causes of high stress and heart attacks.
(B) Studies of the Type A personality are usually based on information obtained from interviews and questionnaires.
(C) Studies have shown that some people fear being successful.
(D) A number of nonambitious people have heart attacks.

Alternatives (B) and (C) can be ruled out on logical grounds. Both (A) and (D) could be considered logically correct (or at least not incorrect), but reflecting different perspectives. Of the two responses, selecting (A) is taken as an indicator of achievement motivation, because to do so reflects a justification that achievement striving is a positive thing. A score reflecting an individual's level of achievement motivation is obtained by aggregating the answers to several of these kinds of items.

The CRT for achievement motivation has been shown to be unrelated to cognitive ability, and reliable and valid for predicting different behavioral manifestations of achievement (average r over 10 studies = 0.44) (James, 1998).

Other-Report Ratings

Other-report ratings are assessments in which others (e.g., parents, teachers, colleagues, friends) rate individuals on various noncognitive qualities. This method has a long history and countless studies have been conducted that employed this methodology to gather information (e.g., Tupes & Christal, 1961/1992). Other-ratings have an advantage over self-ratings in that they aim to preclude socially desirable responding, although they do permit rating biases. Self-ratings and other-ratings do not always agree (Oltmanns & Turkheimer, 2006), but other-ratings are often more predictive of outcomes than are self-ratings (MacCann, Minsky, Ventura, & Roberts, 2010; Wagerman & Funder, 2007).

■ APPLIED METHODS OF NONCOGNITIVE SKILL ASSESSMENT IN EDUCATION

Given the variety of methods for assessing noncognitive skills, it is useful to examine how some of these methods have been applied in education. We highlight four examples: noncognitive assessments for law school applicants, the work of

Neal Schmitt and Frederick Oswald, the ETS Personal Potential Index, and ACT WorkKeys assessment.

Noncognitive Assessments for Law School Applicants

One example of noncognitive skills measurement in education relates to the work of Marjorie M. Shultz and Sheldon Zedeck, who conducted a comprehensive multiyear research program to develop supplemental assessments to assist in law school admissions with the Law School Admissions Council. The research program grew out of an effort to augment the Law School Admissions Test (LSAT) with additional assessments that moved beyond predicting law school grades. The purpose of the study was thus to increase the narrow focus of the LSAT with supplemental skill assessments.

The researchers conducted interviews with lawyers, law faculty, law students, judges, and clients, resulting in a list of 26 effectiveness factors comprising effective lawyering performance. The interviewers also identified 716 behaviors linked to these 26 effectiveness factors, with behavioral examples ranging between poor and excellent performance.

Next, the researchers selected a battery of existing assessments of personality including the Hogan Personality Inventory (HPI; Hogan & Hogan, 2007), the Hogan Development Survey (HDS; Hogan & Hogan, 1997), the Motives, Values, Preferences Inventory (MVPI; Hogan & Hogan, 1996), the Revised Life Orientation Test (LOT-R; Scheier, Carver, & Bridges, 1994), and the Self-Monitoring Scale (SMS; Snyder, 1974). Each of these assessments was selected based on their likelihood to predict lawyering performance, as identified by the 26 effectiveness factors. Each of the assessments selected also relied on self-reports methods using either Likert-type or True/False rating scales.

Three additional assessments were developed specifically for the study: an Emotion Recognition Test (ER) modeled after the Facial Action Coding System (FACS) developed by Paul Ekman (2004), situational judgment tests tailored to measure lawyering effectiveness, and biographical information data.

Regarding the procedure of the study, 1148 participants completed the assessment battery through an online delivery system. This sample consisted primarily of law school alumni at Berkley. Participants completed self-evaluations of their job performance on each of the 26 effectiveness factors and recruited peers and supervisors to also complete evaluations on these dimensions.

In terms of results, in general, scores on each of the noncognitive assessments did not differ by race or gender. In addition, SJTs, biodata, and several HPI scales predicted many of the identified dimensions of lawyering performance, whereas the LSAT and grades did not. In this way, the results show that not only do noncognitive assessments predict valuable educational outcomes, but that assessments that were designed to be faking resistant predicted performance above and beyond LSAT and GPA.

Noncognitive Assessments in Higher Education

Another body of research relating noncognitive skills to higher education outcomes appears in the work of Neal Schmitt and Frederick Oswald, who demonstrate in a series of studies that noncognitive skill assessments provide incremental validity over cognitive ability in predicting educational outcome variables. Schmitt et al. (2009) gathered data from over 2771 freshman students across 10 colleges and universities, as well as follow-up data from 593 of these students 3.5 years later. Similar to the approach of Zedeck et al., the researchers gave students a battery of noncognitive assessments designed to be resistant to faking.

Among these assessments were a biodata instrument (consisting of 112 multiple-choice questions assessing 12 dimensions of student performance) and a 36-item situational judgment test measuring the same 12 dimensions (examples of the dimensional factors include interpersonal skills, leadership, perseverance, adaptability, and ethics). The researchers also collected outcome data that included cumulative GPA, SAT/ACT scores, self-reported performance ratings using a behaviorally anchored rating scale, organizational citizenship behavior, absenteeism, and graduation status.

The overall results of the study indicate that the SJTs and biodata assessments, each of which was designed to be resistant to faking, incrementally predicted GPA above and beyond standardized test scores (SAT/ACT). Additional outcomes such as self-reported performance and absenteeism were also predicted by the noncognitive biodata and SJT assessments.

ETS® Personal Potential Index

The Personal Potential Index (PPI) is a rating system for assessing a graduate school applicant's suitability for graduate study. The PPI works as a rating form for mentors (e.g., faculty or employers) to rate students on various personal attributes, and is designed to be the first personal attribute assessment to play a role in high-stakes admissions decisions in graduate school. These ratings are aimed to systematically measure many of the qualities reported in letters of recommendation. The PPI consists of six subscales: *Knowledge and Creativity, Communication Skills, Teamwork, Resilience, Planning and Organization, and Ethics.* Ratings are made on a five-point Likert-type scale, ranging from below average to truly exceptional. Although the PPI does not explicitly measure personality, the subscales for Resilience (e.g., Works extremely hard) and Planning and Organization (e.g., Organizes work and time effectively) presumably capture important aspects of conscientiousness. In this way, the PPI encompasses several of the noncognitive domains that have been shown to be related to educational outcomes.

ACT WorkKeys®

WorkKeys® is a skills assessment used in schools and workplaces developed by ACT that measures "real world" skills identified as crucial for job success (e.g., teamwork, listening, and readiness). The chosen skills were content validated based on consultations with educators, employers, and labor organizations. The WorkKeys® assessment has been used in educational contexts to prepare students for jobs after graduation, identify skill levels, and provide remediation. Educational institutions that have made use of the WorkKeys® assessment include a number of public schools in Chicago, Syracuse University, and Aims Community College.

Summary

Overall, each of these examples demonstrates how noncognitive assessments are currently playing a role in both educational research and practice. In each example, efforts have been made to account for the risk of faking that is likely to occur for high-stakes self-report assessments, whether through the use of situational judgment tests, biographical data, or other reports. In this way, the examples serve as signals of not only the rising presence of noncognitive assessments and measures of 21st century skills in education, but also the mounting need for ways to account for intentional faking in education. The remainder of the chapter discusses a parallel concern in education: unintentional faking.

■ UNINTENTIONAL FAKING: SELF-ENHANCEMENT IN EDUCATION

As discussed in the chapter introduction, self-assessments may be inaccurately inflated for reasons other than intentional faking. If this is the case, countermeasures designed to deal with intentional faking that do not take this consideration into account may at times prove ineffective in uncovering true scores. Below, we discuss some examples of unintentional faking effects, most of which come from research in social psychology, and how they can influence educational outcomes. We also discuss some possibilities for reducing these effects.

Every day people make important judgments about themselves. When they do, however, they tend to say that they have better skills and abilities, are more likely to experience positive (and less likely to experience negative) events, and are more often correct than is warranted (see Alicke & Govorun, 2005; Dunning, Heath, & Suls, 2004 for reviews). Although these judgments may appear to be intentionally faked, they are at times the result of one or more psychological processes that cause people to believe that their inflated self-judgments are indeed accurate. This view is consistent with Paulhus's (2002) notions of unintentional faking in the forms of *Self-Deceptive Enhancement* and *Self-Deceptive Denial*. Self-deceptive enhancement is the tendency to overestimate our standing on agentic traits—leading to inflated scores on traits such as fearlessness and emotional stability. Self-deceptive denial is the tendency to deny socially deviant impulses—leading to inflated scores on traits such as agreeableness and dutifulness. Below, we review findings on three additional types of unintentional faking: *Above-Average Effects*, *Unrealistic Optimism*, and *Overconfidence Effects*. As we will discuss later, this unintentional faking may have significant consequences for education.

Above-Average Effects

The finding that people believe they are above average as compared to their peers is likely one of the most robust in psychology, having been replicated across several populations and abilities. Typically above-average effects are revealed when participants directly compare their abilities to the average person in their peer group (for example, on a percentile scale), or when they rate their abilities and the average person's abilities separately and then the two judgments are compared. In the percentile example, an accurate set of responses should logically average at the 50th percentile. In practice, however, judgments typically average significantly greater than the 50th percentile for desirable abilities.

One of the earliest and most cited above-average effect findings comes from a 1976–1977 College Board survey of over 800,000 high school students, which revealed that students believed they were skilled to an unrealistic extent on several abilities (College Board, 1976–1977). For example, 89% of students said they were above average at getting along with others, 70% said they were above average in leadership, and 57% said they were above average in mathematics. Mattern, Burrus, and Shaw (2010) recently replicated the results for mathematics in two samples of high school students. That is, 76% of a sample of over 150,000 high school students and 64% of a second sample of over 650,000 high school students estimated that they were above average in mathematics. Other notable examples of often-cited above-average effects include the following: 88% of Americans stated that they were above-average drivers (Svenson, 1981), 94% of university professors stated that were above-average teachers (Cross, 1977), and college students stated that they were more likely to possess desirable traits (e.g., cooperative, considerate) and less likely to possess undesirable traits (e.g., disobedient, snobbish) than the average college student (Alicke, 1985).

Who is it that most overestimates themselves? Interestingly, it seems that the above-average effect is most pronounced in those who are *below average* (Austin & Gregory, 2007; Ehrlinger, Johnson, Banner, Dunning, & Kruger, 2008; Kruger & Dunning, 1999, 2002; Mattern et al., 2010). For example, Kruger and Dunning (1999) found that when asked to estimate their ability to use proper grammar, college students who were in the bottom quartile of ability overestimated their ability more than those in the other three ability quartiles. Although this work was originally criticized as simply an artifact of regression to the mean (Krueger & Mueller, 2002), other work ruled out the regression interpretation, instead providing evidence that this effect is a product of the unskilled individual's lack of metacognitive awareness (Ehrlinger et al., 2008; Kruger & Dunning, 2002). Ehrlinger et al. (2008) replicated this finding for more ecologically valid tasks, such as gun club members estimating their knowledge of gun safety. Furthermore, other research found that the most unskilled pharmacy students overestimated both their clinical knowledge and communication skills the most (Austin & Gregory, 2007). Additionally, in the samples described above, Mattern et al. (2010) replicated this finding with high school students' estimates of their mathematics ability.

Do students really believe they are above average or are their reports simply wishful thinking or intentional faking? Recent research has provided evidence that, in these cases, students are in fact unintentionally faking. That is, they truly believe that they are above average (Williams & Gilovich, 2008). In this research, college students completed a fake personality inventory that ostensibly measured their intelligence, creativity, maturity, and positivity. Next, they estimated how they compared on each of the four traits with the average student at their school. Results revealed that students demonstrated the typically found above-average effect. They were then asked to place a bet; they could either compare their score to a randomly selected student's score or they could convert their estimate to a number and draw a number from an urn of 100 numbers (e.g., if they said they were in the 60th percentile in intelligence, they could convert that number to 60). They would win $1 per category if the randomly selected student scored lower than them, or if they drew a number at or below their estimate (if they chose to convert their number). Thus, if students truly believed their estimate, they should have demonstrated no preference for keeping their estimates or converting them, but if their estimates were simply wishful thinking or intentional faking, they should demonstrate a preference to switch. Students demonstrated no preference, providing evidence that they truly believed that they were above average. Thus, it seems that inflated self-estimates are in fact, at least at times, a product of unintentional faking.

Unrealistic Optimism

Not only do people believe that they have greater abilities than they actually do, they also overestimate the likelihood that positive events will happen to them and underestimate the likelihood that negative events will happen to them. For example, Neil Weinstein (1980) found that college students thought that, on average, they were more likely than the average student to own their own home, get a good job offer before graduation, and live past 80 years. Furthermore, they also thought that they were less likely than the average student to get a divorce, be fired from a job, and drop out of college.

Future teachers are also unrealistically optimistic about their ability to teach. For instance, in one study, teacher education students about to begin student teaching were asked several questions about their expectations about the first year of teaching (C.S. Weinstein, 1988). Specifically, they were asked about how difficult they thought 33 teaching responsibilities (e.g., dealing with work load, maintaining discipline, relating to parents) would be for themselves and their peers. The future teachers were overwhelmingly unrealistically optimistic, predicting that they would have fewer problems handling each of the 33 responsibilities than the average teacher.

Overconfidence Effects

Finally, people also tend to overestimate the extent to which answers they give are correct and to which their predictions about the future will prove to be accurate. For example, a now classic study in overconfidence demonstrated that college students who were 65% to 70% confident that they correctly answered various knowledge questions were in reality correct only 50% of the time (Lichtenstein & Fischhoff, 1977). In fact, follow-up research revealed that participants were still wrong about 30% of the time when they stated that they were 100% certain they were correct (Fischhoff, Slovic, & Lichtenstein, 1977). More recently, 15-year-old British students were overconfident in their performance on the 2003 Program for International Student Assessment (PISA) mathematics section (Chevalier, Gibbons, Thorpe, Snell,

& Hoskins, 2009). Additionally, Chevalier et al. (2009) found that first year college students also tended to be overconfident in their mathematics performance. People also tend to be overconfident with respect to their predictions of other peoples' behavior, even when they live with the people they are making predictions about (Dunning, Griffin, Milojkovic, & Ross, 1990). For instance, Dunning et al. (1990) found that college students were overconfident in their ability to predict how their roommates would respond on a questionnaire (Dunning et al., 1990). Perhaps surprisingly, expertise does not provide immunity to overconfidence. To provide just a few examples, overconfidence has been identified in engineers (Kidd, 1970), clinical psychologists (Oskamp, 1965), and lawyers (Wagenaar & Karen, 1986).

Of note, Stankov and Lee (2008) recently proposed that confidence is a trait in itself, distinct from both the Big Five and from cognitive ability, and reported data that suggested that confidence is only modestly correlated with these constructs. If it is the case that confidence is a trait that remains relatively stable across individuals over time, it should be possible to create assessments of confidence to be used to adjust self-assessments thought to be influenced by unintentional faking.

Possible Implications of Unintentional Faking in Education

Successfully navigating school requires students to assess themselves constantly. For example, to successfully complete homework or pass tests students must assess both their current level of knowledge and ability and the amount of work required to learn the new material. In addition, effectively applying for college requires students to at least somewhat realistically assess their chances of acceptance. And once a student knows which college he or she wants to attend, information about himself or herself must be provided to people who make admissions decisions. At each step of the way, unintentional faking may have an impact. Above-average, unrealistic optimism and overconfidence effects may all have similar outcomes for students and teachers. However, because above-average and unrealistic optimism effects likely have a similar genesis, we discuss those two effects in conjunction. We then discuss implications of overconfidence. As many of these effects we discuss below have yet to be studied empirically, this is a potentially fruitful area for future work.

Above-Average and Unrealistic Optimism in Education

It is clear that above-average and unrealistic optimism effects can have an impact on students' motivation to work hard on homework and tests. Students' expectations that they are more intelligent and better prepared than other students, and that they are more likely to achieve a good grade than other students, may have an influence on how hard, and how often, they feel they should study. What is unclear is what the nature of that influence would be. On the one hand, overestimating yourself may be related to self-efficacy (the belief that one has the skills to complete a desired action), and a great deal of research has found that self-efficacy is positively related to academic outcomes (e.g., Bandura, 1977, 1993). On the other hand, those who overestimate their knowledge and the likelihood they will succeed may put forth less effort than they otherwise would.

Recently published research suggests that those who overestimate their ability perform better in college than those who underestimate themselves (Mattern et al., 2010). High school students estimated their mathematics ability as compared to their peers. These estimates were then compared to their true mathematics ability as indexed by their SAT mathematics score, and students were tracked through their college careers. At each level of true ability, persistence to the second year of school, first year GPA, and graduation increased as students' self-estimates of their ability increased. Additionally, at times students who overestimated their ability outperformed students who were more highly skilled (e.g., scored higher on their SAT mathematics examination) but who underestimated that skill, providing evidence that overestimating yourself may have positive consequences for education. Effects, however, were small (e.g., each scale point a student went up in self-estimated ability corresponded to a 3% greater chance of graduating), and thus further research is needed.

Not only can self-estimates of ability influence academic outcomes, they may also have an influence on students' *reactions* to academic outcomes. Simply put, student feelings regarding the outcome of an examination or test can vary as a function of whether that outcome meets prior expectations. As such, if a student believes that he or she is more skilled than his or her classmates and expects to outperform them, the student will be unsatisfied with an outcome if his or her grade does not meet those expectations and may even feel that the outcome is unjust. For example, *equity theory* states that an outcome will be perceived as fair if the ratio of inputs (e.g., the work a student puts into assignments and examinations) to outcomes (e.g., grades) is equal to the ratio of others' inputs to outcomes (e.g., Adams, 1965). The implication of this is that students will tend to feel that their grades are unfair to the extent that they inflate their inputs. Feeling that you have been fairly graded may be especially important for schools. For instance, distributive fairness has been found to be related to several important outcomes in organizations, such as withdrawal and organizational citizenship (Colquitt, Conlon, Wesson, Porter, & Ng, 2001), and it is reasonable to assume that it should be related to similar outcomes in schools.

Unintentional faking can also manifest itself in the personal statements students write for admission to undergraduate and graduate programs, and in any self-ratings they are asked to provide. Because students are motivated to be accepted into the programs they are applying to when completing these self-ratings, intentional faking is a potential problem. However, we believe unintentional faking in the form of above-average and unrealistic optimism effects can also come into play when students write about themselves in personal statements and give self-ratings, and those making acceptance decisions should keep these effects in mind in their evaluation process.

Students are not the only ones susceptible to unintentional faking. As demonstrated above, preservice teachers are also unrealistically optimistic about their ability to handle the job of teaching (C.S. Weinstein, 1988). As Weinstein herself speculated, these unrealistic expectations can contribute to high amount of stress that new teachers often feel when they realize that teaching is much more difficult than they had imagined. To the extent that such overinflated self-assessments are a contributing factor in teacher turnover—up to 40% of teachers resign from their school district within their first 2 years on the job (Watt & Richardson, 2008)—this has tangible consequences for the educational system.

Countering Above-Average and Unrealistic Optimism Effects

There are several possibilities for designing interventions to improve the accuracy of student and teacher self-assessments. One strategy for creating effective interventions is to first look at the moderating factors and mechanisms for these effects and to consider how they might be applied. As such, some factors that influence above-average and unrealistic optimism effects are reviewed below, along with potential applications to interventions.

First, because the criteria for evaluating ambiguous traits are difficult to evaluate, above-average effects are more pronounced for them than for more objective traits (e.g., Alicke & Govorun, 2005). For instance, it is more difficult to evaluate moral traits than to evaluate ability in sports, and thus people should demonstrate more pronounced above-average effects for traits such as morals (e.g., Allison, Messick, & Goethals, 1989). When students evaluate their moral standing, for example, they can focus on the fact that they recently donated $5 to charity and conveniently ignore the fact that they copied from their friend's last mathematics homework. However, when they evaluate their athletic ability, it is more difficult to ignore the fact that they were recently cut from the basketball team. One implication of this fact is that students can be made to more accurately assess themselves if they are asked to consider only objective traits and abilities. Furthermore, if students are asked to rate themselves on more ambiguous traits and abilities, these traits and abilities can be broken down into their more objective components (e.g., morality partly consists of both giving to others *and* not cheating) when students rate themselves.

Second, above-average and unrealistic optimism effects are larger when people compare themselves to average others rather than individual people (e.g., Alicke, Klotz, Breitenbecher, Yurak, & Vredenburg, 1995). This is the case even if we do not know the individual to whom we are comparing ourselves; for example, Alicke et al. (1995) found that above-average effects were smaller when people compared themselves to the person they were sitting next to in a laboratory study than if they compared themselves to the average student at their school. Thus, one way to get students and teachers to more accurately assess themselves is to have them compare themselves to another student or teacher who is like them rather than the "average" student or teacher.

Third, there is some evidence that these effects at times occur as a result of people selecting inferior others to compare themselves to (see Alicke & Govorun, 2005; Perloff & Fetzer, 1986). For example, when asked to estimate their reading ability, students may choose to compare herself (perhaps unintentionally) to other students who are poor at reading, thus giving her an inflated sense of her reading ability. This suggests that asking a student to compare herself to a student who is like her (such as her best friend) would be one way to get her to more accurately assess herself. Indeed, research evidence exists that suggests that this type of manipulation does work to reduce the above-average effect (Perloff & Fetzer, 1986).

A fourth factor in above-average and unrealistic optimism effects concerns the focus of attention in the comparison. People tend to be egocentric processors of information in that they tend to focus more on their own abilities and likelihood of experiencing events than on others' (e.g., Chambers, Windschitl, & Suls, 2003, Kruger, 1999; Kruger & Burrus, 2004). For above-average effects, this means that people will have a tendency to overestimate their relative standing on easy abilities because they will tend to neglect the fact that abilities that are easy (e.g., driving) are also easy for others. This can lead to above-average effects because people tend to be asked about abilities that are relatively easy (Kruger, 1999). The same is true for unrealistic optimism (Chambers et al., 2003; Kruger & Burrus, 2004). People tend to neglect the fact that frequently occurring events are as likely to occur for others as they are for them, and infrequently occurring events are as unlikely to occur for others as they are for them. Because desirability of event tends to be confounded with event likelihood in optimism questionnaires, unrealistic optimism usually is displayed. The implication is that people at times will claim to be *below average* and will be unrealistically *pessimistic* if they are asked about difficult abilities and rare events. Thus, a student or teacher self-assessment that includes these types of abilities and events may lead respondents to give a (if not more accurate) more varied picture of their skills, abilities, and likelihood of success.

Relatedly, another factor in these effects is focalism, or the fact that the focus of comparison tends to receive more weight in the comparison than the referent of the comparison (e.g., Kruger & Burrus, 2004). In most social comparisons, the self is the focus of the comparison and the other is the referent. Thus, the self is weighed more heavily in the comparison than is the other. This means that above-average and unrealistic optimism effects should be attenuated when the other is made the focus of the comparison. For example, Kruger and Burrus (2004) asked some students to compare their likelihood of experiencing several events with that of the average student and asked other students to compare the average student's likelihood of experiencing several events with their own. Unrealistic optimism effects were attenuated when the other was the subject of the comparison (although they did not completely reverse, suggesting that egocentrism was still present). The implication is simple; any manipulation that leads students and teachers to think more about the comparison group should lead to more accurate self-assessments.

In high-stakes selection situations (e.g., undergraduate or graduate admissions decisions), the problem of faking can potentially be alleviated by having another person, such as a counselor or professor, rate the candidates rather than the candidates rating themselves. The assumption is that an other-recommender is less motivated to fake an assessment than are the candidates themselves, and thus the assessment should be more accurate. This is the logic behind both the letter of recommendation and the PPI discussed above. Although on the surface recommendations may be perceived to be more accurate than self-reports because they may be immune to intentional faking, a closer look at the social comparison literature suggests that other raters may not be immune to unintentional faking.

The *local-comparisons-general* standards (LOGE) model is a model of comparison that states that when people are asked to compare a person to a target group (the local comparison), they actually compare the person to a group that is an amalgamation of both the local comparison and the more general standard (e.g., Klar, 2002). For example, a professor who is asked on a recommendation form to compare a student with other students applying to graduate school will in reality tend to compare the student to a comparison group that consists of an average of both students applying to graduate school and the average college student. This means that because students applying to graduate school tend to be superior to students who are not, almost *every* student applying to graduate school will be rated as an above-average student. For example, in one study, a small group of friends was asked to compare a randomly selected group member with other members of the group on a set of socially desirable traits (Klar, 2002). Results revealed that because group members were in reality compared to an average of other group members and the average nongroup member, every group member was rated more positively than the average group member. This basic finding has been confirmed in several experiments and applies to nonsocial comparisons as well (Giladi & Klar, 2002). Because recommenders are typically asked to compare students to others like them, this presents a real problem. Although more research should be conducted on implications for recommendations, one possible fix would be to anchor recommenders' ratings by giving them a hypothetical individual with which to compare the aspiring graduate student, rather than comparing them to a generalized other student. Another related possibility would be to employ the anchoring vignette technique described above.

Overconfidence in Education

In their review on self-assessment, Dunning et al. (2004) discussed two ways overconfidence influences student study habits. The first concerns massed versus distributed training, and the second concerns the assessment of reading comprehension. Because Dunning et al. thoroughly review these two issues in their paper, we provide only a short summary of their review below.

When it comes to learning, distributed training is superior to massed training (e.g., Willingham, 2002). It is now a well-known fact that memory for information is improved if studying is spread over a number of short sessions rather than "crammed" into one long session. Despite this, most students prefer cramming to spreading study sessions over a longer period of time. Undoubtedly, procrastination is one reason for this. However, another possible reason is that students tend to be overconfident that they have learned the material as a result of massed training. That is, students and teachers alike tend to believe that material that has been learned quickly will tend to be remembered (Bjork, 1994, 1999). Simply put, people confuse speed with proficiency and thus become overconfident in their learning (Dunning et al., 2004). Massed training tends to create the impression that a student has learned something very quickly.

Dunning et al. (2004) also discuss how overconfidence can tend to occur when students assess how well they have understood their reading assignments. For example, Glenberg, Wilkinson, and Epstein (1982) had college students read several texts and found that the students stated that they were very confident that they understood the readings, although several parts of the text were intentionally contradictory.

This overconfidence can be a severe problem because the amount of time students spend studying tends to vary as a function of how much they feel that they have understood (Dunning et al., 2004).

Countering Overconfidence Effects

Dunning et al. also outline several possible ways to counter overconfidence in students so that they learn more efficiently. One way is essentially to disrupt massed training so that it becomes distributed training (Bjork, 1994, 1999). For example, a student could purposely plan to study over several sessions, plan on studying several different topics in each study session, and study in several different environments (e.g., study in the library at some times and study in groups at the coffee shop at other times). There are also several ways to improve reading comprehension. For example, self-testing can help but only if there is a delay between studying and self-testing. This is the case because students may overestimate the amount of knowledge they have because presumably information will come to mind more easily if it was just studied (Benjamin, Bjork, & Schwartz, 1998). Another strategy that can be useful is for teachers to periodically stop their students and ask them questions pertaining to their understanding of the material (Koch, 2001). Finally, students can also be shown exactly what a high performance on an assignment or examination looks like as they are working (e.g., Farh & Dobbins, 1989). This "benchmarking" process allows students to assess the quality of their performance more accurately as it leads them to judge their work using objective standards rather than mental heuristics regarding ease of mental retrieval of information.

■ CONCLUSIONS

The temptation to fake has always been a problem in education. As pressure increases on students to be accepted to, and excel in, top colleges and universities, we expect this temptation to grow. The recent emphasis on noncognitive constructs in education, combined with the fact that fake-resistant assessments of noncognitive constructs have yet to be fully developed, further increases the temptation, and opportunity, to present an inaccurate picture of our abilities and personality traits. As such, it may not be surprising that an entire book has been devoted to the problem of intentional faking.

We would like the reader to at least consider the possibility, however, that at times inflated self-assessments may be unintentionally faked. Several psychological processes may lead students and teachers alike to overestimate their ability, their likelihood to experience positive future events, and their confidence that they are correct in their judgments. A fuller consideration of these unintentional faking effects may lead to more effective counters against inflated self-judgments.

In education, the consequences of faking vary in severity and consequence. For example, if not caught, students that plagiarize are unfairly rewarded as compared to their peers, and if caught, are expelled from school. Furthermore, it is undoubtedly the case that students who are admitted to universities based on faked information are more likely to drop out, wasting thousands of university dollars. In addition, first year teachers who overestimate their ability to teach may find themselves dissatisfied with their jobs, potentially contributing to the teacher retention problem. The list could go on, but for the sake of brevity we stop there.

We conclude by introducing a final bit of food for thought. Faking, and intentional faking in particular, may potentially have additional, more insidious effects than previously considered in this or other chapters. Those who fake may be more likely in the future to behave unethically (Gino, Norton, & Ariely, 2010). Simply put, faking may beget faking. In several recent experimental studies, Gino et al. found that people who wear counterfeit products are more likely to lie and judge others as unethical in subsequent tasks. This suggests that there is value in future research not only in designing assessments that are resistant to faking but also in creating manipulations that reduce the *temptation* to fake in the first place. Furthermore, educators may want to consider the possibility that a system that encourages faking may also encourage unethical behavior in other contexts. As such, counters to faking in education may be even more important than previously considered.

References

Ackerman, P. L., & Heggestad, E. D. (1997). Intelligence, personality, and interests: Evidence for overlapping traits. *Psychological Bulletin, 121,* 219–245.

Adams, J. S. (1965). Inequity in social exchange. *Advances in Experimental Social Psychology, 62,* 335–343.

Alicke, M. D. (1985). Global self-evaluation as determined by the desirability and controllability of trait adjectives. *Journal of Personality and Social Psychology, 49,* 1621–1630.

Alicke, M. D., & Govorun, O. (2005). The better-than-average effect. In M. D. Alicke, D.A. Dunning, & J. I. Krueger (Eds.), *The self in social judgment* (pp. 85–106). New York: Psychology Press.

Alicke, M. D., Klotz, M. L., Breitenbecher, D. L., Yurak, T. J., & Vredenburg, D. S. (1995). Personal contact, individuation and the better than average effect. *Journal of Personality and Social Psychology, 68,* 804–825.

Allison, S. T., Messick, D. M., & Goethals, G. R. (1989). On being better but not smarter than others: The Muhammad Ali effect. *Social Cognition, 7,* 275–296.

Austin, Z., & Gregory, P. A. M. (2007). Evaluating the accuracy of pharmacy students' self-assessment skills. *American Journal of Pharmaceutical Education, 71,* 1–8.

Bandura, A. (1977). Perceived self-efficacy in cognitive development and functioning. *Educational Psychologist, 28,* 117–148.

Bandura, A. (1993). Self-efficacy: Toward a unifying theory of behavioral change. *Psychological Review, 84,* 191–215.

Benjamin, A. S., Bjork, R. A., & Schwartz, B. L. (1998). The mismeasure of memory: When retrieval fluency is misleading as a metamnemonic index. *Journal of Experimental Psychology: General, 127,* 55–68.

Bjork, R. A. (1994). Institutional impediments to effective training. In D. Druckman & R. A. Bjork (Eds.), *Learning, remembering, believing: Enhancing human performance* (pp. 295–306). Washington, D.C.: National Academy Press.

Bjork, R. A. (1999). Assessing our own competence: Heuristics and illusions. In D. Gopher & A. Koriat (Eds.), *Attention and peformance XVII. Cognitive regulation of performance: Interaction of theory and application* (pp. 435–459). Cambridge, MA: MIT Press.

Buckley, J. (2008). Survey context effects in anchoring vignettes. Retrieved February 10, 2010 from http://polmeth.wustl.edu/workingpapers.php.

Chambers, J. R., Windschitl, P. D., & Suls, J. (2003). Egocentrism, event frequency, and comparative optimism: When what happens frequently is "More likely to happen to me." *Personality and Social Psychology Bulletin, 29*, 1343–1356.

Chevalier, A., Gibbons, S., Thorpe, A., Snell, M., & Hoskins, S. (2009). Students' academic self-perception. *Economics of Education Review, 28*, 716–727.

Christiansen, N. D., Burns, G. N., & Montgomery, G. E. (2005). Reconsidering forced-choice item formats for applicant personality assessment. *Human Performance, 18*, 267–307.

College Board. (1976–1977). *Student descriptive questionnaire*. Princeton, NJ: Educational Testing Service.

Colquitt, J. A., Conlon, D. E., Wesson, M. J., Porter, O. L. H., & Ng, K.Y. (2001). Justice at the millennium: A meta-analytic review of 25 years of organizational justice research. *Journal of Applied Psychology, 86*, 425–445.

Conference Board. (2006). *Are they really ready to work? Employers' perspectives on the basic knowledge and applied skills of new entrants to the 21st century U.S. workforce.* Retrieved 3rd September, 2008, from http://www.conference-board.org/knowledge/workforceReadiness.cfm.

Crede, M., & Kuncel, N. R. (2008). Study habits, skills, and attitudes: The third pillar supporting collegiate academic performance. *Perspectives on Psychological Science, 3*, 425–453.

Cross, K. P. (1977). Not can, but will college teaching be improved? *New Directions for Higher Education, 17*, 1–15.

Dictionary.com. (2010). Faking. Retrieved May 21, 2010 from http://dictionary.reference.com/browse/faking.

Dunning, D., Griffin, D. W., Milojkovic, J. D., & Ross, L. (1990). The overconfidence effect in social prediction. *Journal of Personality and Social Psychology, 58*, 568–581.

Dunning, D., Heath, C., & Suls, J. (2004). Flawed self-assessment: Implications for health, education, and the workplace. *Psychological Science in the Public Interest, 5*, 69–106.

Ehrlinger, J., Johnson, K., Banner, M., Dunning, D., & Kruger, J. (2008). Why the unskilled are unaware: Further explorations of (absent) self-insight among the incompetent. *Organizational Behavior and Human Decision Processes, 105*, 98–121.

Ekman, P. (2004). *Emotions revealed: Recognizing faces and feelings to improve communication and emotional life*. New York: Macmillan.

Farh, J. L., & Dobbins, G. H. (1989). Student self-assessment in higher education: A meta-analysis comparing peer and teacher marks. *Review of Educational Research, 59*, 395–430.

Fischhoff, B., Slovic, P., & Lichtenstein, S. (1977). Knowing with certainty: The appropriateness of extreme confidence. *Journal of Experimental Psychology: Human Perception and Performance, 3*, 552–564.

Giladi, E. E., & Klar, Y. (2002). When standards are wide of the mark: Nonselective superiority and inferiority biases in comparative judgments of objects and concepts. *Journal of Experimental Psychology: General, 131*, 538–551.

Gino, F., Norton, M. I., & Ariely, D. (2010). The counterfeit self: The deceptive costs of faking it. *Psychological Science, 12*, 712–720.

Glenberg, A. M., Wilkinson, A. C., & Epstein, W. (1982). The illusion of knowing: Failure in the self-assessment of comprehension. *Memory & Cognition, 10*, 597–602.

Griffith, R. L., Chmielowski, T., & Yoshita, Y. (2007). Do applicants fake? An examination of the frequency of applicant faking behavior. *Personnel Review, 36*, 341–357.

Guzzardo, J. (2010). Prosecutor: Ex-Harvard student pleads not guilty to faking credentials. Retrieved May 21, 2010 from http://www.cnn.com/2010/CRIME/05/18/massachusetts. harvard.student/index.html?hpt=T2.

Heggestad, E. D., Morrison, M., Reeve, C. L., & McCloy, R. A. (2006). Forced-choice assessments of personality for selection: Evaluating issues of normative assessment and faking resistance. *Journal of Applied Psychology, 91*, 9–24.

Hogan, J., & Hogan, R. (1996). *Motives, Values, Preferences Inventory manual*. Tulsa, OK: Hogan Assessment Systems.

Hogan, R., & Hogan, J. (1997). *Hogan Development Survey manual*. Tulsa, OK: Hogan Assessment Systems.

Hogan, R., & Hogan, J. (2007). *Hogan Personality Inventory manual* (3rd ed.). Tulsa, OK: Hogan Assessment Systems.

Hooper, A. C., Cullen, M. J., & Sackett, P. R. (2006). Operational threats to the use of Situational Judgment Tests: Faking, coaching, and retesting issues. In J. Weekley and R. Ployhart (Eds.) *Situational Judgment Tests* (pp. 205–323). Mahwah, NJ: Lawrence A. Erlbaum,

Howard, A., & Choi, M. (2000). How do you assess a manager's decision-making abilities? The use of situational inventories. *International Journal of Selection and Assessment, 8*, 85–88.

James, L. R. (1998). Measurement of personality via conditional reasoning. *Organizational Research Methods, 1*, 131–163.

Kidd, J. B. (1970). The utilization of subjective probabilities in production planning. *Acta Psychologica, 34*, 338–347.

King, G., Murray, C. L., Salomon, J. A., & Tandon, A. (2004). Enhancing the validity and cross-cultural comparability of measurement in survey research. *American Political Science Review, 98*, 191–207.

Klar, Y. (2002). Way beyond compare: Nonselective superiority and inferiority biases in judging randomly assigned group members relative to their peers. *Journal of Experimental Social Psychology, 38*, 331–351.

Koch, A. (2001). Training in metacognition and comprehension of physics texts. *Science Education, 75*, 858–868.

Krosnick, J. A., Judd, C. M., & Wittenbrink, B. (2005). Attitude measurement. In D. Albarracin, B. T. Johnson, & M. P. Zanna (Eds.), *Handbook of attitudes and attitude change* (pp. 21–76). Mahwah, NJ: Erlbaum.

Krueger, J., & Mueller, R. A. (2002). Unskilled, unaware, or both? The better-than-average heuristic and statistical regression predict errors in estimates of own performance. *Journal of Personality and Social Psychology, 82*, 180–188.

Kruger, J. (1999). Lake Wobegon be gone! The "below-average effect" and the egocentric nature of comparative ability judgments. *Journal of Personality and Social Psychology, 77*, 221–232.

Kruger, J., & Burrus, J. (2004). Egocentrism and focalism in unrealistic optimism (and pessimism). *Journal of Experimental Social Psychology, 40*, 332–340.

Kruger, J., & Dunning, D. (1999). Unskilled and unaware of it: How difficulties in recognizing one's own incompetence lead to inflated self-assessments. *Journal of Personality and Social Psychology, 77*, 1121–1134.

Kruger, J., & Dunning, D. (2002). Unskilled and unaware—but why? A reply to Krueger & Mueller. *Journal of Personality and Social Psychology, 82*, 189–192.

Kuncel, N., Hezlett, S. A., Ones, D. S., Crede, M., Vannelli, J. R., Thomas, L. L., Duehr, E. E., & Jackson, H. L. (2005). *A Meta-Analysis of Personality Determinants of College Student*

Performance. 20th Annual Meeting of the Society of Industrial-Organizational Psychology, Los Angeles, CA.

Kyllonen, P. C., & Lee, S. (2005). Assessing problem solving in context. In O. Wilhelm & R. W. Engle (Eds.), *Handbook of understanding and measuring intelligence* (pp. 11–25). Thousand Oaks, CA: Sage.

Lafontaine, D., & Monseur, C. (2007, August). Why do noncognitive variables better predict mathematics achievement in some countries than in others? *A methodological study of PISA 2003*. Earli Conference, Budapest.

LeBreton, J. M., Barksdale, C. D., & Robin, J. (2007). Measurement issues associated with Conditional Reasoning Tests: Indirect measurement and test faking. *Journal of Applied Psychology, 92*, 1–16.

Legree, P. J. (1995). Evidence for an oblique social intelligence factor. *Intelligence, 21*, 247–266.

Lichtenstein, S., & Fischhoff, B. (1977). Do those who know more also know more about how much they know? The calibration of probability judgments. *Organizational Behavior and Human Performance, 20*, 159–183.

Lievens, F., Buyse, T., & Sackett, P. R. (2005). The operational validity of a video-based situational judgment test for medical college admissions: Illustrating the importance of matching predictor and criterion construct domains. *Journal of Applied Psychology, 90*, 442–452.

Lievens, F., & Coestsier, P. (2002). Situational tests in student selection: An examination of predictive validity, adverse impact, and construct validity. *International Journal of Selection and Assessment, 10*, 245–257.

MacCann, C., Minsky, J., Ventura, M., & Roberts, R. D. (under review, 2010). Mother knows best: Comparing self- and parent-reported personality in predicting academic achievement. *Personality and Social Psychology Bulletin.*

MacCann, C., & Roberts, R. D. (2008). Assessing emotional intelligence with situational judgment test paradigms: Theory and data. *Emotion, 8*, 540–551.

MacCann, C., Wang, L., Matthews, G., & Roberts, R. D. (under review, 2010). Examining self report versus other reports in a situational judgment test of emotional abilities. *Emotion.*

Mattern, K. D., Burrus, J., & Shaw, E. J. (2010). When both the skilled and unskilled are unaware: Consequences for academic performance. *Self and Identity, 9*, 129–141.

McDaniel, M. A., Morgesen, F. P., Finnegan, E. B., Campion, M. A., & Braverman, E. P. (2001). Use of situational judgment tests to predict job performance: A clarification of the literature. *Journal of Applied Psychology, 86*, 730–740.

Mumford, M. D., & Owens, W. A. (1987). Methodology review: Principles, procedures, and findings in the application of background data measures. *Applied Psychological Measurement, 11*, 1–31.

Noftle, E. E., & Robins, R. (2007). Personality predictors of academic outcomes: Big Five correlates of GPA and SAT scores. *Journal of Personality and Social Psychology, 93*, 116–130.

Oltmanns, T. F., & Turkheimer, E. (2006). Perceptions of self and others regarding pathological personality traits. In R. Krueger & J. Tackett (Eds.), *Personality and psychopathology: Building bridges* (pp. 71–111). New York: Guilford.

Oskamp, S. (1965). Overconfidence in case-study judgments. *The Journal of Consulting Psychology, 29*, 261–265.

Oswald, F. L., Schmitt, N., Kim, B. H., Ramsay, L. J., & Gillespie, M. A. (2004). Developing a biodata measure and situational judgment inventory as predictors of college student performance. *Journal of Applied Psychology, 89*, 187–207.

Paulhus, D. L. (2002). Socially desirable responding: The evolution of a construct. In H. I. Braun, D. N. Jackson, & D. E. Wiley (Eds.), *The role of constructs in psychological and educational measurement* (pp. 49–69). Mahwah, NJ: Erlbaum.

Pauls, C. A., & Crost, N. W. (2005). Effects of different instructional sets on the construct validity of the NEO-PI-R. *Personality and Individual Differences, 39,* 297–308.

Perloff, L. S., & Fetzer, B. K. (1986). Self-other judgments and perceived vulnerability to victimization. *Journal of Personality and Social Psychology, 50,* 502–510.

Poropat, A. E. (2009). A meta-analysis of the five-factor model of personality and academic performance. *Psychological Bulletin, 135,* 322–338.

Prelec, D. (2004). A Bayesian truth serum for subjective data. *Science, 306,* 462–466.

Prelec, D., & Weaver, R. G. (2006). *Truthful answers are surprisingly common: Experimental tests of Bayesian truth serum.* Paper presented at the ETS Mini-conference on Faking in Noncognitive Assessments. Princeton, NJ: ETS.

Robbins, S. B., Lauver, K., Le, H., Davis, D., Langley, R., & Carlstrom, A. (2004). Do psychosocial and study skills factors predict college outcomes? A meta-analysis. *Psychological Bulletin, 130,* 261–288.

Scheier, M. F., Carver, C. S., & Bridges, M. W. (1994). Distinguishing optimism from neuroticism (and trait anxiety, self-mastery, and self-esteem): A reevaluation of the Life Orientation Test. *Journal of Personality and Social Psychology, 67,* 1063–1078.

Schmitt, N., Keeney, J., Oswald, F. L., Pleskac, T., Quinn, A., Sinha, R., & Zorzie, M. (2009). Prediction of 4-year college student performance using cognitive and noncognitive predictors and the impact of demographic status on admitted students. *Journal of Applied Psychology, 94,* 1479–1497.

Schmitt, N., & Kuncel, C. (2002). The effects of required elaboration of answers to biodata questions. *Personnel Psychology, 55,* 569–587.

Schmitt, N., Oswald, F. L., Kim, B. H., Gillespie, M. A., & Ramsay, L. J. (2003). Impact of elaboration on socially desirable responding and the validity of biodata measures. *Journal of Applied Psychology, 88,* 979–988.

Seipp, B. (1991). Anxiety and academic performance: A meta-analysis of findings. *Anxiety Research, 4,* 27–41.

Snyder, M. (1974). Self-monitoring of expressive behavior. *Journal of Personality and Social Psychology, 30,* 526–537.

Stankov, L., & Lee, J. (2008). Confidence and cognitive test performance. *Journal of Educational Psychology, 100,* 961–976.

Stark, S., Chernyshenko, O. S., & Drasgow, F. (2005). An IRT approach to constructing and scoring pairwise preference items involving stimuli on different dimensions: An application to the problem of faking in personality assessment. *Applied Psychological Measurement, 29,* 184–201.

Stark, S., Chernyshenko, O. S., & Drasgow, F. (in press, 2010). Constructing fake-resistant personality tests using item response theory: High stakes personality testing with multidimensional pairwise preferences. In M. Ziegler, C. MacCann, & R. D. Roberts (Eds.), *Faking in personality assessment: Knowns and unknowns.* New York: Oxford University Press.

Steinberg, J., & Zezima, K. (2010). Campuses ensnared by "life of deception." Retrieved May 21, 2010 from http://www.nytimes.com/2010/05/19/education/19harvard.html?adxnnl=1&adxnnlx=1274450878-WxlqfsOaPHKgzJeVP4dcCA.

Sternberg, R. J., Forsythe, G. B., Hedlund, J., Horvath, J. A., Wagner, R. K., Williams, W. M., et al. (2000). *Practical Intelligence in Everyday Life.* New York: Cambridge University Press.

Svenson, O. (1981). Are we all less risky and more skillful than our fellow drivers? *Acta Psychologica, 47,* 143–148.

Tupes, E. C., & Christal, R. E. (1961/1992). Recurrent personality factors based on trait ratings. *Journal of Personality, 60,* 225–251.

Viswesvaran, C., & Ones, D. S. (1999). Meta-analyses of fakability estimates: Implications for personality measurement. *Educational and Psychological Measurement, 59,* 197–210.

Wagenaar, W. A., & Karen, G. B. (1986). Does the expert know? The reliability of predictions and confidence ratings of experts. In E. Hollnagel, G. Manici, & D. D. Woods (Eds.), *Intelligent decision support in process environments* (pp. 87–103). Berlin: Springer Verlag.

Wagerman, S. A., & Funder, D. C. (2007). Acquaintance reports of personality and academic achievement: A case for conscientiousness. *Journal of Research in Personality, 41,* 221–229.

Wang, L., MacCann, C., Zhuang, X., Liu, L., & Roberts, R. D. (2009). Assessing teamwork and collaboration in high school students: A multimethod approach. *Canadian Journal of School Psychology, 24,* 108–124.

Watt, H. M. G., & Richardson, P. W. (2008). Motivations, perceptions, and aspirations concerning teaching as a career for different types of beginning teachers. *Learning and Instruction, 18,* 408–428.

Weinstein, C. S. (1988). Preservice teachers' expectations about the first year of teaching. *Teaching & Teacher Education, 4,* 31–40.

Weinstein, N. (1980). Unrealistic optimism about future life events. *Journal of Personality and Social Psychology, 39,* 806–820.

Williams, E., & Gilovich, T. (2008). Do people really believe they are above average? *Journal of Experimental Social Psychology, 44,* 1121–1128.

Willingham, D. T. (2002). How we learn. Ask the cognitive scientist: Allocating student study time. "Massed" versus "distributed" practice. *American Educator, 26,* 37–39.

PART SIX

Conclusions

18 Faking in Personality Assessment

Reflections and Recommendations[1]

CAROLYN MACCANN, MATTHIAS ZIEGLER, AND RICHARD D. ROBERTS

The intention of this book was to address several questions on faking: Whether people fake, whether it matters, and whether faking can be detected, corrected, or prevented. To address this intention we invited contributions from selected experts who had published extensively on these issues. It is clear from the respective chapter contributions that some of these issues are close to consensus, whereas others are still open to a diversity of opinion and contrasting perspectives. In line with our aim of presenting multiple viewpoints, we designed the book to include two independent summary chapters: The present one and Chapter 19 by Paul Sackett. These were written as entirely independent attempts to synthesize the diversity of viewpoints presented, and thus represent independent points of view on the current state of affairs in faking research and practice. The current chapter represents our best efforts to summarize these contributions into a series of recommendations to form a blueprint for future theory, research, and practice.

WHAT IS FAKING? REACHING CONSENSUS ON A DEFINITION OF FAKING

The foundation that underpins all other issues is the definition of faking. The question of whether faking occurs, matters, can be controlled, stopped, or corrected depends crucially on what is actually meant by "faking." An agreed-upon definition would mean that researchers are using the same language when talking about the phenomenon. Table 18.1 paraphrases the definitions of faking offered by the various contributors to this volume. A brief examination of the salient points shows that there are several key points of agreement that can be distilled to create a consensual definition of faking: (1) faking is a behavior rather than a trait, (2) faking requires motivation (i.e., it is goal-oriented), (3) faking behavior results in an inaccurate or enhanced impression, and (4) faking involves the interaction of person (traits) and situational factors (environmental influences). In addition, nearly half of the chapters viewed faking as a conscious or intentional behavior,

---

1. The views expressed here are those of the authors and do not reflect those of the University of Sydney, Humboldt Universität zu Berlin, or the Educational Testing Service.

TABLE 18.1 *A Summary of Definitions of Faking from This Volume*

Chapter Number, Author, and Definition	Elements
1. **Ziegler, MacCann, and Roberts**: Faking represents a response set aimed at providing a portrayal of the self that helps a person to achieve personal goals. Faking occurs when this response set is activated by situational demands and person characteristics to produce systematic differences in test scores that are not due to the attribute of interest.	• Interaction of multiple situation and person factors • Involves motivation • Inaccurate or deceptive
2. **Ellingson**: Faking is a volitional and effortful behavior (rather than a trait) in which individuals will engage when both individual and environmental factors motivate the individual to provide an inaccurate characterization or façade.	• Inaccurate or deceptive • Involves motivation • Behavior rather than a trait • Conscious/deliberate • Interaction of multiple situation and person factors
3. **Griffith and Converse**: Faking represents an attempt to present a more favorable appearance on personality measures than is warranted. The degree to which faking is present in any sample is influenced by motivation and will depend on many moderators such as sample characteristics, the construct measured, and the measurement format.	• Inaccurate or deceptive • Involves motivation • Interaction of multiple situation and person factors
4. **Smith and McDaniel**: Faking is motivated impression management through the use of intentional response distortion.	• Involves motivation • Conscious/deliberate • Inaccurate or deceptive
5. **Holden and Book**: Faking is intentional misrepresentation in self-report, and involves the interaction of three key features: (1) faking is intentional, such that faking behavior occurs with active awareness in a conscious or deliberate manner, (2) faking has some degree of deception associated with it, and (3) faking is oriented toward others (as opposed to deceiving the self).	• Conscious/deliberate • Inaccurate or deceptive • Oriented toward others
6. **Heggestad**: Faking involves two key elements: (1) faking is a behavior influenced by dispositional, attitudinal, situational, and demographic factors (rather than a psychological construct) and (2) faking is, at its core, a measurement issue. That is, faking is a set of systematic factors that influences a person's observed score to a greater degree in motivated than in nonmotivated settings.	• Involves motivation • Behavior rather than a trait • Conscious/deliberate • Interaction of multiple situation and person factors
7. **Kuncel, Borneman, and Kiger**: Responses to a personality test item are based on a test taker's goals to be (1) impressive, (2) credible, and (3) true to the self. Faking on a personality item occurs when the need to be impressive interacts with the other needs to determine a person's answer on a personality item.	• Involves motivation • Interaction of multiple situation and person factors
8. **Zickar and Sliter**: Faking is a behavior that occurs at the item level, with faking having a complex effect on item characteristics (i.e., faking affects not just item difficulty, but many other characteristics).	• Behavior rather than a trait • Involves motivation • Interaction of multiple situation and person factors
9. **Reeder and Ryan**: Faking is socially desirable responding (conscious distortion by presenting oneself as possessing higher levels of desirable traits and lower levels of undesirable traits).	• Behavior rather than a trait • Conscious/deliberate • Inaccurate or deceptive
10. **Paulhus**: Faking is the motivated distortion of self-reports for the purpose of self-presentation. Some types of faking (self-enhancement or impression management) involve exaggerating positive qualities and/or denying negative qualities, whereas others (e.g., malingering) involve exaggerating negative qualities.	• Inaccurate or deceptive • Involves motivation

(Continued)

TABLE 18.1 *Continued*

Chapter Number, Author, and Definition	Elements
11. **Ventura**: Faking behavior involves conscious inhibition mechanisms relating to social desirability.	• Behavior rather than a trait • Inaccurate or deceptive • Conscious/deliberate
12. **Dilchert and Ones**: Faking is an overly positive self-presentation that occurs when active and conscious attempts are made to distort one's responses in response to motivational demands.	• Involves motivation • Inaccurate or deceptive • Conscious/deliberate
13. **Bäckström, Björklund, and Larsson**: Faking encompasses both person-level traits and situational influences that affect the extent to which test takers portray themselves in a socially desirable way. Faking is related to the test takers' reaction to the evaluative content of the item, rather than the descriptive content, and is sensitive to motivational influences.	• Involves motivation • Interaction of multiple situation and person factors • A function of evaluative item content rather than descriptive item content
14. **Stark, Chernyshenko, and Drasgow**: Faking involves answering in a socially desirable way to improve one's test score to gain a desirable outcome.	• Involves motivation • Inaccurate or deceptive
15. **Lukoff**: Faking involves a false answer that did not arise naturally, but arose due to an intention to gain a particular score or create a particular impression.	• Involves motivation • Inaccurate or deceptive • Conscious/deliberate
16. **Hall and Hall**: Malingering includes both the fabrication of clinical symptoms and/or diagnoses and the gross exaggeration of symptoms for the purpose of obtaining a specific secondary gain, often in a legal context.	• Inaccurate or deceptive • Involves motivation
17. **Burrus, Naemi, and Kyllonen**: Faking represents an attempt to conceal defects or create an appearance of greater attractiveness, interest, or value, usually to deceive.	• Inaccurate or deceptive

rather than something unconscious or outside of awareness. Only Burrus, Naemi, and Kyllonen (Chapter 17) explicitly discussed the concept of unintentional faking. They distinguish between intentional and unintentional faking, somewhat analogous to the distinction between Paulhus' (2002) self-deceptive enhancement and impression management, respectively.

It thus seems that most experts view faking as a deliberate act, distinguishing this from other forms of response distortion that may not be conscious and intentional. Faking is thus a deliberate set of behaviors motivated by a desire to present a deceptive impression to the world. Like most other behavior, faking is caused by an interaction between person and situation characteristics. Starting from this definition, it makes little sense to try and identify "trait" faking (i.e., to classify people as "liars" or "fakers" across all situations and motivational conditions), or to assume that situational influences on faking will play out the same way for all people. The fact that situational influences will not affect all people equally points to the limits of current methods and interpretations of results in faking research. In laboratory studies, telling participants to fake will not have the same effect on all participants. In field studies, the fact that a person is an applicant does not mean that he or she can automatically be considered part of the quasiexperimental group of fakers (see Zickar, Gibby, & Robie, 2004).

■ DO PEOPLE FAKE?

The critical role of motivation was in fact the most common point of agreement in defining faking: Faking requires an incentive, motivation, encouragement, or inducement. In short, for faking to occur, there must be some reason to fake. Empirical studies of faking comparing applicants to incumbents or applicant-incumbents to research volunteers implicitly assume that the motivational component is so strong that it can be used as a proxy for faking behavior itself. That is, the applicant group can be operationally defined as the "fakers." Ellingson (Chapter 2) points out that this assumption is not necessarily the case, and expands on the implications this has for existing research methods. Although faking almost certainly involves motivation, motivation alone is not sufficient for faking to occur. Both person and situation factors will influence whether faking occurs. Heggestad (Chapter 6) provides a summary of the empirically-supported influences on faking. His summary includes both person factors (e.g., lack of Conscientiousness, Emotional Stability, integrity, and rule-consciousness) and situation factors (e.g., importance of the outcome, knowledge of job requirements, and knowledge of how the test will be used).

Even with an incentive to fake, not everyone will fake, and there will be large differences in the extent of faking. As Griffith and Converse (Chapter 3) convincingly argue, it is clear that at least some people can and do fake when they are motivated to do so. However, it is equally clear that not all people motivated to fake will actually fake in practice. There are both individual differences in the willingness to fake, and in the strength of situational cues as an incentive to fake. Trait differences in willingness to fake are *not* equivalent to differences in faking behavior, since faking is also influenced by situational factors. In addition, the interaction between person traits and situational demand is not an all-or-nothing question of faking versus no faking. The extent or degree of faking is a function of the person–environment interaction.

Consensus on the Prevalence of Faking

Because it is clear that not everyone will fake just because they have a reason or motivation to do so, the (multi-)million-dollar question is *how many* people fake to a substantial degree in common high-stakes situations. Holden and Book (Chapter 5) reference studies that estimate the prevalence of faking at 14% to 27% for employment selection and Griffith and Converse (Chapter 3) estimate the prevalence rates at 20% to 40% of job seekers. Hall and Hall (Chapter 16) cite similar prevalence ratings for faking medical or neuropsychological conditions, with faking suspected for 30% of personal injury cases, 30% of disability claims, and 19% of criminal evaluations. The general consensus seems to be that about one in four people will fake in a high-stakes situation. This has obvious consequences for these one in four people who may be hired for jobs that are beyond their competence, admitted to a course that they subsequently struggle to master, or compensated for nonexistent injuries or illness. This may also have serious consequences for the three in four people who do not fake. The nonfakers may be displaced by higher-scoring fakers for favorable jobs or educational opportunities, and may collectively bear the costs of supporting malingerers who falsely obtain compensation or benefits.

■ THE IMPACT OF FAKING: DOES FAKING MATTER?

The impact of faking may be stronger for some situations than others. As Holden and Book (Chapter 5) point out, different paradigms for faking research find differences in the extent and magnitude of faking. Laboratory studies on instructed faking conclusively show that faking affects means, correlational structures, and validity. Results from real life applied settings are less clear. Holden and Book (Chapter 5) point out that faking may be job specific and multidimensional. In addition, Smith and McDaniel (Chapter 4) also point out that applicant groups may self-select into jobs for which they are temperamentally suited. Thus, applicants may obtain higher scores than comparison samples on desirable personality traits because they actually have these personality traits (and therefore applied for a job that required such traits), and not because they are faking.

Both these perspectives suggest that when looking at the effects of faking using samples from applied contexts, it is important to isolate homogeneous subgroups (i.e., groups applying for the same job). Otherwise the impact of faking on the psychometric properties of the test used might be obscured. In that sense, previous studies using samples from applied contexts should be interpreted with this distinction in mind. Another important issue is distinguishing between the psychometric validity of a scale (e.g., correlations between test scores and criteria) and the interpretation of an individual's test results. Holden and Book (Chapter 5) are clear on this issue: no matter what the effects of faking might be on validity evidence, faking is detrimental to the validity of an individual's score interpretation. This proposition has important implications for practitioners, as the applications for which there is most motivation to fake are also the applications that consider *individual scores* rather than group trends (i.e., selection decisions). For example, suppose 10% of people fake good on a workplace climate measure intended to identify teams with low morale. The resulting policy decisions are likely to be just as valid as if no one had faked (assuming equal rates of faking across teams). However, if 10% of people fake a Conscientiousness measure administered to job applicants for a prestigious executive position, the resulting hiring decision may be completely invalid if one of the fakers was chosen.

Consensus on the Impact of Faking

The broad consensus is that faking will affect the interpretation of individual scores in high-stakes conditions but may not strongly affect interpretations of correlation-based findings (e.g., test-criterion correlations). When faking occurs, interpretations of individual scores of fakers will not be accurate. Given that about a quarter of people will fake in high-stakes settings, this means that the interpretation of individual scores will be inaccurate about a quarter of the time. In addition, if norms are calculated using samples from high-stakes settings, scores may be slightly depressed for the three quarters of test takers who do not fake their responses. In essence, faking may be a big problem for the fairness and accuracy of selection decisions, but may not be a problem for correlational research aimed at test-criterion relations.

How Much Do Scores Increase under Faking?

The lower bound for an individual's score increase due to faking can be estimated from meta-analyses of the mean difference between applicants' and nonapplicants' personality scores. A meta-analysis by Birkeland, Manson, Kisamore, Brannick, and Smith (2006) found that job applicants scored higher than nonapplicants on Extraversion ($d = 0.11$), Openness ($d = 0.13$), Agreeableness ($d = 0.16$), Emotional Stability ($d = 0.44$), and Conscientiousness ($d = 0.45$). These estimates are likely to be a lower bound for several reasons. First, only a proportion of the applicant group will actually fake. Second, applicants may fake differently for different personality facets, which may obscure findings on the domain level (Ziegler, Danay, Schoelmerich, & Buehner, 2010). For example, an applicant who fakes high on Extraversion Assertiveness but low on Extraversion Excitement-Seeking may show no mean difference on his or her overall Extraversion score. Third, Birkeland et al. identified job type as a moderating influence on the effect size. Thus, within more homogeneous subgroups (i.e., applicants for the same job) effect sizes can be smaller or larger. In fact, the best estimate is that around a quarter of applicants fake, so that the best estimate of how much an *individual score* will increase under faking is likely to be four times the size of this group effect. For example, applicants who *do* distort their responses may increase their Conscientiousness scores by around 1.8 standard deviations (assuming they have enough rating scale left and have not reached ceiling). Score differences this large would result in very different interpretations of honest and faked responses.

■ DETECTING FAKING

Contributors to this volume have outlined a number of different methods for detecting faking: social desirability scales, appropriateness indices, aberrant response patterns, bogus items, the Bayesian truth serum, linguistic analysis, response latencies, and decision trees. The fact that faking detection methods require both a high detection rate *and* a low rate of false positives to be used in applied settings is pointed out by Kuncel, Borneman, and Kiger (Chapter 7), Stark, Chernyshenko, & Drasgow (Chapter 14), and Zickar and Sliter (Chapter 8). In high-stakes applications, any methodology that falsely accuses honest responders of faking may (1) decrease the accuracy of selection decisions, (2) be legally indefensible, and (3) be detrimental for a company's personnel marketing. The tension between correctly detecting faking and inaccurately labeling honest people as fakers reflects the tension between validity in a research context and validity in a real-world context of high-stakes decision making. In the laboratory, an error rate of 5% is standard. In the world outside the laboratory, an error rate of 5% might result in litigation by the 5% of people who were falsely accused of faking. The risk of inaccurate measurement, unfairness, and potential litigation also hinge on the strategy that is used once faking is detected. Reeder and Ryan (Chapter 9) suggest that there are four courses of action available once faking is detected: (1) score adjustment, (2) exclusion of detected fakers, (3) verification or retesting, and (4) cautious interpretations of substantive personality scores. If people accused of faking have their scores adjusted downward, or are excluded from an employment or educational opportunity, any percentage of false positives is legally indefensible. Any method that results in inaccurately penalizing a proportion of innocent people simply cannot be used in practice.

So far, none of the faking detection mechanisms described in this book would stand up to the "no false positives" test that one might take as important for applied use. This is an important point for practitioners, particularly in a legal context. In short, practitioners may be better off retesting or cautiously interpreting possible "faked" scores than adjusting scores or excluding the "fakers." Practitioners may also be better off investing in mechanisms to *prevent* faking in addition to mechanisms to *detect* faking. However, stating that faking detection mechanisms are not currently appropriate for applied settings is *not* synonymous with stating that these mechanisms are useless. As Heggestad (Chapter 6) points out, understanding the processes and nature of faking is a vitally important goal in improving the science of selection, and many of the paradigms described in the preceding chapters are useful tools for this purpose. In the sections below, we evaluate some of the major paradigms in faking research, outlining the purposes for which these might be most useful.

Social Desirability Scales

The authors in this volume are virtually unanimous in their view that social desirability (SD) scales are not an accurate or defensible method for detecting or correcting faking. Sometimes also termed lie scales, unlikely virtues, or impression management scales, SD scales are hugely popular and frequently used in applied settings, especially in personnel psychology. However, SD scales suffer from a number of empirical and conceptual shortcomings. In fact, these problems are important enough to indicate that SD scales are inappropriate both for applied purposes and for the purposes of researching the mechanisms and processes underlying faking behavior.

Problem 1: SD Scales Are Related to Substantive Personality Traits

The idea that SD scales are capturing substantive aspects of personality is repeated by Smith and McDaniel (Chapter 4), Holden and Book (Chapter 5), Kuncel et al. (Chapter 7), Reeder and Ryan (Chapter 9), and Dilchert and Ones (Chapter 12). Empirical evidence from multiple sources suggests that scores on SD scales are correlated with personality traits such as Emotional Stability, Agreeableness, and Conscientiousness (Li & Bagger, 2006; Ones, Viswesvaran, & Reiss, 1996). This holds true across multiple types of SD scales (e.g., social desirability, response distortion, impression management, self-deceptive enhancement, and unlikely virtues). If scores on SD scales are in fact correlated with socially desirable personality traits, then excluding job applicants with high SD scores excludes the very people that actually have desirable personality traits and should be hired. Such overlap between SD scales and personality traits also indicates that there is really no foolproof way to determine whether high scorers on SD scales are liars or unusually virtuous people.

Problem 2: Empirical Evidence Does Not Support the Suppressor Effect for SD Scales

The practice of using SD scores to "correct" scores on substantive personality traits generally assumes that SD scores act as a statistical suppressor, such that controlling for SD variance should increase the personality-criterion relationship. Reeder and Ryan (Chapter 9) describe the criteria for suppression in detail, pointing out that SD scales do not meet these criteria. In fact, using SD scores to adjust personality scale scores results in either a negligible or negative effect. After corrections are applied, the correlation between personality scores and criterion variables either remains about the same or in fact decreases. That is, using SD scales to correct for faking behavior actually *lowers* the test-criterion relationships, and the usefulness of test scores in predicting outcomes such as job performance. The fact that correcting personality scores with SD scale scores does nothing to improve the accuracy of personality tests is pointed out by Reeder and Ryan (Chapter 9), Dilchert and Ones (Chapter 12), and Stark et al. (Chapter 14).

Problem 3: Test Takers May Not Interpret SD Items in a Strictly Logical Manner

Kuncel et al. (Chapter 7) point out that the underlying logic of SD scales may be flawed. Typical SD items present a behavior or attitude that is obviously undesirable but extremely frequent, so it can be assumed that most people would endorse the item if they were being 100% honest (e.g., "Have you ever stolen anything, even a pin or a button?"). Because most people have at some point used someone else's milk from the office fridge, taken a pen or shower-cap from a hotel room, or engaged in other trivial thefts, the strictly logical answer would be "yes" for almost all people. However, Kuncel et al. point out that people may not perceive items in this way. As every good test developer knows, the purpose of a psychometric test item is to identify differences between people, such that an item that everyone endorses is useless. Kuncel et al. propose that test takers may hold a similar attitude, implicitly assuming that test items are intended to sort test takers into groups. With such an attitude, SD items such as "Do you always tell the truth?" or "Have you ever stolen anything?" are interpreted to index the extent of lying or theft, rather than the literal truth of the statement. As such, endorsement of SD items may represent test takers' evaluation of their honesty or obedience to social norms rather than lying about socially undesirable behaviors. This interpretation is supported by the correlations of SD scores with Conscientiousness and Agreeableness.

Bogus Items and the Overclaiming Technique

The best-known and most systematic use of bogus items to detect faking is the overclaiming technique, described in some detail by Paulhus (Chapter 10). The technique asks test takers to rate their familiarity with a number of concepts (e.g., scientific terms). Amid several real concepts are some nonexistent "foils." Indices of over-claiming can be calculated by comparing the proportion of real concepts claimed to the proportion of foils claimed using formulas from signal detection theory. Evidence to date indicates that overclaiming may be a reasonably accurate measure of a certain type of faking: faking greater knowledge of a particular field (e.g., science) than one actually has.

Usefulness of the Overclaiming Technique

Just as SD scales are confounded with real personality variance, overclaiming may be confounded with real knowledge. Foils that sound like real scientific terms may be overclaimed by people with more science knowledge compared to those with less science knowledge. For example, knowledge of the chemical "chlorine" may prime test takers to claim they are familiar with the nonexistent term "cholarine" (Paulhus, Harms, Bruce, & Lysy, 2003). In addition, identifying overclaiming in a particular field of knowledge would be useful for applications only if there were no way to accurately measure the real extent of knowledge in that field. For example, if it is possible to test people's knowledge of information technology (IT), it is not necessary to determine whether they exaggerate their IT skills. For most purposes, the resources required to construct an overclaiming measure for a particular field of knowledge seem about equal to the resources required to construct a (nonfak-able) knowledge test for a particular field. Thus, although the overclaiming tech-nique is a useful research tool for examining the nature of faking, overclaiming may not be operationally useful in applied settings such as selection testing.

The Bayesian Truth Serum Technique

The Bayesian Truth Serum (BTS) calculates how often people endorse item content they perceive as unusual. For example, people who often agree with unpopular attitudes or behaviors are assumed to be adjusting their answers based on social desirability, rather than an honest appraisal of the item content. The extent of agree-ment with unpopular items can be taken as an index of truth telling. Both Kuncel et al. (Chapter 7) and Burrus et al. (Chapter 17) describe the operational details and empirical proof of the BTS in some detail. Similar to the overclaiming technique, the BTS promises to be a useful research tool for examining the processes and nature of faking, but is not yet at a stage to be practically useful or defensible for applied use.

Usefulness of the BTS Technique

The BTS requires two pieces of information for every item: (1) the test taker's endorsement of the item and (2) the proportion of others that the test taker estimates would endorse the item. Estimating the beliefs of other people is meta-cognitively complex, and may be subject to frame-of-reference effects as to who these "others" are considered to be [other job applicants, other people the test taker personally knows, other people of similar socioeconomic status (SES) and demographics to the test taker, or all other people in the world]. For these reasons, the BTS may not function accurately for test takers with poor meta-cognitive skills or test takers using an unusual frame of reference. In addition, collecting additional information doubles the test-taking time since twice as many questions are asked.

Appropriateness Indices and Aberrant Response Patterns

Zickar and Sliter (Chapter 8) discuss the use of item response theory (IRT) to develop appropriateness indices that may be used to identify aberrant or unusual response patterns. Appropriateness indices are measures of how well an individual test taker's response pattern fits a particular model of responding. People who attempt to fake high scores may have unusual response patterns and therefore be detected by appropriateness indices. Different kinds of appropriateness indices or statistical modeling may have different levels of accuracy: Zickar and Sliter claim that (1) the standardized log-likelihood index can detect fakers at only about 10% better than chance; (2) appropriateness indices may be accurate, but also result in a high rate of false positives (e.g., appropriateness indices can detect about 20% to 40% of fakers if the "false-positive" rate is restricted to be no more than 5%, but higher detection rates will also result in higher false accuracy rates); and (3) mixed Rasch-latent class modeling is reasonably effective at judging whether people had faked good, faked bad, or answered honestly.

It seems clear that detection rates and false-positive rates for these IRT models are not adequate for applied use. Nevertheless, using IRT to research differences between "fakers" and instructed "honest responders" can be much more informative than using classical test theory approaches, as the effect of faking on the discrimination and pseudoguessing parameters as well as item difficulty can be examined. Zickar and Sliter point out that faking does not just shift the item difficulty, but affects other properties of the item. Item response theory also examines the effects of faking at an *item level* rather than a total test level, and thus may provide a more nuanced view of how faking affects test responses.

Linguistic Analysis

Ventura (Chapter 11) proposes an innovative use of linguistic analysis to detect faking. Based on the linguistic inquiry word count (LIWC) method of Pennebaker, Francis, and Booth (2001), Ventura suggests that faking could be detected by examining the language that people use in samples of free-response text. Potential applications of this proposed technique include identification of faking in free-response measures of personality (e.g., autobiographical descriptions or diary methods), documents (e.g., cover letters or statements of job experience, letters of recommendation), or spoken language (e.g., job interview responses). Existing research suggests that LIWC methods of deception detection are more accurate than human judgment (68% accuracy for LIWC versus 30% for human judgment; Newman, Pennebaker, Berry, & Richards, 2003). This research also demonstrates that LIWC methods may result in fewer false positives than human judgment, where people are truthful but are identified as deceptive (32% false positives for LIWC versus 71% for human judgment). Thus, Ventura's suggestions may improve the detection of faking relative to human judgment, but accuracy and false-alarm rates fall far below what would be acceptable for applied use. The LIWC method is at present an untested paradigm in faking research, so that the potential usefulness for research and practice is unknown. However, the paradigm may prove useful for elucidating the processes underlying faking behavior.

Decision Trees

Lukoff (Chapter 15) describes how machine-learning algorithms can be developed by analyzing response patterns from known faked and nonfaked data. These algorithms can then be used to detect faking via a decision tree model. In these models, a particular path of responses over several items might be used to estimate whether faking has occurred. Lukoff notes that accuracy rates for faking detection are up to 70%, but that these differ for different scales (e.g., detecting faking from Assertiveness scales resulted in lower accuracy rates than using an Achievement Striving scale). Again, these rates are too low to be used as exclusion criteria in practical applications, but may be useful for research purposes, and eventually for other applications (e.g., test takers could be warned not to fake when detection probabilities reached a critical threshold).

■ PREVENTING FAKING

The previous paradigms described several methods for *detecting* faking. Once faking has been detected, there is then the question of how to proceed: in essence, what to do with the potentially faked scores? An alternative range of methods focuses on preventing faking in all test takers, rather than detecting it in a proportion of test takers. If these methods work, they have an advantage over faking detection methods in that there is no contingent decision about what to do with the "fakers," and no potential concerns about legal defensibility over the false-positive rate. Methods for preventing faking fall into two camps: (1) using "fake-proof" testing methods (e.g., observer reports, verifiable biodata, or forced-choice testing methods), and (2) attempts to decrease test takers' motivation to fake (e.g., warnings).

Observer Reports

Both Lukoff (Chapter 15) and Burrus et al. (Chapter 17) discuss the use of observer reports (also known as other-reports or third-party reports) as a method for minimizing faking on personality assessments. The logic of observer reports in preventing faking is that the test taker has no personal gain from a high or low score, and therefore will give an unbiased evaluation. Observer reports are relatively common in human resources for development or promotion, and are often collected from peers, supervisors, or subordinates in 360-degree or multirater designs. As discussed in Burrus et al. (Chapter 17), observer reports of noncognitive constructs are also becoming more common-place in educational testing. Currently,

320 New Perspectives on Faking in Personality Assessment

The Personality Potential Index (PPI) developed by the Educational Testing Service (ETS) uses faculty ratings to assess the noncognitive abilities of graduate school applicants, and represents a large-scale, operational standardized observer report protocol.

There are two potential roadblocks for observer reports as fake-proof measures of personality. First, to obtain an accurate observer report requires an appropriate observer—someone who is familiar enough with the target's attribute-relevant behaviors, attitudes, thoughts, and values to provide accurate ratings. This is not always possible, particularly for large-scale recruitment. Second, other reports do not necessarily provide an unbiased evaluation, as both Lukoff (Chapter 15) and Burrus et al. (Chapter 17) discuss. Co-workers may conceivably try to fake desirable scores to help a well-liked peer get into a valued job, and faculty members may well exaggerate the positive qualities of their students to help them get into desirable graduate schools. For these reasons, observer reports are not a panacea for faking, although the use of observer reports in conjunction with self-reports may both help identify response distortion and help provide a more accurate assessment of personality traits.

Biodata, Elaboration, and Verifiable Responses

Several chapters discuss the fact that items that are potentially verifiable (such as biodata) are less susceptible to being faked in practice. This issue is touched on by Lukoff (Chapter 15), Griffith and Converse (Chapter 3), and Burrus et al. (Chapter 17). A test taker is far more likely to fake on the item "I take on extra work" compared to the potentially verifiable item "How many hours of overtime did you perform last month," as the latter can potentially be checked. Verifiable items that require elaboration are even less likely to be faked (e.g., "How many computer languages are you proficient in? Name these languages"). Although some attributes are difficult to measure with biodata or verifiable facts, this approach seems promising in preventing faking.

Manipulations of Item Desirability

Bäckström, Björklund, and Larsson (Chapter 13) outlined a manipulation of the evaluative content of personality test items that they refer to as *evaluative neutralization*. The essence of evaluative neutralization is very simple: Desirable-sounding and undesirable-sounding items are rephrased to sound more neutral and test takers will not be tempted to alter their responses. Bäckström et al. showed that (1) the neutralized scale measured the same attributes as the original scale (correlations between sub-scales were reasonably high) and (2) neutralized scales showed less of an increase in a fake-good context, although the difference was small. Such results suggest that evaluative neutralization may reduce, but not eliminate, faking in high-stakes situations. One possible concern with this method is whether neutralized test scores maintain a useful level of heterogeneity. If all items are rephrased so as to sound neutral, it is possible that few extreme items (those endorsed by very few people) will remain, such that it is not possible to identify people at the extremes of normal human personality.

Within the constraints of ensuring test heterogeneity, test developers of new psychometric tools might consider implementing evaluative neutralization as part of the test development process (e.g., collecting ratings of social desirability and/or job desirability of each item and excluding or rephrasing those with high values). This may be a particularly important part of assessment development if tests are intended for use in high-stakes applications. Including such a process may reduce the extent of faking, although certainly could not be relied upon to eliminate faking altogether.

Situational Tests

Burrus et al. (Chapter 17) review several methods for reducing faking that revolve around situation-based testing. The first and most direct of these is the situational judgment test (SJT). The SJT method of measurement presents the test taker with a situation and several possible responses to evaluate. There is some evidence that faking is less severe on SJTs compared to rating scales, possibly due to the higher cognitive demands of evaluating the social desirability of a specific behavioral response compared to a generalized statement (Nguyen, Biderman, & McDaniel, 2005). However, it is still demonstrably possible to fake a higher score on an SJT. Burrus et al. also discuss the conditional reasoning paradigm as a potential fake-proof measurement paradigm. Conditional reasoning tests present test takers with a situation or premise and ask them to select which of several options represents a logical conclusion. Unbeknowst to the test taker, one of the options is logical only if they have a particular *justification mechanism* that colors their thinking. For example, aggressive people may believe that "everyone is out to get me", which would affect the way they process or view everyday situations. The conditional reasoning test measures the presence of these justification mechanisms (and hence can be used to measure any construct with known justification mechanisms). Preliminary research indicates that test takers are unable to fake good on a conditional reasoning measure of aggression (LeBreton, Barksdale, Robin, & James, 2007).

Forced-Choice Item Formats

Dilchert and Ones (Chapter 12) and Stark et al. (Chapter 14) discuss the possibility that forced-choice item presentation may prevent test takers from faking high scores on personality tests. The logic of a forced-choice item format is that test takers are forced to choose between several equally desirable items, and cannot endorse them all. In an example for a pair-comparison item, test takers may be asked which of "I work hard" or "I am a natural leader" best reflects them. Test takers cannot agree with both items, so cannot increase their scores on both positive dimensions. There are several possible forced-choice formats, with research indicating that forced-choice presentation of items may prevent the worst excesses of faking (e.g., Jackson, Wroblewski, & Ashton, 2000; but see Heggestad, Morrison, Reeve, & McCloy, 2006 for an opposing viewpoint). However, Dilchert and Ones (Chapter 12) point out that forced-choice measurement results in ipsative or partly ipsative properties of test scores. Essentially, personality dimensions are not independent: one cannot be high on all of them. This poses a problem for test takers who really *are* high on multiple personality dimensions, or employers who want to select individuals based on high scores on more than one personality dimension.

However, Stark et al. (Chapter 14) propose a number of IRT-based processes for constructing forced-choice items that solve the ipsativity problem. For example, in the sequential approach to developing a multidimensional pairwise preference (MDPP) measure, we first determine both social desirability and item parameters of a large number of items presented in conventional format. Social desirability ratings and item parameters may then be used to develop pairs of statements that act as a pair-comparison item (e.g., "I work hard" versus "I am a natural leader"). An important feature is that most pair-comparison items are drawn from two different personality domains (e.g., a Conscientiousness item is compared to an Agreeableness item). However, at least for some pairs the items belong to the same domain. That way, it is possible to compute scores that also have a normative value, i.e., can be used to differentiate between people. Empirical evidence to date suggests that tests constructed and scored using the MDPP method appear resistant to faking, and that normative rather than ipsative information can be recovered from this process. In this way, an empirically based procedure for item selection and test development combined with new statistical modeling techniques seems to produce the best of both worlds: fake-proof tests that also lack the ipsativity that plagued earlier operationalizations of forced-choice measurement.

Warnings

Before or during the test, the test taker may be warned that deception can be detected, particular consequences will result from detection, deceptive responses may lead to suboptimal outcomes for the test taker, deceptive responses are counterproductive to the purpose of selection, or that deception is morally wrong. These warnings to test takers are assumed to decrease their motivation to fake, as faking is seen as riskier, less worthwhile, and more reprehensible. Both Lukoff (Chapter 15) and Dilchert and Ones (Chapter 12) discuss different taxonomies of warnings that have been used in the literature. An early distinction differentiated between detection warnings and warnings relating to the consequences of faking, with warnings related to consequences shown to decrease the extent of faking (Dwight & Donovan, 2003). A more detailed taxonomy of warnings was later proposed by Pace and Borman (2006), who included five types of warnings: (1) detection warnings, (2) consequences warnings, (3) reasoning warnings constructed to convince test takers that answering honestly is in their best interests, (4) educational warnings that try to convince test takers of the validity of the tests and selection procedures, and (5) moral warnings that try to appeal to the conscience of the test taker. These different types of warnings may be differentially effective for different types of situations. For example, reasoning warnings may be appropriate in a context of low unemployment where the job seeker has the opportunity to select from many available jobs, but may not be appropriate in high unemployment times, when there is little work available.

Although research indicates that warnings generally decrease the extent of faking, there are several troublesome issues with warnings. First, warnings may affect the responding of honest but anxious test takers, who may in fact give less desirable responses than they actually believe are true (so as not to get "caught"). Second, the content of the warnings themselves may not actually be true. Given that no faking detection mechanisms are 100% accurate, warning that all faking will be detected is in fact a lie. This may potentially be a legal problem, and should prompt practitioners to consider the exact wording of the warnings with great care. On the positive side, warnings take few resources to implement, and do seem to reduce the extent of faking (although clearly they do not ameliorate faking altogether). In balance, a carefully considered system of warnings is probably beneficial to the goals of an accurate selection process.

■ APPLICATIONS AND REFLECTIONS ON FAKING

One of the clear messages to come out of this book is that motivation is a key determinant of whether faking will occur. Several contributors made the point that the social desirability of an item may be distinct from job desirability of an item, and that different items may in fact be job desirable for different types of jobs (e.g., Dilchert & Ones, Chapter 12). However, there is no formal theory that outlines the distinction between social desirability and job desirability, or the item characteristics that influence desirability in different contexts. Most of the chapters in this volume and much of the published research on faking assume a context of employment selection. This is partly a reflection of the historical use of personality assessment for employment selection rather than educational selection or other purposes. However, personality assessment is increasingly being used in other high-stakes contexts, as discussed by Hall and Hall (Chapter 16) and Burrus et al. (Chapter 17). Motivational conditions may be quite different in different contexts. To take an obvious example, test takers may be motivated to "fake bad" (or malinger) rather than "fake good" on personality tests that diagnose psychiatric conditions that result in disability compensation, or diminish the penalty for a crime (see Hall and Hall for a detailed discussion of malingering). More subtle differences may occur in faking a dating website's personality test compared to a faking for job selection. A test taker's evaluation of desirability of the items will be framed by different contexts. For example, certain aspects of Agreeableness may be considered much more important in an interpersonal relationship than an employment context. Similarly, certain aspects of Openness may be considered much more important in an educational than a job selection context.

Motivation to fake is usually considered in terms of high-stakes and low-stakes testing situations. Despite the acknowledged importance of motivation for faking behavior, the current paradigm for discussing and interpreting situational motivators is blunt and simplified at best, addressing only whether the test has consequences (high-stakes) or does not (low-stakes). Kuncel et al. (Chapter 7) suggest developing a theory of test-taking motivation based on a more nuanced taxonomy of stakes. They drew inspiration from psychological models of interpersonal goals (e.g., Fitzsimons & Bargh, 2003), implying that the effect of motivation on faking behavior may be qualitatively different for different types of goals. For example, goals such as self-presentational concerns, success in life, getting along, establishing relationships, and self-benefit might each result in a different likelihood of faking, or in qualitatively different types of faking. That is, different sources of motivation may result in both different probabilities of faking and different kinds of faking. In addition, faking prevention mechanisms such as warnings may be differentially effective for different types of test taker motivation. In fact, different types of warnings may be more useful for some types of motivation than others. Developing better models of test taker motivation may be one way to increase understanding of what is going on when people fake. Given that motivation is subject to situational influences, research uncovering the underlying situational dimensions that lead to a particular appraisal of the situation would be immensely useful in exploring faking.

On a practical note, faking may be much more of a problem for selection decisions if personality tests are used to "select-in" rather than to "select-out." Fakers will displace people at the top of the distribution, but are not necessarily from the bottom of the distribution themselves. Using personality tests to "select-out" rather than "select-in" would mean that rank-order changes occurring in the top would be less detrimental. A study by Griffith, Chmielowski, and Yoshita (2007) suggests selection ratios larger than 50% are necessary to avoid disruptive effects of faking on rank order. Thus, it seems more reasonable to use self-reports of personality to discard the worst 10% to 20% than to select the best.

A further reflection on practical implications for faking relates to the assumed linear relationship between personality traits and workplace or scholastic performance. Selection ratios and norm-referenced decisions implicitly or explicitly assume that more is always better. Logically, this may not be true. Levels of Conscientiousness that are excessively high may result in obsessive-compulsive behavior rather than useful organization and industriousness. Levels of Emotional Stability that are excessively high may result in a complete lack of anxiety about vital outcomes that may be counterproductive for consequential decisions. The concept of a curvilinear relationship between personality and performance may affect the way that people fake. Individuals trying to fake an ideal score may not simply try to score as highly as possible, but try to aim for a score that is high but not *too* high. Much of the research on faking implicitly assumes a linear model and examines mean differences rather than response pattern differences. If individuals are faking in a more nuanced way, this suggests that research based on item response theory or latent class detection may be more conceptually appropriate than classical test theory for understanding and detecting faking—a point taken up by Zickar and Sliter in Chapter 8 of this volume. Moreover, research correlating any operationalization of faking with other criteria should consider such curvilinear relationships.

A further theme in many of the chapters in this volume is the distinction between what happens in the laboratory and what happens in the "real world." Motivational conditions of applying for a job are difficult if not impossible to replicate in a laboratory setting. The implication of this is that any research findings from laboratory studies (usually based on instructed faking, although sometimes on experimentally manipulating faking motivation) must be replicated in real, high-stakes settings. The processes underlying faking behavior may be subject to very different influences for a person who needs a job to feed their family compared to a research volunteer who is following instructions for course credit, a cash reimbursement, or general interest in research. Motivation is obviously vastly different and, thus, laboratory research will always need to be replicated in the field to ensure that results generalize.

■ RECOMMENDATIONS FOR RESEARCH AND PRACTICE

Although there are still several unknowns in faking research, and several of the paradigms still require refinement before applied use appears likely, several general principles emerged consistently across chapters in this volume. We believe that there is enough of a consensus on these issues to form a set of broad recommendations for research, theory, and practice, as follows:

Recommendation 1. Social desirability scales should not be used as indicators of faking behavior in either research or practice. Use of social desirability scales to index faking behavior is inaccurate, and use of social desirability scales to correct personality scores may do more harm than good.

Recommendation 2. When existing detection methods suggest that faking has occurred, practitioners are advised to retest or to interpret scores cautiously rather than to exclude the identified fakers or try to correct their scores. This caution is due to the inevitable presence of false positives when detecting faking.

Recommendation 3. Practitioners are better advised to implement strategies designed to minimize faking (e.g., using verifiable biodata or observer reports) rather than to detect and/or correct for faking once it has occurred.

Recommendation 4. Practitioners are better advised to use personality scales as a "screen-out" tool (to exclude those with inappropriately low levels of desired attributes) rather than a "screen-in" tool (to select those with exceptionally high levels of desired attributes). This method will give "fakers" a smaller chance to displace desirable test takers in the selection procedure.

Recommendation 5. When tests are developed for high-stakes applications, test developers should consider implementing formal processes to neutralize the evaluative content of test items to reduce faking motivation. However, test developers should also take care that such a process does not reduce the test's bandwidth, such that identification of extreme individuals is still possible.

Recommendation 6. Research might usefully consider developing more sophisticated models of test taker motivation that expand on the high-stakes versus low-stakes dichotomy and head toward a taxonomy of situational appraisals that acts as motivators for faking behavior.

Recommendation 7. Research might usefully concentrate on developing a theoretical model of faking that incorporates (1) a taxonomy of motivational conditions (as in the previous

recommendation), (2) a taxonomy of individual differences traits
relevant to faking behavior, and (3) a process model of the way that
faking behavior occurs.

Recommendation 8. Research findings from laboratory studies should
be replicated in the field to ensure that results generalize to motivated
real-life contexts.

■ THE FUTURE OF FAKING RESEARCH

Although the contributions in this volume indicated considerable consensus on
some issues, it is clear that there is a long way to go before the faking problem can
be solved and put away. The silver lining for researchers is that even after all the
years of investigation there are still many open questions that allow faking researchers the opportunity to leave their mark. However, the field has become so broad
that we believe it might be advantageous to specify some areas in which research
might most fruitfully be directed.

Based on the arguments stated throughout the book, it seems clear that the
greatest need might be to establish a common understanding and language to
communicate about the faking phenomenon. As long as all kinds of different definitions and operationalizations are used, it seems almost impossible to arrive at a
commonly accepted set of "truths." Much like the early problems caused by having
no common framework in personality research, faking research might also be
hampered by lacking a common definition. Such a commonly accepted definition
does not have to explain all features. Rather, it must provide a general framework.
Our earlier list of agreed-upon elements of faking, distilled from 17 disparate perspectives, might be seen by researchers as a common ground from where to start a
systematic research agenda.

Another important and closely linked step would be to establish process models
that describe the unfolding of actual faking behavior. As noted throughout the
volume, we have a pretty clear idea of faking antecedents and some ideas regarding
its impact on the validity of test scores and selection processes. However, the actual
process remains widely unclear. Here we call for a broadening of perspectives and
methods. Qualitative approaches such as think-aloud techniques might provide
key information. More broadly, borrowing theory and methods from fields such as
social psychology, personality, behavioral economics, and cognitive psychology
might offer unique insights into the faking process.

Finally, a more nuanced approach to personality may be called for in faking,
moving beyond the Big Five broad domains to examine the effects of faking on the
more specific facets of personality. This may be particularly important for high-
stakes applied settings where task demands map to a profile of personality that is
more detailed than five broad domains. In addition, this may also be a necessary
condition for the development of within-domain forced-choice assessments or for
biodata measures targeting narrow traits.

In the end, it is our opinion that only a clear understanding of the faking process will allow the development of means to prevent or correct its occurrence or at
least determine its exact influence.

References

Bäckström, M., Björklund, F., & Larsson, M. R. (2011). Social desirability in personality assessment: Outline of a model to explain individual differences. In M. Ziegler, C. MacCann, and R. D. Roberts (Eds.) New perspectives on faking in personality assessment (pp. 201–213). New York: Oxford University Press.

Birkeland, S. A., Manson, T. M., Kisamore, J. L., Brannick, M. T., & Smith, M. A. (2006). A meta-analytic investigation of job applicant faking on personality measures. *International Journal of Selection and Assessment*, 14, 317–335.

Burrus, J., Naemi, B. D., & Kyllonen, P. C. (2011). Intentional and unintentional faking in education. In M. Ziegler, C. MacCann, and R. D. Roberts (Eds.) New perspectives on faking in personality assessment (pp. 282–306). New York: Oxford University Press.

Dilchert, S., & Ones, D.S. (2011). Application of preventive strategies. In M. Ziegler, C. MacCann, and R. D. Roberts (Eds.) New perspectives on faking in personality assessment (pp. 177–200). New York: Oxford University Press.

Dwight, S. A., & Donovan, J. J. (2003). Do warnings not to fake reduce faking? *Human Performance*, 16, 1–23.

Ellingson, J. E. (2011). People fake only when they need to fake. In M. Ziegler, C. MacCann, and R. D. Roberts (Eds.) New perspectives on faking in personality assessment (pp. 19–33). New York: Oxford University Press.

Fitzsimons, G. M., & Bargh, J. A. (2003). Thinking of you: Nonconscious pursuit of interpersonal goals associated with relationship partners. *Journal of Personality and Social Psychology*, 84, 148–164.

Griffith, R. L., & Converse, P. D. (2011). The rules of evidence and the prevalence of applicant faking. In M. Ziegler, C. MacCann, and R. D. Roberts (Eds.) New perspectives on faking in personality assessment (pp. 34–52). New York: Oxford University Press.

Griffith, R. L., Chmielowski, T., & Yoshita, Y. (2007). Do applicants fake? An examination of the frequency of applicant faking behavior. *Personnel Review*, 36, 341–357.

Hall, R. C. W., & Hall, R. C. W. (2011). Plaintiffs who malinger: Impact of litigation on fake testimony. In M. Ziegler, C. MacCann, and R. D. Roberts (Eds.) New perspectives on faking in personality assessment (pp. 255–281). New York: Oxford University Press.

Heggestad, E. D. (2011). A conceptual representation of faking: Putting the horse back in front of the cart. In M. Ziegler, C. MacCann, and R. D. Roberts (Eds.) New perspectives on faking in personality assessment (pp. 87–101). New York: Oxford University Press.

Heggestad, E. D., Morrison, M., Reeve, C. L., & McCloy, R. A. (2006). Forced-choice assessments for selection: Evaluating issues of normative assessment and faking resistance. *Journal of Applied Psychology*, 91, 9–24.

Holden, R. R., & Book, A.S. (2011). Faking does distort self-report personality assessment. In M. Ziegler, C. MacCann, and R. D. Roberts (Eds.) New perspectives on faking in personality assessment (pp. 71–84). New York: Oxford University Press.

Jackson, D. N., Wroblewski, V. R., & Ashton, M. C. (2000). The impact of faking on employment tests: Do forced choice offer a solution? *Human Performance*, 13, 371–388.

Kuncel, N. R., Borneman, M., & Kiger, T. (2011). Innovative item response process and Bayesian faking detection methods: More questions than answers. In M. Ziegler, C. MacCann, and R. D. Roberts (Eds.) New perspectives on faking in personality assessment (pp. 102–112). New York: Oxford University Press.

LeBreton, J. M., Barksdale, C. D., Robin, J., & James, L. R. (2007). Measurement issues associated with conditional reasoning tests: Indirect measurement and test faking. *Journal of Applied Psychology*, 92, 1–16.

Li, A., & Bagger, J. (2006). Using the BIDR to distinguish the effects of impression management and self-deception on the criterion validity of personality measures: A meta-analysis. *International Journal of Selection and Assessment, 14*, 131–141.

Lukoff, B. (2011). Is faking inevitable? Person-level strategies for reducing faking. In M. Ziegler, C. MacCann, and R. D. Roberts (Eds.) New perspectives on faking in personality assessment (pp. 240–252). New York: Oxford University Press.

Newman, M. L., Pennebaker, J. W., Berry, D. S., & Richards, J. M. (2003). Lying words: Predicting deception from linguistic style. *Personality and Social Psychology Bulletin, 29*, 665–675.

Nguyen, N. T., Biderman, M. D., & McDaniel, M. A. (2005). Effects of response instruction on faking a situational judgment test. *International Journal of Selection and Assessment, 13*, 250–260.

Ones, D. S., Viswesvaran, C., & Reiss, A. D. (1996). Role of social desirability in personality testing for personnel selection: The red herring. *Journal of Applied Psychology, 81*, 660–679.

Pace, V. L., & Borman, W. C. (2006). The use of warnings to discourage faking on noncognitive inventories. In D. Svyantek, R. L. Griffith, & M. H. Peterson (Eds.), *A closer examination of applicant faking behavior* (pp. 283–301). Greenwich, CT: Information Age.

Paulhus, D. L. (2002). Socially desirable responding: The evolution of a construct. In H. I. Braun, D. N. Jackson, & D. E. Wiley (Eds.), *The role of constructs in psychological and educational measurement* (pp. 49–69). Mahwah, NJ: Erlbaum.

Paulhus, D. L. (2011). Overclaiming on personality questionnaires. In M. Ziegler, C. MacCann, and R. D. Roberts (Eds.) New perspectives on faking in personality assessment (pp. 151–164). New York: Oxford University Press.

Paulhus, D. L., Harms, P. D., Bruce, M. N., & Lysy, D. C. (2003). The over-claiming technique: Measuring self-enhancement independent of ability. *Journal of Personality and Social Psychology, 84*, 681–693.

Pennebaker, J. W., Francis, M. E., & Booth, R. J. (2001). *Linguistic Inquiry and Word Count (LIWC): LIWC2001.* Mahwah, NJ: Erlbaum.

Reeder, M. C., & Ann Marie Ryan (2011). Methods for correcting for faking. In M. Ziegler, C. MacCann, and R. D. Roberts (Eds.) New perspectives on faking in personality assessment (pp. 131–150). New York: Oxford University Press.

Smith, D. B., & McDaniel, M. (2011). Questioning old assumptions: Faking and the personality–performance relationship. In M. Ziegler, C. MacCann, and R. D. Roberts (Eds.) New perspectives on faking in personality assessment (pp. 53–70). New York: Oxford University Press.

Stark, S., Chernyshenko, O. S., & Drasgow, F. (2011). Constructing fake-resistant personality tests using item response theory: High-stakes personality testing with multidimensional pairwise preferences. In M. Ziegler, C. MacCann, and R. D. Roberts (Eds.) New perspectives on faking in personality assessment (pp. 214–239). New York: Oxford University Press.

Ventura, M. (2011). The detection of faking through word use. In M. Ziegler, C. MacCann, and R. D. Roberts (Eds.) New perspectives on faking in personality assessment (pp. 165–174). New York: Oxford University Press.

Zickar, M. J., & Sliter, K. A. (2011). Searching for unicorns: Item response theory-based solutions to the faking problem. In M. Ziegler, C. MacCann, and R. D. Roberts (Eds.) New perspectives on faking in personality assessment (pp. 113–130). New York: Oxford University Press.

Zickar, M. J., Gibby, R. E., & Robie, C. (2004). Uncovering faking samples in applicant, incumbent, and experimental data sets: An application of mixed-model item response theory. *Organizational Research Methods, 7,* 168–190.

Ziegler, M., Danay, E., Schoelmerich, F., & Buehner, M. (2010). Predicting academic success with the Big 5 rated from different points of view: Self-rated, other-rated, and faked. *European Journal of Personality, 24,* 341–355.

19 Faking in Personality Assessments

Where Do We Stand?

■ PAUL R. SACKETT

In this chapter I offer thoughts on a number of topics based on reading all of the chapters prepared for this volume. I have not taken the "critical discussant" role; this is not a chapter-by-chapter set of critiques. Rather, it is intended as my take on where we stand on a series of important questions related to faking informed by material in the chapters. It is intended to be readable on its own (i.e., the reader is not expected to have first read all of the prior chapters in the volume). I also note that although personality assessment can be done in any number of contexts, the focus of most authors in this volume is selection decisions in organizational or educational contexts, and I also focus on faking in the context of selection decisions.

■ WHAT IS FAKING?

I view an observed score on a personality item (or aggregate of items constituting a scale) as having multiple systematic variance components, including at least the following:

1. Mean true score across situations
2. Situationally specific true departure from grand mean
3. Cross-domain erroneous self-perception
4. Situationally specific erroneous self-perception
5. Cross-domain consistent impression management
6. Situationally specific intentional distortion.

To illustrate, consider a single item from the International Personality Item Pool Openness scale: "have excellent ideas" (Goldberg Johnson, Eber, Hogan, Ashton, Cloninger, & Gough, 2006). The mean true score across situations would be conceptualized as the actual quality of one's ideas across domains (e.g., work, family, community). True situational variance would reflect real differences in the quality of ideas across domains. You might have outstanding insight into child-raising, and have consistently excellent ideas about courses of action in that domain, yet have only average quality ideas in a particular workplace setting.

An additional component of variance would reflect any erroneous self-perception. This could be domain general (i.e., a consistent tendency to overevaluate the quality of one's ideas) or domain specific (e.g., an accurate perception of the quality of one's ideas in the domain of child-raising but misperception of the quality of one's ideas at work).

Cross-domain consistent impression management might reflect, say, a tendency to give yourself the benefit of the doubt (e.g. "if unsure whether I'm a 4 or a 5, go with the higher") or a tendency to respond in terms of your "best self" rather than your "typical self." A key notion here is that these response tendencies are consistent across situations, and likely are largely automatized. I speculate that it is possible to create a setting that pushes the individual out of this automatic response mode and into a controlled processing mode in which these response tendencies are acknowledged (which is what differentiates this from the prior category of truly erroneous self-perception).

The final component of variance is situationally specific intentional distortion. This most clearly reflects the idea of faking in response to perceived situational demands (e.g., "I'll overstate my virtues in the interests of getting this job").

I suggest that both conceptually and operationally, faking can be viewed as the difference between the score obtained in the situation of interest to the researcher (e.g., the score obtained as an applicant for a specific job) and some other score. I believe that there is inconsistency in how faking is conceptualized, and that various operationalizations of faking implicitly reflect different views of what sources of variance are relevant to the faking estimate.

Consider how various authors in this volume conceptualize faking. I will not extract a definition from all chapters, but rather will sample a few. In Chapter 2, Ellingson defines faking as a behavior in which "individuals knowingly choose to answer personality questions in a manner that provides an inaccurate characterization or façade." This considers faking to be the difference between the operational score (reflecting all six variance sources) and a score reflecting the first five sources. This is similar to Holden and Book's (Chapter 5) view of faking as "intentional misrepresentation in self-report." In these views, erroneous self-perception and automaticized impression management are not part of faking. I see this as the most common view among authors in this volume. It is not, however, universal. Griffith and Converse in Chapter 3 view faking as an "attempt to present a more favorable appearance than is warranted." Here the implied difference is between an operational score and a true score. In Chapter 17 Burrus, Naemi, and Kyllonen differentiate between intentional faking and unintentional faking, and thus do include erroneous self-perception within the domain of faking.

I concur with the view of faking as the sixth source in variance in the list above, namely, situation-specific intentional distortion of responses. This is not to diminish the importance of the other sources of variance as part of a broad goal of fully understanding how individuals respond to personality items. But it is important to be clear as to the phenomenon of interest. Once we differentiate faking (i.e., intentional distortion) from other sources of variance, we are in a position to be clear as to what we are and are not doing with various interventions. Example 1: "preventing faking" does not mean that what is observed is true score plus random error. Example 2: when the use of a social desirability scale to adjust a personality score is investigated, it is important to be clear as to whether the goal is to remove only the effects of intentional distortion, or whether elements of erroneous self-perception are targeted as well. Example 3: a research strategy of comparing individuals' responses as a job applicant with the same individuals' responses in a "research only" setting attempts to isolate intentional distortion, while a strategy of comparing self-ratings with other ratings is something very different, as self-ratings may differ from other ratings due to sources of variance other than intentional distortion (e.g., erroneous self-perception). As this example shows, the various research design strategies that have been brought to bear in examining faking are not always comparable in terms of the question they are addressing, and the questions addressed by different designs should be carefully attended to in comparing research findings across designs.

■ FAKING DEPENDS ON TEST TAKER GOALS, AND THESE VARY

In Chapter 1, Ziegler, MacCann, and Roberts state that "faking represents a res⁻ ponse set aimed at providing a portrayal of the self that helps a person to achieve personal goals." The notion of personal goals is important, as it is useful to view all responses to personality items as aimed at one or more personal goals. I found the framework offered by Kuncel, Borneman, and Kiger (Chapter 7) particularly helpful in thinking about personal goals. Kuncel et al. suggest that "responding to a single item comes down to wanting to be impressive, credible, and true to the self. Being impressive involves giving the response to a given item that is believed to be viewed as maximally desirable by the target audience without violating short- or long-term credibility or providing responses that are too inconsistent with the subject's 'self.' " While Kuncel et al. approach motivation to faking from a goals perspective, Ellingson (Chapter 2) adopts an expectancy theory perspective. I believe the two can be readily integrated: These three goals can be viewed as outcomes whose valence can vary across individuals and across situations within individuals. Similarly, the instrumentality of various response strategies for achieving these goals can vary across individuals and across situations.

I believe that taking this personal goals perspective into account has considerable potential for a better understanding of faking. First, it is safe to assert that there are individual differences in the relative importance of these goals. Concern for impressing others is an interesting personality characteristic in and of itself. Although many may be willing to engage in some degree of faking in the interests of achieving an objective (e.g., getting a job offer), others may take a "this is who I am—take it or leave it" approach. For example, colleagues and I conducted a study in which individuals received false feedback indicating they had failed a personality test, and were then offered the opportunity to retest (Hooper, Sackett, Rootes, & Rigdon, 2008). Although most reported that they changed their response strategy on the second attempt (and succeeded in improving their scores), 17% reported that they did not change their strategy.

Concern for credibility is likely to reflect individual differences, and may be linked to differences in factors such as (1) short-term versus long-term thinking and (2) impulsiveness. Test takers taking a short-term view may be concerned only with the short-term objective of getting a high score. In contrast, those taking a longer-term view may limit the degree to which they distort responses based on perceiving a need to reconcile the plausibility of the image they present on the test with the image that they will present in subsequent direct contact with the organization (e.g., interviewers, supervisors).

Concern for being true to the self is also likely to vary across individuals. Landers, Sackett, and Tuzinski (2011) report a study in an organizational setting in which a coaching rumor arose about a response strategy that, if executed correctly, could result in obtaining a "perfect" score on a personality test. The response strategy (involving using only the extreme poles of a five-point scale for all items) reflects abandoning any semblance of giving responses reflective of your perceived self. Although only about 7% of candidates attempted to use this extreme version of faking, the finding does indicate that some individuals are willing to discard concern for being true to yourself.

Second, in addition to individual determinants of variation in concern for each of these goals, there are likely to also be situational determinants. The perceived value of responding in a manner intended to impress may be quite different in settings seen by a candidate as very selective ("I need to score in the top 1%") versus settings in which the candidate believes a test is being used in a screen-out fashion ("I need to avoid scoring in the bottom 10%"). The importance of credibility may vary by the context in which testing is done (e.g., as part of a psychological assessment in which the candidate knows that the testing will be followed by an in-depth interview with a psychologist versus completing a test on-line as part of the initial screening for a position). The importance assigned to being true to yourself may also vary by context. For example, in the Landers et al. (2011) study, candidates who were retested after initial failure were much more likely to follow the coaching rumor and use the extreme response strategy than candidates being tested for the first time.

Third, the research designs used in studying faking may in and of themselves influence concern for each of these goals. The instructions given to participants in instructed faking studies often directly or indirectly address these goals. For example, some instructions say "respond as you would as if you were applying for a job you really wanted" (which primes the "impress" goal), whereas others much more directly ask the participant to respond in a way that will obtain a high score and explicitly state that participants should not be concerned about the honesty of their responses. Note that in such studies the meaning of the "impress" goal changes from "impress the employer by looking good for this job" to "impress the researcher by showing that you know how to identify desirable responses." I note, though, that a colleague and I were surprised to find no difference in mean faking effect sizes for direct ("get a high score") versus indirect ("respond as an applicant") in a meta-analysis of the instructed faking literature (Hooper & Sackett, 2008).

In sum, if we pair the suggestion of Kuncel et al. (Chapter 7) that three common test taker goals are to impress, to be credible, and to be true to one's self with an examination of potential individual, situational, and research design sources of variance in these three goals, we see that framing the question as "do test takers fake: yes or no?" is not productive. Some do, some don't, and the questions of interest are "who does?" and "when?" Careful consideration of how these goals vary across the setting in which different studies have been done may help shed light on inconsistencies in the literature.

■ DOES FAKING OCCUR IN OPERATIONAL SETTINGS?

There is a clear consensus that examinees can fake if instructed to do so, but differing views as to the presence and extent of faking in actual selection settings. Although the editors of this volume invited authors to take opposite sides on this issue, the authors reframed their tasks, and so the strong "faking does not occur" position is not championed in this volume. For example, Ellingson (Chapter 2) reframed her task as addressing "when do applicants fake?" rather than "do applicants fake?" Griffith and Converse (Chapter 3) offer a strong and spirited argument in support of the position that faking does occur, and offer an overall estimate that on average about 30% of candidates fake. They offer multiple lines of evidence, including applicant-incumbent mean score comparisons, applicant-incumbent criterion-related validity comparisons, rates of endorsement of bogus statements on tests, examinees self-statements regarding their involvement in faking, and within-subject studies in which scores as an applicant are compared with scores in a research setting with the instruction to respond honestly. Although each of these designs can be critiqued, the use of such a wide variety of research strategies and the convergence of findings across strategies are, in my opinion, quite compelling. Individually, each research design does not rule out one or more plausible alternate explanations for the observed findings. But when findings converge across multiple strategies it becomes less and less likely that the findings are artifactual.

There is one research strategy beyond those examined by Griffith and Converse that I find most interesting, namely, studies in which candidates retest after initial failure. This is the design that is the basis for Hogan, Barrett, and Hogan's (2007) strong statement that faking is not a problem in applied settings. They used this design with a large sample, and found no change (mean d across dimensions = −0.02). I am aware of three other studies that use this design, with retest improvement of $d = 0.86$ (Landers et al., 2011), $d = 2.8$ (Young, 2003), and mean d across dimensions = 0.30 (Hausknecht, 2010). There is clearly much variability here, and it is not as yet fully clear what the key features are that lead to large versus small differences upon retesting. Although a full understanding of the reasons for this variation requires further research, I view the sizable change upon retesting in some studies as strong evidence that faking does occur in at least some applicant settings. Thus we can move past the question of whether or not faking occurs. It does occur, and at least in some settings it occurs to a substantial degree. As we are not in a position to determine in advance whether a given setting is one in which the extent of faking will be relatively high or relatively low, it seems prudent to approach any selection setting with the perspective that some degree of faking is likely and to carefully consider what should be done about it. This leads to the next issue: Does faking matter?

■ DOES FAKING MATTER?

To address this question we must specify what it means for faking to "matter." The outcomes of interest must be clearly understood to answer the question, and my sense is that there is not consensus as to these outcomes. For some, the outcomes of interest are criterion-related validity or extensions of criterion-related validity into a utility framework (e.g., Smith & McDaniel, Chapter 4). For others, outcomes are broadened to include construct validity (i.e., whether the observed score represents the examinee's standing on the construct of interest) and to consequences of lack of construct validity, such as concerns over the unfairness if individuals who fake displace individuals who do not fake (e.g., Holden & Book, Chapter 5).

If the outcomes of interest are restricted to validity and utility, then a case can be made that faking does not matter—or at least does not matter much. A key research finding is that for correlations in the range we commonly encounter in selection work, the correlation coefficient is startlingly robust to score distortion. This is best reflected in simulation studies that systematically examine the effects of different features on the resulting correlation (e.g., Berry & Sackett, 2009; Komar, Brown, Komar, & Robie, 2008; Zickar, Rosse, Levin, & Hulin, 1996; also see Reeder & Ryan, Chapter 9). Such studies generate samples of applicants in which the correlation between nonfaked responses and a criterion is specified (say, $r = 0.30$), and then alter scores to simulate faking. These studies commonly vary features such as the proportion of applicants that fakes, the mean degree of score change attained when faking, and the variability in the amount of score change among applicants who fake. Although all reach the logically necessary conclusion that the correlation is reduced when faking is added (assuming that, consistent with the literature, faking is not in and of itself positively related to the criterion), the reduction is generally modest unless extreme scenarios are examined (e.g., very high proportions of applicants faking paired with very high mean score change due to faking and with very high variability in the degree of score change among those who fake). So although preventing or detecting faking would be helpful in moving toward maximizing the potential level of criterion-related validity attainable with a given personality measure, the failure to do so does not negate the value of using the personality measure. In most settings, personality measures retain at least 75% of the predictive power that they would have in the absence of faking.

In contrast to the validity/utility perspective, which focuses solely on the interests of the organization, is a perspective focusing on the fact that the lack of construct validity produced by faking has consequences for individual applicants. The concern is that faking will result in an altering of the rank ordering of applicants, with fakers with lower true scores supplanting deserving applicants with higher true scores. A number of studies have examined the effects of faking on the rank ordering of candidates (e.g., Ellingson, Sackett, & Hough, 1999; Rossé, Stecher, Miller, & Levin, 1998). For example, in Ellingson et al. military recruits completed a personality measure twice, under respond honestly and respond as a job applicant instructions, in counterbalanced order. The rank ordering of examinees based on honest condition scores was compared with the rank orderings in which the honest condition scores were replaced with applicant condition scores for varying proportions of examinees to simulate the effects of faking by varying proportions of the applicant pool. The effects of faking varied by the percent of applicants faking and the selection ratio, but for plausible scenarios [e.g., 30% faking, matching the Griffith and Converse (Chapter 3) estimate, paired with a 30% selection ratio] more than half of those selected were individuals who would not have been selected if their honest condition scores had been available.

Thus, if the outcomes of interest include consequences for individual candidates, the displacement of honest respondents by respondents engaging in faking is an outcome that may be seen as unacceptable. Test administrators typically instruct candidates to respond honestly; however, those who accept those instructions have their chances of being selected diminished, whereas those who ignore those instructions improve their chances. That candidates who ignore these instructions are rewarded is troubling, and may make some organizations uncomfortable with the use of personality measures. Even though personality measures retain much of their validity in the presence of faking, the fact that fakers displace nonfakers is seen as unfair.

Sackett and Lievens (2008) noted that most research modeling the effects of faking has focused on top-down selection. However, in many operational settings such measures are used with a relatively low fixed cutoff as part of initial screening. In such a setting, faking may result in an undeserving candidate succeeding in meeting the threshold for moving on to the next stage, but that candidate does not necessarily supplant a candidate who responds honestly on a rank order list, as would be the case in top-down selection. Berry and Sackett (2009) model the use of personality in this screen-out fashion, and show that there are methods for setting a cut score that can overcome the problem of deserving candidates being supplanted by less deserving candidates. Note that this approach does not identify or weed out fakers, and some fakers do indeed move on to the next stage in the selection process along with individuals who do not fake. But using this approach can overcome the concern that the use of the personality measure per se displaces deserving candidates in favor of candidates engaging in faking.

In sum, the question of whether faking matters requires specification of the outcomes of interest, and users of personality measures can differ as to the outcomes of concern. If the outcomes are limited to criterion-related validity, then faking matters in the sense of reducing validity to some degree but may not matter if even that somewhat reduced level of validity is deemed useful. If outcomes are expanded to include concern over the displacement of honest respondents by those who engage in faking, then faking can indeed be a real problem. But the degree to which deserving candidates are displaced varies as a function of the way the personality measure is used. Displacement can have dramatic consequences when the measure is used in a top-down fashion, but can be essentially a nonissue in settings in which the measure is used with a relatively low cut as part of the initial screening. This highlights the importance of considering the context in which personality measures will be used, an issue that has not received adequate attention to date.

■ THE EFFECT OF CONTEXT ON FAKING

This section elaborates on themes that have been introduced above regarding contextual issues that may affect the extent of faking. As noted earlier, faking is a domain in which widely divergent findings are seen, and reconciling these is important for the field to move forward. One contender for the most dramatic example of this is the difference in findings between studies that on the surface appear to use a similar research strategy, namely examining score changes for individuals who retest after initial failure. As noted above, retest d scores vary from –0.02 to 2.8. I do note one provocative finding, namely that there is a very close correspondence between (1) the Time 2 – Time 1 d for those retesting after failure and (2) the d between those passing and those failing on the initial attempt. This latter d reflects primarily the weight given to the test in question in the pass-fail decision: A d of zero would be expected for a test given no weight in the selection decision and a d in excess of 2.0 would be expected if the test was the sole determinant of the pass–fail decision. Values for these two ds are –0.02 and 0.04 for Hogan et al. (2007), 0.30 and 0.48 for Hausknecht (2010), 0.86 and 0.86 for Landers et al. (2011), and 2.8 and 2.8 for Young (2003). So the greater the role of the personality scales in the pass–fail decision, the greater the score improvement upon retesting.

I offer some speculation on the processes behind this pattern of findings. In the Hogan et al. (2007) study producing negligible change upon retest the personality measure was part of a larger selection battery including cognitive ability and English comprehension tests. In the Young (2003) study producing an extremely large change upon retest, the personality measure alone was the basis for the initial failure. I suggest that in the absence of explicit feedback linking failure on the overall selection battery to the personality measure, applicants are more likely to attribute their failure to their performance on the cognitive portion of the battery than to the personality portion. On cognitive tests examinees generally have a sense that there were items for which they did not know the correct response (for example, examinees behave differently if they believe there is a penalty for guessing than they do if number right scoring is used). Thus, there is a readily available attribution for failure, namely, incorrect answers on the cognitive portion of the examination. However, when the personality measure is the sole basis for failure, it is clear that the responses given failed to impress organizational decision makers, prompting a reassessment of one's response strategy. Clearly, empirical work is needed, but I suggest that one key contextual feature is the use of a personality measure alone as the basis for decision making versus the use of a personality measure embedded in a larger test battery.

Moving to a second example of conflicting findings, one outlying finding in the faking literature is the large N study by Ellingson, Sackett, and Connelly (2007), discussed by both Griffith and Converse (Chapter 3) and Smith and McDaniel (Chapter 4). In this study, samples of individuals took the same personality measure twice, in either a selection context (with scores provided to the organization for decision-making purposes) or a development context (with scores going only to the individual, not to the employing organization). The study was based on the premise that the motivation to impress the hiring organization in a selection context was not present in a development context, and thus that the difference between the two settings would estimate the degree of faking in the selection context. The finding of a small mean d across dimensions of 0.075 suggested that faking was quite limited.

One potential explanation for the difference between the findings of Ellingson et al. (2007) and other within-person studies discussed by Griffith and Converse (Chapter 3) is that in the data set of Ellingson et al. the personality measure was commonly administered in the context of comprehensive individual assessment, in which a series of tests was followed by an interview with a psychologist. In terms of the goals framework of Kuncel et al. (Chapter 7), the anticipation of a follow-up interview may prime concern for the credibility goal, thus limiting the degree to which candidates engage in faking. Again, empirical work is needed, but I suggest that another key contextual feature is the setting in which a personality measure is administered (e.g., closely linked to an interview process that candidates may view as intended to test the credibility of responses to the personality items versus an on-line screening setting prior to any direct contact with any organizational representatives and without any information about subsequent steps in the selection process; see also Reeder & Ryan, Chapter 9).

In sum, the large variation in estimates of the extent of faking may reflect real differences in the extent of faking across settings, due to various contextual features. Two contextual features highlighted here are (1) the use of personality measures in settings in which decisions are based on the personality measure alone versus decisions based on multiple factors, and (2) the use of personality measures in settings closely linked to processes that may be seen of corroborating or as challenging the image presented in the responses to the personality items versus settings that do not highlight the concern for credibility. There are clearly many more contextual features that merit attention; see Heggestad (Chapter 6) for other factors proposed in the literature.

■ CAN FAKING BE PREVENTED?

The two faking prevention strategies receiving most attention in this volume are the use of warnings to deter faking and the use of test formats designed to render faking more difficult. Warnings are treated in Stark et al. (Chapter 14), Lukoff (Chapter 15), and Dilchert and Ones (Chapter 12). What I conclude from those chapters is that (1) there are different types of warnings (e.g., those that state or imply that attempts to fake will be detected versus those that exhort the examinee to respond honestly), (2) warnings may reduce faking under some circumstances, but such a reduction is likely to be modest, (3) warnings may lead to more nuanced faking, rather than more blatant forms such as always endorsing the response viewed as more desirable, and (4) computer administration of personality measures permits real-time warnings linked to individual response patterns, thus linking warnings as a prevention strategy with some type of faking detection method. In other words, if a pattern suggestive of faking is identified in responses to early test items, a warning can be given in hopes of altering the response strategy. But warnings will not "solve" the faking problem.

The second strategy examined in this volume involves changes in test design with the goal of reducing faking. Dilchert and Ones (Chapter 12) suggest the use of subtle items as a promising response strategy; similarly, Bäckström et al. (Chapter 13) suggest the use of more neutral (and thus less obviously socially desirable) items. More extensively studied is the use of forced-choice formats, a literature reviewed in Stark et al. (Chapter 14), Dilchert and Ones (Chapter 12), and Burrus et al. (Chapter 17). This is an approach that has a long history, with a mixed record of findings. Some studies report evidence suggesting that forced-choice formats are resistant to faking, whereas other equally compelling studies show evidence of successful faking. Dilchert and Ones (Chapter 12) broaden the discussion to include a variety of other concerns about forced-choice methods (e.g., validity in comparison to using the same items in single-item rather than a forced-choice format). The big new development in this literature on forced-choice methods is the work by Stark et al. (Chapter 14), which involves the use of a sophisticated item response theory (IRT)-based psychometric model as the underpinnings for multi-dimensional paired preference tests. Stark et al. present promising initial results, and describe ongoing operational research in a military environment that promises to provide very useful information as to the effectiveness of the approach. They are appropriately cautious in terms of the in-progress nature of the work.

My sense is that the larger the number of dimensions that are assessed and valued, and the harder it is to discern dimensions valued by the organization, the more faking-resistant forced-choice methods will be. Forced-choice methods change the task facing a candidate who hopes to impress by faking from identifying the valued response for each item to identifying which dimensions are valued by the organization and then choosing responses indicative of high standing on those dimensions. It should be easier for a candidate to succeed in achieving the goal of, say, appearing conscientious than to achieve the goal of attaining high scores on 10 dimensions.

In sum, although warnings and forced-choice formatting may reduce faking in some settings, neither is likely to consistently and completely prevent faking. Thus, on the assumption that faking may occur, the next question is whether it can be detected.

■ CAN FAKING BE DETECTED?

Multiple chapters outline one or more proposed faking detection methods. Reviews of multiple methods are found in Dilchert and Ones (Chapter 12), Kuncel et al. (Chapter 7), Reeder and Ryan (Chapter 9), and Burrus et al. (Chapter 17), whereas other chapters focus on specific approaches (e.g., the treatment of overclaiming by Paulhus in Chapter 10 and Zickar & Sliter's treatment of IRT approaches in Chapter 8). The array of approaches is extensive, and individual critiques are beyond the scope of this chapter. Some have a long history (e.g., social desirability scales, response latencies), whereas others are novel proposals as yet relatively unexplored and likely new to many readers of this volume (e.g., over-claiming methods, the Bayesian truth serum approach, and Kuncel's idiosyncratic item response approach). Each of these novel methods shows initial promise, but the question is whether that promise will be fulfilled as they are subjected to further scrutiny. The older methods (social desirability scales and response laten-cies) have been subjected to such scrutiny, and, particularly in the case of social desirability scales, are generally rejected as useful approaches to identifying fakers.

Similarly, Zickar and Sliter (Chapter 8) are not optimistic about the promise of IRT approaches to detecting faking.

Several points are worth making about faking detection methods. First, they differ in terms of the data needed to render a judgment about faking (Reeder & Ryan, Chapter 9). Some, such as the idiosyncratic response method of Kuncel et al., use the item responses to the personality scales as the basis for a scoring key to identify faking. Others require the collection of additional information. For example, in the overclaiming approach examinees report their degree of familiarity with a range of items, some of which are nonexistent. The Bayesian truth serum approach, by contrast, requires examinees to make two responses to each item: their own response and their estimate of the proportion of the population that would respond in the same way. This need for additional data raises pragmatic concerns. There are some settings in which the time available is at a premium, and others in which, say, doubling testing time to permit collecting additional data from each examinee is more feasible. Thus, even approaches that prove useful may not be universal solutions.

Second, a concern commonly raised is the possibility of false positives (i.e., individuals falsely labeled as faking). I see no prospect of an approach that will identify fakers with certainty, and thus false positives are inevitable. Of interest is the convergence between different methods. With a single approach we can always question whether a given examinee is misclassified. But if an examinee was identified as faking via multiple independent approaches, the case would be more compelling. Of course, it is possible that each approach effectively identifies a distinct portion of those engaging in faking, in which case convergence would not be expected. But a comparison of detection approaches both empirically and conceptually would be useful.

In sum, we are not at the point at which methods of identifying individuals engaging in faking are available for use in operational settings. Some very clever and sophisticated approaches have been proposed, and it will be very interesting to monitor how research progresses.

■ CAN SCORES BE ADJUSTED TO REMOVE THE EFFECTS OF FAKING?

This section can be quite brief, as successfully adjusting scores first requires that faking be detected. As the above section notes, a new generation of potential detection methods has been proposed, but much work remains to be done before we are in a position to pass judgment as to their effectiveness in operational settings. So without a reliable and valid detection method, scores cannot be adjusted to remove the effects of faking. (Note that Reeder and Ryan, Chapter 9, also view removing a candidate from the applicant pool as a correction strategy, in addition to adjusting scores.)

As chapters in this volume document (e.g., Reeder & Ryan, Chapter 9, and Dilchert & Ones, Chapter 12), the use of social desirability scales to adjust personality scale scores is a widespread operational practice. There is emerging consensus among scholars in this area that this is not effective. Much of the work on this topic focuses on the effects of score adjustment on criterion-related validity. Although that is certainly a useful issue, I call attention to the discussion in an earlier section of this chapter on the relative insensitivity of criterion-related validity coefficients to the effects of faking. Similarly, we would not expect that an effective correction for faking would have a large effect on validity coefficients. Given the concern of at least some for issues of construct validity, the effects of score correction on construct validity merits more consideration than it has received in the past. Even if criterion-related validity was only minimally affected, an increase in construct validity (e.g., corrected scores showing closer correspondence to scores obtained in situations with minimal motivation to impress) would be an important achievement. Note that Reeder and Ryan (Chapter 9) report being able to identify only one study of the effects of score adjustment on construct validity, namely, Ellingson et al. (1999). As research on score detection methods continues, research on construct as well as criterion-related validity is encouraged.

■ SO WHERE DO WE STAND?

As this volume illustrates, there continues to be a high level of activity in terms of research on issues related to faking. The research domain looks very different than it did a decade ago, with an expansion of the range of research strategies used to study faking, increasing quantitative sophistication in the tools brought to bear to model faking and to study its effects, and a great deal of creativity in evidence as new potential methods of designing personality measures and identifying faking are put forward and examined. That said, in terms of current operational practice, the tools available to us have at best a modest effect on preventing faking and we do not have evidence of their effectiveness in identifying faking. This may change in the future as research progresses.

What does this imply for current operational use of personality measures? I suggest that this depends on the context in which the personality measure is used. In some contexts, faking appears far more an issue than in others. Consider three ways of using a personality measure. The first is to use the personality measure as the sole basis for selection decisions, and to rank order candidates and select in a top-down fashion. The second is to use the personality as an initial screen, requiring candidates to exceed some relatively low cutoff in order to proceed to the next stage of the selection process. The third is to use the personality measure as part of a broad and integrative selection system in which a decision maker integrates information from the personality measure with other methods aimed at providing insight into the same dimensions (e.g., biodata, work samples, interviews).

In the first setting faking would appear most problematic, at least for those concerned with the displacement of deserving candidates by those who engage in faking. Although this setting is commonly modeled in faking research, my sense is that it is, in fact, quite rare in operational settings. The second way of use appears far more common in high-volume selection settings: The personality measure is not the only measure used, and it is used in a screening fashion rather than in a top-down fashion. As noted earlier, Berry and Sackett (2009) show that there are ways of setting the cutoff such that candidates who do not engage in faking would not be wrongly displaced by candidates who do fake. Some individuals who fake do move on to subsequent stages, but not at the expense of those who do not fake. Although a higher mean level of criterion performance among those eventually selected would be expected if faking could be prevented or corrected, the presence of faking does not negate the predictive value of the personality measure, nor does it cause concerns about unfairness to nonfaking candidates that is present when top-down selection is used. Similarly, in the third way of using personality measures (e.g., in conjunction with other methods, thus permitting triangulation among methods providing input on a given dimension) the integration with other information provides an opportunity to seek corroboration of the information obtained via the personality measure. Of course, this method puts the burden of integration and decision making on the individual decision maker, but there is at least the potential for checks and balances, rather than simply taking the personality score at face value.

In sum, although improved methods of preventing, detecting, and correcting for faking will be welcome developments, it is not the case that there is a need to suspend operations while waiting for these developments. The chapters in this volume do a marvelous job of assessing the current state of the literature and highlighting promising directions for the future.

References

Bäckström, M., Björklund, F., & Larsson, M. R. (2011). Social desirability in personality assessment: Outline of a model to explain individual differences. In M. Ziegler, C. MacCann, and R. D. Roberts (Eds.) New perspectives on faking in personality assessment (pp. 201–213). New York: Oxford University Press.

Berry, C. M., & Sackett, P. R. (2009). Faking in continuous flow selection systems: Tradeoffs in utility vs. fairness resulting from two cut score strategies. *Personnel Psychology, 62,* 833–861.

Burrus, J., Naemi, B. D., & Kyllonen, P. C. (2011). Intentional and unintentional faking in education. In M. Ziegler, C. MacCann, and R. D. Roberts (Eds.) New perspectives on faking in personality assessment (pp. 282–306). New York: Oxford University Press.

Dilchert, S., & Ones, D. S. (2011). Application of preventive strategies. In M. Ziegler, C. MacCann, and R. D. Roberts (Eds.) New perspectives on faking in personality assessment (pp. 117–200). New York: Oxford University Press.

Ellingson, J. E. (2011). People fake only when they need to fake. In M. Ziegler, C. MacCann, and R. D. Roberts (Eds.) New perspectives on faking in personality assessment (pp. 19–33). New York: Oxford University Press.

Ellingson, J. E., Sackett, P. R., & Connelly, B. S. (2007). Personality assessment across selection and development contexts: Insights into response distortion. *Journal of Applied Psychology, 92,* 386–395.

Ellingson, J. E., Sackett, P. R., & Hough, L. (1999). Social desirability corrections in personality measurement: Issues of applicant comparison and construct validity. *Journal of Applied Psychology, 84,* 155–166.

Goldberg, L. R., Johnson, J. A., Eber, H. W., Hogan, R., Ashton, M. C., Cloninger, C. R., & Gough, H. C. (2006). The International Personality Item Pool and the future of public-domain personality measures. *Journal of Research in Personality, 40,* 84–96.

Griffith, R. L., & Converse, P. D. (2011). The rules of evidence and the prevalence of applicant faking. In M. Ziegler, C. MacCann, and R. D. Roberts (Eds.) New perspectives on faking in personality assessment (pp. 34–52). New York: Oxford University Press.

Hausknecht, J. P. (2010). Candidate persistence and personality test practice effects: Implications for staffing system management. *Personnel Psychology*, *63*, 299–324.

Hogan, J., Barrett, P., & Hogan, R. (2007). Personality measurement, faking, and employment selection. *Journal of Applied Psychology*, *92*, 1270–1285.

Hooper, A. C., & Sackett, P. R. (2008). *Self-presentation on personality measures: A meta-analysis*. Paper presented at the conference of the Society for Industrial and Organizational Psychology, San Francisco, CA.

Hooper, A. C., Sackett, P. R, Rootes, M. A., & Rigdon, J. L. (2008). *Retaking personality measures after failure: Changes in scores and strategies*. Paper presented at the conference of the Society for Industrial and Organizational Psychology, San Francisco, CA.

Komar, S. G., Brown, D. J., Komar, J. A., & Robie, C. (2008). Faking and the validity of conscientiousness: A Monte Carlo investigation. *Journal of Applied Psychology*, *93*, 140–154.

Kuncel, N. R., Borneman, M., & Kiger, T. (2011). Innovative item response process and Bayesian faking detection methods: More questions than answers. In M. Ziegler, C. MacCann, and R. D. Roberts (Eds.) New perspectives on faking in personality assessment (pp. 102–112). New York: Oxford University Press.

Landers, R. N., Sackett, P. R., & Tuzinski, K. A. (2011). Retesting after initial failure, coaching rumors, and warnings against faking in the use of personality measures for selection. *Journal of Applied Psychology*, *96*, 202–210.

Lukoff, B. (2011). Is faking inevitable? Person-level strategies for reducing faking. In M. Ziegler, C. MacCann, and R. D. Roberts (Eds.) New perspectives on faking in personality assessment (pp. 240–252). New York: Oxford University Press.

Paulhus, D. L. (2011). Overclaiming on personality questionnaires. In M. Ziegler, C. MacCann, and R. D. Roberts (Eds.) New perspectives on faking in personality assessment (pp. 151–164). New York: Oxford University Press.

Reeder, M. C., & Ann Marie Ryan (2011). Methods for correcting for faking. In M. Ziegler, C. MacCann, and R. D. Roberts (Eds.) New perspectives on faking in personality assessment (pp. 131–150). New York: Oxford University Press.

Rossé, J. G., Stecher, M. D., Miller, J. L., & Levin, R. (1998). The impact of response distortion on preemployment personality testing and hiring decisions. *Journal of Applied Psychology*, *83*, 634–644.

Sackett, P. R., & Lievens, F. (2008). Personnel selection. In S. T. Fiske, A. E. Kazdin, & D. L. Schacter (Eds.), *Annual review of psychology* (pp. 419–450). Palo Alto, CA: Annual Reviews.

Smith, D. B., & McDaniel, M. (2011). Questioning old assumptions: Faking and the personality–performance relationship. In M. Ziegler, C. MacCann, and R. D. Roberts (Eds.) New perspectives on faking in personality assessment (pp. 53–70). New York: Oxford University Press.

Stark, S., Chernyshenko, O. S., & Drasgow, F. (2011). Constructing fake-resistant personality tests using item response theory: High-stakes personality testing with multidimensional pairwise preferences. In M. Ziegler, C. MacCann, and R. D. Roberts (Eds.) New perspectives on faking in personality assessment (pp. 214–239). New York: Oxford University Press.

Young, M. C. (2003, June). *Effects of retesting on a new army measure of motivational attributes: Implications for response distortion, test validity, and operational use*. Paper presented at the annual meeting of the International Public Management Association Assessment Council (IPMAAC), Baltimore, MD.

Zickar, M. J., & Sliter, K. A. (2011). Searching for unicorns: Item response theory-based solutions to the faking problem. In M. Ziegler, C. MacCann, and R. D. Roberts (Eds.) New perspectives on faking in personality assessment (pp. 113–130). New York: Oxford University Press.

Zickar, M. J., Rosse, J. G., Levin, R. A., & Hulin, C. L. (1996, April). Modeling the effects of faking on personality tests. In C. Hulin (Chair), *The third discipline in psychology: Computational modeling in organizations.* Symposium presented at the annual conference of the Society for Industrial and Organizational Psychology, San Diego, CA.

Ziegler, M., MacCann, C., & Roberts, R. D. (2011). Faking: knowns, unknowns, and points of contention. In M. Ziegler, C. MacCann, and R. D. Roberts (Eds.) New perspectives on faking in personality assessment (pp. 3–16). New York: Oxford University Press.

■ INDEX

Page numbers followed by *f*, *t*, or *n* indicate figures, tables, or notes, respectively.